PRACTICAL PROFESSIONAL GASTRONOMY

PRACTICAL PROFESSIONAL GASTRONOMY

H. L. Cracknell, F.H.C.I.M.A., A.C.F.

and

G. Nobis, B.A.(Hons), M.H.C.I.M.A.

Introduction by Michael Maclagan,
Trinity College, Oxford

MACMILLAN

First published 1985

Published by
MACMILLAN EDUCATION LTD
Houndmills, Basingstoke, Hampshire RG21 2XS
and London
Companies and representatives
throughout the world

Printed in Great Britain by
Camelot Press Ltd, Southampton

British Library Cataloguing in Publication Data
Practical professional gastronomy
1. Food   2. Caterers and catering
I. Title   II. Nobis, G.
641.3'0024642   TX353
ISBN 0–333–36103–2
ISBN 0–333–36104–0 Pbk

Contents

Appendixes

List of Illustrations

x

Preface

The subject of gastronomy as a body of knowledge is one that gives rise to much controversy, the main difficulty being to confine its scope within clearly defined parameters of conventional disciplines as associated with culinary practices.

This book is written to give guidance to those engaged in the provision of food and drink so that they may improve their knowledge, extend the frontiers of the art and science of gastronomy, and achieve yet higher standards.

The approach is interdisciplinary and an attempt is made to transcend the conventional boundaries of present practice. The axis is the interconnection between man, his food and drink, the environment and the development of cookery practices. All these factors have to be considered in the light of the prevailing cultures of mankind and be based on the accumulation of nutritional knowledge that shapes our eating habits.

It is hoped that the contents of this book will stimulate a desire to learn more about the eating habits of nations and why means of nourishment are often imposed by geographical chance. Such studies can be a means of gaining a closer understanding of our fellow men and strengthen the brotherhood of man. A knowledge of man's physiological needs and of his psychological characteristics is considered necessary in order to understand the way in which present-day eating practices including table manners and other forms of etiquette, have come about by a prolonged process of progression of all the many strands that go to form the subject of oenogastronomy.

On a more practical plane, it is suggested that a basic knowledge of the principles of menu composition is essential because it is fundamental to every gourmet occasion. It is essential that the menu and wine list is absolutely right before any of the other aspects of gastronomy are planned.

The authors believe that the pleasures that can be obtained from a knowledge and love of good food and drink are not the sole prerogative of the wealthy. The knowledge of good food and drink can be applied right across the wide expanse of catering activities and at all levels as a means of making man's journey through life more pleasurable.

H. L. C.
G. N.

Acknowledgements

The authors and publishers wish to thank the following for permission to reproduce illustrations:

BBC Hulton Picture Library
Bodleian Library, Oxford
Borough of Brighton Royal Pavilion, Art Gallery and Museums
Christmas Archives and Photo Library
Guildhall Library, London
Mansell Collection
Museo Nazionale Napoli
National Monuments Record
National Railway Museum

The publishers have made every effort to trace the copyright holders, but if any have been overlooked, the necessary arrangements will be made at the first opportunity.

Introduction

I first met Mr Harry Cracknell, one of the joint authors of this book, in 1972. The occasion was an interesting one, for with a colleague he had organised a gastronomic dinner in the Department of Catering Management at the Oxford Polytechnic. Thus was founded a Society 'devoted to furthering the Appreciation of Good Food and Wine', which at its second meeting adopted the name of Brillat-Savarin. The preparation of the carefully selected menus gave a rare opportunity to the students to produce dishes of the highest expertise; furthermore, each feast was followed by an opportunity for the diners to express their opinions on what they had been eating.

In this volume the authors have a comparable dual approach. The consumption of food and wine is very properly seen as an art, but it is viewed from the point of view of the cook and the restaurateur as well as from that of the diner. Certain primitive tribes, we are assured by anthropologists, regard the act of eating as indecent and only to be performed in private while other functions may freely be exercised in public view. I do not share their views, nor do the authors of this highly informative book. On the contrary they share the view of Anthelme de Brillat-Savarin, which adorned the menu of which I wrote above:

> The pleasures of the table belong to all times and all ages, to every country and every day; they go hand in hand with all our other pleasures, outlast them, and remain to console us for their loss.

I count myself fortunate to have been brought up in a family where both food and wine were taken seriously, and then to have lived much of my life in Oxford where the same conditions have prevailed. As one looks back over the years of consumption, it is simple to see how personal tastes are conditioned by events outside one's control. Even today I am not over-fond of brains, and I think this goes back to the end of the First World War when they were (I believe) not rationed and thought to be wholesome for children. On the other hand, I like my game well-hung: this may go back to my mother's father, whose prescription was simple, if perchance extravagant: 'Hang two pheasants up by the beak: when one falls off, eat the other.' Two very large changes have occurred in the provision of food within my memory. One is the revolution of transport, which has brought *exotica* from every land to our tables; the other is the considerable replacement of small suppliers by multiple concerns with a consequent elimination of the unusual or the specialised. My mother, herself an excellent cook, would feel aggrieved if she could not get that admirable fish, John Dory – the *Poisson St Pierre* of legend – from our local fishmonger in South Kensington. When on festive occasions she bought from him what nowadays are ubiquitously styled 'scampi' they went under the more appropriate name of Dublin Bay Prawns. And in truth the large prawn of home waters is not the same as its cousin of the Venetian lagoons. Viewing a modern retailer of fish one sometimes feels that one would welcome more products from home waters and fewer 'Pacific prawns'. How gladly would I trade many imported cheeses for a regular supply of Blue Vinney.

The authors of this book have cast their net wide. Food from every area of the world comes under their scrutiny, as does also its preparation from the age of Greece and Rome. But the scientific aspects are by no means neglected. It would seem that we all need a regular intake of five chemical substances in recognisable proportions. I think I was vaguely aware that I required a daily intake of two and a half litres of water, though I am always prepared to compromise by ingesting some of it in the form of wine. After all it is not necessary to drink wine of the highest class all the time. There is a little to be said for the attitude of Mr Mountchesney in Disraeli's *Sybil*: 'I rather like bad wine, one gets so bored with good wine.' However, I had no conception that I needed a daily intake of ten to fourteen megajoules of energy every day. Strict vegetarians should perhaps add to their diet vitamin B12, which is only present in animal sources of food.

It is to the credit of the authors that they do not shirk the practical side of constructing a menu. In a fixed-price menu, the main dish should take some 62 to 72 per cent of the total cost. It is an interesting reflection that restaurants as we understand them, that is true eating places as opposed to inns and taverns, only came into existence in the eighteenth century. Even then certain practices which we would expect were slow to become common. According to family tradition, it was only in the 1870s that an English diplomat, Sir William Barrington, persuaded the great establishments of Paris that hot plates contributed to the better enjoyment of great food.

Some of the historic meals which the two authors have discovered make fascinating reading; they range from a dinner at York contrived by the great Alexis Soyer using 180 fowls but only cooking the tiny portion known as the '*sot l'y laisse*' (often in English usage 'the oyster') to a French meal organised by President Loubet which entailed the consumption of 50000 bottles of wine and the washing up of a quarter of a million plates!

Mercifully, fashions change from age to age and vary from continent to continent. In the Middle Ages whale was esteemed a delicacy, but it could not recover that qualification in the last war. In New Zealand (I was delighted to discover) the flesh of the sheep is described by its age – hogget, shearing, and so on.

Less attention is paid nowadays to the gastronomic requirements of abstinence on fast days or in Lent. My grandmother, a sister of the diplomat mentioned above, preserved a menu from Paris for Good Friday 1877.

LE MENU

Potage de Purée de Pois Faubonne

Cassolettes de Laitances de Carpe à la Flamande

Turbot sauces Crevettes et Hollandaise

Quenelles de Merlans à la Béarnaise

Timbales d'Oeufs Princesse

Mayonnaise de Filets de Sole à la Bagration

Pommes de Terre Farcies Soufflées

Salade de Romaine

Eperlans frits à la Colbert

Pâté de Saumon aux Truffes

Asperges en Branches sauce Hollandaise

Haricots Verts sautés au Beurre

Gâteaux Montmorency Chauds

Soufflés Vanille frappés

Glace Danicheff

It will be observed that this simple little repast is indeed '*maigre*' throughout by the strictest rules.

It is tempting to quote further from the extensive variety of sources employed in this fascinating and truly 'free-range' volume, but the reader must do his own research. For myself I wish the book every success. It balances splendidly the interests of those who consume and those who prepare.

MICHAEL MACLAGAN

xviii

1 A Study of Foods and the Development of Eating Habits

The Evolution of Practices – Fulfilment of Requirements – Man's Food Materials – People and Environment – Food Supply and Man's Eating Habits – The Genesis of Eating Habits – Effects of Taboo and Religion – Religious Acceptances and Restrictions of Alcohol Consumption

THE EVOLUTION OF PRACTICES

Present-day eating habits, the menus on which meals are listed and the cookery practices that produce the meals we eat, are the result of a long, slow evolutionary process that corresponds with the civilisation of mankind and reflects his fight for survival, his physiological and psychological adaptation to prevailing climatic conditions and his ambition for good health and a long life.

At the metaphysical level the driving forces of man are his genes which are the hereditary units which replicate the phenotype, so that man is better equipped to cope with his environmental conditions. Thus, mankind living in the polar regions is of short and stocky build whereas he who lives in the warm regions of the world is more likely to be tall and slender of build. In equatorial regions man is dark-skinned, the dark skin filtering the light into his body flesh, while in the temperate and colder zones of this globe he is light-skinned so that more sunlight can be trapped and converted into beneficial Vitamin D for his skin.

1

FULFILMENT OF REQUIREMENTS

Man's basic drives are aimed at satisfying his biological needs for food and drink and any shortfall of these creates a state of arousal in specific centres in the brain, which respond by prompting a desire to remedy the situation. Thus hunger causes a chemical change in the bloodstream that leads to a demand for it to be satisfied which shows that man's basic drives shape his eating habits. To understand how to fulfil his requirement for food requires some knowledge of (i) his physiological and psychological characteristics as to whether his body may reject certain foods as being obnoxious, or his cultural background rejects others as being forbidden, and (ii) the environmental conditions in which he lives and the flora and fauna that flourish around him; these may become modified by scientific research and the technological advances of production which give mankind more control over his resources of food.

Man needs to derive from the resources about him, a well-balanced diet that will bring him good health and, if possible, longevity, so enabling him to multiply. These local resources will enable him to develop suitable food habits and culinary practices. He will experiment and decide upon appropriate processes to render the products more digestible, including the addition of seasonings and flavourings that satisfy his palate. He will need to bear in mind any religious requirements of his race, the social etiquette in force in his area, and of course any prevalent economic pressures which can change year by year, such as the success of the harvest.

There are a number of natural limitations that affect man's selection of his diet. Geographical boundaries and transportation facilities may affect choice and availability of certain foods; what may thrive in one part of the world may not grow in another and despite the improvements in production, preservation and transference, man's food habits are handed down from one generation to another and he is reluctant to change them, even though he may transfer from one part of the world to another.

MAN'S FOOD MATERIALS

Cereals

The environment and climate dictate what foods can be grown in a particular country and these largely decide what the basic diet will consist of. It is well known that rice is the staple food of people of the East and wheat that of the people of the West, but there is a big difference between the agro-climatic requirements for these two crops. Rice grows best in alluvial soil with impervious subsoil to hold abundant moisture and a warm climate to germinate and ripen.

2

Wheat requires heavy loam soil, a cool temperature and moist conditions. Both these cereals have played an important part in the development of the eating habits of nations but human beings cannot live on one or the other or even both, to the exclusion of all else.

Vegetables and Fruit

After cereals, vegetables form a major part of the diet of many nations and religious sects. Some vegetables act as staples in the diet as for example potatoes which are used in many countries as an important part of most main meals; also beans and lentils which are the major ingredients of many diets and the main source of protein. Fruit plays an important part as well because of its place in the menu as the sweet course to be eaten raw, usually instead of a more fattening pudding or ice-cream dessert. Many fruits are the source of Vitamin C and certain minerals, also of fibre which is regarded as beneficial to the entire digestive tract.

Meat

The availability of animals for food is dictated by geographic location and by the religious rules and beliefs of the church of a country. Countries in the equatorial belt have difficulty in raising domestic animals because of diseases borne by insects such as the tsetse fly which carries sleeping sickness in cattle in Africa and the cattle tick which attacks herds in South American countries. Cattle prosper in more temperate zones and the countries in these regions rely upon them not only for nourishment but also for their milk, their hides and even their dung for fuel.

Pigs flourish in temperate zones and pork is a popular meat in many countries. In some countries, because of the fact that a pig can thrive on a diet of garbage, the animal is rejected as being unclean and therefore unfit to eat as food by the entire population, or by a religious sect.

Sheep need good pasturage which means they thrive in moist areas such as New Zealand where the country's economy is hinged on their export to many different parts of the world. Mutton is the only food of animal origin that is accepted in every country and by almost every religious and ethnic group.

Poultry is produced in most areas of the world and with the exception of strict vegetarianism, there are no religious or social restrictions attached to any of the foods that come into this category. In some countries the country people still buy birds with the feathers on but practically all poultry is now marketed in clean, ready-to-cook form either fresh, chilled or frozen.

Outside those zones where domesticated animals do not thrive, man has to hunt wild animals and game birds in order to satisfy his hunger. According to his country of birth, he accepts as a matter of course that his meat is that of a

3

goat, llama, buffalo, yak or reindeer; his milk will be from the same indigenous animal. The Eskimo is accustomed to eating seal meat as his main source of food and his children would rather have a piece of seal blubber than a bar of chocolate as a treat.

Whale-meat is consumed in many countries in the form of red meat for roasting or grilling and is perfectly acceptable in place of beef which it resembles. Whale-oil is used to manufacture margarine and is healthier than animal fats.

Fish

Many ethnic groups have a preference for fish which they recognise as an excellent source of protein food whether it be salt-water, fresh-water or shellfish. The structure of ordinary fish is delicate which means that it is always tender and easily digestible. Shellfish are much firmer and become tough and indigestible during cooking especially if cooked for too long, so more care is necessary. The seas around the coast of North West Europe provide cod, haddock, herring, mackerel, sole and whiting whereas the Mediterranean provides mainly pilchards, tuna-fish and sardines. The Pacific Ocean provides large quantities of anchovies, herrings, mackerel, sardines and more exotic fish such as octopus and squid.

To the Japanese, fish is more important than meat or cheese because their country is difficult to cultivate and cannot be put to arable use, but it is surrounded by the sea which is their natural source of protein food. The Chinese too, are very fond of fish but because of the large land-mass, inland transportation of this perishable commodity presents difficulties so the demand is not fulfilled. The Norwegians rate fish very highly in their diet.

Water

Water is essential to every form of life, for plants as well as animals, yet a large part of the world's surface receives as little as 2.5 cm in the course of the year. The amount of rainfall is dependent upon the rate of evaporation which is affected by temperature, humidity, air movement and natural drainage. Water is essential for the cultivation of crops but can be provided or supplemented by irrigation and does not depend entirely on rainfall. Irrigation can be supplied through catchment water, natural surface water from lakes or rivers and from springs and wells. In these forms water has enabled new crops to be grown in parts of the world where it was previously thought impossible, thus affecting prevalent eating patterns.

PEOPLE AND ENVIRONMENT

Man as an organism is dependent for his survival upon an intrinsic ability to adapt to the prevailing environmental conditions to which he is exposed; this essential process of adaptation is explained in the Darwinian theory of the survival of the fittest.

With man, the main consideration is that he must 'fit' the prevalent climatic condition for his well being and survival, and the human body has demonstrated this magnificent ability for adaptation. Thus from the Equator to the Polar Zone, indigenous man demonstrates dramatic changes in his characteristics which permit successful adaptation to the external environment.

Within the equatorial belt where scanty clothing is required in order to maintain a balance of coolness he is tall, slender, long-limbed and dark-skinned, traits which assist in performing efficiently in conditions of extreme heat and that also filter excessive sunlight. On the opposite extreme within the polar zone we find that man tends almost to assume the spheric shape ideal for environmental protection; that is, he is short and stocky hence releasing a minimal amount of body heat in the extremely unfavourable cold climate, where the balance of the external temperature tends to be some 50°C below normal body temperature. His skin colour tends to be extremely light so that he can convert the sun's rays into Vitamin D efficiently thus making him self-sufficient, especially in a situation where many of the items rich in Vitamin D are missing from the diet. Another feature of the inhabitants of these intensely cold regions is the flat look of the face which possesses a layer of fat just below the skin affording protection when exposed. Although their noses have a flat appearance, the inner nasal passages are very long so as to help to warm the intake of cold air. Another well-known fact is that they possess an inner ability of increased blood flow to the facial area and hands which prevents frostbite. Within these two extremes many examples, less pronounced but equally important as signs of adaptation, exist.

Given that man's adaptation to the environment is so pronounced in physical characteristics, it follows that also at less visible levels, adaptation to the environment has been equally active. Using the same example of the two extremes of climate it is apparent that man's indigenous diet reflects this adaptation factor. Man living within the equatorial belt appears to be able to perform efficiently on an almost totally vegetarian diet, taken at frequent intervals, which provide much-needed fluids and minerals and is of low calorific value so as to prevent perspiration by raising the metabolic rate during the digestive process. This diet even though it is extremely low in fat and protein substances, seems adequate for the climate.

On the opposite side, man in the Polar regions tends to live on an intensive diet of meat and fat alone, and still lives to a good old age. Within these two extremes many examples of adaptation exist, and man's instincts appear to guide him whenever possible to seek a balance to his physiological requirements and

5

also certain additions to his diet to restore the equilibrium, whenever a deficiency exists. Salt is one of such additions; where man has adapted to a diet of cereals and vegetables which provides an excess of potassium over sodium in relation to his body fluids, salt becomes a highly esteemed commodity, whereas to people such as the Eskimo who live entirely on a carnivorous diet, salt is super-fluous and they demonstrate a dislike for it.

The environment and its topographic features have also been influential in developing early pastoral or farming communities which show the interaction of man and his land in the form of preferred nourishment. Pastoral communities have developed a diet based on meat from certain animals which could be easily moved to more suitable pasture as required whilst farming communities came to rely more on domesticated animals, cereal and vegetables.

Other communities living on a mountainous terrain and in close proximity to the sea have come to rely on fish as the basis for their diet. These practices came later to be seen as the eating habits of nations which developed a cuisine around the available commodities.

FOOD SUPPLY AND MANS EATING HABITS

The boundaries, real or imaginary, that restrict the availability of some foods to man are further confounded by the amount of cultivable space which is reckoned to be only one third of the earth's surface, or some 6 million square miles. From within this limited space man has to obtain all the food he needs to carry out his work, mainly by growing it and by rearing it, although in contrast to the total animal kingdom those he has managed to domesticate are still small in number.

In the beginning man learned by cautious exploration of his surroundings what foods suited him. He had to do this by trial and error, experimenting with toxic foods in his search to accumulate knowledge that would set a pattern of eating habits. He continued to widen his range of nutrients but ensured that succeeding generations adhered to established codes of eating.

The complex organism that is man is born with the ability to see and to speak, and in all probability to avoid poisoning himself with dangerous foods, a fact demonstrated by his innate dislike of bitter tastes often associated with toxic alkaloids. Against this is the almost universal acceptance of sweet-tasting foods exemplified by the universal liking for fruit.

The colour of food similarly affects acceptance, for instance anything that is blue – the colour normally associated with poison – is unacceptable unless very pale in colour. A description of colour acceptance is given in Chapter 2 and Chapter 6.

It is possible that man's experiments with safety in food occurred at the same time that he stumbled on the use of fire to cook it. It is estimated that he was carnivorous as long as 70 000–100 000 years ago.

THE GENESIS OF EATING HABITS

Man's need for food led him to examine the great number of plants growing until he decided which were safe; these then became his staple foods because nature had made them available and any new ones would be needed only in times of scarcity. The use of fire contributed to food hygiene since thorough cooking destroys micro-organisms and, to an extent, some toxic chemicals contained in foodstuffs; in addition the result was more tender and digestible food that had a better taste than when raw. Washing and processing food by drying or smoking also made it safer to eat.

Dairy farming has been in existence since about 4000 BC but milking animals and the consumption of their milk has not been universally adopted. China, the nation that influenced good gastronomic practices the world over makes little use of milk products.

Milk does cause some people discomfort in the form of stomach cramp, diarrhoea and dysentery whereas to others milk is one of the most important foods. The derivatives of milk are usually enjoyed more than the liquid itself. Other foods have a more valuable therapeutic effect on some groups of people than on others, for example it is an established fact that porridge is a more beneficial food to Irish and Scottish people than to other nations who may eat and enjoy it.

Recent research carried out at the University of Kentucky College by Dr James Anderson has demonstrated that for people suffering from heart disease, high blood pressure and diabetes, oats made into porridge helps in lowering the blood cholesterol to a safe level.

The 'gumminess' that is produced when porridge is made is formed by the fibrous nature of the bran of the oats used and this gummy fibre material reduces the blood cholesterol by a third; it also reduces the blood sugar and fats. The populations of Scotland and Ireland have largely abandoned this traditional dish as being the mainstay of their breakfast meal and have adopted the use of convenience cereals based on wheat bran which contains cellulose and lacks the gummy nature of oats.

Scotland now has the unenviable reputation of being one of the most unhealthy nations in the western world, particularly in the matter of deaths caused by heart disease. There is a case for recommending the return of porridge for breakfast, not only during the winter but all the year around.

If it is accepted that it is the environment which first establishes man's choice of foods then it is necessary to find out how the body interacts with the food and the environment. The answer does not lie entirely with nutrition for although a nutritionist can determine physiological requirements for differing conditions and provide an accurate analysis of the constituents of a food he cannot always determine what happens to it when it has been consumed. Food reacts in different ways in various groups of people; for some it provides heat and energy, to others it causes discomfort, and it can pass through the system of others

7

without leaving any nourishment. There is considerable evidence which shows that the ability to derive energy and nourishment from food varies considerably from one group to another. It is suggested that some ethnic groups can derive benefit from certain foods but that these benefits cannot be derived by other groups. Some food causes violent sickness, not because of any physiological reason but because the food is unfamiliar or the dish contains some unknown ingredient.

It is a fact that man possesses a set of rules which tell him what he can and what he cannot eat. Abstinence from certain foods leads not only to dishabituation of certain aspects of the digestive system which act as catalysts but also in creating a state of mind which can lead to an abhorrence of certain foods, hence rejection or violent sickness is caused through the prevailing mental state.

A notable distinction between local food preferences lies in the way food is flavoured. Certain herbs that are widely used in one area may play no part in the cookery traditions of another. It is possible to summarise the cooking of a nation in very few words, but it would be impossible to describe Italian cookery without mentioning garlic and tomatoes and most Greek dishes traditionally require the addition of oil and lemon.

Anyone can make an empirical assessment that will encompass the cookery of a particular country, indeed it can often be encapsulated in one word, for example, curry epitomises India, Bangladesh and Pakistan to some people; paprika Hungary, chillies represent Mexico and so on. Such particular flavours predominate as the expression of the national taste of a country and although they are symbolic they may put in an appearance in only a few of the country's best-known dishes. It may not even be the case that the flavourings were adopted in the first case because of their nutritional value or as an aid to digestion – it was simply that they were available locally and proved acceptable.

There is evidence that some flavourings are beneficial in the diet and are an aid to digestion. Onion is probably the most widely used flavouring and can assist in breaking down fatty acids in meat thus reducing the amount of cholesterol in the body. The lemon juice used in connection with fish, veal and many other dishes neutralises the effects of salt concentration. Many cookery writers appear to be besotted with freshly-ground black pepper in their recipes but there is sound logic in what they advocate because this spice does have a stimulating effect on the gastric juices and is therefore a valuable aid to digestion. Some of the well-known flavourings were originally used to preserve and prevent foods from going bad, the most common ones being salt, sugar, acid and spices, also sulphur dioxide.

Smoking is a way of preserving food and air-drying is often used in conjunction with it as for example pemmican which is smoke-dried, powdered buffalo meat used to provide instant nourishment when on a long trek. Cereals, fruits and vegetables are air-dried to preserve them for future use.

It may have been during the course of dehydrating grapes that the first discovery was made of the keeping property of fermented grapejuice and that this led in turn to the first wine-making. In Greece, resin from the pine tree is still

8

added to wine because it was originally thought it would act as a preservative; the Greeks developed a taste for it, although to others there is a connotation of pharmaceutical flavouring.

Cheese-making is a means of using surplus milk by rendering it into a condensed and more nutritious form; fats and oils originate from various plants or animals and are made into cheeses which keep for a far longer time than the product from which they derived.

EFFECTS OF TABOOS AND RELIGION

The rules that indicate what man should or should not eat may originally have evolved when epidemics threatened whole races and were thought to be caused by eating certain foods. Future avoidance of the suspect food led to an abhorrence of it and this laid down the rule, enforced by custodians, that it should not form part of the diet. The well-being of a race had to be maintained so that it could prosper and multiply which meant that food which deteriorated rapidly was unhygienic and should not be consumed.

Some kinds of animals and certain foods were deemed to be sacred such as the cow which is a deity in the Hindu religion because it could be reborn as a man and so beef is forbidden in their diet, although there are several hundred million cattle in India. The sacredness comes from *ahimsa* which means the respect for life and non-injury. Cattle provide the main form of domestic fuel with their dung, they also provide milk and its by-products as well as traction power, which justifies their keep as useful animals.

Although they have some things in common, there is sufficient difference between the various religions as regards dietary restraints, to keep their identity. As regards the eating of meat, many religions impose some restraints, often forbidding the consumption of pork. The fact that meat from a pig can cause trichinosis may not have been understood by the custodians of nations but they saw that pigs were scavengers and therefore classed them as being unclean. This early observation of the rules of hygiene caused several religions to proscribe the consumption of pork and there is a very long list of other foods considered unsuitable and many sound reasons given for deeming them to be so. These religious decrees have saved nations from extinction and they also show how for example vegetarianism can be a form of protection while still providing sound nourishment.

Any Roman Catholic person of more than thirty years of age can recall the restrictions which applied to what they were allowed to eat on Fridays. Until 1967 Friday meant fish for dinner because right from early Christian times it was deemed a day of penitence and fish rather than meat was the main meal. An English Act of Parliament in 1548 ordered abstinence from meat on all the sixteen days listed in the Book of Common Prayer, as well as every Friday and

9

the forty days of Lent. Observance of this is still ordered for Ash Wednesday and and Good Friday, every week-day during Lent and nearly every Friday. Caterers working in the welfare sector tend to cling to old habits and their customers are generally glad they do, and look forward to their fish and chips on Fridays even though there may be alternative meat dishes. Even young people under the age of thirty appear to appreciate having one day during the week when the diet is disciplined.

Not all flesh was forbidden on Fridays and for the duration of Lent the Roman Catholic church considered some game birds acceptable as Lenten dishes. These were the waterfowl of all species which could taste fishy because of their eating habits but when skilfully cooked and garnished could be transformed into dishes fit for a Pope. In Roman Catholic households and in restaurants of Roman Catholic countries no meat was ordered during Lent which meant that the stock for making soups and sauces was made from fish bones as nineteenth century recipes for example Sauce Espagnole Maigre, or Lenten brown sauce, bear witness.

A religion is the practice of beliefs in a supernatural force or divine being and it regulates man's activities within a moral code of practice that has been handed down by the earthly representatives of the supreme power. The main religions are Christianity, Hinduism, Buddhism, Judaism and Islam with many branches in each.

Christianity

This religion has some nine hundred million followers in the Roman Catholic, Protestant and Eastern Orthodox churches, over half being Roman Catholics. In general most Protestant denominations have little or no restrictions but there are some sects such as the Adventists who live on a lacto-ovo-vegetarian diet and consider stimulating drink and tobacco to be harmful to their health. In the calendar for the Eastern Orthodox Church there are many periods of fasting including Lent and Advent. Total abstinence from animal food is observed during the forty days of Lent and only fish is permitted on Annunciation Day and on Palm Sunday. Easter is celebrated with the Pascal lamb. The Greek Orthodox Church uses symbolic foods such as the holy bread *prosphoron* and the whole grains of wheat mixed with almonds, parsley, pomegranate kernels, raisins, sesame seeds, spices and sugar, called *koliva*, eaten in honour of the death of Christ.

Judaism

The Torah is the body of law given orally by God to Moses for the Jewish religion, as recorded in the first five books of the Old Testament. It includes the dietary laws as laid down by Moses in Leviticus, Chapter 11, verses 1–47,

10

and gives an exhaustive list of what animals, birds and fishes may not be eaten. These include the camel, the swine, the horse, the hare, the eagle, the osprey, the raven, the cuckoo, the cormorant, the great owl, the pelican, the swan, the heron, the stork and the bat. All molluscs, crustaceans, the tortoise and eels are forbidden. All the permitted animals must be killed according to prescribed rules, and processed in a ritual fashion. If they died naturally they become forbidden.

Islam(Muhammadism or Muslim religion)

This is the major religion of the Middle East founded by the Prophet Muhammad in Mecca in 622. It has more than five hundred million followers not only in the the countries of Arabia, but also in Eastern Europe, Africa, Afghanistan, India, Pakistan, Malaya and Indonesia. The Muslim religion is contained in the Koran, a compilation of 114 chapters, in the second of which the revelations of God to Muhammad regarding the dietary laws are given. All alcoholic drinks are forbidden, meat must be slaughtered ritually but pork is forbidden. One of the pillars of Islam is to observe the annual fast during the lunar month of Ramadan when the faithful are forbidden to eat or drink between dawn and dusk.

Hinduism

This is the name given to the cults and beliefs of most of the people living in India. Hindu society is based on a caste system under the dominance of the Brahmins in which all Hindus have been unalterably placed in a class structure and cannot move out of it, even by marriage. The caste system as well as creating a hierarchy also makes for tolerance and non-violence. The practice of dietary law says that meat cannot be obtained without causing injury to other creatures and that there is no greater sinner than the man who seeks to increase the bulk of his own flesh by that of other beings. This means that the faithful are mostly lacto-vegetarians but avoid eggs because they contain the live embryo; although a Benghali may eat fish, a southerner may not. The less orthodox eat meat but not beef; pork and chicken are used sparingly. Ghee, which is clarified butter made from buffalo's or cows' milk, is widely used and held in high esteem.

Buddhism

The Buddha lived from 563 to 483 BC and the religion he founded spread from India to Sri Lanka, China, Japan, Korea, Tibet and through Central and South-East Asia. The arrival of the Muslims in India brought about the virtual disappearance of Buddhism and led to the destruction of many of their temples,

11

monasteries and shrines. Love and compassion are its central virtues, and hatred and brutality which can result in the slaughter of animals are vices.

RELIGIOUS ACCEPTANCES AND RESTRICTIONS OF ALCOHOL CONSUMPTION

Further to the bodies of rules which regulate which foods can be consumed, the community of man has also established bodies of rules, in many parts of the world, which restrict the consumption of intoxicating liquor. Records of ancient Babylon indicate that laws regulating the sale of alcohol existed as far back as 1770 BC. Similarly, ancient Greek writings provide ample evidence of warnings given against alcoholic excesses.

Students of religious developments believe that water was the original fluid offered to the gods, but that when the religious orders became aware of the state of ecstasy produced in the participant by the use of alcohol in religious ceremonies, this became more widely used and the effect was attributed to divine intervention. Records of Egyptian and Mesopotamian cultures indicate how alcohol was then transferred from religious rituals to common use.

Ancient nations attempted to restrict the widespread use of alcoholic consumption. The Canaanite Jews, although approving of wine as a gift from God and accepting wine-drinking in all their major religious rituals, disapproved of drinking solely for the after-effects of alcohol. However, records show that all the ancient Mediterranean cultures – Greek, Roman and Jewish – drank copiously. The wines were not drunk in their pure form but diluted with water; even so they had a high alcohol content. This pleasure from drinking led the Romans to institute and worship Bacchus the God of Wine, and great festivals were given in his honour which involved several weeks of continual drinking.

The Roman Catholic Church accepted the consumption of alcohol as part of its heritage, which is manifestly symbolised in the communion rite that demonstrates the union of God and man through bread – the Body – and wine – the Blood – of Jesus Christ.

When the schism occurred in the Roman Church, Protestantism had a period of doubt about wine and alcoholic consumption, but no sanction against it was ever introduced and as in the Roman Catholic Church, drinking became the accepted behaviour.

Many religions and many nations do however, impose restrictions on alcohol consumption, yet it is consumed by people in India, Sri Lanka, the Philippines, China and Japan, even where the prevalent religion restricts its consumption. For example under Hinduism, the Brahmin caste abstains from alcohol; in Buddhism, devout followers of Buddha abstain from alcohol. Under Islam, Muhammad condemned wine and with the spread of the Koran all his followers were forbidden to drink alcohol, under the threat of heavy penalties, a feature which is still the custom in those Middle Eastern countries where Islam is the national religion.

Thus is can be seen that a number of natural, cultural and physiological factors have affected the development of eating habits and consequently the rise of gastronomic practices in various parts of the world. It should also have become apparent that gastronomy, like many art forms, has a local appeal and that what may be considered by people in one culture as pleasant, attractive and desirable may be totally rejected by another group possibly through lack of knowledge, suspicion or abhorrence.

The validity of the gastronomic occasion is thus almost culture-specific. These factors indicate that the provider of food and beverages requires above all else to be completely familiar with, and well-informed on, what is and what is not acceptable to his patrons. Failure to appreciate this would certainly lead to many dissatisfied customers and at times even to national embarrassment.

14

2   Man's Senses

THE DIETARY CONNECTION

Any evaluation of man's senses and his choice of food cannot be fully com-
prehended solely from a knowledge of his present diet but would have to be
based on his inborn food habits and beliefs because it is from these that a
person's present choice, acceptance and practice regarding food, stems. Food
habits of families and nations are inherited and play a large part in people's likes
and dislikes from one generation to the next.

It is thought that the beneficial aspects of certain foods were first known
to the Chinese as long ago as 2700 BC. The first references to *Yin* and *Yang*
foods – the foundations of Chinese medicine as practised today – were made
during the reign of the Emperor Huang-Ti (2697-2597). *Yin* is the principle of
darkness and cold, and *Yang* is that of light and warmth. *Yin* and *Yang* represent
the negative and positive forces of life as symbols of the balance of nature and
every item of food is either *Yin* or *Yang*. When a person feels unwell and consults
his doctor, the doctor will diagnose the cause of the illness and recommend a
Yin or a *Yang* diet to effect the cure, using opposing foodstuffs. Confucious,
who lived from 551-479 BC, held food in high esteem and encouraged his
followers to discuss the nature of foods and their quality, flavour, texture and
appearance. During the long reign of the Chou Dynasty the philosophy known
as **The Way (Taoism)** was developed which was a means of achieving harmony
and peace with nature. The opposing forces of *Yin* and *Yang* were the balancing
elements of all aspects of life, not only of the diet. During the Han Dynasty

15

from 202 BC–220 AD the concept of five elements of wood, fire, earth, metal and water, was developed. These elements were held to be the essential substances of the world and parallels were drawn with the five flavours of food and with other factors such as the planets, the seasons, humours and the organs of the body.

About 150 years later Claudius Galen (c 130–201 AD) the Greek physician, made his pronouncement that the natural world consisted of the elements of air, fire, water and earth, each with its own characteristics. In his scheme earth was dry, water was moist, fire was hot and air was cold and a combination of these produced hot and moist, cold and moist, hot and dry, and cold and dry. In order to retain good health, Galen pronounced that a balance of these was required in the body and any imbalance would lead to bodily disorders that would require drugs or food to restore to perfect balance. He went on to re-propose the Aristotelian dictum that humours of temperaments were blood, bile, phlegm and black bile which nowadays would be rendered as sanguine, choleric, phlegmatic and melancholic states. This concept was later adopted by the German philosopher Immanuel Kant (1724–1804), in his definition of personality.

With the dissolution of the Roman Empire the centre of learning shifted from Rome and many of Galen's writings were lost; those that survived were translated into Syriac, then into Arabic and again into Latin to form *Materia Medica*, the book that established the pattern of medical study until the earlier part of the nineteenth century.

During the eleventh century the centre of learning shifted to the Italian city of Salerno where the first school of medicine was founded by Robert Guiscard of Hauteville in Normandy. The Salerno dietary practices became known throughout Europe as the Salerno Regimen and were based on the Galenic principles that some kinds of food were essential for the well-being of man and helped to maintain balance and self-control. Foods were classified in a manner not dissimilar from the *Yin* and *Yang* practices, as possessing various properties, lettuce being the lowest element in *Yang* and chilli pepper the maximum in *Yin*.

In the Salerno Regimen foods were classified according to their qualities, cold food being recommended to cure a choleric disposition and hot food to provide courage and boldness. Fruit was considered cold and moist and associated with stomach upsets and therefore unsuitable for children, expectant mothers and wet-nurses. But fruit was highly esteemed by others for its digestive properties which is probably the reason for its present popularity in countries around the Mediterranean where it is eaten at the end of a meal rather than at the beginning as is commonly done in most other countries.

The School of Salerno thrived for 400 years until it was overtaken by the newly-prosperous states of north Italy, in particular the Venetian province which became the new centre of medical learning. In the climate of the Renaissance the School of Padua achieved fame with the appointment in 1543 of Vesalius to the chair of anatomy and surgery at the University of Padua, founded in 1222. His first task was to challenge many of the assumptions of the School of Salerno which had become ossified by religious interventions, and

16

to revitalise the teaching of medicine. The teaching of the School of Padua was logical and scientific and the subject of dietary habits and the understanding of eating practices were researched. Padua maintained its importance until it was overtaken by the medical schools in Protestant countries where innovations or new concepts did not automatically incur the wrath of the church.

René Descartes (1596-1650) the French philosopher, published a *Discourse de la Méthode* concerning human and animal behaviour which laid the foundations for concepts which still influence psychological thought. These include the dualism of mind and body, the location of the mind and the separation of activity centres within the mind which led to the basis for the study of senses and sensation.

René Antoine Ferchault de Réaumur (1683-1757) the French lawyer and scientist, made a study of the process of digestion, using his pet bird. His work was adopted by L. Spallanzani, Professor of Mathematics and Physics at the University of Reggio, who demonstrated that digestion was a chemical process. In 1787 Antoine Laurent Lavoisier (1743-94) studied the respiratory process and measured the amount of oxygen used by a fasting man at rest. He also showed how the amount required increased during the digestive process and concluded that the three factors that contributed to the consumption of oxygen were temperature, digestion and work, thereby laying the foundations of a quantitative approach to the study of human metabolism. In 1824 the English physician, William Prout, demonstrated the existence of hydrochloric acid in the stomach and showed its action in the digestive process.

In 1653 Nicholas Culpeper published his book on herbs in which he described their qualities and gave guidance on their use in the cure of various diseases. His descriptions were familiar in that he described the temperament of herbs as being hot, cold, moist, dry or temperate, thus reinforcing the concepts of the Salerno Regimen. It was at this time that research was concentrated on the primary components of foods and the French scientist Francois Magendie (1783-1855) demonstrated that protein as we now call it, was essential to life and health. The first textbook on biochemistry appeared in 1842, written by Justus von Liebig (1803-73). He demonstrated that it was not carbon or hydrogen that was burned in the digestive process but fats and carbohydrates. Fat received attention and it was Marcellin Berthelot (1827-1907) the organic chemist, who described the enzyme that split lipids into fatty acids and glycerol.

In 1866 Sir Edward Frankland gave accurate calorific values for a wide range of items. Later Casimir Frank studied the discarded matter from a rice-polishing mill and found it contained substances which could cure beriberi, the wasting disease caused by a shortage of thiamine which is contained in the husk and membrane of rice. It was he who proposed that such essential sources be called vitamins from *vita* meaning life and *amine*, their supposed chemical compositions. All these factors combined and led to a theoretical formula of man's basic food requirements and the modern science of nutrition.

THE SENSES AND GASTRONOMY

During the past hundred years a lot has been learned about man's five senses and it is known that an ability to put their function into context can be of use in the study of eating practices and processes. This is the realm of the psychologist whose findings can be of use to students of gastronomy for a better understanding of this important study.

The senses – sight, hearing, smell, taste and touch – depend upon the physiological system which affects the body as a whole insofar as it maintains a correct balance of nutrients which will culminate in a state of equilibrium, or homeostasis, which is the perfect control function. It stems from the hypothalamus which has the power to satisfy hunger from stored sources within the body. The hypothalamus has two distinct aspects – the lateral which initiates the eating process and the ventromedial which acts as a satiety centre.

THE VISUAL SENSE IN GASTRONOMY

Sight is of particular importance in gastronomy since it gives the first reaction to the food as presented and predisposes the other senses to a particular reation. Familiar foods are recognised and the sight of unfamiliar ones gives rise to a state of alertness which lasts until they are tasted and, one hopes, approved.

In Chapter 1 it was suggested that man possesses an inbuilt mechanism which decides which foods are safe to eat and which are unsafe; this is obviously connected with vision, and colour is of importance in this reaction. The colours of foods and meals have an effect on appetite by creating an emotional predisposition either for acceptance or rejection. Colours in the violet and blue spectrum are associated with toxic alkaloids so foods in this range are normally rejected. There is an association of colour with flavour as shown by an experiment in which various flavours of fruit jelly were coloured incorrectly with the result that it was impossible to describe the taste correctly. Many children and their parents say that a bar of white chocolate is not so 'chocolaty' as the normal chocolate-coloured bar. Similarly a dining-room that is decorated in a mixture of diffused colours can increase the customers' expectations of an enjoyable meal and be an aid to his digestion.

When carrying out product taste tests, panellists are usually blindfolded. This is how a blind person has to discern the quality of meals he is served, with the advantage that his other senses have been heightened by the disability.

In processing certain foods the original colour can become modified and unless it is restored by artificial means the result can be unacceptable, but this must be done very carefully. In this country table margarine has to be coloured

18

pale yellow to make it similar to butter, while in Germany and Italy where mostly unsalted butter is used, margarine is white like the butter.

THE AUDITORY SENSE

The eyes are stimulated by electromagnetic energy but the ears respond to mechanical energy, or pressure changes in the molecules in the atmosphere. The human ear hears normal frequencies ranging from 500–4000 Hz per second, although the most familiar measurement is given in decibels.

The auditory sense has not been given as much attention as the others and most restaurants sell food smells, rather than sounds. The sound of people guzzling and enjoying their food is considered bad manners and it is the sound made by the food itself that is pleasurable. Such sounds are few – the sizzle and spume of fish cooked *à la meunière* may not last till it gets to the customer, the crackle of a breakfast cereal soon subsides, the snap of *crudités* is momentary and the pop of a bottle of champagne being opened ought not to be accompanied by the noise of froth. Not even the preparation of a *flambé* dish should cause noise to rise above the sound of customers talking. When the background of noise in a room rises above 70 decibels it can cause stress and detract from what should be the pleasurable sensation of eating; too much noise whether made by customers or waiters can be the cause of an over-emotional state amongst everybody present.

THE TASTE OF FOOD

Taste is a highly personal attribute and as the Romans said '*De gustibus non est disputandum*', there is no accounting for it. The level of development of Man's taste in food and the accompanying sensitivity differ greatly from one society to another over specific periods of time, and from one individual to another, according to culture, food habits, taste training, knowledge of food, age and education.

Jean-Anthelme Brillat-Savarin suggested that taste could be considered under three headings:

1. in physical man it is the apparatus by means of which he is able to distinguish various flavours;
2. in moral man it is the sensation which stimulates the organ at the centre of his feelings which is influenced by any savoury body;
3. its own significant taste is the property possessed by any given substance which can influence the organ and give rise to sensation.

19

In eating food several judgements are brought into play and involve not only the flavour or taste but also the quality and the harmonious blending of the different foodstuffs that make the dish; it should all combine to aid digestion. Obviously each food has its own particular odour – both the natural smell and any that is added during its processing into a meal – and this helps to increase the flow of saliva that is essential in digestion.

TASTE PERCEPTION IN MAN

The taste of food is perceived by the taste-buds of the tongue which are the papillae or small protuberances of which there are four groups, some more sensitive than others. The fungiform papillae are located near the surface whilst the circumvallate and filiform or fibrous papillae are in the grooves. Our taste-buds live for only a few days before becoming degenerate and being replaced by new ones. As people grow old so the regeneration of taste-buds becomes slower with a consequent decrease in sensitivity to the real taste of foods and a need for stronger flavours.

Taste-perception is very limited and only the four main tastes of bitter, sweet, saline and acid are markedly noticeable and although the number of taste sensations is extremely large they stem from these four. This means they need to be assisted by the sense of smell to be fully effective.

The taste-buds are distributed around the tongue, the top being capable of sensing all the tastes but mainly the sweet ones; bitter tastes are felt by the back and the sour and salty ones by the centre and edge of the tongue. The concentration of the taste and the temperature of the food both have an effect upon the taste sensation.

THE SENSE OF SMELL

Since the smell of cooked food may reach the customer before he actually sees it, odour can have a stronger influence than taste upon acceptance or rejection. The smell of food should create a state of pleasurable anticipation that causes the saliva to flow.

The noses of normal people are extremely sensitive and can recognise low odour concentrations because they are aided by the memory which acts as a template of classification. It is more difficult to quantify a smell because, as merely a sensation it can only be measured by comparison. Carl Linnaeus (1707-78) the Swedish botanist who published the binominal classification of species called the *Systema Natura* has distinguished various smells which are still valid and form the basis of most smells.

The nose contains olfactory receptor cells which are also primary sensory nerve cells and it is their excitation as promoted by the overall size and shape of the odour molecules which is the determining factor in the characteristics of any smell, whether it be food or any other item.

Much depends on the ability of a person's olfactory organ to make a measurement of any smell and its intensity. Once the body has attained its optimum level of nutrients in the balanced form, its sensitivity to the smell of food decreases, thus reducing the appetite. It is possible to postulate a phenomenon of selective perception in which one individual will note only certain factors whilst, in another, many factors will filter from the system thus preventing it from becoming overloaded and therefore not capable of coping with too great an amount of incoming information. Once a possible tissue deficiency has been satisfied, sensitivity to smell should decrease.

More importance is given to the senses of sight and hearing than to that of smell, yet it is the source of as much pleasure as the first two combined and is the most primitive of them all as it enabled man to find his first foods. A man's calling may cause him to develop a smell–discrimination that assists him in his job, be it as gardener, farmer, fruit grower, wine maker, chef, perfume chemist, tea blender or in one of many other trades. According to his practical or professional training he can acquire an extremely selective perception of smell which never fails excepting for distractions of a nervous or medical nature. Memory retention can be achieved providing it is part of a regular routine; its extension will depend upon a person's perseverance.

THE SENSE OF TOUCH

In terms of gastronomy it is the mouth which acts as the organ concerned with tactile sensation. With the tongue, it makes decisions on viscosity, texture, moisture and temperature of the food offered to it. A highly-trained food-taster is able to discriminate between the most minute particles as small as 0.01 mm and to describe the viscosity of a liquid even when it is at very low concentration. The sensation of pressure is exercised by the form of compression of the teeth which ranges from 10 kg at the incisors to 45 kg at the molar teeth. Those groups of people who are accustomed to living on a diet of tough food are capable of exercising even more pressure in mastication.

Mastication breaks food into chunks that can be easily digested, exposing it to enzymatic action that assists digestion. Continuous mastication of tough food does not result in additional flavour release but certainly speeds up the work of the stomach in absorbing it. George Bernard Shaw (1856-1950) the playwright and critic, ascribed his good health and longevity to the facts that he chewed every mouthful of food a hundred times before swallowing it, and that he was a vegetarian. The moist or oily nature of a food will make it easier to rotate on the palate creating a pleasurable or unpleasurable experience, as the case may be. The condition of the teeth is the main reason why some people tend to choose dishes requiring little or no mastication such as made-up, tenderised, comminuted, tumbled and re-formed foods.

TEMPERATURE AND TASTE

The temperature at which food is supposed to be served has a bearing on its acceptance and the pleasure to be derived from eating it. All too often, the diners' anticipation is dashed by food being served lukewarm when it should be hot, and by cold dishes being either too cold or lukewarm. From childhood we learn to expect food to be served at the optimum temperature for complete enjoyment.

The location of the temperature sense is in the tongue and soft palate where there are specific receptors for either cold or warm sensations. The two extremes of taste – bitter and sweet – cannot readily be perceived in food served at extremes of temperature, that is, below freezing point and above 60°C.

The ideal range of temperatures for recording degrees of sweetness-intensity is between 16°C and 35°C and any sweet dishes eaten at temperatures below or above this range have to linger in the mouth to reach 36.8°C before they can be correctly described. Bitter tastes register best at low temperatures from 3°–16°C and decrease by as much as a third at temperatures from 16° to 42°C.

SENSITIVITY TO PAIN

Pain fulfils the important function of warning that something is wrong with the body or that an injury has been caused. In eating, pain can be caused by very hot food which at a temperature of 45°C, or below freezing-point, can damage body cells. Serving syrup tart as it comes from the oven will burn the mouth and the practice of flashing food under the salamander or in a microwave oven can hurt the palate and is as bad as serving food that is not hot enough.

Food that requires excessive effort in mastication, fillets of fish that contain bones, and splinters of bone in poultry dishes, can all cause pain unnecessarily as can extremes of seasoning of salt, pepper and spices and excessive concentration of a sauce or of a stew which has been cooked for too long.

22

ORGANOLEPTIC ASPECTS OF QUALITY RECOGNITION

When the functions of the various senses have been understood it is then possible to calculate the interaction of food and drink and to assess quality recognition, quality being measured in terms of consumer satisfaction.

Organoleptic perception is the registration of a sense upon a perceptor, or in other words, the impressions gained by the receipt of imposing factors upon any of the senses. From this the mind gains an appreciation of what is being transmitted to it by its sensory perceptors. A person's sensory perception enables him to appreciate what is in effect, his own highly personal evaluation and appreciation of what is being offered up.

HABITUATION OF THE SENSES

When a person first goes into a room where there is a clock with a loud tick he is extremely aware of it for a brief period and may find that the noise distresses him. After the first abrupt awareness the ticking seems to stop or rather the person no longer notices it. This common phenomenon is referred to as 'habituation'.

Habituation results from a continuous exposure of an organism, nerve cell or sensory receptor to a continuous or constant stimulus. Constant exposure to a stimulus, be it colour, sound, taste, smell, temperature or texture, results in a gradual decrease or dulling of its emphasis. This means that a variety of sensations are required that will emphasise the range of nutrients, cooking processes, methods of presentation and contrast of food combinations. This contrast of resources needs to be controlled in a sensible manner so as to achieve maximum effect and avoid dissipation. Reference could be made to the composer of an opera who follows the standard pattern of an overture, the crescendo, gentle cavatina which is a melodious song, to the cavaletta or heroic response, leading to the dramatic conclusion of the opus.

Similarly, in order to create an enjoyable meal, the caterer needs to give due consideration to the conventional pattern of courses and the way in which the sequence relates to the consumer's senses. There is an ascending order of intensity, liquid to solid, light to heavy, delicate to more highly-seasoned, leading to a dramatic conclusion that leaves a sense of well-being and fulfilment. Of course, the combinations of dishes and their composition as well as the consumer's reaction to them, varies from one culture to another but the principles of menu sequence generally apply.

MEALS AND HABITUATION

To be properly appreciated a meal should provide an intensity of sensations, beginning with the aesthetic presentation or aroma of the first course because even at this early stage the consumer will make up his mind about the quality of the entire meal and assume an attitude of complete reception or rejection.

If the course is approved it is likely to be eaten quickly not so much to satisfy a depth of hunger as to avoid the senses' habituation to a pleasurable sensation which would result in a decrease in the pleasure. Should any dish be so poorly presented that it fails to please the eye, the whole system will react and the pace of eating become slow. The salivary glands will not flow easily thus rendering the process of eating more difficult and time-consuming.

METHODS FOR AVOIDING HABITUATION OF THE SENSES

The complete enjoyment of a meal therefore demands the occurrence of various sensations throughout it, whether the occasion is one of gastronomic importance or an everyday affair. Certainly it is more difficult to keep the senses alert during an ordinary occurrence than during a gourmet meal in which there are usually a number of traditional classical garnishes to make it more of an occasion.

Suggestions on how to carry this out in practice might include the following examples:

Hors-d'Oeuvre - the varied flavour and texture of, say, Parma ham and melon in which the dry and salty nature of the cured ham contrasts strongly with the cool fresh flavour and high moisture content of the melon.

Smoked salmon in the Norwegian style - the richness of a thin slice of smoked salmon with its deep orange colour contrasts with the delicate and mild soft egg mixture.

Bread is the normal adjunct to most main meals, being regarded as a filler by those people with a large appetite. In fact its role is more that of palate-cleanser as it helps to avoid a constant flavour in contact with the taste-receptor. The habit of eating it with butter is mainly confined to countries in the cool temperature zones because the butter ensures a good intake of energy, however undesirable this habit may be. A plainly cooked dish of pasta or fish really needs a sauce to provide a contrast and stimulation of tastes. The vegetables served with a main dish can act as a contrast so causing repeated stimulation and the avoidance of habituation. A salad served with a roast or grill has the same effect.

Accompanying relishes such as mustard, pickles, chutney and proprietary sauces make their contribution to variety and add contrast. The British habit of pounding a bottle of sauce over most foods is frequently decried but is justified because we cook plainly and in trying to avoid over-seasoning, have become accustomed to adding the extra flavouring sensation of a spicy sauce. The popularity of 'fast food' comes not just from the informality of the eating experience but from the adjuncts that liven up the mundane food and give it a flavour sensation.

Food temperature provides contrast and an ice-cream sweet can give a sensation of lightness because of the ice-cold state in which it is served and its consequent effect upon the senses.

Thus it can be seen that variation in food is necessary in order to ensure complete consumer appreciation; no one item should be allowed to have an adverse effect upon another but merely to complement it or contrast with it.

WISDOM AND FALLACY OF FOOD CHOICE

Patterns of food choice are determined by both cultural and instinctual habits yet the eating habits of many ethnic groups include many inexplicable practices which not only replenish lost energy but contribute to good health. Many people are averse to offal and reject all these nutritional organs; the reason for this is not apparent but may stem from the time when these parts of animals were used as sacrificial offerings to the gods because they were then held high in estimation. Since the use of offal was primarily for this purpose it is possible that ordinary people left them alone because they regarded them as food for the gods.

THE SEQUENCE AND CONTENT OF COURSES

There is some logic in the way that the order of courses in the menu has evolved over the ages. The principles of menu-planning serve to ensure an ideal way of distributing the necessary intake of food in the most practical manner.

To start with a soup makes good sense as it is easy to digest and can be as light or heavy as required by the consumer. It can be a refreshing or filling course according to climatic conditions. The almost universal practice of serving vegetables with meat and fish as a main course is to provide a variety of taste-sensations and a more balanced intake of nutrients than if the meat was to be consumed on its own. Various vegetables have different attributes so it is important to use those that are in keeping with the main item. Onions however can be used in almost every savoury dish as they assist in the digestion of fatty foods and exert a small beneficial effect by reducing the amount of cholesterol in the blood; they also contain prostaglandin which is capable of reducing hypertension. Garlic is also beneficial in the diet although it is used in very small amounts as a flavouring rather than as a vegetable. It too can destroy cholesterol in the blood and reduce hypertension. As onions and garlic are normally used only in small amounts for flavouring other ingredients their remedial effect is minimal.

Similar experiences have been noted when other nations or consumer groups have moved away from the staples of their traditional diet to other foods in which the body did not find the same essential nutrients. The move can show up quite quickly with undesirable results and it would appear that man comes to rely upon indigenous foods for his well-being and although the benefits may not be thoroughly understood it could be a more complex matter than a simple physiological replenishment. Established dietary practices should not be abandoned until any adverse effect has been proven.

The present-day trend of limiting lunch to a hamburger bun or a sandwich can be dangerous although there are many who state that there is nothing wrong with this new form of diet; only time will prove the validity of the pros and cons of the argument. Yet nutritionally the meal is not only unbalanced, but the main danger is that young people are being trained to accept a meal-substitute rather than a proper meal.

THE FLAVOURING OF FOODS

At first glance there would not appear to be any sound nutritional justification for the additional flavouring of foods other than possibly increased sensory pleasure. It is well known that the addition of certain flavourings aid the digestive process and it has been proved that when spices such as curry or pepper are deleted from a traditional diet there is malfunction of the digestive system, leading to a general state of malaise. When evaluating the role of chillies in the diet of those groups of South Americans who use them widely, it was found that the vitamin A content of chillies is of great importance because the normal diet is low in protein. It appears that chillies provide important micronutrients essential to the well-being of people in those countries. Even herbs, although used in very small amounts, make a contribution to good health and certain herbs and spices have definite bacteriostatic qualities which act as preservatives and so help to extend the shelf-life of a commodity. Their continuous and consistent use may have helped to adapt the digestive system to their everyday use and the consequent desire for their particular flavour characteristics. This originated in the availability of those ingredients in a local area but has since been extended to worldwide acceptance.

This chapter has shown that the basic rules of dietary practice emanated from the Far East and that developments in eating practices have been very slow, proceeding at an evolutionary rather than a revolutionary pace. It has also shown that the interpretation of man's needs as expounded by Galen over 2000 years ago were still dominant until the beginning of the nineteenth century. That his thinking has not been entirely replaced is evidenced by the large number of health-food stores that have opened to supply the demand for wholesome natural foodstuffs and sensible additives that fulfil a need in present-day diets.

Over the centuries man has constantly validated his previous assumptions regarding food acceptance, rejecting many that failed him but keeping the wisdom as exemplified in many traditional practices because they made good sense.

28

3 Nutrimental Aspects

Eating as a Necessity – Man's Nutritional Requirements – Innate Food
Characteristics – Dietary Requirements – Digestion – Considerations of
Digestion – Environmental Effects – Cultural Limitations – Societal
Influences – The Meal and the Occasion – Good Food and Bad Food –
Alcohol

EATING AS A NECESSITY

This chapter considers the dietary needs of mankind in terms of nutritional
requirements and food selection. The important of a working knowledge of
nutrition cannot be over-stressed; nutrition is a practical subject carried out
every day by those who compose menus and chefs who put them into effect.

One of the major problems facing our society in the western hemisphere is
malnutrition. It is not that we suffer from hunger but rather that we are prone
to excessive intake of food and drink which can lead to obesity, coronary heart
disease, hypertension, diabetes, and cirrhosis of the liver.

Any discussion of a topic such as malnutrition may appear out of place in a
textbook devoted to the study of gastronomy because the very word conjures up
the implication of gluttonous feasting. But gastronomy is also concerned with an
intelligent study of the effects of eating food, which is what nutrition is about.
The concern expressed by the medical profession about the foods people eat
means they want caterers to do something about it; certainly the public will
demand action, such is their worry about health. It is only too easy to fall into
bad food habits and to eat junk foods and fun foods because they need little or
no preparation and are suitable for any time of day or night.

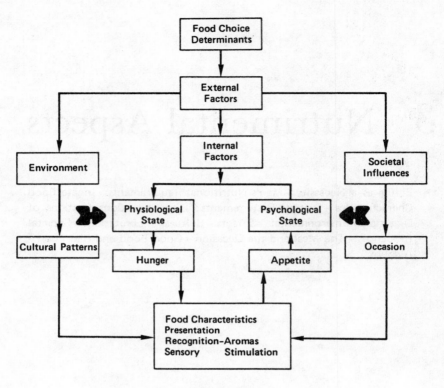

Figure 3.1
FOOD CHOICE DETERMINANTS

Fig. 3.1 illustrates the grouping of the three main factors which exert an influence on man's interaction to food and thus to his food choice. Many of the points in the diagram are dealt with in depth later in this chapter and it is suggested that the diagram will act as a frame of reference in placing the topics into context as they are discussed.

The three main factors that interact in food choice are (i) the totality of external factors, (ii) man himself, and (iii) the food available. It is then necessary to take note of the individual sub-units within the three major groupings which as shown, are not static but subject to various degrees of continuous modification. Their importance can shift in relation to each other hence no one of them can be pinpointed as being the single most important factor and any one of them can be more important than the others under different circumstances. As an example, when considering the external factors, the environment in particular, it is necessary to take into account not only the season when a food becomes available but also the thermal conditions of the place where it will be consumed because of the demands that thermal conditions make on the body.

Similarly, societal restraint can affect food supply and price just as it can the

30

occasion. For example, a wedding feast will have a different effect on the state of mind of participants from that which would be engendered at a funeral repast.

Thus it can be confidently stated that the internal subgroupings of factors is partially dependent on the external factors in terms of priorities, especially those of hunger, appetite and mental and physical well-being, and the interaction of these factors with the food. Should a person who is very hungry be presented with a food that his culture totally rejects, he will suffer hunger rather than accept. On the other hand, if a person has only a slight appetite when presented with an attractive dish which exhales a splendid aroma, this may cause his appetite to undergo such a state of arousal as to cause a very definite state of hunger. For this to be achieved, food preparation and presentation must always be such as will create a feeling of desire to eat and so enhance the chance of acceptance.

MAN'S NUTRITIONAL REQUIREMENTS

The body is a complex unit which requires five main chemicals to keep in good order. Its mechanism is in continuous use even when the body is at rest. It needs to be kept at a constant temperature which necessitates a constant input of food to replenish the energy expended by continuous biological action. The harder a person works the more food he needs to eat to produce the necessary energy. On average the daily requirement of energy is 10–14 Megajoules and also 2.5 litres of water. When exposed to extremes of temperature or subjected to increased activity more energy is needed in the form of food in order to maintain the balance of body constituents. The intake must be chosen carefully so as to ensure that the correct proportion of the five chemicals is maintained; these five are found in the body in the following proportions: protein 18 per cent, fat 13.5 per cent, carbohydrates 1.5 per cent, minerals 6 per cent and water 61 per cent; a minute quantity of micronutrients is also present. This leads to a nutritionally-balanced diet, derived preferably from a variety of foods so that the person maintains an interest in the meals he eats.

An interest in food and the experiences that eating can give ensures that the body is provided with the necessary nutrients and micronutrients to give good health and longevity. It is nature's way that guides man to satisfy his primary need for food, however there are a number of variables which intervene and have an effect upon the acceptance of some desirable nutrients and may cause people to choose only familiar and therefore more acceptable items.

These variables can be broadly divided into three areas: (i) the innate characteristics and sensory properties of foods, (ii) the physical and mental state of the individual at the time of making the choice, and (iii) the inbuilt cultural and societal practices which affect the combination, preparation, cooking, serving, and sharing of the eating experience.

INNATE FOOD CHARACTERISTICS

There are two aspects to this study, (i) regarding food as a nutrient or chemical substance, and (ii) regarding it as being the source of pleasurable sensations derived from the texture, flavour and aroma of a prepared dish. The five main nutrients have to be looked at from both these aspects as follows:

Protein

This is made of a number of macromolecules called *amino-acids* which are essential for both the growth and repair of tissues of the body either as part of its organic structure or as indispensable components of a specific reaction taking place in the organism.

The two kinds of protein are (i) *primary protein* which is derived from animal sources including the flesh and organs of all animals and their by-products such as eggs or milk, together with derivatives of these such as cheese, and (ii) *secondary protein* which is derived from vegetable sources and their derivatives such as textured vegetable protein.

It is essential that the diet provides the body with all the essential amino-acids which alone provide growth and repair, as there are some which cannot be synthesised by the body from other nutrients, although some exceptions have been noted.

The characteristics of primary protein are derived from a number of factors all of which have an effect upon acceptability and quality. The following are the points that may exert an influence:

1. the specific species of animal such as Aberdeen Angus or Charolais-cross cattle which are ideal for fattening;
2. the method of husbandry used, such as how the animals are fed and how the amount of exercise determines the proportion of lean meat;
3. the natural nutrients available in a locality, such as grass of the pampas or any alternative method of feeding;
4. the age of the animal at slaughter, which can affect the concentration of nutrients;
5. the quality of the cut of meat, either lean muscle or an active organ such as the liver;
6. the variation of nutrients in fish according to whether it is the white or the oily kind, and its treatment and preservation by smoking, salting or deep freezing, all of which have different effects.

PREPARATION AND COOKING OF ANIMAL PROTEIN

Different cuts of meat require different cooking processes and the same applies to the various kinds of fish; the method of cooking also affects the preparation procedures. The ultimate objective is to provide a tasty dish that is easy to eat and digest and the food should also stimulate the sensory apparatus.

The Need for Fat

Fat plays an important part in the diet of man by performing a specific function in the cells; even as small an amount as one gram per day is essential because the body cannot manufacture it. Fat is composed of fatty acids, a total absence of which may have serious consequence.

Fatty acids are in two main forms:

1. *saturated fatty acids* which are mainly of animal origin and contain more hydrogen atoms; when cold they solidify;
2. *unsaturated fatty acids* which are mainly of vegetable origin and remain in a liquid state when cold.

Fat has a higher calorific value than the other nutrients but the present belief is that people living in the Western world are consuming too much fat, particularly saturated fats which, unlike the unsaturated fats, leave a heavy deposit in the circulatory channels.

The uses of fat in the diet depend on a number of factors including the nature of the fat itself. Saturated fat comes from animal and dairy sources, for example, 'marbling' of a steak, streaky bacon and the fat content of a kipper; milk, butter and cream. Unsaturated fat is obtained from such plants as olives, nuts, soya beans and sunflower seeds. *Margarine* used to be made almost entirely from vegetable oils but is now made mainly from animal fats, including whale oil.

SATURATED FATS

The treatment and method of preserving the fat is also one of the factors determining its use and flavour intensifiers – such as adding salt to butter – are used to make fat more acceptable. Butter made by churning appears to have a different flavour and consistency from that produced by the centrifugal method. *Butter* is considered the best quality fat because of the presence of *butyrin* the volatile fat which gives it the special flavour. Its low melting-point is an asset. *Ghee* is widely used in Indian cookery to provide flavour and richness and is made mainly from clarified butter altough some vegetable oils are used.

UNSATURATED FATS

The quality of *olive oil* depends not only on the actual olives but on the way they are treated. The finest quality is called virgin olive oil and is obtained by rolling the olives between boards with very little pressure. Ordinary quality olive oil is obtained after a second pressing with hot water to pulp the olives, the result being treated and clarified in a refinery.

33

Fat has a special role in gastronomy because it contributes to the acceptance and palatability of a large number of the dishes we eat. When food is deep-fried, the heat of the fat adds both crispness and flavour which is useful if the basic ingredient is bland or neutral. A dry piece of meat benefits from being cooked in fat and delicate fish benefits from a butter or oil sauce such as Hollandaise and mayonnaise. Asparagus is considered to be a luxury vegetable but without the hot butter, vinaigrette or other appropriate sauce is merely another vegetable and hardly worthy of a solo appearance on the menu. Likewise, bread without butter is not considered adequate in England.

Carbohydrates

This nutrient forms a staple in the diet of the majority of the world's population and is often the main source of body energy. Carbohydrates can be obtained in the form of *sugar, starch, cellulose, pectin* and *glycogen* and from other compounds which contain carbon, hydrogen and oxygen. Glycogen is the only form of carbohydrate which is not produced by plants.

Sugar is the simplest form of carbohydrate and is classed as (i) *monosaccharides* or simple sugars, and (ii) *disaccharides* which consists of two monosaccharides linked together. Monosaccharides are subdivided into *glucose, fructose,* and *galactose,* and disaccharides into *lactose* and *maltose.*

Starch is a *polysaccharide* and is obtained only from vegetable products which is the form in which most of our intake of carbohydrate is found. Plants manufacture sugar by the process of photosynthesis and then store it in the seeds, roots or stems as minute granules of starch. These granules need to be processed or cooked prior to ingestion as they would not otherwise be made available to man.

Cellulose is the covering which envelopes the starch grains in the plant tissue and is not available to man in its natural form and must be processed to provide any food value. Ruminants can break it down into valuable food material and it may thus be made available to man indirectly.

Pectin is a polysaccharide obtained from green fruits and certain vegetable roots. It has no direct food value to man but is useful for its gelling (or setting) properties in making jam or jelly.

Glycogen is the only carbohydrate that is of animal origin and is manufactured in the body from glucose and stored as a reserve carbohydrate within the liver and muscle tissue of animals and fish.

The function of carbohydrates with a few exceptions, is to provide the main source of energy in the diet, and it is therefore very important. With the exception of glycogen, the sources of supply are cereals, fruits and vegetables which are also providers of secondary proteins, minerals and various vitamins.

34

For the purpose of providing energy, carbohydrates have to be converted into glucose before they can be digested, either during the processing or within the body. Carbohydrates are essential for certain body tissues such as the brain which can use only carbohydrate or glucose as its source of energy; they are also required to ensure the complete metabolism of the fat intake. A knowledge of the role of carbohydrates in the diet and their sources of supply is of value in the study of gastronomy.

Foods are composed of a variety of basic chemicals and the majority of them contain a combination of the chemicals already indicated. When properly selected and assisted by an intake of dairy products such as milk and eggs, carbohydrates provide the total nutritional requirements, the only shortfall being some of the essential amino-acids found only in meat. Many vegetarians live to a ripe old age, which can pose the question as to whether the body is able to manufacture certain chemicals when they are not made available through the diet.

The factors that contribute to the characteristics of carbohydrates include:

1. their specific botanical species; from a low calorie and nil protein content in citrus fruits to a high calorie and protein content as found in pulses, cereals and nuts;
2. the prevailing climatic conditions which govern the ability of various plants to extract their nourishment from the soil;
3. climatic conditions which affect growth with the mineral content varying according to the amount of daylight, sunlight, relative humidity and rainfall and the prevailing temperature;
4. the type of soil and its nutrients and the method of farming;
5. the method of harvesting and the period of time from then, through storage to usage;
6. the processing that the food undergoes such as washing, drying or freezing which may lead to a loss of vitamins;
7. any refining process that may eliminate some valuable nutrient content.

Vitamins

The human organism requires not only protein, fat and carbohydrate but also one other vital element, known as *vitamins* whose role is to act as a biochemical catalyst which carries out a variety of conversions within the body cells. A lack of vitamins in the diet is serious, but happily a well-balanced diet which includes fresh foods usually provides the recommended daily intake although strict vegetarians may suffer from a lack of Vitamin B_{12} which is only available from animal sources. Poor cooking practices and a lack of fresh fruit and vegetables may cause a shortage of Vitamin C and caterers should strive to supply and not to destroy this essential element of the diet.

Water is essential for all the bodily biochemical processes and for facilitating the discharge of waste materials. Under normal conditions approximately 2.5 litres of water are required daily but in a very hot climate where the loss through perspiration can be as much as 0.5 litre per hour, this loss must be replaced at the same rate.

Mineral salts are important in the chemical reaction with the body cells, two of them, *calcium* and *phosphorus* being important in bone formation, especially for young people. Iron is required to maintain the blood cells in a healthy state and caterers should recognise those foods that are good sources of supply.

DIETARY REQUIREMENTS

Man in Western society has learned over the centuries how to combine the nutrients into an acceptable meal and he did this long before the science of nutrition was understood. Many cooking methods have evolved to such a degree of perfection that there is no serious loss of nutrients as for example with vegetables that are kept very slightly underdone thus retaining maximum vitamin content which was being done long before the word 'vitamin' had been invented. The practice of serving vegetables with meat is long-established and makes good nutritional sense.

In addition to a practical application of nutrition through the menu, caterers should be aware of the way in which various groups of food are reconverted to their basic elements within the body and how they are utilised for energy and maintenance of the body system. This aspect should be borne in mind when composing menus as any imbalance – for example, an excessive amount of fat, protein or very salty items – may have an adverse affect upon the digestive process so spoiling the pleasure of the meal by unpleasant after-effects.

DIGESTION

There are a few experiences worse than that of leaving the dinner-table with a feeling of over-fullness, nausea and general malaise, caused by poor digestion. The food we eat has to be broken down in the digestive system into its individual basic constituents so as to be absorbed.

The digestive system begins in the mouth where the digestive juices are promoted by the taste of the food, it is however necessary to distinguish between appetite and hunger. *Hunger* arises when the body is depleted of energy and the stomach is empty. Pangs of hunger caused by muscular contraction inside the stomach, energise the organism to seek replenishment. The vision and aroma of food will stimulate the flow of gastric juices which are alerted in readiness for intake. *Appetite* is more subtle than hunger and the flow of gastric juices needs to be promoted early in order to assist digestion. It has been suggested that rituals such as changing in readiness for dinner, a chat over cocktails, the sight of the table set in readiness and the glow of candlelight all contribute to a state of mind that leads to the fulfilment of expectations of pleasurable sensation. The next stage is the presentation of the food in the best possible manner so that nothing stops the further flow of the juices by being of unpleasant appearance or obnoxious smell.

Food is broken down by the teeth and moistened by the saliva which helps the tongue to rotate it until it reaches a stage when it can be swallowed easily and passed down the gullet. The saliva contains the enzyme *pythalin* which converts starch into glucose but doughy masses are not easily penetrated by the pythalin and are therefore more difficult to digest. An emotional state such as anger, fear or worry will decrease the flow of saliva so impairing digestion.

When the masticated food moves towards the stomach it can be affected by the state of arousal of the person; when he is angry or distressed the stomach may hang low in the abdomen thus impairing digestion. The stomach can stretch to receive the amount of food sent to it but this capacity can be affected by the person's state of mind at the time of eating. Only when he is relaxed and able to give full attention to the meal is the condition for good digestion created. The stomach has three functions to fulfil: (i) temporary storage; (ii) mixing and breaking down food; (iii) the release of food at intervals to the next stage of digestion.

Storage is necessary as otherwise we would need to eat something every twenty minutes or so. While food is in the stomach the muscles contract gently and continuously, churning it against the walls where *gastric juice* is released through the numerous glands which line the stomach. The gastric juice is composed of 99 per cent *water*, 0.02–0.04 per cent *hydrochloric acid*, and 0.5 per cent *pepsinogen*, which combine to produce the enzyme *pepsin* which acts on the foods. From the stomach only water, alcohol and salts are absorbed, the main nutrients being taken during the next stage which occurs in the small intestine. Muscular contractions push the partially digested food or chyme along the duodenum towards the large intestine. The pancreas gland releases some of its juice into the small intestine and bile flows from the liver to split or convert the foods they are designed to treat.

After some three to four hours in the small intestine food passes into the large intestine where further breakdown of as yet undigested substances such as cellulose takes place. After this all that is left is faeces to be expelled after having been something up to twenty-four hours in the making.

CONSIDERATIONS OF DIGESTION

The person who composes menus and is concerned for the well-being of his customers should give some consideration to the facts concerning digestion. The process of digestion is driven by energy and does not happen of its own volation. Any energy left is that which is surplus to the digestive process so it follows that food items which tax the system will mean less energy available for external release. Thus foods of less nutritive value but easily digestible properties may be more beneficial.

A large meal will cause extra work in the stomach both during the churning process and in pushing it into the small intestine. A large intake of liquid, including wine, will dilate the stomach and reduce its working efficiency by diluting the secreted enzymes. This is one reason why soup may require more time to digest than a solid meal.

Food should be prepared so that it stimulates a desire to eat by causing a state of anticipation. It can be prepared so that some of the chewing has been eliminated by mechanical means such as in making sausages and beefburgers. Raw meat is actually more readily digestible than well-done meat as for example in *Steak Tartare* or an underdone steak but there is possible danger from bacterial contamination from a diet of uncooked meat.

Starches need to be thoroughly cooked to become digestible because the cellulose which envelopes the starch grains is not soluble by the digestive fluid and the cooking process must rupture the cells. Purées of vegetable are obviously easier to digest than whole vegetables.

A beaten raw egg is easier to digest than a cooked one yet is equal in nutritional value; but it is still advisable to cook foods until fairly well done so that they become safer to ingest. Overcooked protein tends to become dry and denatured thus making it difficult to digest.

Protein and fat require more time to pass through the digestive system than does carbohydrate so it is advisable to limit the amount of these in the diet. Rich foods such as fat and cream have a high satiety value which creates a feeling of fullness in the stomach, sometimes even before the meal is completed. They should therefore be used with discretion.

Cold drinks lower the temperature inside the stomach thus retarding digestion so the traditional practice of serving a sorbet midway through a long meal may be good for refreshing the palate but bad for the digestive process.

Warm food and spiced foods serve to encourage the release of digestive enzymes so facilitating the enjoyment. Too much strenuous exercise can affect all the organs of the body and interfere with good digestion whether the exercise is taken before or after a meal. This would indicate the need for a pause between the time when the meal ends and dancing begins at a dinner dance.

ENVIRONMENTAL EFFECTS

The effect of the environment on standard dietary practices is outlined in Chapter 1 and it is important to remember that this has an effect upon food choice on a daily basis. Customers are affected by variations of season and climate as shown by the popularity of salads in summer because of their cool appeal whereas in winter there is a desire for warming foods to maintain the correct body-surface temperature. Seasonality of foods in the temperate regions is a factor that guides conscious choice towards foods available – and at their best – at a particular time of year. The place where food is eaten also has a considerable effect on the food choice.

CULTURAL LIMITATIONS

From the moment of birth each one of us is exposed to and enveloped within the confines of our society. The language that we learn as our initial means of communication and our patterns of behaviour are there before us and reflect the accumulation of knowledge and standards of our ancestors.

This knowledge has been codified and is reflected in the social institutions which guide our pattern of interaction within the standard and the wills of the majority. In accepting these standards we enter into a social contract with our fellow citizens, and any deviation will incur not only the disfavour of others but also create a sense of self-dissonance which could affect our well-being. The power of these conventions is as strong in the matter of food acceptance as in our dealings with the outside world.

In the western world marriage is a union between one man and one woman and bigamy is punished, yet in other societies polygamy is accepted. As for food, what is acceptable to one culture may be looked upon as totally abhorrent by another and to try to make people eat a food they have never tried can cause physical sickness and a state of malaise.

The culture of a society and its prejudices and taboos limit the choice of foods and a caterer needs to know what these are, especially when dealing with an international gathering. To serve an unknown or unacceptable food, even though it may be an insignificant item of garnish, may cause suspicion and fear in the member of a particular ethnic group so making the entire meal an unpleasant experience. Flavourings have to be acceptable and it should be borne in mind that pungent herbs such as mint and sage and powerful flavourings such as onion and garlic are not universally popular and that spices must be used sparingly for some groups of people. The skill of French chefs in the way they use flavours elegantly and judiciously has been one of the factors that has raised French cooking to such a high standard.

SOCIETAL INFLUENCES

The culture and tradition of various groups of people have set parameters of food acceptability that are perpetuated by succeeding generations even though they may be living in a new environment and different society from that of their forebears. The fact that a new situation exists seldom appears to have much effect upon food laws even though the abandonment of ancient rules and beliefs may lead to loss of identity.

The society entered by a newcomer from another society or country is bound to exert an influence on him and it can take a long time to settle. A person may move to a richer or to a poorer country than the one in he was brought up, so having to adjust his expectations to certain aspects of a new environment. For example:

1. the economic power or disposable income of a western country will appear enormous to somebody going there from say, a remote village of India;
2. State legislation of the adopted country may be connected with the national religion and forbid him to carry out some of his customary practices, such as the method of animal slaughter;
3. methods of farming and animal husbandry may offer a bewildering abundance of food choices;
4. different values placed in the meal ritual such as using a knife and fork rather than the fingers.

The newcomer will normally adapt himself to the situation and if it is the pattern to consume three meals per day then he will drop whatever was his previous habit and adopt that of his host-country or society. The same applies to furnishing a home and, to a certain extent, to bringing up a family; it is really a case of 'when in Rome, doing as the Romans do'.

Means of communication and cheapness of holidays and transport help people of one country to appreciate the customs of other countries while the availability of imported foodstuffs encourages people to experiment and so widen their choice of dishes.

THE MEAL AND OCCASION

From the very earliest times man has commemorated important happenings by a ceremonial meal that marked the occasion in an emphatic manner. Such special events as the capture of a large animal that could be shared among the whole of a nomadic tribe or, as later in history, the celebration of a birth or marriage, were sufficient excuse to warrant a special meal. The gathering of a good harvest justified a celebration meal with more than the usual amount of food being served, thus befitting the occasion.

40

The discovery of fire and the fashioning of cooking utensils gave a new emphasis to communal eating; the emerging leader of a community could justify his position by obtaining a rich choice of food to underly the importance of the special occasion and so reinforce the allegiance of his supporters.

The celebration of a special occasion also implied the use of special foods; a gathering of people to share the experience of a meal acquired a symbolic value, often associated with religious beliefs. The Sabbath day was the day for rest and prayers but it was also the day of the week for a celebratory meal at which the whole family gathered. As part of the ritual, grace was said before the meal to give thanks to God for providing the food they were about to enjoy, and also at the end of the meal.

The protocol of washing the hands before eating is not only for hygienic reasons but a symbolic gesture of cleansing and purifying before partaking of a gift from God. Sharing the meal with the family was also symbolic of the unity and value of family life.

The dining table was the centre point of the home and when guests were welcomed to partake with the family they were offered the best that could be afforded. The *banc* was the bench on which people sat to eat and is the origin of the word *banquet*. Thus food was not eaten solely for sustenance but also to extend hospitality and social warmth.

As groups and societies grew in size to cities and states, leaders of the community made every effort to provide extra special meals for distinguished visitors. It is now internationally accepted that a worthy person is given a banquet in his honour as the most appropriate way of paying respect.

GOOD FOOD AND BAD FOOD

Food means all the nourishing things we eat for enjoyment and to stay healthy. Under normal conditions good sound food provides a balanced diet but any item that is bad or dirty is unacceptable except under extreme conditions of deprivation when items that are normally unacceptable have to be consumed.

Certain groups of people can safely ingest putrid eggs or meat and derive pleasure from them yet these same people are likely to be violently sick if given fresh milk or a piece of cheese to eat because of gastro-intestinal irritation or malabsorption.

Foods that are considered good for one group may have an adverse effect on a single member of that group. an allergy may result and to that person, the food is bad.

A large intake of food of any kind can cause an unpleasant effect to anybody, more especially if the food is of one nutrient, for example an excess of protein or fat. Excessive consumption of alcohol is well-known as being the cause of sickness and the body's normal tolerance is limited approximately 500 ml over a short period of say, one hour and a quarter. A habitual drunkard is likely to suffer organ damage such as cirrhosis of the liver. Some people are affected by consuming certain fruits such as figs, grapes, plums, and rhubarb, and vegetables such as pimentoes, Brussels sprouts and spinach because these have an unpleasant effect upon the digestion. Dried pulses, hard cheese and fats because of their high satiety value, can also be hard on the digestion.

'Good' foods are those that conform to quality criteria in relation to their physical properties of maturity for an intended purpose. Quality is judged by colour, odour, freshness and suitability for the meal.

ALCOHOL

The word *alcohol* is derived from the Arabic word *alkohl* which is the eye shadow used by women. The word was initially used to describe spirit distilled from wine but now means all kinds of intoxicating liquor.

Alcohol is produced during the fermentation process by minute organisms in the yeast which split the sugar consisting of carbon, hydrogen and oxygen, into two substances, carbon combining with part of the oxygen to form carbonic acid gas (CO_2), the remainder of the carbon mixing with the hydrogen and oxygen to form alcohol.

Alcohol is similar to other carbohydrates in that it releases heat and energy for work and can therefore be considered as a food and it has a specific action upon the nervous system. Taken in small amounts, alcohol is a stimulant and yet it helps relaxation by releasing inhibitions and by stimulating the appetite.

The therapeutic value of alcohol is offset by its action as a depressant upon the nervous system and as the concentration in the body increases so does its narcotic effect. A concentration of only 1 per cent in the blood (which is equivalent to approximately three normal measures of gin or whisky or about three pints of beer) will impair sensory and motor-functions. A level of more than 80mg / 100 ml of blood alcohol concentration is sufficient to incapacitate a person for driving a car and he will be guilty of driving 'under the influence'.

Alcohol taken in moderation has a definite beneficial effect and can speed up metabolic processes so contributing to a feeling of well-being; excessive drinking acts against a pleasant gastronomic experience.

To enjoy a meal to the full, a state of alertness is necessary and the only way to keep alert throughout, is to drink sparingly and to savour each sip. One aperitif and a maximum of three glasses of wine each holding approximately 1.5 decilitres is sufficient to provide an impression of well-being; it should be remembered that coffee is also a stimulant.

From time immemorial, wine has made a major contribution to gastronomy and an understanding of it is essential to the study. References can be found in the Old Testament such as that Moses advised that vines be planted on the slopes

42

instead of on flat ground near water. Wine was produced in Egypt, the vines probably being brought from Armenia and Syria, although none of these countries now produce wine. The Etruscans introduced the art of wine-making into Italy and the Romans held it in great esteem both as a beverage and a food. The Romans added all sorts of things such as tar, resinous matter and gypsum, to their wine as a means of preserving it, additions that would not be very acceptable today!

The Roman Legions were paid in salt, (*salarium*) hence the word 'salary', and in wine. The cost of transporting large quantities of wine to wherever the legions were operating was overcome by planing vines in the occupied countries, or by bringing it from a nearby one that produced it. From this the habit of drinking wine, especially with meals, was firmly established throughout most of Europe, so founding this aspect of gastronomy.

OPERA DI M.
BARTOLOMEO
SCAPPI, CVOCO SECRETO
DI PAPA PIO QVINTO,

DIVISA IN SEI LIBRI.

Nel primo si contiene il ragionamento che fa l'Autore con Gio. suo discepolo.

Nel secondo si tratta di diuerse viuande di carne, sì di quadrupedi, come di uolatili.

Nel terzo si parla della statura, e stagione de pesci.

Nel quarto si mostrano le liste del presentar le viuande in tauola, così di grasso come di magro.

Nel quinto si contiene l'ordine di far diuerse sorti di paste, & altri lauori.

Nel sesto, & vltimo libro si ragiona de'conualescenti, & molte altre sorti di viuande per gli infermi.

Con il discorso funerale che fu fatto nelle essequie di Papa Paulo III.

Con le figure che fanno bisogno nella cucina, & alli Reuerendissimi nel Conclaue.

E IL MIO FOGLIO

QVAL PIV FERMO

E IL MIO PRESAGGIO.

SIBYLLA

Col priuilegio del sommo Pontefice Papa Pio V. & dell'Illustriss. Senato Veneto per anni XX.

4 The Progression of Gastronomy

Food Habits of Ancient Greece – Eating in Ancient Rome – The Egyptian Contribution – Eating in Great Britain in Early Times – Elizabethan Meals – The French Approach and Contribution – Cooking Methods through the Ages – The British at Dinner – The Pattern of Living of the Wealthy – The London Season – Domestic Staff – The Influence of Cookery Books – The Great Chefs – The Influence of Food Guides – Restaurant Gradings – Culinary Associations – Gourmet Societies – Food Writers – Museums

FOOD HABITS OF ANCIENT GREECE

When the ancient Greeks first began to enjoy the pleasures of the table they were gourmands rather than gourmets – in other words they ate heartily but fed badly by trying out all kinds of combinations of foodstuffs, mostly incompatible. Vast sums of money were spent on buying food and the cook employed in private service was instructed by his master or mistress on the method of preparation leaving the cook with no authority to correct the prevalent extravagances and excesses. Gastronomy was outclassed by gluttony and the connoisseur by the gourmandiser.

As time went by, the Greeks became more discriminating and selective in their choice of food and eventually they allowed their cooks to use their acquired skills and knowledge in deciding what were the most appropriate food combinations. The cooks were thus able to keep their masters in better health and this in turn made them more agreeable to serve and at the same time, saved them money since the cooks were allowed to exert full authority over the organisation of their kitchen.

At that time many of the cooks working in Greece had been brought from Sicily. The flair and innovatory skills of Sicilian cooks was such that they had made a reputation for themselves in the culinary arts by their ability to prepare

45

eye-catching displays of food from very simple ingredients. They created many new dishes and as each was invented the creator held the copyright of it for a year before any other cook was allowed to feature it.

This led to prodigality as each master urged his cook to produce ever more sumptuous dishes for the feasts to which he invited his friends. Such functions set an increasingly high standard of cooking by making even greater demands on the skill and creativity of the cooks.

There was no shortage of labour for the kitchens of Greek noblemen as slaves were used for all the dirty and heavy kitchen work. The head cook merely sat on a throne in the centre of his kitchen directing the efforts of his team of cooks, shouting instructions amidst the noise and the dust and fumes produced by the fires. The cooks brought their dishes to him to show how they had inter-preted his instructions, some of them being those received from his master or mistress and probably still somewhat outlandish by his standards.

Feasts were held to celebrate any and every event such as the birth of a baby or the triumphal return of a warrior from war; these were sufficient excuse to warrant a great feast to which hundreds of family and friends could be invited. Gradually the rich changed their gluttonous habits and through the influence of their Sicilian cooks, developed as gourmets.

Festivities were further enhanced by the introduction of a musical back-ground although it was not allowed to interfere with the eloquent flow of conversation about the food and drink. The Greeks came to regard cookery as an art, with eating and drinking as its manifestation. Great men studied the appetite so as to classify its various forms and suggested that a good chef could stimulate it even when it was already satiated.

Epicurus the philosopher, who lived from 342–270 BC, told his fellow-countrymen to 'Eat, drink and merry, for tomorrow we die'; they listened to his edict and were pleased to carry it out in practice.

EATING IN ANCIENT ROME

In Rome after it had been rebuilt in 390 BC the very rich vied with one another for the high quality of the dishes they presented at their dinner parties. The range of food products was constantly increased by new ingredients brought back from each new country conquered.

Lucullus (110–57 BC) was one of the conquerors and he brought so many rare foodstuffs back to Rome that his fame as a general was surpassed by his reputation as being the greatest gourmet of all times. He spent his wealth on giving sumptuous feasts for which these rare and exotic commodities were cooked by the most intricate methods and ornamented in the most elaborate style. Nowadays we speak of a 'Lucullan feast' as meaning an epicurean occasion at which the standard of food, cookery and service are of the highest order and a restaurant named after Lucullus would obviously be a high class one.

(Ed.ne Alinari) N.º 26089. — Imm.ti TARQUINIA. — Dintorni. Tombe Etrusche. Affresco nella Tomba dei Leopardi.

1. A banqueting scene from a fresco in an Etruscan royal tomb, dating from the sixth century BC

47

The Romans ate their feasts from a reclining position rather than seated at the table and plenty of space was allowed for the entertainment that became an integral part of the feast. Lucullus and other notables liked to offer guests such performers as dancers, clowns, singers, magicians and raconteurs to amuse, excite or titillate guests in order to generate an atmosphere that would cause the event to end as an orgy, so satisfying all the senses. Such events were confined to the very wealthy but to some extent they can be said to have led to the fall of the Roman Empire because these excesses became an integral part of the life of the rich, causing social degeneration in later years. There was no middle class of citizens and the way of living of the poor classes of slaves and conscripts was in complete contrast to that of their masters.

In preparation for going out to dine, guests began with a bath and massage and special attention to their hair and teeth. On arrival, slaves would pour

2. Fish formed an important part of the Roman diet; the Mediterranean provided a rich harvest, as this first century mosaic from Pompeii shows

48

scented cold water over their hands, take off their outdoor shoes and replace them with slippers, after bathing their feet. A special banquet dress was worn to replace the outdoor toga and the guests were then bidden to take their places on the couches around the room, their hair was sprayed with perfume and the room itself scented with various essences and spices. After thanks had been said to the Gods, the musicians would start playing and the voluptuous serving girls would bring in the food and serve the drink.

The Romans used a so-called *liquamen* known as *garum* in many of their savoury foods; it was made from the guts of fish together with anchovies, sprats and red mullet which had been cured by salting and drying in the sun. The first course might be a selection of small titbits of various meats, poultry and game made in the form of what we now call *piroguis*, rissoles and *rastegais*, or olives, radishes and hard-boiled peacock-eggs which when opened, revealed a roasted bunting or other exotic delicacy. The second course consisted of several species of fish cooked in many ways, and various kinds of meat, poultry and game in the elaboration of which one kind of meat was dressed to look like another; they were brought in and carved whilst slaves poured out glasses of wine flavoured with spices and honey, probably rather like present day sweet vermouth.

The guests drank toasts to one another and it was then time for the dessert course which often consisted of fresh or preserved exotic fruits from other countries, many kinds of pastries and sweetmeats all made attractive both to the eye and mouth. For the dessert, a very sweet and highly concentrated liquid made from dried grapes and grape-must was served; this was known as *passum*. By this time the brow of each guest had been adorned with a garland of sweet-smelling leaves as being an heroic trencherman and the vomitoriums would be in constant use. There are no Roman influences left on our cooking or eating today, although there are a few in Italian gastronomy.

We still use the names of the illustrious people of these days, for example Lucullus, Epicurus and Cadmos who was chef to the King of Sidon in Phoenicia, as garnish names for outstanding dishes created for special occasions.

EGYPTIAN CONTRIBUTION

Food in ancient Egypt was both abundant and varied, even for the poorer classes and long before were any imported foods from abroad. The general view of Egypt being a desert where nothing much thrived or grew is erroneous and meat and fish, cereals, fruit and vegetables were produced. Being well-nourished did not mean that they were obese, in fact obesity even among the rich was looked upon as objectionable; the hard-working peasant class could hardly be expected to put on weight although beer was freely obtainable. The eighteenth dynasty of of the Pharaohs, 500 years before the birth of Christ, saw Egypt at the height of its power and richness.

49

It might be thought that at this time the only source of meat was from the hunt but in fact the ancient Egyptians had learned to use cattle for work and as food and drink. Beef was eaten by the upper classes and the poorer people ate mutton, goat, and poultry, either roasted or boiled; pork was acceptable though not in widespread use, pigeons, doves, geese, duck and quail were used and fish (usually freshwater species) were salted or sun-dried to preserve them for later appreciation. Locusts were (and are still) considered a delicacy; honey was used for sweetening purposes.

EATING IN GREAT BRITAIN IN EARLY TIMES

Britons have always had simple tastes in food and their normal diet at the time of the Roman invasion in the 1st century BC still consisted mainly of meat. This was of course, looked down on by the Roman conquerors who, as we have seen, were used to eating a much wider variety of foods as a result of their conquest of various parts of the world.

Although the native diet was improved and expanded by the various invaders, the influence they exerted did not affect Briton's tastes to any marked degree. The Romans introduced the vine and by the time the Domesday Book was completed there were no fewer than thirty-eight vineyards listed, which continued to flourish until Tudor times. Many of the fruits and vegetables we now accept as a normal part of our everyday diet were first introduced by the Romans. The ancient Britons had developed a taste for oysters and so had the Romans who helped to improve methods of cultivation in order that there was a plentiful supply for all to eat at every meal.

The English developed further eating habits under the Saxons who conquered Britain in the 5th century AD, and their tastes included nearly all the various kinds of meat and poultry as used today as well as the same kinds of game animals and birds. Both fresh and salt-water fish were eaten and there was quite a good selection of fruit and vegetables to choose from. Herbs and spices were used in cooking, although at that time most of the meat was spit-roasted. Bread was made from stone-ground flour and cheese was used even then as a course in its own right, usually accompanied by wine or ale, both of which were plentiful and cheap. Mead was more expensive so was drunk mainly by the rich.

The Danes, whose attempt to conquer Britain began around 850 AD were a hard drinking race who liked their food and were stout trencherman. Both King Alfred and King Canute who reigned during this period were reputed to be monarchs who loved the pleasures of the table. The Danish invaders were integrated into the English race as were their food habits.

The conquest of England in 1066 by William I exerted a Gallic influence on English eating habits that was much more considerable than that of any of the conquerors who had come before them, because in comparison with for example, the Danes, the Normans were very dainty eaters. They enjoyed good food but it had to be served ceremoniously with the special feast days celebrated in the proper manner. On such occasions the boar's head would be borne into the dining room to the sound of trumpets and drums and the singing of a choir; it was normally accompanied by roasted birds such as cranes, geese, peacocks or swans, served on great platters and surrounded with elaborate garnishes.

The fish that Britons ate included whitebait, herrings (both fresh and salted), eels, salmon and occasionally, whalemeat. The meat was generally highly spiced and seasoned which helped to disguise any off-flavour caused by poor storage facilities, but it was usually cooked until well-done so as prevent any indisposition of the partakers.

The bread was good and totally unlike the factory-produced loaf to which we are accustomed nowadays. It was very crusty and coarse in texture. Many spiced breads were made; Simnel cake flavoured with saffron, and *pain perdu*, often called French toast, were popular. Although several kinds of cheese were readily obtainable they did not play quite such an important part in the diet as it does today. Fruits in season were used but dessert was not a feature of everyday meals because the eating quality of many fruits was not sufficiently good. There was ale, beer, cider and wine to drink. The ale was made without hops and as it did not taste very nice it became the custom to immerse a toasted apple in it to enhance the taste. From this habit comes the phrase to 'toast' a person by drinking his health. Cider had been drunk since the eleventh century and had become so popular that during the fifteenth century there were as many cider-houses as there were alehouses in London.

During the reign of the Tudor monarchs from 1485 to 1663 there was an improvement in the quality of foods produced mainly brought about by better husbandry, but not in the variety. In the rural areas people lived by being virtually self-supporting, rearing and growing for their immediate needs and preserving any surplus for use out of season just as today a good housewife gets the urge to preserve food to stock her larder against the possibility of being cut off from normal supplies. In those days practically all the processing of food was done in the kitchen; meat was slaughtered, flayed, plucked or drawn; fish was gutted and filleted, butter was churned and many foods were smoked, dried, cured and dealt with totally. But as Henry J. Heinz said when he first set up his factory in 1900, housewives were happy and willing to pay for someone else to take over a share of the more tedious kitchen chores thus making their lives more congenial. In towns the supply of perishable commodites was prone to the vagaries of weather, transport and storage facilities. Cattle were kept for use as draught animals rather than being reared especially for the table which would indicate that the roast beef of old England might have been rather tough to eat. Fish and meat and other commodites were improved by being cured but they often needed to be marinated with spices and herbs to mask the fact that they were past their pristine freshness. Vinegar was widely used to preserve and marinate meat and to wash off signs of staleness.

Soup has been an important part of the British diet from early in the thirteenth century; according to the skill of the cook, it ranged from thin watery gruel to a thickly-garnished broth but as in France, it served as a source of sustenance and often as a meal in its own right. Pulses were used as a base and fennel became one of the favourite flavourings, possibly because it was considered to be a cure for fever but mainly because it was a widely cultivated vegetable. Salad vegetables were grown and olive oil and wine vinegar were imported to make salad dressings. Flowers and buds were much used in salads and to add aroma to other dishes; they were also candied or made into conserves.

The quality of flour was improved, making it possible to produce better bread, cakes, biscuits and puddings. Dried fruit was imported but the sweetening agent was local honey; eggs and butter were readily available for making rich cakes. Certain areas, including **Bakewell**, **Banbury** and **Shrewsbury**, became famous for the biscuits or cakes they produced. The wide range of boiled puddings which are such an attractive feature of British menus, did not become popular until the seventeenth century. Game was more widely used than it is now and just as the Greeks and Romans had enjoyed the thrills of the chase and considered it an honourable sport, so the English have always loved shooting and hunting and shown an appreciation of the taste of the flesh of game, both feathered and furred. Game was an ideal commodity because it could be kept for some length of time whilst it matured and became more tender; it was the practice to bury it unplucked in the earth until it developed a high flavour and aroma. The other reason for its popularity was because many of them are excellent for presentation purposes, for example a boar's head, a roasted capercailzie or a haunch of venison presents a challenge to the cook as to the ways in which he can lustre, bedeck and display it.

ELIZABETHAN MEALS

The picture of the eating habits of the ordinary people of those days from 1558 to 1603 when Elizabeth was queen is that they ate substantial meals comprised of a fairly restricted range of commodites which they used quite extravagantly. In fact this is a distorted image and although the family meal included a large number and variety of dishes at each of the two courses comprising the full dinner, the large number of dishes were there to provide a choice rather than an abundance. Members of the family took what they wanted of the dishes nearest to them, probably only two or three items, rising to half a dozen on feast days, and the surplus food, with the exception of the joints, was served to the household staff to supplement their more restricted meals.

In those days there was a law stipulating that fish be served on two days each week, but Sunday was a meat day and Sunday dinner was a substantial midday meal and the most important and formal repast of the whole week, a tradition

3. A sixteenth-century kitchen (from Bartolomeo Scappi's *Opera* of 1570)

that has carried right on, gaining further emphasis during Victorian times, to our own days when it is still the custom for the family to sit down to a 'joint and two veg.' followed by a tart or pudding.

THE FRENCH APPROACH AND CONTRIBUTION

In other civilised countries, catering followed a similar pattern to that of the United Kingdom. In France the *auberges* or inns existed as long ago as Roman times and the abbeys welcomed travellers right up to the time of the French Revolution in 1789. The post-houses where the stage-coaches stopped overnight or waited whilst the horses were changed, increased in number until the arrival of the railway age.

The inn acted as a centre where the villagers could come into contact with the outside world as travellers brought news, gossip and rumours and exchanged information. Thus the inn played both a social and a political role. To attract and retain the valued business of customers the *aubergiste* fed them well and at all times, by keeping the place open all day.

The signs outside the inns were similar to those in England, being named after either the owner, the local landowner, the main profession of its patrons (such as *Hôtel du Commerce*), historical persons (such as *Hôtel Saint-Louis*), a friendly country (for example *Hôtel d'Angleterre* - the first to be so named was in 1784 as the result of peace between the two countries) but there was less use of facetious or meaningless inn names than in England.

Until the sixteenth century the progress of catering in France was similar to that of Great Britain but then a big change came about as a result of the marriage of Catherine de Medici of Florence to Henry II of France in 1533. She brought her own cooks and domestic staff to the French court and they introduced their own florentine specialities and other Italian culinary practices which helped to refine and improve the then standards of French cookery. Gradually France overtook Italy as the foremost country in the art of cooking and began to lead the world in matters of gastronomic excellence.

Restaurants, as separate places from inns and hotels, started to open in Paris about 1770 and became so popular that they spread across France and to other countries in Europe. Antoine Beauvilliers, a chef, became the first well-known restaurateur because of his pleasant personality and good memory for names and faces; his dining-room was elegantly decorated and furnished, the waiters were smart and he kept a good cellar, so his establishment became the first successful enterprise at this high level. The advantages of having a restaurant separate from an inn were that it was open all day whereas the inn usually offered set meals at set times, the customer had a wider choice than in the set meal at the inn, the atmosphere was greatly different, and the client could decide what he wanted to pay and so eat accordingly.

54

COOKING METHODS THROUGH THE AGES

Cooking equipment and the methods of cooking have played almost as important a role as the foods themselves. Once man was able to create fire and keep it alight, he soon learned how to render inedible raw materials palatable and also to preserve them for future use by smoking. So it was that hot roast meat was the staple food of Stone Age man.

The first kinds of fuel were wood and peat and their use might indicate that cooking was a smelly, smoky business when carried out in a cave but if wood is well-seasoned and properly prepared it need not be obnoxious. The use of the right kind such as ash, beech, cherry or hawthorn wood gives a hot clear fire that both cooks and warms. To roast a whole beast indoors over an open fire would have made a mess so such a size of 'joint' was usually cooked outdoors. Only when it was understood that a chimney was needed not purely as an exit for the smoke and smell but also to create a draught, was it possible to instal a spit indoors; the fire could then be set into the wall rather than in the centre of the room.

Charcoal was used both to cook on and to heat the rooms of the house by placing it in a portable brazier which might be either a bucket with holes or a purpose-made iron basket. Charcoal gives off a lot of heat without much smoke or smell and leaves very little ash; it is thus ideal for use in a grill or barbecue.

The spit was a slender iron or steel rod on which a whole carcase or several joints and items of poultry were impaled; for very small birds a spit with prongs was used so as to keep them steady. The spit was turned constantly over or in front of an open fire, by means of a turnspit; this could be a person who was either too old or too young to be useful elsewhere in the kitchen, a dog, or some form of jack which turned the spit mechanically. The fat and drippings ran into a pan underneath and were used to baste the meat to prevent the exterior from drying although it has been dredged with flour or breadcrumbs beforehand to give a crisp coating while keeping it moist and succulent within.

When man learned how to form iron into pots, it became possible to cook food by boiling and a cauldron was placed over the fire, standing on its legs or hanging from a hook or bar in the fireplace. A complete meal can be cooked by boiling if the component parts are separated in nets, baskets or cloths. The household way of baking was on the hearth among the ashes, on hot stones, or on an iron girdle plate. Later on, brick ovens were installed in large establishments and commercial bakehouses; the fire was kindled in the oven chamber and had to be cleared out before anything could be put to cook.

The open range made it possible to cook by all the known methods of cooking and although the open range was originally wood-fired, concern at the loss of so many forests being chopped down for fuel spurred the search for an alternative source of heat. Coal largely replaced wood as the fuel for cooking and this led to the development of the closed range by about 1830. A range is a composite item of cooking equipment designed to perform several functions – that of baking

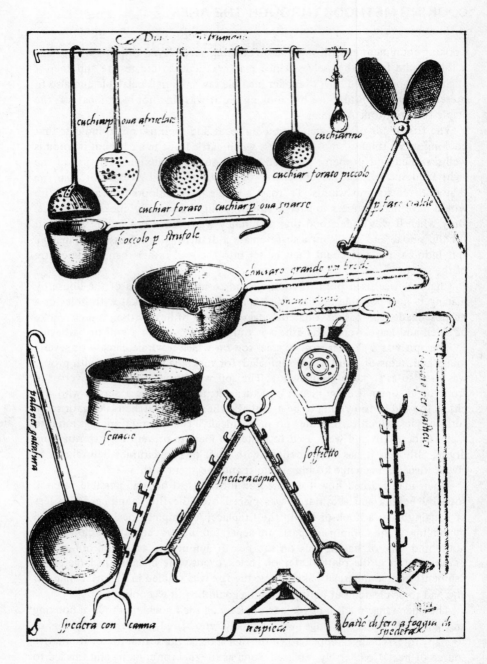

4. Mestole, schiumarole and other utensils (from Bartolomeo Scappi's *Opera* of 1570)

and roasting in the oven at one side of the fire, boiling and frying on the solid top, the provision of hot water from a boiler at the side and a steam pipe to feed a hot closet for long slow-cooking and for keeping food hot. On Sundays the housewife could have the joint cooked at the baker's shop whilst the family attended church and she could also get the baker to cook her home-made bread.

Cooking by gas did not become popular until many years after it had been used to illuminate streets and houses; this was in spite of the fact that it was so much cleaner than any other fuel then available and that it was much easier to regulate and always readily available by putting a penny in the gas meter. Gas cookers only became popular in the 1880s although they were first used commercially in 1850 when Alexis Soyer, the head chef of the **Reform Club** in Pall Mall, had gas-fired equipment installed in the kitchen he had redesigned. Electric stoves came into use in the 1890s and at this time were merely coal- or gas-cookers that had been converted to use electricity by means of sealed heating elements rather like lamps. It was not until about 1930 that electricity began seriously to challenge gas as a fuel for cooking, as it was only at this time that pans designed specifically for use on electric elements were introduced.

THE BRITISH AT DINNER

For centuries little regard had been paid to the niceties of table manners and it was usual to eat with the fingers. Forks had been used in the kitchen from as far back as Norman times but they did not come into general use for eating purposes until 1652 and even then the fashion had spread from Italy. Before that noblemen took their own knives when they went out to dine and used the pointed end to spear what they wanted from the foods displayed on the table, to cut it up and convey it to the mouth, and to pick their teeth.

The *nef* was a set of cutlery that was a person's own property which was in use mainly on the continent; in England a casket containing cutlery, condiments and napkin was sometimes put in front of each person's place at the table. On the tablecloth, in the centre, stood the salt-cellar, a large and ornate utensil that marked the dividing line between those persons who were of some importance and those who were of lesser importance and sat 'below the salt' at a part of the table where the wine did not circulate. Pepper and mustard containers were introduced later to form a cruet and with sugar casters and toothpick holders became the table accoutrements.

By the end of the Middle Ages in the fifteenth century it became the habit to place various other ornaments on the table to make it look more effective and formal; these were made of silver, gold, mother-of-pearl, enamel and other materials and were kept solely for the purpose of decorating the table. They can often be seen today as part of a town's civic collection, as the mess silver of a Corps of HM Forces, or in the collection of a city livery company, being

57

brought out on all formal occasions. The *épergne* which is an elaborate central ornament consisting of several dishes on branches from a central stem, did not come into use until much later; it was left on the table throughout the meal and held various titbits to fill any vacant spaces in the appetite.

By the end of the Middle Ages edible centrepieces made from marzipan, cake, sugar, rice and other ingredients were used to add interest to the table setting. These included Saint George slaying the dragon, birds in flight, beasts at bay, castles, in fact anything that the pastrycook could fashion as a centrepiece. When Carême moved to England to work for the Prince Regent in 1816, not only his display pieces but almost every dish on the menu was highly ornamented, garnished and displayed to the extent that the actual food was disgused and became subordinated in the overall design. Carême spent a lot of time designing appropriate settings as part of his wonderful dishes almost to the extreme of making cookery a branch of architecture or one of the *beaux arts*. Carême worked in an age when the pedestal, socle, and carved border together with elaborate garnishes, were extremely important. Ornamental skewers set off the finished dishes which became more like presentation pieces and works of art than say, mere dishes of sweetbreads or calf's brains. Carême and his contemporaries worked in a more leisurely and elegant age than did Escoffier who to a great extent had to correct the situation as he found it being carried on by Carême's successors. Further information about Carême is included in Chapter 12.

Escoffier had to change methods of presentation because of the changing demands of a more businesslike clientèle who did not have the time to admire the decorations around the food. Centrepieces still have their uses, despite the remarks of those experts who deride them as monstrosities left from a former age. Apart from the interest they add to culinary exhibitions they contribute an added dimension to a display of food at a buffet, for the presentation of certain dishes, and in the same way as does a birthday or anniversary cake, convey a personal note of esteem at a special celebration meal. Whether carved in fat, ice or salt, fabricated from nougat, gum paste, marzipan, chocolate, or pulled and blown sugar, they demonstrate the skills of the kitchen staff and invariably draw gasps of amazement at their artistry from guests, which is always a good sign as it has made them take more notice of what they are eating on this special occasion.

Dining in Victorian and Edwardian times was a more elaborate occasion than during any other age and even in lower middle-class family circles, the routine of eating was hedged about with etiquette and formality. The table was laid with great precision with ornamented cutlery, glass and crockery. Ornaments included candelabra, statuary, and an *épergne* for the display of flowers, fruit and titbits; very often there was a further display of some of the family silverware on the side-table for guests to admire as they passed fron drawing-room to dining-room in orderly procession.

The accoutrements of the table, the menus and place cards were of the best quality the hostess could afford and the food the best that the cook could produce on the budget. The daily menu was usually quite a lengthy one with alternatives on some of the courses. The dessert was quite an important course consisting of a nice array of fruit and nuts in season with finger-bowls, which had been introduced from Italy in the late eighteenth century, to put in front of each guest.

After the meal was over it was the custom for the ladies to rise and follow their hostess into the drawing-room; the gentlemen stood whilst the ladies left, then sat down again to drink vintage port, smoke a cigar and enjoy some masculine conversation. They rejoined the ladies to listen to the muscial part of the evening's proceedings, either amateur talent by some of the guests or professional performers singing or playing.

THE PATTERN OF LIVING OF THE WEALTHY

During the latter part of the nineteenth century and up to the end of the 1920s the British aristocracy and the very wealthy followed a set routine that filled most of their time in pleasurable pursuit of a range of activities that brought them together with their continental and American counterparts to a particular resort at a specific time each year. To be considered as one of this select international society meant being seen at and holding parties in an hotel or a private villa in one of the fashionable places on the itinerary, which stretched from this country through France and Germany to places as far away as Egypt. This meant that hotels opened only for the season with the head waiter and head chef moving on with his brigade to the next place on the itinerary favoured by the high society. It was in this way that César Ritz became well-known, as he transferred from Monte Carlo to Switzerland to France, opening up hotels in time for the arrival of those rich and great ones. The result was that he gained such a following that Richard D'Oyly Carte, owner of the **Savoy Hotel** saw that if he could persuade Ritz to run the **Savoy,** the princes and potentates of every nationality would follow him to London. This proved to be so when in 1890 Ritz and Escoffier both came to England and helped to found the reputation of this great hotel. Ritz went on to found the hotel group that bears his name, including the Ritz hotels in London and Paris.

THE LONDON SEASON

The London Season was an important source of business for hotels and restaurants in England because it was the time when 'everyone who was anyone' visited London to participate in the round of events that filled the months from Easter to August; after that they went back to the shires in time for the shooting season.

For their daughters the most important thing was to show themselves off, mainly in the hope of finding a husband, but also to be presented at Court when the reigning monarch held a number of Drawing Rooms at which the débutantes were presented. This auspicious event was the main reason for the season being held and the girls were then said to have 'come out' and were in effect put up for auction in the marriage market by their mothers, to the most suitable eligible young men of title or fortune. The débutantes' balls were held at private houses and in hotels and as much depended upon the amount of money spent by a girl's father as upon her own personality and manner towards prospective suitors that made her chances of finding a husband.

It was a season of much gaiety that embraced many different events both in and out of London; opera at Covent Garden, concerts, exhibitions, plays, riding in Hyde Park, as well as going to the Races at Ascot and Goodwood, boating at Henley and watching cricket at Lord's. The organisers of the many balls vied with each other to put on the most spectacular events by transforming the room into a special scene or giving it a theme; some balls contributed funds to a charity but all were for the benefit of the débutantes with food and drink of the finest quality and the event going on until daybreak after the participants had danced the night away.

Although the presentations at Court were discontinued in 1958, 'coming out' still brings business to hotels and caterers, although it is no longer confined to six weeks of the year.

DOMESTIC STAFF

Before the outbreak of the First World War in 1914 domestic servants outnumbered the workforce of any other industry in England. Domestic work employed more people than did the shipyards, cotton mills and coalmines together.

For many young women, domestic service was the only career open and it was the practice for them to leave home as soon as schooldays were ended to go to work as a general servant (like a Cinderella) doing all the housework for a private family. This sort of job nearly always involved living-in and the hours of work were long. The work was arduous and many domestic servants were grievously exploited and badly paid, but then so were the workers in many other trades. There was some slight consolation in that good private service offered the opportunity to experience a more superior way of life than that of a poverty-stricken home background. Domestic servants saw how the other half lived and could profit from it, at least in terms of manners, speech and taste. They gained an appreciation of good food and enjoyed a fairly tranquil way of life.

60

In the large private houses where the number of servants rivalled the strength of a battalion of soldiers, there was a rigid class distinction between the various grades. Each senior member of staff was a dignitary in his or her own right and even the master entered the butler's pantry only with his permission as did the mistress into the kitchen where the cook reigned as undisputed monarch. These members of staff were respected not only by their own underlings but by the members of the household, their guests and by the suppliers who provided them with goods and services.

Waiting at table, cleaning the silver, decanting the wine, polishing shoes, blackleading the grate, in the same way as doing the cooking, were actually part of an honourable and dignified calling that could provide a satisfying career for life.

In medieval times the sons of gentlemen did not feel demeaned when called upon to do service for their lord whether it was at table, in the bedchamber or the field of battle; proud noblemen were honoured to be called to wait upon the king. Such was domestic service in feudal times.

In England the contemporary prejudice against domestic service acts against the interest of hoteliers and restaurateurs as many people are made to feel that it will lower their dignity to have to serve their fellow human beings. In the ideal egalitarian society there will still be a need for some to render service to others and catering above all others, is, a service industry. The old 'upstairs–downstairs' distinction in conditions and the unequal master–servant relationship have both disappeared forever and even determined egalitarians have to agree that service is no longer a menial job. In practice a job in catering can facilitate social mobility within the different classes. Catering will always remain as a service industry despite the introduction of automation, and most countries in the world are heavily dependent on the continued growth of their catering and tourist industries. This can come about only if there is a complete change of attitude on the part of potential recruits in the advanced countries with diminishing reliance on immigrant staff from the less industrialised parts of the world.

As recently as the early nineteenth century the musicians in private service were regarded as servants; they managed to get themselves recognised as artists whereas the chef or cook and his underlings have failed to achieve recognition as anything other than domestic servants. This is partly their own fault but partly also because of the puritanism in our make-up which does not acknowledge the enjoyment of food as part of a cultured life in the same way that the enjoyment of music is accepted.

THE INFLUENCE OF COOKERY BOOKS

Cookery books show us the foods that were available at the time when the books were first printed and reading them helps us to learn about the eating habits of people living at a particular period. Not all cookery books are just a collection of recipes. Some contain far more than formulas and, like Mrs Beeton's *Book of Household Management*, include recipes, cookery theory, menus, details on dietary matters, staffing, legal aspects, medicine and so on.

One of the best-known but least-read of early works on English cookery is *The Forme of Cury*, a collection of recipes by the master-cooks of Richard II, published in 1390. Written on a long roll of vellum it contains nearly 200 recipes for *potages*, fish, meat and sweet dishes as served at the royal court. The *Liber Cure Cocorum* was written early in the fifteenth century in verse and gives a good insight into how the ordinary people lived in those days. The first book to be written about **dietetics** was issued in 1490; entitled *The Gouvernayle of Healthe*, it gave advice on healthful living and warnings and recommendations about various foods.

The Boke of Kervynge by Wynkyn de Worde, the Alsace-born pioneer of printing, published in 1508, was a manual for the use of the carver who was a very important member of staff of every great household. It consisted of a series of instructions for cutting every kind of joint, bird and fish and gave the verbs accordingly, such as to **sply** a bream, **display** a crane, **dismember** a heron and **tranche** a sturgeon, instead of merely to carve them. It also gave an outline of the general duties of the butler as regards the preparation and clearing of the dining table. *The Accomplish't Cook*, written by Robert May, contained the substance of more than fifty years of experience including his time as chef to Charles II; it appeared in 1660 at the time during the Restoration when French cookery was the dominating culinary influence in England.

The first lady to become well-known for her books on cookery was Mrs Hannah Woolley who wrote *The Ladies' Directory* in 1661, going on to write *The Gentlewoman's Companion* in 1673. More prominent amongst women writers was Mrs Hannah Glasse with her famous book, *The Art of Cooking Made Plain and Easy*, written in 1747, in which she castigated French chefs, then working in England, for their extravagances. Mrs Elizabeth Smith, Mrs Elizabeth Raffald, Mary Smith, Mrs Elizabeth Acton and the best known of them all, Mrs Beeton, whose first book was published as a weekly part-work in 1859 and has never been out of print since, were other notable women writers.

Stuart times are reflected in the collection of recipes published by Sir Kenelme Digbie in 1668 as a result of his life-long habit of inspecting the kitchens of his well-to-do friends to find out what their chefs got up to. Many more books were published in the early part of the eighteenth century; in 1703 there was Henry Howard's *England's Newest Way in all Sorts of Cookery*; in 1709, '*The Queen's Royal Cookery*, by T. Hall and in 1710, *Royal Cookery* by P. Lamb who had served royalty during four reigns. In 1723 R. Smith wrote *Court Cookery* and in the same year J. Nott's *The Cook's and Confectioner's Dictionary* appeared. The books written during the eighteenth century laid the foundations for all that have since been written. The authors wrote from many and varied backgrounds; some were professional people who used their experience to write the book, some were by persons who had never had to do any work, let alone in a kitchen

62

5.   Mrs Beeton: a photo used in Nancy Spain's *Life* of her grandmother

but could copy and adapt from previously published books; other books were compiled from contributions from either named or anonymous writers with the compiler given as author. It is perfectly possible to write a cookery book with only a slight knowledge of cooking by worming recipes from chefs or waiters when dining at gourmet establishments, or by soliciting famous people to give their favourite recipe, and so on. But such dilettante writers, although their books may be literary masterpieces and of much interest, do nothing to advance the development nor to codify the fundamentals of cookery.

Here we are concerned with books written for the professional caterer rather than for the housewife, where the information given is in the form of stern instructions rather than as opinions. Such books must prove their value by the successful end-results achieved by following the method and organisation set down by the writer. At the professional level the selection of recipes is bound to be international rather than for a national palate and the use of French terms can hardly be avoided because so much of the everyday language of the kitchen is technical French.

Handing down and refining professional information has been largely in the hands of French chefs, some of whom worked in England during the nineteenth and early twentieth centuries. In addition to running the kitchen of a great hotel or restaurant some of them found time to produce a codification of the then state of their cuisine, yet most of these were men who had little education and had quite likely been born of peasant or artisan stock in remote villages of France. Such was their concern for the well-being and further advancement of their craft that they willingly passed on their knowledge in the books they wrote and the articles they contributed to culinary journals.

The main route followed by classical professional cooker was from Carême via Felix Urbain-Dubois and Jules Gouffé to Escoffier, each adding further advancements and removing any dead wood while still retaining the sound practices that had been handed down to them. Carême had codifed the works of the eighteenth century writers such as Marin and Menon. All this was in French but was readily available to chefs in this country in the original or in translation.

Some of the French chefs who spent their working lives in England also made their contribution but in the English language. The influence of Soyer and Francatelli may not be so strongly felt today as those mentioned already, but they were extraordinarily influential in their own day and did much to encourage their fellow chefs to enhance the standards of culinary practice. Some other authors were successful in bridging the wide gap between writing for the professional cook and for the housewife, by producing a book that was suitable for both. Escoffier did this quite successfully in 1934 when he published *Ma Cuisine* with the French housewife, chef and restaurateur in mind and basing it on his *Guide Culinaire*. In his introduction to *Ma Cuisine* he says that good sound cooking, even though it may be simply done, makes for a contented home.

The first two books on cookery were printed as long ago as the fifteenth century, both in Latin - *De Re Culinaria* supposedly written by Coelius Apicius

64

ɔf Cury,	the French cooks of King Richard II	1390
ιayle of Health		1491
of Cookery	Richard Pynson	1500
of Kervynge	Wynkyn de Worde	1508
ɟl of Helthe	Sir Thomas Elyot	1539
ɟish Housewife	Gervais Markham	1615
of Cookery Refined and Augmented	Joseph Cooper	1654
mpleat Cook	H. Butler	1655
ɔle Body of Cookery Dissected	William Rabisha	1656
ɔomplish't Cook	Robert May	1660
dies' Directory	Hannah Woolley	1661
oset Opened	Sir Kenelme Digby	1668
entlewoman's Company	Hannah Woolley	1673
in-Physick	Thomas Cocke	1676
ria	John Evelyn	1699
ɪnd's Newest Way in all Sorts of Cookery	Henry Howard	1703
Queen's Royal Cookery	J. Hall	1709
Royal Cookery	P. Lamb	1710
Court Cookery	R. Smith	1723
The Compleat Housewife	Elizabeth Smith	1727
The Compleat City and Country Cook	Charles Carter	1732
The Art of Cooking Made Plain and Easy	Hannah Glasse	1747
The London Cook	W. Gilleroy	1762
The Experienced English Housekeeper	Elizabeth Raffald	1769
The Complete Housekeeper and Professional Cook	Mary Smith	1772
The English Art of Cookery	R. Biggs	1788
The London Art of Cookery	John Farley	1790
A New System of Domestic Cookery	Maria Rundell	1806
The Cook's Oracle	Dr William Kitchener	1816
Modern Cookery	Elizabeth Acton	1845
The Book of Household Management	Isobella Beeton	1859

Many books by French authors written in English or translated are also available, including works by Vincent La Chapelle, Alexis Soyer, Charles Francatelli, A. Suzanne and L. E. Ude.

BOOKS IN FRENCH

Title	Author	Date
Le Viandier	Taillevent, chef to Charles V	1370
Le Pâtissier Français	F. P. La Varenne	1653
*Le Nouveau Cuisinier Royal et Bourgeois	F. Massaliot	1691
*Le Cuisinier Moderne	Vincent La Chapelle	1735
Les Dons de Comus	F. Marins	1739
La Cuisinière Bourgeoise	Menon	1746
Les Soupers de la Cour	Menon	1755
Le Cuisinier Instruit	Menon	1758
Histoire de la Vie Privée des Français	Le Grand d'Aussy	1782
Manual des Amphitryons	Grimod de la Reynière	1808
Le Parfait Cuisinier	A. Raimbault	1814
Le Pâtissier Royal Parisien	A. Carême	1815
Le Maître d'Hôtel Français	A. Carême	1822
Le Cuisinier Parisien	A. Carême	1828
Le Nouveau Cuisinier Royal	Beauvilliers	1835
Nouveau Manual du Cuisinier	A. Chevrier	1837
La Grande Cuisine Simplifiée	M. Robert	1845
Histoire des Hôtelleries	Edouard Fournier	1851
La Cuisine Classique	F. Urbain-Dubois and Emile Bernard	1856
Le Cuisinier Practicien	C. Reculet	1859
Le Nouveau Pâtissier-Glacier	P. Lacam	1865
*Le Grand Dictionnaire de Cuisine	Alexandre Dumas	1873
Ecole des Cuisiniers	F. Urbain-Dubois	1887
La Grande Cuisine Illustrée	Prosper Montagné	1900
*Le Guide Culinaire	Auguste Escoffier	1902
Le Grand Livre de la Cuisine	Prosper Montagné	1903
*Larousse Gastronomique	Prosper Montagné	1938

*also translated and published in English

66

was first printed in 1470 and *De Honesta Voluptate* by Platina in 1474. Apicius was a rich Roman senator who lived in the first century AD and his book is a good guide to the professional food preparation of Rome and shows clearly that the Romans liked the original pure taste of their foods to be changed by the addition of sauces and other ingredients so that no single flavour predominated. It was evidently written for professional chefs or was a collection of formulas from several chefs, most of them Greek; it is a pretentious book for its time having been compiled *circa* 200 AD. Platina was a Roman Catholic historian and librarian at the Vatican under Pope Sixtus IV; his real name was Bartolommeo de'Scappi and his book was adapted from the work of a Roman master cook. The *Bibliographie Gastronomique*, by Georges Vicaire, published in 1890, contains details of some 2500 books on food and drink that had been published from the time when printing first began up to the year when the bibliography was compiled. It is possible to have access to some of these books and others by means of a ticket that authorises the use of the reading room at the **British Library** in **London**, the **Ashmolean** at **Oxford**, the **Preston Collection** in the **Brotherton Library** at the **University of Leeds**, the **John Fuller Collection** at **Oxford Polytechnic**, and the **Library of the Cookery and Food Association**, amongst other centres. Lists of the most notable cookery books written in English and French are appended.

THE GREAT CHEFS

The chefs who left their mark on gastronomy over the centuries seldom received much recognition in their lifetime other than in their local circle. In the main only those who found time to write a book on the cookery of the times in which they lived, are remembered; of all the rest perhaps only those who worked in royal service are recorded, the remainder being unsung and long-forgotten.

During the seventeenth and eighteenth centuries, chefs seldom achieved fame or fortune as they did during the nineteenth century and as they do today. Their working conditions in the kitchen were far from salubrious, the hours of duty were long and the work was hard. The climb up the ladder of promotion took a great many years and the prospects of a *commis chef* improving his knowledge was limited because those holding senior positions were reluctant to pass on their hard-earned expertise. Many chefs would have echoed Carême's words *'le charbon nous tue, mais hélas, qu'importe, le moin de jours le plus de gloire'* except that the only glory they could expect to achieve would have been posthumous. Even the patron saint of chefs, the thirteenth century Franciscan monk Saint-Roch is virtually unknown amongst his followers so perhaps it is as well that there is another patron saint of chefs, Saint-Fortunat whose saint's day is 13th December.

One way that chefs can improve their status and their prospects is by being the *chef-patron* of their own business. They can make a name for themselves more quickly and permanently by running a restaurant of their own than by serving a grand establishment for years whilst slowly moving upwards to the rank of head chef.

The pattern of chefs moving from a large organisation or out of private service into their own establishment has a long history going back over 200 years to the time when Antoine Beauvilliers left the service of Louis XVI's brother in 1782 to open his own restaurant in the *rue de Richelieu* in Paris, thus becoming the first known *chef-patron*. Gourmets soon get to hear of these places and willingly make the journey no matter how remote the location; they are always on the alert for news of any eating place worthy of a pilgrimage to seek an outstanding meal, no matter how modest the facilities.

The cult of the chef is not a recent phenomenon and it has long been recognised that he can foster good public relations if prepared to come out of his kitchen and talk to members of the media and the public about himself and his job. The image of the chef has improved tremendously and chefs are now given a bigger say in the running of their establishments. They are stars and expect to be treated as such. The general public likes to catch a glimpse behind the scenes of an hotel or restaurant, as evidenced by the success of Arnold Bennett's book *Imperial Palace*, first published in 1930, in which he takes his readers through the buying office, kitchen, restaurant, laundry and offices of an hotel; this book later became the basis of a successful television series. Arnold Wesker's play, *The Kitchen*, depicts a day's work in the kitchen of a busy popular restaurant and doing so very realistically and dramatically. It is based upon Wesker's own experience as a chef.

LIST OF GREAT CHEFS

Beauvilliers, Antoine	1752–1820	After working as a chef he opened his own restaurant in Paris in 1782; had a strong personality and a good memory. Wrote *L'Art du Cuisine*.
Bernard, Emile	1826–97	Head chef to William I of Prussia; collaborated with Urbain-Dubois in several books.
Carême, Antonin	1784–1833	Trained as a pastrycook and later became head chef to Talleyrand, the Czar of Russia, the Prince Regent and the Rothschild family. He was the first chef to wear a tall hat, when working at the **French Embassy** in Vienna. Author of several cookery books. He was a very pretentious man who expected to be remembered for his books rather than as a chef.

De Gouy, Louis	d. 1947	Famous head chef in New York for thirty-five years and author of eleven books; worked under Escoffier in London.
Diat, Louis	1885-1960	Worked with César Ritz at the **Ritz Hotels** in Paris and London then went to the **Ritz-Carlton** in New York where he spent the rest of his life.
Donon, Joseph	1888-1982	Pupil of Escoffier at the **Carlton** in London then went to USA; in service with the Vanderbilts; supported the establishment of the *Musée Escoffier* at Villeneuve-Loubet.
Dugléré, Adolphe	1805-74	Chef at the *Restaurant Les Provenceaux* in Paris, then the *Café Anglais*; also worked under Carême.
Dunand, J.	late 18th, early 19th c	Worked for the Prince de Condé where his father had been chef, then became chef to Napoleon; created *Poulet Sauté Marengo* in 1800.
Dutrey, Marius	d. 1975	Worked for most of his life in London and was head chef at the **Langham, Savoy** and **Westbury Hotels**; wrote *Calendriere Gastronomique*; an artist.
Escoffier, Georges Auguste	1847-1935	Came to England in 1890 and worked at the **Savoy** with César Ritz until 1898, then at the **Carlton** from 1900-19. Author, with Fétu and Gilbert of *Le Guide Culinaire*.
Fétu, Emile	contemporary of Escoffier	Contemporary and collaborator of Escoffier in *Le Guide Culinaire*, was *chef de cuisine* at the **Langham**, and the Traveller's Club.
Francatelli, Charles Elmé	1805-76	Born in England, worked in Paris under Carême; author of several cookery books. 1852-9 head chef of **Reform Club** and **Crockfords**. Head chef to Queen Victoria 1841-2.
Gilbert, Philéas	1872-1925	Collaborated with Escoffier on *Le Guide Culinaire* and wrote several books on his own.
Gouffé, Jules	1807-77	Author of the *Royal Cookery Book* in 1869 and several other books; worked at **Jockey Club** in Paris and

		from 1840–55 ran his own restaurant. Worked with Carême.
Gouffé, Alphonse	1812–83	Brother of Jules, translator of his *Royal Cookery Book*; worked as pastrycook to HM Queen Victoria for years.
Herbodeau, Eugène	1888–1981	Came to this country as a *commis chef* at the **Carlton** under Escoffier; head chef at **Metropole, Brighton, Ritz** in London and back to the **Carlton** as head chef in 1928. Then opened his own restaurant, *à l'Eçu de France*, in London.
Lacam, Pierre	1836–1902	One of the best known pastrycooks of the nineteenth century, author of several books.
Laguipiere	c. 1750–1812	Chef to Murat and to Napoleon; he died during the retreat from Moscow.
Latry, François	1889–1966	Head chef of **Savoy**, from 1918–42, then returned to France and opened a restaurant with his son who had also worked at the **Savoy**.
La Chapelle, Vincent	b. 1742	Chef to Lord Chesterfield and to William of Orange, author of several books.
La Varenne	1615–1678	Chef to Henry IV' sister, author of four books including *Le Vrai Cuisinier Français* 1651 and *Le Pâtissier Français* in 1653. Chef to Marquis d'Uxelles.
Malet, Henri	d. 1969	Head chef at **Grosvenor House** 1928–34; previously at the **Reform Club**.
Marin, François	18th c	Chef to Prince de Soubise. Wrote *Les Dons de Comus* in 1739.
Menon	18th c	Author of *La Cuisine Bourgeoise*, a best-selling book of the eighteenth and nineteenth century.
Montagné, Prosper	1865–1948	Worked in kitchens of his father's hotel in Toulouse, then in Paris, Monte Carlo and at the *Grand Hotel* in Paris until 1907. Prolific author, works include *La Grande Cuisine Illustrée*.
Pelleprat, H.-P.	1869–1949	Chef at *Café de la Paix* and at *Lucas*, then for thirty years an instructor

		at the *Cordon Bleu* School in Paris; author of several cookery books.
Perrin, Fernand	active in London 1920–60	Head chef of the **Park Lane** from 1926-58. Worked under Escoffier at the **Carlton** and at **St Ermin's, Coburg, Claridges**, and the **Grand Hotel**, all in London.
Ranhofer, Charles	1836-1899	Chef at **Delmonico's** in New York for thirty years, wrote the **Epicurean**; previously chef to Napoleon III.
Senn, Hermann	c. 1850-1934	Born in Switzerland, founded the **Cookery and Food Association** in 1885; advisor to the Home Office, War Office and helped in forming Westminster College in 1911. Demonstrator; lent his name for publicising proprietary sauces etc. Was chef at the **Reform Club.**
Soyer, Alexis	1809-1858	Worked for Duke of Cambridge 1831, became chef at the **Reform Club** in 1837; went to Crimea War zone with F. Nightingale; wore a black velvet cook's hat with a tassel, to be different, also worked for Crosse and Blackwell's.
Soyer, Nicolas	late 19th and early 20th c	Grandson of Alexis, worked in private service then chef at **Brook's Club**; popularised paper-bag cookery in Edwardian days.
Taillevent, dit Tirel	d. 1395	Chef to Philip IV and Charles VI of France.
Ude, Louis Eustache	19th c	Chef to Laetitia Bonaparte then to the Duke of York, the **United Services Club** and **Crockfords**.
Urbain-Dubois, Felix	1818-1902	Chef to the German Emperor and the Czar of Russia. Wrote several books.
Virlogeux, Jean-Baptist	1885-1958	Chef at **Claridges**, head chef at **Savoy** and **Dorchester**; also worked at the *Elysée Palace* and the *Crillon* in Paris and the **Hermitage** in Moscow.

This list gives the names of many of the best known chefs throughout the ages and, as may be seen, many of them are French but the majority of those listed are chefs who worked in England. French chefs have filled many of the top positions in England, first in the private service of rich and powerful families and later in hotels and restaurants, ever since the time of the French Revolution in 1789. England has always attracted chefs from France, not because the working conditions and pay are any better than at home, nor that a head chef's job in England carries more prestige than in France, but because the emigation of French chefs to all parts of the world is an accepted part of France's contribution to the civilising nature of gastronomy. The fact that the head chef is French is often of importance to the hotel as it helps to give the establishment an image of epicurean expertise.

This is not to say that a French chef is better at managing and motivating kitchen staff than one of another nationality; it is simply the fact that the French, above all others, are gifted with a special aptitude for food. Many of them have a special flair and seemingly inborn understanding of the right way of treating raw ingredients and possess an ability to turn them into delectable dishes. Gastronomy is of international creation but it is French chefs who have contributed the most to its present state of perfection. Well may the words of Carême be echoed 'La cuisine, c'est l'homme'.

INFLUENCE OF FOOD GUIDES

Food guides have played a large part in the cult of the chef, listing as they do, the merits of an establishment and giving the name of its chef. This encourages the pursuit of the coveted rosettes, crowns, toques or stars which the various inspecting bodies award to restaurants which reach their very high standards. These are very difficult both to attain and to maintain, and the head chef has to prove to these usually anonymous but very influential food critics who always arrive unannounced, that he can keep up the same standard on which he is judged, every day of the week and every week of the year.

The Michelin Guide has been established for more than eighty years and is the most widely-used; its judgements have always erred on the side of over-caution and this part of the tyre firm is a very self-effacing and unobtrusive organisation. The Egon Ronay organisation is thorough, indefatigable and very publicity-conscious; its guidebooks like to give narrative descriptions of the meal-experience of the establishment in addition to judging the merits of its food. The Good Food Guide has a less professional approach than the Michelin and Ronay guides because it is written by correspondents who are lay people who love good food, rather than professional inspectors.

The *Gault et Millau Guide to London* was written originally for French tourists and is very forthright in its comments, to the extent that its guide to restaurants in France has left many great restauranteurs quaking since it has never spared even the greatest of names. It was started in 1982 and sells well over 200 000 copies each year. It covers nearly 5000 restaurants. Its highest reward is four toques which are awarded for the food rather than for the décor and the atmosphere, as is the case with many other guides. Head chefs regard its two authors with great respect because they know they do not allow amateurism, whether it be a fancy fashionable restaurant run by a dilettante or by a supposedly fully-training head chef who does his job in an unprofessional way. They abhor the pseudo-chic and unfinished character of even some of the most brilliant productions of *cuisine nouvelle*, or as they might put it, *pseudo-cuisine nouvelle*.

The *Harper's and Queen Magazine's 300 Best Hotels in the World*, edited by Rene Lecler, gives a highly personal estimate of the restaurant and other amenities of the de luxe five-star hotels in some fifty countries.

The *Automobile Association* classifies hotels by the award of a number of stars, restaurants by a range of one to five crossed items of cutlery and the cooking by a range of one to three rosettes; its gradings and comments are highly professional under the guidance of the editor, Ian Tyers, who is a member of the professional body of caterers. Its guidebook Hotels and Restaurants in Britain appears annually.

RESTAURANT GRADINGS

In some countries the government, through its Ministry of Tourism, exerts a close control over the catering industry in the way that establishments are run, the prices they can charge and their grading. In some instances, only persons who can prove their knowledge of the job by their references and experience, are allowed to operate a catering establishment.

As well as being vetted by the government office, the hotel and restaurant association of the country may exert some influence on standards. In Jersey the Tourism Committee runs an annual competition in which a panel of judges has a meal in each participating restaurant and awards a diploma carrying from one to four toques according to the standard achieved. All categories of catering establishment may enter, from de luxe hotel restaurants to fish and chip places and hamburger bars. The criteria are value for money, standard of service, quality of food, and hygiene, although it is not usual for these judges, or indeed any of those from the guides, to look too closely at the kitchen premises.

CULINARY ASSOCIATIONS

Under this title is meant the culinary societies founded by chefs for themselves rather than those founded by gastronomes for which membership is an appreciation of gourmet meals. Throughout the centuries chefs in many countries have felt the need to form themselves into a guild or association as a means of proving their professionalism both to employers and the general public. Membership of a well-established, recognised and properly organised association confers status as it is accepted that only those who are properly qualified can join. In France such an association was formed in 1599 when *Les Maiêstres-queux-portes-chappes* conferred distinction upon a band of élite chefs who had designed for themselves a distinctive uniform of a long gown which they wore at work to distinguish themselves from lower grades of cooks who worked in aprons! In 1737 a separate society was formed for master roast-cooks – *Les Maiêstres Rôtisseurs* which some years later amalgamated with the older association of Master Chefs.

In England the chefs of the Oxford colleges formed themselves into a guild in 1482. In fact, at that time there were two guilds, the other being for the cooks of the inns and hostelries of the city. Being the chef of a college of the University was a position of some importance which entitled him to ride in procession to Saint Peter's in the East for the annual service each Whit Sunday.

Before Escoffier settled in London for the most important part of his career, he had helped to found the *Societé Culinaire Française* because he felt there was a need to improve the image of the chefs of France. This was in 1882 and in the columns of its journal, *L'Art Culinaire*, regret was expressed at the low social rank accorded to chefs and the need to improve the standard of culinary artistry as a means of raising their standing in the social order. Urbain-Dubois and Suzanne were the first editors and the journal and the society are still flourishing.

During the thirty years that Escoffier worked in London he constantly sought to raise the status of both his French and British colleagues. This he did by personal example in his own life, as the head chef of the hotels in which he worked, and by exhorting his fellow chefs to promote and develop their professional standing. With Fétu he was a founder-member of the *Association Culinaire Française de Grande Bretagne* which was formed in 1903 as a club where members could meet during their off-duty hours. It is still going strong and confers awards upon its members according to their level of ability and experience; membership is open to people only by virtue of the position they hold. Other professional associations include the *Master Chef's Institute*, the *Culinary Institute of America*, the *Societé des Pâtissiers de Paris*, the *Societé des Cuisiniers de Paris*, the *Federation Mondial des Sociétés Culinaires*. There is also a British branch of the *Academie Culinaire de France*, founded in 1951, which is open to practising professional chefs who 'uphold the desire to ensure a more comprehensive representation of the development of the culinary arts and encourage

74

initiative in promoting the prestige of the association as well as assisting in modernising old recipes and creating new ones'. There is even a Club des Chefs des Chefs open only to those in the service of Kings, princes and presidents!

In France there are hundreds of societies, clubs and *confrèries* connected with cooking and drinking and the *Grand Livre de Sociétés et Confrèries Gastronomique de France* by J. Wontez, gives details of most of these. Amongst them are the *Academie de Gastronomes Brillat-Savarin*, the *Amis de Curnonsky*, the *Cercle des Amitiés Gastronomique International* and the *Club des Cent* which was founded in 1912 by a group of motorists to search for and recommend good placed to eat and stay. The *Cercle des Gourmettes*, founded in 1929 for female gastronomes, the *Club Prosper Montagné* which organises an annual culinary competition, the *Les Disciples d'Antonin Carême* and the *Société Mutualiste des Cuisiniers de Paris* founded in 1840, are other professional bodies.

In England there is the **Cookery and Food Association** founded by Eugène Pouard chef to Queen Victoria's bodyguard and Hermann Senn in 1885, the **Worshipful Company of Cooks** formed by Royal Charter in the reign of Edward IV (1442–83), the **Chefs and Cooks Circle** and the **Guild of Chefs** which is affiliated to the **Cookery and Food Association**.

The *Worshipful Company of Cooks* was incorporated in 1482 and ranks thirty-fifth of the eighty-three Livery Companies. It originally had its own premises, **Cooks' Hall** in Aldersgate Street but this was destroyed by fire in 1771 and the Company has used other livery company halls ever since. There were cookshops from the twelfth century and the Worshipful Company was set up by the owners who at one time had control over all cooks and caterers employed in the City of London.

Such associations as these do much good by helping to advance the standing of members in the places where they work and in so doing, to improve the state of gastronomy for the benefit of customers. Surprisingly, there are no such associations for head waiters probably because they have little time to spare from their lucrative jobs and see no need to preserve their status.

GOURMET SOCIETIES

In addition to the chef's associations that exist in most countries there are very many epicurean and gastronomic societies to which people connected with hotels and other areas of the food industry and those who appreciate the value of good food, belong. Even some of the chef's associations extend membership at honorary level to noted gastronomes, food writers and others who have contributed to the advancement of the culinary art.

As long ago as 1683 there existed a gourmet society known as *L'Ordre de la Máduse* which had been founded by French naval officers based at Marseilles. It held monthly meetings to which wives were invited and those present ate, drank, sang and laughed in honour of good food and wine. It became such a popular society that branches opened all over France.

There are many branches of a society called *Les Amis d'Escoffier* and another called *Les Disciples d'Escoffier*, particularly in the United States but also elsewhere, which hold regular meetings in various restaurants that take the form of a meal for the enjoyment of members and also as a challenge to the head chef and the manager to produce a gourmet occasion for some very knowledgeable and exacting customers.

The Wine and Food Society was formed by André Simon and the writer A. J. A. Symons, and held its first meeting at the **Café Royal** in 1933. Fifty years later it has branches both in England and overseas.

The *Réunion des Gastronomes* was formed in 1899 in London with the object of bringing together proprietors, directors and managers of all branches of the catering industry who possess sound knowledge and experience. It aims to develop and support the culinary art and to raise the status of hotel-keeping and catering so that members may feel proud of their profession. The first president was Mr Judah who at that time owned the *Café Royal* and César Ritz and Auguste Escoffier were members in the early days. Membership is limited to two hundred persons so making it a great honour to belong. Meetings take the form of a monthly supper held at a different restaurant each time and it is the tradition that the chef of the establishment creates a new dish in their honour, very often giving the recipe on the menu card and signing his name to it. An annual banquet is also held and it is expected that the chef will put himself out for such a distinguished company, creating something unusual in the knowledge that members will note and appreciate the extra efforts made on their behalf.

Examples of the menus of the monthly suppers illustrate how simple they are and yet how recherché the individual courses are, entirely in keeping with the unwritten laws of gastronomy. At the same time they show that the members take this meal in their stride because they habitually eat on these lines in their everyday life!

In its early days the *Réunion des Gastronomes* admitted suppliers to the catering trade into membership but like other associations, once well-established, it was able to exist without them. In 1923 membership was tightened with the result that thirteen suppliers of food and wine in London formed their own gastronomic association to hold club meetings. The great Escoffier was their guest at the inaugural lunch and the **Thirteen Club** has continued to run on very similar lines to the *Réunion*, meeting for gourmet luncheons at different restaurants.

FOOD WRITERS

The job of being a food writer is not quite the sinecure that it might seem to be; indeed, it is a very responsible one that necessitates a sound knowledge of the principles of oenogastronomy and of the contents of Saulnier's *Repertoire* and to have the necessary stamina to be a powerful wielder of knives and forks and lifter of glasses. Many daily papers and a lot of magazines feature a food writer whose job is to visit restaurants and act as critic by giving his or her views on the standard of food and service. Quite often they write under a pseudonym so as to preserve their anonymity and if possible to prevent recognition when entering a restaurant. An article in a journal with a large circulation can have a tremendous effect upon the restaurant featured and the review may make or break its reputation. The writer has therefore to be completely impartial, must not have any violent dislikes of food and must be able to sum up a restaurant and write about it in very readable prose.

In a capital city there will be several thousand restaurants to cover, with each one keen to have the unsolicited praise of a food writer and the consequent increase in business. As an example, there are over three thousand eating places in London, without counting the public houses! A conscientious food scribe may need to visit any one restaurant half a dozen times before committing himself to passing judgement on it. To cover all those establishments that merit a review can mean the writer having to eat forty or fifty gourmet meals each month, no easy task, quite apart from the enormous expenses bill to the owner of the journal!

Over the years there have been many food writers whose work has greatly influenced gastronomy by praising those places that have genuinely made some contribution to it, perhaps the doyen of them all being Robert Courtine of *Le Monde*; he is the most erudite of French food critics and a writer of many books on gastronomy. Although writing for a daily or weekly newspaper may appear to be a very ephemeral form of literature, in some cases it does survive in a fairly permanent form by being collected and published in a book. Colonel Newnham Davis wrote about the London Restaurants of his day for the *Sporting Life* and many of his articles were collected and published in a book. His method was simple – he discussed the restaurant's location and ambience, its senior staff, the menu and wine list, what he and his guest chose to eat, and the final bill. He never introduced a critical note into his articles thus he was guide rather than critic but nevertheless his work still affords a knowledgeable account of the restaurants of late Victorian and early Edwardian days.

Books such as these which are really literary guides to actual places have always found a market amongst gourmets. Robin Douglas and Eileen Hooton-Smith are amongst those who have chronicled the restaurants of the days between the two World Wars.

The other kind of food writer is the person who writes a regular cookery article mainly for female readers of a journal. It is designed to instruct in the art of cookery in a witty and elegant manner that can also be read for entertainment by those who do not relish doing the cooking. The weekly article can deal with a particular aspect of cookery such as a commodity and how it can be used in various ways, a course of the menu, the cookery of a region or country, the preparation of a complete meal and other such topics.

There is also the specialist writer on wine who sets out to educate his readers by discussing the merits of and recommending certain wines. There are wine magazines for the trade and for the general public with articles on many aspects, some of them dealing with food. **The Masters of Wine**, some of whom write such articles, bring a wealth of knowlege to their discussions on the manifold aspects of oenology.

There is a world-wide association of food writers with its headquarters in Paris. It is the *Fédération International de la Presse Gastronomique Vinicole et Touristique* with some 500 members in twenty countries, the vast majority being in France. The association may award its own diplomas to establishments that have made a significant contribution to gastronomy. Some of its members are capable of forming an international team of judges at *Salons Culinaires*. Its memberhsip also extends to radio and television per~onalities connected with food and drink programmes.

In addition to their work of writing about restaurants, many food writers act as book reviewers of the hundreds of cookery books published each year in most countries. They can bring their experience to a discussion of the good and not-so-good points of a book and their views will be of some significance to the sales. Many food writers and cookery specialists subscribe to or write for a small publication entitled *Petits Propos Culinaires* which, because of its investigative articles on little-known aspects of food and drink, has a wide circulation in many English-speaking countries. The company, Prospect Books, also issues reprints of early and rare cookery books.

CULINARY MUSEUMS

The *Fondation Auguste Escoffier* is the body of people that looks after the *Musée de l'Art Culinaire* at Villeneuve-Loubet, which is housed in the master's birthplace, between Nice and Cannes. Every year thousands of visitors go there from all over the world to view the unique collection of culinary objects. The curator Monsieur Parrot is pleased to help visitors seeking to widen their knowledge and understanding of the great chef.

At Carcassone, south of Toulouse, the *Musée Prosper-Montagné* has been set up in temporary premises in the *rue Aimée-Ramon*. At present it is open only during the summer but will eventually move to a permanent site in the Old Town quarter and remain open throughout the year.

In England there are many stately homes where the fully equipped kitchens are still intact and open for viewing. These include **Waddesdon Manor**, near Aylesbury, **Ham House** at Richmond and **Apsley House** at Hyde Park Corner as well as the **Royal Pavilion** at Brighton. Many museums have collections of old kitchen equipment, including the **Castle Museum** at York and the **Castle Museum** at Norwich.

There are museums with displays of kitchen equipment and instruments for eating at Amsterdam, Antwerp, Bruges, Cologne and Paris, as well as many other cities.

5 Considerations of the Menu and Wine List

The Purpose of the Menu – Need for Originality – Menu Layout – The History of Menus – Means of Communication – Meals of the Day – Classes of Establishment and Staff – The Qualities of Waiting Staff – Briefing of Waiting Staff – Correct Dress for the Customer – Food Preferences – Prices on Menus – Menu Publicity – Merchandising the Meal – Food Standards – Food Additives – *Menu Truquage* – The Role of Standardised Recipes

THE PURPOSE OF THE MENU

A menu is composed to carry out the following objectives:

1. list the dishes that will be served and the prices that will be charged;
2. act as a showcase by listing all that is available for sale;
3. govern the range of foodstuffs that have to be made available in order to prepare the dishes;
4. authorise production by the kitchen staff.

In other words, it is the master plan that governs the operation of the kitchen and restaurant. It is an offence not to display a menu with the prices marked on it in a place where prospective customers can read it *before* entering the restaurant, as the menu is supposed to provide customers with sufficient information for them to decide if an establishment is the kind of place that suits them. A brief study of a menu should enable a knowledgeable customer to obtain a fairly clear idea of the extent of the menu, its content and the prices charged, all of which help to show what style of place it is.

A customer's expectations are often guided by the name of the restaurant and it can be misleading to dub an establishment inappropriately. A customer who enters a restaurant called the 'Ritz-Sheraton' would not expect it to be a cafe with counter service and uncleared tables. A fast food type of restaurant is usually one of a chain or is operated to a standard formula under franchise; which means that all branches are identical no matter whereabouts they are located. Once he has patronised one of them, a customer knows what to expect whenever he sees the particular façade.

It is equally possible to identify other distinct types of restaurants such as Chinese, Indian or other national ones where it is usual for the menu and the décor to follow a set pattern.

Once a customer has glanced at the menu and made an assumption as to the type of place, he will be geared mentally to expect a certain result. In a fast food restaurant he realises that the choice of food is going to be limited, that table settings and etiquette are not prerequisites, and that there will be no delay once he has given his order. At the other extreme in patronising a restaurant where the menu prices seem to him to be high, the customer will expect to be able to choose from a wide selection of first-class dishes and to be served in a relaxed atmosphere and luxurious surroundings.

Between these two kinds of establishments there is the moderately-priced place where the eating experience may be less positively identifiable and the expectations less clear-cut and where therefore the menu should assist by playing a big part in setting the scene.

In the welfare catering sector there is usually a captive clientele so the larger the number being served the greater should be the choice of foods. This is because of the danger of monotony setting in as the range of low-cost dishes is limited, with many of them falling into the category of the nondescript where there is difficulty in identifying the main ingredient. In some establishments it is the practice to make one particular ingredient, say minced beef, serve for several different dishes by finishing it in different ways. It is not uncommon for a cook to produce just one kind of gravy or sauce to go with a number of different foods, whether it is entirely appropriate or not. It often happens that two or more rather unpopular dishes appear on the same menu thus giving no choice to anyone.

Behind the scenes, a menu plays a different role from that displayed 'out front'; in the production area it acts as the indicator of what dishes are to be prepared, the number of portions to be produced, and who is to do them in accordance with the system of kitchen organisation. It will be written in its most basic form.

NEED FOR ORIGINALITY

As has been stated, the menu and wine list must be composed so as to be in keeping with the nature of the establishment; this means that they should be a reflection of the company's policy. The policy as drawn up will have identified a market need and will have set out to meet it by supplying the kinds of food and wines most likely to satisfy the customers it is hoped to attract.

This policy finds its expression in the form of the two lists that tell customers what is on offer and if the market has been thoroughly researched it should produce a menu and a wine list that are original and unique. It is unprofessional to copy a menu of another similar establishment, for even though it may work successfully at the original place there is no certainty that it will do so elsewhere. Menus and wine lists are not usually covered by copyright although the total package of, say, a fast food operation could well be. No one has ever taken the trouble to copyright an actual recipe; it is the *book* of recipes as written by an author that is copyright, so anyone may take a recipe which appeals to them and use it as it is or in a modified form, without fear of having to pay a royalty.

The originator of *cuisine nouvelle* is Paul Bocuse and his ideas on how it should be done are original, but no-one pays him any fees for adopting his methods which are in widespread use in many countries. In fact the inventor of a new dish or new method is usually proud to see it become well-known and widely used by other chefs.

The compilation of both menu and wine list should be done in an original form and the only way to make it so is by giving deep thought as to what the customer wants and how to satisfy this in a unique and imaginative way. In an establishment where it is intended to keep the à la carte menu and the wine list in use over a period of time, probably because of the transient nature of its clientele, it is essential to get everything correct so as to avoid the need to cross off dishes or alter prices during the period of time it is in existence. Certainly there is a big saving on printing by having long-life menus.

MENU LAYOUT

By tradition nearly all menus are laid out in a neat pattern under the heading of the various courses so as to group like with like. Even within the choices of a particular course the accepted pattern of courses should apply; for example, in the first or starting course of a Table d'Hôte menu where a number of choices are offered they should be listed in the order of, fruit juice or soup, *not* soup followed by fruit juice. Similarly for the main course the choice of, say, egg, fish or meat should follow in that order and not as often written, Steak and kidney pie, Fried Cod and lemon, and Cheese Omelette – these should be placed in their correct sequence where a knowledgeable customer would expect to find them. When there are hot and cold choices, the hot ones should precede the cold. When having menus printed or typed with each dish being given a line of its own, the name of each item should work from the centre of the page outwards so that a pattern emerges as follows:

Consommé Royale

Timable de Sole Nantua

Volaille de France Dorée aux Truffes Fraîches

Pommes Noisettes

and so on.

THE HISTORY OF MENUS

The menu as we know it today in the form of a card to be handed to or placed in front of each customer, is said by Herman Senn to have originated as long ago as 1541 when an early Duke of Brunswick was observed to be studying a sheet of paper on which one of his retinue had written down the list of dishes for that evening's meal. He was obviously both a gourmand and a gourmet and did not want to miss any of the fine dishes served up by his chef at the Court in Dresden. But there are many references to menus much earlier than this. The original word for a menu was *Escriteau* or *Escriptieau* and there are many examples in existence dating back to the sixteenth century although some of them are really only lists for use in the kitchen.

The menu that was served in 1363 to Hugh IV of Cyprus, Edward III of England, David of Scotland and Waldemar of Denmark and John of France, who had been brought as a prisoner, by Sir Henry Picard, a vintner who was said to be the richest man in London, has been recorded. It consisted of four courses, each a full meal in itself with a selection of soups, fish and meat dishes in each. Sir Henry saw to it that the wines from his cellar were in keeping with the quality of his food. One of the drinks served was *hippocras* made of spices, honey and red wine, cleared by filtering.

At that time it was the pattern of meals at home to serve two main courses which comprises the repast – the *entrée* and the *relevé*. Each was in fact a meal in itself with a variety of dishes set out neatly on the table for diners to help themselves. It was not the intention that everybody should have a full helping of each dish but that they should partake of those nearest, eating soup, fish, meat or sweet in any order. There were so many different dishes on the table that it would have needed a very long piece of paper to write them out in correct menu order. The Duke of Brunswick's idea of having a bill of fare therefore made it possible for him to have what he wanted even though it may have been away down the table. Menus must have been in use in the kitchen ever since cooks were first employed to produce more than a small selection of dishes,

6. The kitchens at Christ Church Oxford in the eighteenth century

although for a simple meal with no alternatives it is hardly necessary to commit the menu to paper as both cook and server can easily remember what is on and the customer can be told what he is going to get.

It has long been the pattern for the cook to see the mistress early each day to discuss and decide on the day's menus; where no set menu is operated a decision on what dishes to prepare is taken in the knowledge of what is in stock or on order. The pattern of a cook buying at the early morning market and making up the menu from what he or she has purchased is still quite usual, especially with the *chef-patron*.

Reference to the use of menus can be seen as far back as the twelfth century. A thirteenth century book gives the *Escripteau* for a banquet and details of the order of dishes of a menu served in ancient Rome are given in a book published in 1797. Robert Briggs gives bills of fare for each month of the year in his book, *The English Art of Cookery*, published in 1791. Honoré Blanc wrote a *Guide du Dîners* in 1814 which gave the menus of notable Parisien restaurants. Baron Brisse, the famous gastronome, included a daily menu in his newspaper, *Liberté*, and published the collection as a book in 1867. At the *Telegraph Eating-House* in the City of London in the 1870s there was a show-board outside the door on which was painted the bill of fare, which never changed. In keeping with the traditions of the City which are as valid today as they were 170 years ago, the menu listed four roast joints, various grilled chops and steaks and three kinds of soup; with bread and a pint of ale the bill for a lunch would come to about two shillings, or 10p.

MEANS OF COMMUNICATION

According to the kind of establishment, there are several ways of acquainting customers with what is available to eat:

1. by word of mouth;
2. a printed or hand-written menu card;
3. by means of illustrations such as colour photographs or drawings of the various dishes;
4. by displaying the list of dishes written on a board or on a screen where everyone can see it;
5. by displaying sample meals on the service counter.

Each method demands the same underlying menu composition. An establishment will use the means of communication most suitable for it so that it does the job of selling in the most effective way. There should be some compatibility between the chosen means of communication and the establishment; for special function menus there must be compatibility between the menu and the occasion. For instance the menu for the dinner of a yacht club could be done in the form of sails and flags, that for an academic reunion on a blackboard with a card resting on a miniature cardboard easel and so on.

In her *Book of Household Management*, Mrs Beeton warns her readers how provoking it is when a guest partakes of something for which he does not care to the exclusion of something he particularly liked, because lacking a menu, he does not know that it is yet to come. She goes on to say that a hand-painted or etched card is much nicer than a bought one since it will be looked upon as a token of attention and a desire to please and will probably be taken away as a souvenir of a pleasant party.

Mrs Beeton goes on to provide menus and table displays showing how the dishes should be set out for:

1. a wedding breakfast of thirty dishes,
2. An everyday breakfast which includes cutlets, kidneys, rissoles and fried soles;
3. a buffet lunch of eleven warm dishes and eight sweets;
4. six-course dinners in which she shows the dessert on display throughout the meal as a table decoration, a soup at the head of the table and one at the foot but of different flavours, and two more for the second course (she calls this the 'old-fashioned manner' because the Russian style of service was already making headway when her book was published in 1861;
5. staff menus;
6. several five- or six-course menus that can be reduced to four by combining soup and fish or fish and meat;
7. a six-course fish dinner;
8. a game dinner with fifteen different kinds of game in four courses, followed by sweet and dessert;
9. Ball suppers;
10. a buffet supper.

Altogether there are 104 pages of menus both for special functions as above and for every day of the year. Mrs Beeton thus gives a valuable insight into the way people of various social classes lived in Victorian times.

It is not always essential to have a menu in order to know what there is to eat. When Ritz and Escoffier were working at the Savoy Hotel they introduced the novel idea of set-priced menus. The customer informed the head waiter how much he wished to spend per person and Escoffier gave him that price menu, so the customer did not have to bother with choosing any dishes knowing that the Savoy would provide good value for money. This is known as a *prix fixe* menu and is a form of Table d'Hôte, although not every party that booked a table in this way necessarily got the same nenu as it depended on what items were available. Another advantage of this system is that a customer who does not understand French and therefore cannot read a menu or one who finds it difficult to select a balanced meal, is relieved of the problem. With the other kind of menu at the Savoy, the customer left everything to Escoffier, including the price. Given the names of the host and his guests a suitable *'menu à mon idée'*, or *'menu surprise'* was composed on the spot; it may have included dishes from the menu already printed for that meal or others from commodites available in the kitchen. This is where a chef puts his reputation to a severe test since all the blame or praise will be entirely due to him.

MEALS OF THE DAY

These will be outlined in Chapter 6 from the point of view of Menu Planning but are dealt with here in greater detail.

Breakfast

The English breakfast is absolutely in accord with the British character and climate; it is perhaps even more of an institution than the other and larger meals of the day. It is possibly the only meal of the day when the whole family is present to sit down and eat, if only briefly, before going off to school or to work. Even though the pace of modern living may cause many to skip a full breakfast they still hanker for it as those hotels and boarding houses which tried to deny their guests the opportunity of breakfasting, found out. When on holiday and time is on their side tourists insist on a full English breakfast; after all bacon and eggs has been a favourite meal since the sixteenth century when it vied with a chine of beef and a joint of mutton for pride of place.

Secretly we fantasise over this meal and imagine ourselves coming down to the breakfast room and lifting the lids of the silver dishes on the sideboard to choose from bacon, sausages, kidneys, kedgeree and kippers with whole oat porridge to begin with and toast and marmalade to end. No polite conversation is expected at this time of day and it is in order to bury oneself in the morning paper.

Visitors to England delight in finding the perfect English breakfast which is best partaken in the hotel dining-room and not the bedroom, where only a Continental breakfast is really suitable. The dining-room at this time of day should be reverently hushed with only the sound of newspapers being turned. The perfectly-served breakfast will offer butter in dishes and marmalade in pots rather than in portion control plastic containers or foil wrappers. As much care is taken with boiling an egg of the right size to the exact second as with the toast which must be cut to the correct thickness and served hot, neither too soft nor too crisp, and served in a toast rack with a ventilated cover.

People's ideas of the perfect breakfast vary, despite the fact that tradition has outlined the number of courses and list of suitable dishes. The following accounts show how breakfasts have changed over the years.

From the *Ordinances of a Noble Household in 1512*: 'On fast days my Lord and Lady are served with a loaf of bread on trenchers, a quart of beer, a quart of wine, pieces of salt fish, baked herrings and a dish of sprats. On flesh days the fish to be replaced by half a chine of mutton or else a chine of beef boiled'.

Samuel Pepys' breakfast on New Year's Day 1668 was eaten between the hours of six and seven in the morning and consisted of 'dipping into a barrel of oysters, a dish of neat's tongues, one of anchovies, a drink of several kinds of wine and some Northdown ale. Parson Woodforde records in his diary for 1794 that he had ham and tongue, toast, rolls and honey.

Harold Nicolson described breakfasts during the Edwardian era as being a substantial and social affair that was consumed unhurriedly starting with porridge that could be eaten while walking about, then an omelette; fried whiting and devilled kidneys were the hot dishes and tongue, ham and roast ptarmigan the cold dishes. There were scones with marmalade or honey and fresh fruit such as melon, nectarines and raspberries.

Kedgeree was originally an Indian dish consisting of rice, lentils, onion, eggs and spices all mixed together; the flaked finnan haddock was added when the dish was accepted into the British breakfast repertoire.

British Rail consider fried bread and sauté potatoes to be appropriate with the sausage, egg and bacon; some hotels still include fried fish as well as the more usual grilled bloaters and kippers and poached finnan haddock. Other places offer yoghurt as an alternative to the juices, stewed fruit and cereals.

The business man's 'working breakfast' where a group of executives or sales-men come together to save time by combining breakfast and business is some-times stimulated by the serving of champagne which should certainly assist by getting the agenda off to the right start because people are often ill-humoured at the beginning of the day – one reason why there can be more complaints at this meal than at the others. The importance of breakfast to the hotel proprietor can be gauged from the price charged which is almost the same as for lunch yet as the cost of ingredients is much lower it should be a profitable meal to serve.

Lunch

The original meaning of dine was to eat at noon and dinner was the name of the midday meal but this has changed over the centuries and the word lunch has become the accepted name for light refreshments taken between breakfast and dinner. This does indicate that dinner is the main meal of the day so if only a supper is served late in the day then the midday meal is really the dinner and can be so-called.

The French do not distinguish very clearly between breakfast and lunch and use the word *déjeuner* for both, adding *du matin* or *de midi* to denote which it is. In culinary language breakfast becomes *petit déjeuner* and the word *dinatoire* for a substantial midday meal is seldom used. It is sometimes necessary to allocate a certain weighting to the main meals of the day particularly where customers are on full board as in an hotel, hospital or boarding school. In such a case a decision has to be taken as to the relative importance of lunch and dinner and the percentage of the day's allowance to be allocated to each of the meals of the day.

Since the majority of people have to return to their duties after taking a break for lunch it is obvious that the midday meal should not be too big as otherwise the afternoon's production may suffer. But this is not to suggest that a feeling of well-being is inappropriate at this time of day; it is the occasion that matters, as explained in Chapter 6 on Menu Planning.

Dinner

Some lucky caterers have never had to face the problem of what constitutes a *relevé*; this is because they work in that sector of the industry such as a staff canteen where only lunch is served. Nor do they need to worry about what dishes are appropriate for lunch but not for dinner, since they can use any dish for the main meal of the day, in effect, dinner served at lunchtime.

Entrées and *relevés* really only cause problems of dinner menu composition because nowadays a lunch menu, even if it is a banquet, seldom includes two meat dishes. However the service of an *entrée* followed by a *relevé* or 'remove' meaning the dish that succeeds another, is still widely used at dinner. As previously noted, dinner can be an elaborate and leisurely affair for which all the caterers' art needs to be engaged.

CLASSES OF ESTABLISHMENT AND STAFF

As we have already said, a customer can decide if a restaurant is to his liking, without actually entering the dining room by taking a brief look at the menu. Only if the prices on the menu accord with the amount of money in his wallet or the total he wants to pay by credit card, should the customer commit himself inescapably. The way that the menu is printed, as well as the dishes and prices it contains, the location of the restaurant, its exterior, whether there is a commissionaire on duty to open doors and greet customers, if there are plenty of other greeters to take hats and coats and guide to table, all give a good idea of what the meal is likely to cost and if there is going to be a lot of tipping.

In many cases people book a table at a particular restaurant on the recommendation of a friend who has liked his experience there and said how much it cost him. People are just as likely to choose a restaurant from its description in a food guidebook or an article in a magazine in which the specialities of the place and an average cost of a dinner are given. Booking a table does not necessarily guarantee one of the best positions in the dining room but should ensure

7. The kitchens at the Royal Pavilion, Brighton, in their heyday

that if the guest arrives shortly before the stated hour he will not be kept waiting long. Booking the table, the actual meal and the wine by telephone could be a lengthy process and would only be possible on the actual day on the grounds that the reception head waiter is not given the menus in advance and in any case does not have time to study them in depth.

An experienced waiter can quickly size up a customer as to the amount of tip he is likely to leave and will set out to achieve it or even to better his assumption by providing a standard of service in accordance with his estimate. This is not to suggest that somebody who is immaculately dressed and has a prosperous look about him will receive attentive service whereas someone wearing a well-worn suit will be given poor service. Waiters are good psychologists and instantly recognise the small details that distinguish between the various classes of customers such as the cut and the cloth of their clothes, their social graces and whether they appear to be at ease in the environment and show confidence in placing the order. Even casual clothes can convey an idea of the wearer's station in life by their telling look of quality; not that casual clothes and unkempt looks are *de rigueur* for dinner in any but the lowest starred restaurants.

Head waiters like to 'dress' the dining room and a party of people who have taken care of their appearance and who obviously wish to make an occasion of the evening are likely to be well-seated where the eyes of the curious can fall on

91

them. If they look like being good spenders their station-waiter will be one of the best who will play his part in making the meal memorable; customers of less decorative value are likely to be seated near the service doors. Those wanting to be secluded in a corner should not have to ask as the experienced head waiter can sense this and will instinctively guide the couple to a suitable table.

A head waiter should aim to pamper his customers and make them feel as though they were guests in the home of someone they know who owns a mansion; they ought not to be nagged by thoughts of the amount of the bill they will be presented with.

THE QUALITIES OF WAITING STAFF

It may sound rather dated to refer to the personal attributes of waiting staff by insisting on the need for a good standard of hygiene in their person and in their dress. There was a time when staff had to submit to an inspection before each service, not just of hands and fingernails but hair, shoes and uniform; many restaurants would not engage waiting staff who wore glasses. In certain eating places it was the fashion to allow waiting staff to wear what they liked, any objections to this being stifled by their pleasant personality and friendliness. It adds a certain cachet to have, say, actresses or actors whilst resting, débutantes or even, as recently announced by a restaurant proprietor, university graduates to serve the food and wine. Certainly such members of staff would provide erudite service; whether they are allowed to quote classical or biblical sayings in the way they were taught at drama school or college is up to the manager.

The generally accepted custom of making waiting staff take their meal before the commencement of service is a wise one, not so much because a hungry waiter may be tempted to help himself to something destined for the customer or that he will drool over what he in the midst of serving but because he may lose his appetite during the long service period. The means by which waiting staff manage to obtain a good meal for themselves are described hilariously by Ludwig Bemelmens in *Hotel Bemelmens*, a book that should be required reading for every food and beverage manager, as should George Orwell's *Down and Out in Paris and London*.

Although waiting at table may appear to be work of a menial or servile nature with no end-product that can really be evaluated except by the size of the tip; as a well-paid job it does merit some theoretic background study and textbooks on food and beverage service can be of much help in making this a worthwhile career for persons who can apply their professional knowledge in a sophisticated manner without necessarily being obsequious.

BRIEFING OF WAITING STAFF

One way of enabling staff to provide a better service to customers is to make sure that they know what they are serving. It is standard practice in college training restaurants for the lecturer to brief students about the content of the menu before they embark on the service. This includes a definition of the classical names, serving techniques, suitable accompaniments and portion size; the briefing is often combined with an inspection of the table lay-up and of students to ensure they are correctly groomed.

In the industry, where a permanent waiting staff is employed and the menu does not change much from week to week there is no need to hold a twice-daily briefing because staff will be familiar with the range of dishes included in the menus whether they are à la Carte or Table d'Hôte. When a new dish is introduced staff can look it up in the *Repertoire de la Cuisine* which is the standard reference book for catering staff and gives a brief outline of the ingredients of a classical dish.

Even though a menu written in French may also include an explanation in English, customers frequently ask for further information about the dishes and the member of staff should not be at a loss to describe the contents of the dish and how it has been cooked. The description they give should be precise and easy to understand; it should not be given in vague terms that convey little information, nor ought it to be too glowing in case it fails to live up to its description.

Does this indicate the need for waiting staff to be given training sessions in food appreciation and the opportunities to taste the dishes they have to serve? Certainly the person who chooses waiting as a career should try to gain a thorough knowledge of all the service techniques, the composition of dishes, food supplies and seasons, cooking methods and possibly even of basic nutrition. It is obvious that a wine waiter must be able to describe each wine included on the list, doing it in realistic terms rather than to say a wine is dry or sweet, light or heavy. He needs to be able to recommend wines to match foods and vice versa, and all this would indicate the need for practical tasting sessions as part of an on-the-job training programme.

CORRECT DRESS FOR THE CUSTOMER

Restaurant managers distinguish between how they allow customers to dress for lunch and what they think is correct to wear for dinner and good ones do not have to put up notices saying what dress is permitted. At a seaside resort guests will be tempted to come in from the beach and sit down in swimming costume and sandals but as this can offend other guests the head waiter has to make it clearly understood that he does not approve. It may be all right for a pool-side buffet lunch at a one-star Spanish hotel but not indoors in an establishment where good manners are expected and a certain standard of decency is maintained. At one time head waiters kept a stock of secondhand ties to lend to male customers who tried to breach the unwritten code of etiquette that banned open-neck shirts and roll-collar sweaters, no matter how good they looked.

Not so very long ago women wearing trousers, even a trouser suit, were denied admission to some top restaurants, no matter how elegant they looked. The ban on customers dressed in jeans or leather jackets is quite widespread because restaurateurs consider persons wearing this kind of apparel to be potential troublemakers or undesirable because their mode of dress may lower the tone of the place.

FOOD PREFERENCES

Gastronomy conjures up a picture of elegantly dressed men and women sitting around a table pensively chewing every morsel of food and savouring each mouthful of wine to the last drop. This image may well stem from a reversal of Brillat-Savarin's boastful aphorism 'Tell me what you eat and I will tell you what you are', but no one should write as confidently as this because there are far too many variants to distort so simplistic a statement. Not all gourmets are people who need to tuck a table napkin into the collar of their dress shirt; not all fat men live on dumplings, doughnuts and roly-poly pudding; there are many thin people who can eat as many soft-centred chocolates and slices of dripping toast as they like without putting on an extra ounce of weight. As stated in Chapter 1, different nations have different tastes and even inside a country different regions have different food habits.

It is necessary to take account of the various surveys carried out by research companies when compiling menus because these firms spend a lot of time and money on finding out people's preferences. One of these surveys recently revealed that people living in the southern half of Britain drink more fruit juice, eat more fresh meat, frozen vegetables, pasta and fresh fruit than people living in the North. Northerners perhaps surprisingly appear to prefer using canned meat and vegetables, bought pies, milk puddings and syrup puddings and ready-made cake. In Scotland the inhabitants have a great liking for pickles and ketchup possibly to disguise the taste of meats; and also like chocolate biscuits and bought cakes.

That Britain is a land of unadventurous eaters is evidenced by another survey which shows that soup, fried fish and chips followed by ice-cream is typically our favourite lunch meal at almost all levels. We do not do much better at dinner either because the survey conclusively shows that our most representative meal is shrimp cocktail, grilled steak and chips followed by apple pie and custard and since not many placed now offer apple pie we are happy to accept cheese or a slice of *ersatz* Black Forest gateau instead.

The most popular menu items for both lunch or dinner are tomato soup, fruit juice or shrimp cocktail, fried fish, sirloin steak, roast beef or meat pie, served with chips or roast potatoes and peas or cauliflower; then as previously stated, fruit pie, ice cream, gateau or cheese. Even with the cheese, English people are very circumspect and the majority opt for Cheddar. In selecting something to drink with the meal the English know the protocol and choose to drink wine in preference to the national drink of beer but when it comes to choosing the wine the English are not very adventurous and tend to drink those sold under a brand name without worrying where it was produced.

A recent survey carried out in restaurants of all classes showed that nearly a quarter of the total number of places offered more than just one single menu at each meal. In the other 75 per cent of restaurants, which includes public houses, steak bars, Indian and Chinese restaurants and fast-food groups only one menu is used and in these an à la carte menu is used more than the *table d'hôte* although public houses tend to use the latter. Restaurants in hotels usually offer both Table d'Hôte and à la Carte menus.

PRICES ON MENUS

The delicate subject of prices has been solved by some establishments which print a number of menus without the prices. None of the à la Carte items are priced nor does the Table d'Hôte menu carry any indication of what is charged. These unpriced menus are the ones handed to guests, mainly ladies, and the idea is that they can then choose what they want without regard to the cost and without causing any embarrassment by selecting what might be an expensive dish. The host is given a priced menu; thus he can do some mental arithmetic as to the likely amount of the bill and also check the bill against the menu.

There does not appear to be a need to proffer unpriced wine lists as it is the duty of the host himself to order sufficient of whichever wine he considers will be acceptable to his guests. Should a wide range of dishes be chosen some white and some red wine would be ordered. If there is someone amongst the guests who is knowledgeable on wines the host could invite him to do the choosing. It is certainly not the practice to give each person a copy of the wine list.

MENU PUBLICITY

Every week since 1886 the main weekly catering journal has carried a feature entitled *Our Menu File* which originally consisted of a selection of menus submitted by caterers who felt the event was important enough to put on show to their fellow-caterers. Since 1975 comment on the menus has been given by a former editor of the journal who has endeavoured to tighten the standards of menu composition by commending those he considers sufficiently meritorious to be featured in his article, and rejecting those that do nothing to enhance the standard of menu writing.

It is not so much the occasion as the novelty and quality of the menu and the ingenuity of the writer that makes them worthy of mention. The fact that a famous person ate the meal is not so important as the manner in which the menu is written; whatever the language it has to be accurate and novel and it is important that the style of writing should be innovatory rather than humdrum and lacklustre.

In addition to the thrill of seeing one's menu in the pages of the trade journal there is a chance to participate in a monthly competition with a prize awarded for the menu of the function the judges would most liked to have attended. Sponsored competitions for the **Menu of the Year** are also held.

The Menu File is popular with readers because they can see what is being done over a wide range of establishments from the de luxe to the large-scale, and also who is working where. It also presents readers who are practising caterers with a challenge to emulate or to do better than their peers; it can provide new ideas of suitable food combinations and methods of writing and show the range of wines being used and how they complement the dishes listed. For those who submit menus that receive special mention this is the accolade, as they know that only a small percentage of the menus submitted are published and that of those only one or two each week are commented upon as being worthy of praise.

This might mean that the editor has set himself as the arbiter of what is the right way of composing a menu; he has certainly tried to lay down the law as regards the correct form of writing them in French with which not all his readers necessarily agree. Or it might mean that the general standard of menu composition in England is good. In fact despite the editor's wish to tighten the standards that govern acceptance, even those menus that are published seldom appear to have taken advantage of the opportunity to make a really outstanding contribution to gastronomy. The opportunity as afforded, first by the organiser of the function and second by the possibility of showing it to a wider public is not always siezed upon nor profited from. In general, the menus printed do not show evidence of deep thought or sound research; this may mean that chefs and catering managers have not much time to spend on menu composition no matter how auspicious the occasion, or that they do not put in a fourteen-hour day as was commonly done by their predecessors. The real truth may be that there is no book to give proper guidance on the fine art of menu composition. If *Our Menu File* is a genuine reflection of what is being written and being served for special parties then perhaps the rather scathing criticism of standards as voiced by Christopher Driver in his book *The British at Table 1940–1980* may be justified and some of it ought to be heeded.

Several competitions are held every year in many countries for the best menu, whether an actual menu in daily use at a restaurant, or for a special event, or for a perfectly composed menu to be put into operation if it is successful in winning the competition. The winner gains not only the prize and the accolade but valuable publicity that rebounds to the credit of the place where he works.

MERCHANDISING THE MEAL

The menu is often described as a tool of marketing in that it lists the items of food that are available and seeks to entice people who read it to partake of the dishes. The menu should have been composed with the idea that it will appeal to a certain kind of customer and that it will satisfy them when they sample it. A knowledge of psychology as it affects groups of people of different ages, socio-economic backgrounds, sexes and kinds of work, can be very helpful in deciding what foods to offer.

But eating out is not merely a matter of satisfying the appetite with likeable dishes; the meal needs to be eaten in the right surroundings and served by the right type of person. The menu, the wine list, the service, the personnel and the ambience add up to a total meal experience.

It is this total package that is promotable through the menu; a beautifully furnished restaurant that seeks a limited market of wealthy but discriminating customers can show its true nature in the selection of dishes on the menu and wines in the wine list, and in the way both are designed and produced. In the same way, a popular fast-food shop can convey its vitality by the way the dishes are described on the menu, by the vibrant decor and the slickness of the counter staff. The theme of an eating-place identifies the market segment for which it caters; where the package is well-merchandised, then customers will beat a path to its door.

Merchandising food lies also in the way it is cooked and served; Brillat-Savarin's maxim 'Tell me what you eat and I will tell you who you are' could be equally meaningful if turned around to read 'Tell me who you are and I'll tell you what you eat'. This might indicate that not only the dishes but also the prices charged, fit the particular market segment; it is obviously important for there to be some reconciliation between the quality and the price.

Merchandising food can be taken a step further by putting some of the actual food on display, for example, a salad trolley at which the salad is tossed in the selected dressing, a selection of meats for grilling from which the customer may

97

choose and watch it being cooked on a grill in the dining room, a lighted tank of swimming fish, packages of foods as served in the establishment such as wine, petits fours, take-away meals or coffee, all attractively gift-packed with the logo well in prominence.

A menu and wine list may also be used to advertise other services of the restaurant such as outside catering for private functions either on or off the premises, supplying staff to cook and serve, or to give advice on dishes and wines.

But perhaps the best way of merchandising the image of the establishment is by giving an impression of generosity and geniality which is done by serving ample portions at reasonable prices without nonsensical additional charges for so-called extras. There should be no quibbling over complaints and no attempt to exploit customers but an attitude on the part of staff that the customer is always right and that his or her well-being is their most important consideration.

It is important to present the menu and wine list to the customer in the best possible form; if they are to be put inside a plastic or leather cover, this must set them off to good advantage. A display case for showing the menu near the entrance should be exactly the right size and shape to hold the menu, well-glazed and in keeping with the décor around it.

It is useful to do some case studies on menus to see how successful they are. An example could be a restaurant where the chef prides himself on the large number of items on his à la Carte menu and claims they are all available whenever ordered. He employs a large brigade to cope with all these dishes yet is aware that there are quite a number of items that are never asked for and others that are called for only occasionally. As the food is kept awaiting possible customers, it gradually deteriorates until the time comes when it is necessary to dispose of it, either on the Table d'Hôte menu where it makes less profit or worse still, to be served for staff meals. It is interesting to envisage the solutions to this example and ensure that the problems are entirely eliminated.

FOOD STANDARDS

Food must be fit for human consumption and the technology which produces the foods we use is one of the greatest achievements of modern science. Food-stuffs have to comply with certain standards as laid down by law and the various Acts go into considerable detail in governing its fitness for consumption. Before legislation, adulteration of foods was widespread; most foods are now labelled with a list of ingredients contained in the package. The relevant legal requirements are contained in the Food and Drugs Act 1955 and the Food Labelling Regulations 1980.

Some foods give details of the nutritional value even though the nutrients are artificial ones added to the food, because people are becoming more aware of the need to eat a balanced diet. In the United States every hospital, clinic and old person's home has its nutritionist; big companies employ one to care for employees' dietary and even a modest restaurant may engage a nutrition expert to advise customers at meal-times what to select from the menu and what regime to follow. In this country many restaurants offer slimmers' meals and list the calorie content of various dishes, but only the teaching hospitals and the very largest hospitals employ a dietitian. Nutrition is of great importance to the well-being of a nation but unfortunately the way it is taught and presented often detracts from its value and it can demote a gourmet repast to a materialistic meal.

Nutrition is one of the aspects of food science taught at all levels of catering courses and it is usually presented as the fascinating subject it really is. Unfortunately many students appear to regard it as a theoretical subject that belongs to the laboratory rather than as a practical subject that is carried out in every kitchen, not just the diet kitchen.

Good kitchen practice is necessary not only to preserve nutritional content during the cooking process – and portion sizes have a bearing on the actual food value of meals – but also to ensure the hygienic preparation of food. Food poisoning causes many deaths each year, sometimes from contaminated processed foods but more often from food cooked in a kitchen where hygienic standards are low. In addition many people suffer painful illnesses from eating food infected with bacteria, including salmonella and various staphylococci. Hygiene means looking after raw and cooked foods in the proper manner as laid down by food hygiene legislation; it means keeping the kitchen scrupulously clean, preventing infestation and training staff in good hygienic practices. The Food Hygiene (General) Regulations 1970 and the Food and Drugs (Controls of Food Premises) Act 1976 apply to all kitchens.

The good health of those he serves should be dear to the heart of every caterer, his aim being to serve balanced meals that will keep them fit and well. Obesity is common in the West and gluttony is a danger to guard against at any age; the frustration and materialism of modern life cause some people to seek solace in gourmandising. At the other extreme there are young people, usually women who suffer from being underweight, brought about by psychologically-induced self-starvation, known as *anorexia nervosa*. These unfortunate people need to be coaxed into renewing their interest in food by dainty portions of eye-appealing food served in ideal surroundings. Medical and psychiatric intervention is obviously essential as such a problem can be intractable.

It is very easy for people to fall into the habit of eating those foods which are widely available in ready-prepared form and require little or no mastication. 'Junk food' is the name given to the range of foods that come into this category and it is an appropriate title since they contain little nutritional value and are not conducive to continued good health. Among foods that come into this category are potato crisps and other similar snack items, inferior quality ice-cream, sweet biscuits, jam, slush drinks and so on.

FOOD ADDITIVES

The manufacturers of many of our everyday foods deliberately add extraneous ingredients with a view to improving their keeping qualities and flavour. As there are quite a number of these it is necessary to know what they are and the effect they are meant to have on the food they are added to. All are approved by the government Food Standards Committee and are authorised and approved by the Common Market authorities; the list of ingredients should be printed on the package.

Antioxidants, antifoamings, artificial sweeteners, bleaches, colourings, contaminants, emulsifiers, flavour modifiers, flavourings, flocculators, improvers, preservatives, solvents, sweeteners and thickeners and stabilisers may not appear to be the ingredients of gourmet meals but there is no doubt they have a role to play in the quality of many of the foods we have to eat. Many packaged foods bear the numbers of added colourings, preservatives and flavourings approved by the EEC, and including E102 (*tartragine*) E210 (*benzoic acid*) E320 (*butylated hydroxyanisole*) and E400 (*textural aids*).

As we said in Chapter 2 many food flavours cannot be adequately described in words but the use of artificial flavours and colours in recommended amounts can help to make food more acceptable to the general taste. Manufacturers are aware that the senses lose their sensitivity when over-stimulated by excessive amounts, and that customers can lose interest in a stimulus when it is over-used and becomes monotonous.

Food manufacturers have to protect their reputation by maintaining a consistently high standard of quality that conforms to legislation and to their own voluntary code. If the quality slips the consumer will notice and complain or stop buying it.

MENU TRUQUAGE

Menu Truquage means faking foods and substituting similar but cheaper items for the real thing. Many restaurants that enjoy wide recognition for the excellence of their cooking and make enormous profits from the customers who crowd into them make use of it and if their operation was to be analysed or closely inspected, it could well be that the secret of their success rested on dubious activities. In some cases the praise accorded to an eating-place is really self-generated and stems from a continuous stream of advertising that proclaims the quality of the food and the superb skills of the chef. Announcers and reporters may unwittingly be contributing to the propaganda because they fail to fathom what is going on, or they may be a party to it.

Food writers are often freelance, that is, not always in the *employ* of the journal in which their articles appear, being paid a fee for each article published; some write under a *nom de plume* or may use several names. In any case, writers do not often agree on what they say about an eating-place – one may visit it on a day when it is extremely busy and the dishes are being cooked hurriedly, another may be feeling out of sorts and this could impair his judgement. No matter how impartial, these writers are employed because of their ability with words and love of food rather than for their knowledge of how to run a professional kitchen but their judgements must be free from any charge of self-interest. Some chefs have the ability to make third-rate goods taste like top-quality produce, they can pad out small portions to look generous, produce chicken out of rabbit and veal from pork. The soles they serve are not designated as lemon or Torbay but always as Dover soles – or so the high menu price would indicate.

Fortunately, bogus menus where very few of the dishes are true to name are not in widespread use and stretched menus are found more commonly than actual malpractices. Chefs are required to make their kitchen pay and to do this, certain time-honoured economic practices such as collecting used lobster shells for making bisque soup, picking over poussin carcasses for *émincé*, using outside leaves of lettuce for soup, using leftovers for *hors-d'oeuvres* and analogues for other dishes, are acceptable. Even the staunchest bastion of classical cookery where gourmets go into ecstasies over the fine food must generate a golden flow of profit or else become a relic of a bygone gastronomic age. Those who strive to keep gastronomy alive as a public relations exercise or for their own delight inevitably do it a disservice.

THE ROLE OF STANDARDISED RECIPES

A standard recipe whether it be a handwritten or typed sheet of paper kept in a recipe file or in a computer-based catering information system, is a sure method of quality control and an assurance of customer satisfaction. The advantages of a standard recipe are:

1. uniformity of product each time the recipe is used;
2. correct portion size;
3. cost of dish can be known in advance;
4. controls stores issues because exact weights are given out;
5. decides standard purchasing specifications;
6. can be carried out successfully by inexperienced staff; no dependence on any one employee;
7. exact time taken to prepare a given number of portions of a dish is known;
8. consumer assurance of quality;
9. enables even utilisation of kitchen staff and equipment;
10. exact details are fully described on the file card.

Before a recipe is put on file the dish must be tried out with a taste panel, and only if members give unreserved approval of the dishes' appearance, texture, taste and aroma can it be put into mass production.

A standard recipe then is one that establishes the exact ingredients and their amounts, the cookery methods and the equipment to use, thus ensuring a uniform standard of production in a predetermined quantity that yields the correct amount of profit in relation to the selling price, as shown on Fig. 5.1.

Figure 5.1
CATERING PRODUCTION UNIT STANDARD RECIPE NO M43

No. of Portions: 250

Portion Size: 200 g

Costing date:
November 19--

Name: **Goulash of Beef with Gnocchis**   *Time: 4 hours*

Stage	Amount	Ingredient	Equipment	Method	Time (mins)	Unit cost	Cost £	p
1	25 kg	topside of beef	butcher's block	cut into 2.5 cm cubes	40	210	52	50
2	1 kg	lard	bratt pan	heat until smoking, fry meat until brown	30	56		56
3	6 kg	onions, finely chopped		add to meat and fry	5	22	1	32
4	1.5 kg	paprika		mix in and fry lightly	2	270	4	05
5	1 kg	flour*		sprinkle over and mix in	3	27		27
6	750 g	tomato puree		mix in	2	90		67
7	32 lts	white stock		stir in until smooth	3	3	·	96
8	50 g	salt		sprinkle in, cover and simmer	75	12.5		02
9				stir in the poached and drained gnocchis	10			
	Gnocchis							
1	5 lts	water ⎫	boiling pan	place to boil		180	1	80
	1 kg	butter ⎬						
	150 g	salt ⎭			10	12.5		03
2	3.25 kg	flour		add and mix in, allow to cool	10	27		88
3	60	eggs	mixer	add one by one	10	5	3	00
4	400 g	parmesan cheese		mix in; pipe mixture in 2 cm lengths into hot water, cook for 5 mins then drain	40	580	2	32

Total Cost   68   38

Portion Cost   27.4

* if being frozen use 500 g waxy rice flour and 500 g plain flour, dilute with 2 litres cold stock and add at Stage 9 instead of Stage 5 and reduce white stock to 30 litres at Stage 7.

102

A computer can store standard recipes so that all that is necessary when the dish is to be produced is to enter the name of the dish and the number of portions required and the computer will print it out. It will also print out the requisition so that the kitchen is issued with the exact amount of ingredients. The file of standard recipes can be kept in categories that make menu composition easy by grouping under (i) methods of cooking, (ii) the name of the course, for example, soup, meat, pudding, (iii) the main ingredient used, for example, potato or beef, or (iv) the colour of the resultant dish. If required the nutritional content can be added in, either as the kilocalorie count or the total list of nutritional values. This information can be obtained from McCance and Widdowson in *The Nutritional Value of Foods*, published by HMSO, or it can be worked out from other sources such as the DHSS' *Manual of Catering*. Fig. 5.2 shows the same recipe as produced from a catering information system.

Figure 5.2

STANDARD RECIPE AS PRODUCED FROM A CATERING INFORMATION SYSTEM

Recipe No. M43   Name: Goulash of Beef with Gnocchi. Main ingredient: Beef
No. of portions: 250   Portion size: 200 g   Colour: reddish brown
Method of cooking: Stewing   Time 240 mins
Item of equipment: Bratt pan   Kilocalories: 350 p.p.
Cooking temperature: 98°F

Ingredient	Amount	Cost	Total
beef topside, in 2.5 cubes	25000 g	210	5250
lard	1000 g	56	56
onions, diced	6000 g	22	132
paprika	1500 g	270	405
flour	1000 g	27	27
tomato puree	750 g	90	67
stock	32000 ml	03	96
salt	50 g	12.5	02
water	5000 ml	0	00
butter	1000 g	180	180
salt	150 g	12.5	03
flour	3250 g	27	88
eggs, number	60	05	300
cheese, parmesan	400 g	580	232

Ingredient cost: 6838 p
Cost per portion: 27.40 p
Selling price: 69.25 p

103

6 Menu Planning

General Principles – The Profile of the Customer – The Meal and the
Occasion – The Range of Menus – The Sequence of Courses – The
Selection of Dishes – The Availability of Supplies – Capabilities of
Staff – Equipment and Utensils – The Nutritional Aspects – The
Language of the Menu – Food Combinations – Pricing the Menu

GENERAL PRINCIPLES

When sitting down to produce a menu it is necessary to be aware of certain
factors and to have a set of guidelines as otherwise it can happen that the menu
may not suit the operation and will not conform to accepted professional
standards.

Obviously the menu must be written with the customer in mind because he
is the one who is going to consume and pay for it. It must therefore be one that
will tempt and satisfy him. Guidance in the form of a set of rules or principles
of menu compilation will help to make the menu realistic from both the customer's and the caterer's point of view. The factors governing the planning of a
menu would include:

1. the consumer's needs and expectations;
2. any policy decisions regarding the type of menu to be used;
3. the number of meals to be produced;
4. the price to be charged and the anticipated profit rate;
5. the type of establishment or operation.

Over the years a number of principles have been defined and become generally accepted which help those who write menus. Whilst not every one of these
principles applies to all menus and to all operations, they do act as reminders of
the restraints within which menus need to be written. The parameters that were
identified at the planning stage will act as these restraints. The principles, or
rules of menu planning are based on these topics:

1. the profile of the customer;
2. the meal and the occasion;
3. the range of menus to be written;
4. the sequence of courses;
5. the selection of dishes;
6. the availability of supplies;
7. the capabilities of the staff;
8. the equipment and utensils available;
9. the nutritional aspects;
10. the language to be used;
11. food combinations;
12. pricing the menu and portion control.

The bare statement of each principle will be sufficient to act as a guide to someone who is experienced in writing menus but will need to be interpreted for those who come new to the job. It is therefore necessary to fill in the details as follows, also bearing in mind the factors that govern menu composition as shown in Chapter 7.

Any restaurant will have been established to cater for a particular socio-economic group of customers and the whole operation will be geared to satisfying that group's particular needs. This implies that the location, style and décor, amenities, food and prices will be such as to attract and satisfy a class of people as identified by the market research.

The scope and extent of the menus to be offered can be determined by ascertaining the probable spending power of the average type of customer as well as something of his background such as job, income, age, sex and family circumstances. This information will assist in deciding what dishes to feature on the menu, what style of service should be used, and what prices can be charged.

A particular group of customers of a certain religion or culture can have different expectations from another group but since the dividing line between groups is quite narrow and movement up and down betweeen groups is common, it is a disadvantage to be so inflexible as not to be able to cater for the needs of those groups above and below the social strata of customers as originally identified.

In any case, people's needs change, either by the demands of fashion, their financial position and conflicts on the expenditure of income, or through the mobility of the population. In addition there is always the possibility that custom may be lost or changed because of staff turnover. The personality of the manager, head chef or head waiter is crucial to the success or otherwise of a restaurant and he is a deciding factor in the type of clientele that patronise the place. Very often a restaurant loses its food guide awards when the chef leaves.

How consumer's expectations are to be met is embodied in the policy of an establishment and brought to fruition by the ambience and the total dining experience. If the place is run efficiently and is successful in what it sets out to do, this means that the enterprise is on the right course and that customers are happy.

106

Filling in the details of each principle will serve to show their relevance and their close relationship with the others; it serves to show that to ignore any one could detract from the value of the resultant menu. Few can claim that the menus they produce are free from errors and above criticism or that the present standard of menu composition is perfect. Yet by the simple means of observing these few fairly elementary rules the standard could be easily raised for the benefit of staff and customers alike – and it is not always the printer or typist who is at fault when a menu is less than perfect.

THE PROFILE OF THE CUSTOMER

The person who writes the menu needs to know who he is writing it for as its form and content have to be based on this information. In the absence of these facts the menu is likely to end up as a list of unsuitable dishes that will disappoint those who have to choose from them. There are many groups of people with special requirements to whom the normal popular dishes would be unacceptable, some of these being small homogeneous groups whose needs can be easily satisfied even when only a fixed menu is offered. But the larger the group, or the greater the number of clients to be catered for, the more difficult it becomes to satisfy them all. There will always be the majority who willingly accept the average menu but in large-scale catering, some customers are bound to have different tastes, mainly because of cultural differences.

As has been explained in Chapter 2 a person's likes and dislikes are formed during infancy – his country of birth and home surroundings, the person's race, his cultural and socio-economic background and sometimes his religion, all have an effect on food habits although they may not develop to the full until later in life. Education and travel exert their effect, then as we grow older the metabolism rate starts to slow down and the palate's sensitivity and the ability to masticate food properly subsides. Not only age, but also the sex of the clientele must be considered because it is a biological fact that females because of their structure, do not require as many kilocalories as do males.

In a commercial restaurant in a town centre the clientele will be a cross section of the public some of whom happen to be there more by chance than design and who patronise it because they feel in need of a meal. Unless it is located in a commercial centre it is unlikely that there are any regular customers. If it is in a popular tourist area the business could be seasonal; if the location is devoid of nightlife, evening trade could be minimal; if not in a shopping area business could be poor on Saturday and there would have to be a good reason to open on Sundays and Bank Holidays. It is not the pattern any more to have as many homes as business premises in town centres, so for this sort of establishment it would appear necessary to write a menu that will cater for a great many tastes but in fact it is sufficient to feature the most popular dishes at an average price level that suits the majority of tastes and purses.

8. A supper menu from the Savoy, 1903 (printed on silk)

THE MEAL AND THE OCCASION

This principle is concerned with the basic difference between the three meals of the day, more especially, between the menu for lunch and that for dinner. By 'occasion' is meant the experience of eating – away from home – rather than a functional meal, in other words, one that is slightly out of the ordinary everyday routine. Most of the meals we eat are to provide us with energy and for repair and growth of body tissues and a normal diet usually takes care of these requirements of good health. Then there are those special events for which a customer will dress more carefully, for which he will make a special journey, when he is happy to spend more money than usual, and to which he looks forward with keen anticipation of having a pleasurable time. For such a customer the meal will take on the special meaning of being an occasion, whether or not it is incidental to a major attraction such as a visit to a theatre or cinema, or a meeting. To the staff of the restaurant it is just another turn of duty and they may not realise or care about its importance to a customer. But they should always bear in mind that the pleasure of a good meal can be intense and that every customer should be made to feel on leaving that he is exalted, almost as though he had been in church.

A lot has been written and said about eating out in France and surely cooking as the finest of French glories, lies in the thousands of small restaurants, furnished with plain chairs and check tablecloths but which serve good food to a knowledgeable clientele who do not worry if the welcome is warm or austere; they are keen to savour a gourmet meal and in so doing to participate in an edifying occasion that is a rewarding experience. Here, the underlying planning usually consists of a printed menu to which is added a card that lists the *plats du jour* – dishes of the day – which may be made of rechauffé foods or items on sale in the market that morning that were the inspiration for the special dishes of the day.

Lunch is generally considered to be a more functional meal than dinner and it is accepted that people expect to pay less and spend less time over it than is the case with dinner. This might indicate that a luncheon menu is an easy one to compose and that gastronomy does not come into it. In fact it can present more difficulties than a dinner menu because there are some fairly severe restraints which limit the range of possible dishes because of their price and suitability. Certainly customers' expectations differ between these two meals, with lunch usually being regarded as part of normal everyday routine – a brief respite to relax and re-fuel with energy so as to keep mind and body going to the end of the working day. In those places where lunch is the main meal of the day the normal restrictions on selection of dishes should be relaxed as this meal is the main source of the caterer's expenditure. Yet despite this it is difficult to consider it on the same level of importance as dinner not only because of the time of day, but because it does not lend itself so readily to a sense of occasion as does dinner. Yet there are times when a lunch can be made an occasion, and it would be sad if none of the 25 000 or so consumed by a person during his lifetime was never out of the ordinary. It is part of the caterer's job occasionally to do something different or outstanding such as featuring a special dish or gourmet menu at lunchtime, making use of an event in the calendar or presenting the authentic cookery and dishes of a certain region or country.

THE RANGE OF MENUS

As has been stated there are only two basic kinds of menu – the Table d'Hôte and the à la Carte but each has several derivatives so the list is a fairly long one. The policy of the establishment decides which kind of menu will be used, the policy regarding menus being a combination of such factors as hours of opening, days of the week when it is open, type of customer, amenities of the restaurant, anticipated amount of business, prices charged and so on. An à la carte menu is one which contains a list of dishes for each of the courses, each dish being individually priced and usually cooked to order with the choice left entirely to the customer. A Table d'Hôte menu is one with little or no choice and comprises a complete meal of several courses, with an overall charge. In addition to these there are other kinds of menu that are peculiar to a particular establishment or to a catering chain, but are still derived from one of the two basic kinds.

Table d'Hôte Menu

This kind of menu offers a set meal, either with or without any choices, priced for a definite number of courses. In its basic form it has no alternatives and the captive customers have no option other than to eat it or leave it. This stems from the time when travellers sat together at a long table to partake of a meal with the innkeeper playing the role of mine host. The host's table offered what was called the 'Ordinary' of the day which comprises a substantial meal, either lunch or dinner. Charles Dickens wrote a colourful description of the atmosphere of the dining room of a Victorian inn in *The Pickwick Papers*.

Now even establishments that have a regular captive clientele such as schools, hospitals and prisons, feel there is a need to offer alternatives on their table d'hôte menus and the former take-it or leave-it attitude has disappeared, except for banquets and similar functions.

There are two ways in which choices are included in menus for commercial establishments: (i) there is a selection of items on each course but no prices except a total charge for the number of courses; (ii) there is a price marked against each main dish which determines the charge made for the entire meal. Where these kinds of menus are kept in operation over a period of time there is likely to be a need for additional choices which can take the form of a special

110

dish for each day of the week, or by writing a list each day of the *plats du jour*, which may be seasonal items and can be chosen in place of the printed items.

The writer of a Table d'Hôte menu should not be too adventurous, but should use only dishes that have a popular appeal, and choose dishes for the selection that are fairly equal in appeal. This is not only so that the majority of tastes will be catered for but also to prevent running out of any one dish during the service period thus disappointing some customers. Most Table d'Hôte dishes are cooked ready to serve throughout the service period, the only items cooked to order, where included, being egg dishes. Vegetables should if possible be cooked in batches or served by the rechauffé method but otherwise food is kept hot throughout the service.

A forecast of probable numbers of customers helps to avoid under- or over-production but it is obvious that roast and grilled meats will be the most popular. In deciding on the numbers of portions to produce, the figures are likely to follow the pattern of 30 per cent joint, 20 per cent rechauffé dish, 15 per cent fish, 10 per cent eggs (particularly if omelettes), 10 per cent cold buffet and a further 15 per cent will opt for something from the *plats du jour* list or ask for an à la carte meal.

Table d'Hôte menus are certainly the most widely used because the kitchen organisation behind this method is cost-effective and it is possible to serve a large number of people in a limited amount of time with a limited number of kitchen staff. The customer knows what it is going to cost him and is sure that he will be served a normal-size portion of each item he orders.

There is no fixed number of courses on a Table d'Hôte menu and there can be anything from two to seven, but three or four courses is the normal limit for lunch, and five or six for dinner. Some caterers advertise a four-course *table d'hôte* meal at a fixed price but serve only three that consist of food, the fourth being coffee; this is unprofessional as coffee should be regarded only as an adjunct to a meal. Many caterers do not include coffee in the price of a set meal and charge extra.

A practice that can be detrimental to the good image of catering is to advertise the Table d'Hôte menu at a set price which seems reasonable until the customer receives the bill when he discovers that such extras as a cover charge, VAT, and a service charge are added thus making the price less reasonable.

A la Carte Menu

This kind of menu is generally considered to be more prestigious than the Table d'Hôte and many people think it is used only in high-class restaurants; this is because they realise that eating à la Carte will cost them more than choosing a Table d'Hôte meal. This is not actually the case and although exclusive restaurants operate almost solely on à la Carte lines, so do call-order units and other kinds of fast-food establishments because there the food, although simple, is usually cooked to order or just sufficient to cover the envisaged demand over a short period. An à la Carte menu consists of a list of dishes, printed in the order of the normal sequence of courses with each bearing its particular price. Implicit in this list is the understanding that nothing will be cooked, until it is ordered by a customer and that only items which do not take long are used; this is because of their nature and of the fact that there is a good back-up *mise en place*, or advance preparation. If items that take a time to cook are included in the menu it is necessary to have some ready-cooked or to indicate the time it will take, doing this verbally or by printing it on the menu, for example:

Faisan Souvaroff – for two person (45 mins) followed by the price.

This example also demonstrates that it is not possible to prepare every item in individual portion sizes because by their nature they are too large; other examples are a best end of lamb, duck, chicken, and a *Chateaubriand*.

It is correct to say that an à la Carte portion usually weighs more than a Table d'Hôte one but this more generous helping corresponds with the price charged. The person choosing a three course meal from the à la Carte menu can expect to pay up to twice as much as if it were a set Table d'Hôte meal. Not that is is necessary to go through the Carte, indeed, this kind of menu is so flexible that a customer is permitted to consume just one dish and get up and go, the safeguard being a minimum charge per person at any meal.

An establishment that operates an à la Carte menu needs a different system of kitchen and restaurant organisation from that of a Table d'Hôte menu. It requires skilled cooks who can work quickly and have a good memory for what has been ordered from their section, and waiters who can serve these dishes with the flair and aplomb which they merit. It is often said that an à la Carte menu demands a higher ratio of staff to customers and items of equipment different from those used for a Table d'Hôte menu but this is not necessarily true as the majority of restaurants operating an à la Carte menu also feature a Table d'Hôte menu, and vice versa.

There are various means by which the two kinds of menu can be combined, one of the most usual being to have one printed on each side of a centrefold card; but having menus printed daily for each meal can be done by only the most select places. It is less costly to insert or clip a duplicated typed Table d'Hôte menu in the à la Carte one, or to keep the two menus separate.

An à la Carte menu can be so composed that it covers a long period of time with any seasonal items marked as subject to availability. It must not be dated, the card must be durable and any alterations to prices should be entered neatly.

Special Function Menu

This is the most important offshoot of the Table d'Hô te menu being the one that is used for banquets and other special functions where a fairly large number of people all come together to eat at the same time in delightful surroundings.

112

The way the meal is served does not allow any choice so in some respects this is the simplest form of menu composition, yet it is also the most difficult since the menu has to suit everybody, be it for a thousand people. Only when a special function takes the form of a buffet is there any possibility of customers being given a choice.

At a banquet where everybody sits down to eat the same meal at the same time the menu must consist of dishes that all will like yet at the same time include ones that they do not normally have at home and that are worthy of being served at this special occasion. The larger the numbers attending the function the earlier the meal has to be cooked which limits still further the number of suitable dishes since they must be those that will stand up well to storage in the hot-plate.

The same rules that apply to writing a lunch and dinner menu apply to the special function menu, and the time of the day when the function is being held has a definite effect upon the suitability of dishes. In every event a feeling of occasion must be engendered in the participants, a sense of anticipation for the repast to be served as being the highlight of the function so that when they leave, they feel satisfied.

Menus of the Day

During the course of every day the traditional pattern of meals brings customers to the table to partake of food and drink appropriate to the time. The pattern varies according to the type of establishment, with a residential institution having a different sequence from that of a commercial establishment. The menus that have to be composed are those for breakfast, lunch, afternoon tea, high tea, supper, dinner and late-night snack. Some establishments have to have menus for various kinds of special diet and for people who are ill. Some of the meals listed are used only in certain residential establishments where the requirements are peculiar to their inhabitants and there is a big difference between the menu of a place like a hostel that is in operation every day of the year and, say, a college refectory that caters for student's lunches from Mondays to Fridays during only three ten-week terms.

Breakfast Menus

There are two kinds of breakfast menus in England – the traditional English one and the Continental one. Both are set meals composed in Table d'Hôte form. Actually the Continental breakfast as we know it applies mainly to France as other European countries offer cold meat or cheese.

A 'full English breakfast' consists of two courses plus some adjuncts and beverages; each course offers a number of choices and the range of dishes included is governed by the price charged. The first course usually has a choice of several

113

kinds of breakfast cereal, fruit compotes, fruit juices or porridge, and the second course offers a choice of hot dishes including bacon, sausage, eggs and fish, or cold items such as Bath chap or ham. Then there are the bread items with butter and preserves and the beverage. A similar sort of breakfast is served in other parts of the UK, Scotland for example being noted for its morning-baked baps, potato scones and girdle cakes. No wonder overseas visitors are advised to eat breakfast, followed by breakfast, then another breakfast as constituting the delights of British gastronomy, always provided that the three meals are decently cooked and that a different main dish is chosen each time.

By contrast a Continental breakfast is not a patch on the real thing, being some sort of bread with butter and jam and coffee. Some hotels make it less austere by adding fruit juice or yoghurt, serving hot rolls and croissants and by giving a choice of hot beverage. The different prices charged show the difference between the two sorts of the same meal. Fuller details of breakfast menus are given in Chapter 5.

Lunch Menus

The midday meal is not usually regarded as being the important one of the day. There are however many places where lunch is eaten as the main meal and there are many people who, after having a good lunch, want only a snack meal later on. But generally speaking lunch is not as large or expensive a meal as dinner and the foods used are somewhat different. A two- or three-course set lunch is the norm because this meal is accepted as being an austere and unpretentious one as against dinner where a longer menu is more likely to be demanded.

Suitable items for luncheon menus include stews and good quality made-up dishes of a kind that are totally inappropriate for dinner. A garnish served with a lunch entrée should be simple, and ungarnished dishes are the rule. There is likely to be less demand on the à la Carte menu at lunchtime than there is for dinner.

Dinner Menus

This meal is much more of an occasion than is lunch so it is natural to make the dinner menu exploit this by offering a wider variety of dishes and charging higher prices. This is because most people are relaxed after the day's work and have more time to spend over dinner than they have for lunch. It is only in establishments where lunch is designated as the principal meal of the day that dinner has to give way to it. Because customers are prepared to spend more money, the Table d'Hôte menu can be as many as six courses long and certainly the à la carte menu comes more into its own at this meal.

The dishes included on a dinner menu must be better quality than those for lunch. Certainly it is true that many dishes suitable for serving at lunch are

114

equally good for dinner but it is stressed that inexpensive stews and straightforward roast meats are not correct, neither are egg dishes, farinaceous foods, steamed puddings or baked pies whether meat or sweet. These distinctions are not brought about by fashion or tradition but by the rules of good menu planning as being most beneficial to the customer. Escoffier always put his customers first which is why he wrote 'The service of an hors-d'oeuvre at dinner is undesirable and even though this may be oysters it is really only admissible in the absence of soup. Those hors-d'oeuvre which include various types of fish in oil, smoked fish and highly seasoned salads have a very strong taste on the palate and the customer may find that the soup which follows tastes flat and insipid'. He makes an exception if the oysters are served with hock or dry white Bordeaux and for serving caviar at dinner because its fresh nutty flavour will not spoil that of the soup to follow.

It is incorrect to put puddings and pies on as sweets for dinner and this applies to many other hot sweets including milk puddings, fritters and even pancakes. The dividing line between which sweets are appropriate for lunch or for dinner is very fine but it does exist and should be observed. This means that only light, elegant and eye-catching sweets such as fruit and ice cream should be featured for dinner. More details of the structure of lunch and dinner menus are given in Chapter 7.

Afternoon Tea Menus

This delightful meal is a very English affair that follows a traditional menu with some regional variations. It may be taken rather formally sitting at table or informally in lounge armchairs. The quality of dry tea, either Indian or China used in the pot distinguishes the calibre of this meal and as most British people are connoisseurs of a cup of tea it should be properly made. Continental visitors sometimes prefer *tisane*, which is a herbal brew, to our kind of tea because it is supposed to be good for the digestion and relieve headache; there are many different flavours including camomile and jasmine and it is served with lemon. The food at teatime consists of small dainty sandwiches of fish and meat paste, egg and cress, cucumber and tomato followed by a selection of *pâtisseries françaises* which will include éclairs, choux buns, fruit tartlets, frangipane barquettes, Genoese fancies, etc. A slice of fruit cake, seed cake or jam sponge is in order and during the winter, toasted buttered crumpets or teacakes. **Cream tea** includes scones with strawberry jam and whipped cream.

High Tea Menus

This meal replaces dinner for people who retire early to bed and is therefore more substantial than ordinary afternoon tea. It should be a formal teatime meal plus a hot or cold dish in which eggs, cheese, pasta, fish or cold meat can be

115

used. Sometimes this is followed by a sweet, more especially where children are concerned because this meal is sometimes referred to as the children's dinner. Thus some expert knowledge of the requirements of growing children and of the elderly is needed to compose a suitable menu for this meal.

Supper Menus

This meal has several connotations, it can be a snack meal with a bedtime drink, just a sandwich, or a fairly substantial meal as served at any time in night clubs and casinos to people who are still awake the other side of midnight.

As might be expected of a luxurious members' club the menu is normally a limited à la Carte one of hot and cold dishes of excellent quality, substantial yet fairly light. The items included on the menu are quite different from those served for a theatre supper which is really an offshoot of a normal dinner menu; some long-established supper dishes are **Haddock Monte Carlo, Chicken à la King, Club Sandwich, Omelette Arnold Bennett,** also grilled kippers and other breakfast-type dishes because by now it is getting light outside and morning is breaking.

THE SEQUENCE OF COURSES

Before beginning to compose a menu it is helpful to memorise the sequence of courses of which there are as many as twelve. This is not to suggest that caterers should go back to the golden age of gourmandising as done during the reign of Edward VII, the *bon-viveur*, but that they should know how to select from these many courses and put them together in the right order. Knowing the pattern helps when compiling any kind of menu and is beneficial to customers because they like to see them set out in the right order even though they may not realise the distinction between the courses that are appropriate to lunch as against dinner. The sequence is as follows:

Lunch	French Translation	Dinner	French Translation
Hors-d'oeuvre	*Hors d'-oeuvre*	Hors-d'oeuvre	*Hors-d'oeuvre*
Soup	*Potage*	Soup	*Potage*
Egg dish	*Oeuf*	Fish	*Poisson*
Farinaceous	*Farineaux*	Entrée	*1er Plat*
Fish	*Poisson*	Relevé	*2ème Plat*
Entree		Roast	*Rôti*
Roast	*Rôti*	Cold dish	*Buffet Froid*

116

Grill	Grillade	Vegetable	Légume
Cold buffet	Buffet froid	Sweet	Entremet
Vegetable	Légume	Savoury	Savourie
Sweet	Entremet	Cheese	Fromage
Cheese	Fromage	Dessert	Dessert

A sorbet can be added to the dinner list as course number five, this being a minor one that is supposed to act as a pause to rest and refresh the palate and it used to be the signal for guests to smoke a cigarette such as a Balkan Sobranie or a coloured Russian or Turkish one. The custom of smoking has now been virtually abandoned although the sorbet is still used nearly everywhere. It is permissible to replace a sorbet by a spirit or liqueur served very cold; it is put on the menu by its name or in a literary sense such as for example **Le Trou Normande** which indicates a liqueur glass of calvados. It must not be forgotten that coffee is invariably served at the end of both lunch and dinner and as previously stated some caterers insist on listing it as a course. This is incorrect and even if a lovely service of *petits fours* is offered with the coffee it still does not constitute a course since it is after all only a beverage, and nobody would want to eat a whole helping of these sweetmeats. Using the same argument a brandy or liqueur served at the end of a meal would have to be designated as a course.

To use this established sequence of courses the pattern now is to compile the menu with one dish from each group. For lunch the grouping is *hors-d'oeuvre*, soup, egg, farinaceous; fish, entrée, roast, grill, cold buffet; sweet or cheese thus giving three courses. For dinner it is *hors-d'oeuvre*, soup; fish; entrée, relevé, roast, cold; sweet, savoury, cheese, thus giving four courses. A fifth course could be the cheese and if a six-course menu is requested it could be a single vegetable, the savoury or a savoury soufflé. Cheese used not to be included in a dinner menu but is now very popular and with all its accompaniments can be very acceptable. Compilers of menus need to be aware of the continental habit of eating cheese *before* the sweet and also that savouries are peculiar to the British and Americans. The sequence of courses applies to other meals.

Breakfast

Fruit juice or fruit; cereal or porridge; egg, fish, bacon, sausage or cold meat as the main course; preserves, toast, rolls or croissants. This suggests that it is a four-course meal or even five if fresh fruit is served but it is usually only two courses with the toast, butter, preserves and beverage giving their support rather than acting as a separate course.

It should be noted that breakfast can also be a special function organised as a banquet of several courses with champagne served throughout, finishing with fresh fruit and coffee.

Afternoon Tea

Although it would not appear to be necessary for any separate courses there is a definite sequence and if a menu were to be printed it would show it as sandwiches, bread and butter, preserves; pastries, scones, cake, toasted items, and various kinds of tea with milk or slices of lemon. It is not usual to distinguish the actual content of the sandwiches or to name the cakes except perhaps French pastries.

High Tea

It is possible to identify the limited number of courses of this meal but it is not usual to offer much choice. The first course is the main one of fish, farinaceous, cheese, cold meat and salad, all served with bread and butter and a cup of tea; the second course is the sweet but could be a cake of any kind such as a slice of fruit cake or gateau. Since this is invariably a fairly substantial meal and the last one of the day, it is important to provide sufficient nutrients and bulk in the diet and to offer accompaniments where appropriate.

Supper

The sequence of courses is the same as for dinner but using only a limited number by grouping dishes together for example the *hors-d'oeuvres*, soup and eggs as one course followed by the main course and a few sweets. The meal can be three- or four-course one, on Table d'Hôte lines, or as is frequently the case, an à la Carte menu from which the customer may choose as few or as many course as he pleases.

Dual Purpose Menu

It is not necessary to have a different à la Carte menu for each meal of the day as it is perfectly possible to compile one to suit all meals, provided it is carefully planned. The sequence of courses is the same but a compromise has to be made in that egg and farinaceous dishes will have to be available for lunch and for dinner. Many à la Carte menus are written in French so the headings must be given in the same language.

THE SELECTION OF DISHES

When including dishes on a menu for a meal it is necessary to consider it as a whole and not as a range of individual items. Apart from a set Table d'Hôte meal a customer is free to some extent to make up his own menu from the choices offered so the person compiling the menu must consider all the possible permutations to see that they conform to good principles. The points under this heading are (i) colour, (ii) texture, consistency and shape, (iii) flavour, taste and aroma, (iv) cooking method and (v) serving method.

Colour

Colours play an important part in the enjoyment of food, indeed we 'eat' with our eyes before our lips and every caterer should study colour blends. It is only too easy to compile a colourless menu where there are no colour contrasts or one that is the same colour all through. Most food has its own natural colour and the cooking process should retain or enhance it, not destroy it by poor techniques. Bottled or powdered food-colouring should be used sparingly and only if essential to restore a natural colour, not to colour food in an artificial manner.

People associate colours and colour combinations with certain characteristics, for example:

> **green** indicates freshness, coolness, natural flavour;
> **white** – plainness, purity, cleanliness, clinical, frozen;
> **yellow** – healthful, summeriness, freshly-laid eggs, ripeness;
> **red** – pungent, heated, warmth, hot in flavour;
> **brown** – piquancy, spiciness, richness, tastiness;
> **blue** – weak, watery, coldness, chilliness, poisonous.

This means that brown foods such as stews, a roast or a grill exert good eye appeal because of their deep colour but a vary dark brown gives the impression of being overcooked; a white stew though it may taste as good as a brown one is not so aesthetically appealing. This point can be used as an example to show how easy it is to compile a one-colour meal: for example,

Vichyssoise Soup

Fillet of Sole Suchet

Blanquette of Veal with Mushrooms and Onions

Cauliflower and Boiled Potatoes

Vanilla Bavarois

119

A second example might be:

Tomato Soup

Chicken Chasseur

Carrots and Rissolee Potatoes

Cherry Flan

These are good dishes individually but not collectively, unless a customer insists on a one-colour meal.

It is necessary to envisage the meal as it will appear on the customer's plate, disregarding such things as chopped parsley and sprigs of picked parsley and watercress; some chefs now insist on plating all meals in the kitchen so that they can get the colours nicely contrasted and obtain a very artistic presentation. This kind of service is a feature of *cuisine nouvelle*.

Texture, Consistency and Shape

These indicate the feel of food in the mouth whilst it is being masticated; there are several ways of describing this including crisp, crunchy, chewy, tough, tender, lumpy, underdone and overcooked.

Some groups of people need a completely soft diet because they have few or no teeth with which to chew but this is not to suggest that it must be 'slops' as there can be several stages of consistency from very firm to quite runny. Some people associate mushiness with rotten food and hardness with stale food.

This aspect of balance is not solely concerned with the feel of food in the mouth as the eyes also have their part to play by perceiving the shape and size of food. This can be, for example, the finely-diced vegetables in mutton broth, the sippets in a puree soup, the chopped meat in shepherd's pie and the size of the grains of rice served with a curry. It is concerned with the natural shape of a cutlet, the contour of a turned potato and the neatness of properly trussed poultry.

There is a move away from mushy food back to natural crispness, as noted by the way vegetables are now served after the minimum possible amount of cooking, thus retaining the nutritional content. This is similar to the cooking of pasta until it is exactly *al dente* as it is done by the Italians, or stir-fry by the Chinese. Chefs are aware of the need to contrast textures and consistencies as for example, garnishing poached fillets of sole with fleurons and adding fried bread croutons to a *brandade* or *blanquette*. Soups and sauces should be distinguishable by their consistency and getting this right comes only after long study and experience. These aspects of menu planning although difficult to put into practice, are important enough not to be ignored; they are on a part with

120

au bleu, saignant, à point, bien cuit, and other descriptive terms of the degree and method of cooking and the resultant texture.

Soggy foods are a slur on the English national culinary reputation whereas crudités are of the other extreme; somewhere in between lies the happy medium so sought after by true gourmets.

Flavour, Taste and Aroma

Flavour, taste and aroma are present in most foods and require only salt or sugar to help in developing and modifying but not masking them. In addition to these there are a great many seasonings and flavourings used in varying degrees of intensity either to assist the natural features of food or to convert it so that the flavouring matter is predominant. Some seasonings and flavourings and the degree of use are the hallmark of the cookery of a particular region, country or society.

The aroma of food is a selling-point so it is not always good to have powerful kitchen extraction plant removing all smell before it reaches the customer. Smell comes before sight just as sound comes before taste; for example, the smell of bacon being fried assails the nostrils before it is seen and together with the sizzle of it frying can tempt the customer to order it. The smell of roasting and grinding coffee beans can be so appetising as to create the desire to drink a cup. Caterers sell not only adjectives but aromas too! Nevertheless some odours such as rancid oil and the stale smell of cooked cabbage can be obnoxious. The English have still not lived down their reputation as a nation that serves insipid food which requires generous shakings of salt and pepper, lots of bottled sauce, pickles and mustard to provide some flavour. A good chef will produce dishes that are so correctly seasoned for normal tastes that there is no need for a cruet on the table. The principles which the writer of menus must observe are to avoid repetition of flavours in a menu and not to overload the digestion with an excess of them; very highly-spiced foods spoil the taste of wine and can be detrimental to the sale of this profitable accompaniment. Good menu-planning follows a pattern of mildly flavoured but appetisingly tasty first courses that start the saliva flowing, well seasoned, fine but full-flavoured main courses, followed by dainty delicious sweets that are not too filling, and ending with a *bonne-bouche* of cheese or savoury.

Persons employed in the kitchen must acquire a refined, sensitive palate together with an instinct for and interest in food, which will help them to produce the desired results all the time. Over-seasoning is as bad as under-seasoning and chefs should question the need for seasoned salt, flavoured pepper and monosodium glutamate.

On an assignment at the *Hotel Adlon* in Berlin, Escoffier was seen to take something from his pocket and add a little to a dish he was preparing for the Kaiser. Asked what it was he refused to say more than that without the secret ingredient and his magic touch, the result would be as naught – it was probably

121

dried orange peel! But this was before the introduction of standardised recipes which require exact measurement of every ingredient, including the seasonings and flavourings.

Cooking method

Cooking methods used for the several courses of a meal should not be all the same and with a dozen different ways of doing it, there need be no repetition of methods. Having each of the main dishes cooked by a different method is good for the customer, it also ensures that every kitchen **partie** makes its contribution and that all equipment gets even use. Ideally each course of a Table d'Hôte menu should be cooked by a different method as this will lessen the possibility of similarity of tastes between the courses because some cooking methods produce dry results and others wet ones.

Some forethought would obviate the problem of inappropriate vegetables being served with the main dish. There must be some compatibility between the way the components of the main course are cooked but it often happens when serving a party of people that one gets mashed potato and carrots with his deep fried plaice, another has chips spread across a blanquette of veal and the person having the roast is given duchesse potatoes. This can occur when no consideration is given to the selection of vegetables and the way they are cooked as complementing the main dish; it is yet another instance of bad menu-planning.

Caterers must always be on the alert for the possibility of menu habituation attacking the good name of their establishment. It does not come from keeping the same menu going for too long as it is possible for a pizza parlour or a hamburger bar to keep using the same menu year after year without losing popularity, because the clientele is transitory and patronage is not from regulars. On the other hand in a large-scale operation with a captive clientele there is the risk, even when using a cyclical menu, of the charge that the same dish reappears regularly on the menu, always on the same day of the week.

A menu that is ideal for one place will be totally wrong anywhere else which is why it is not possible or necessary to copyright a menu since it is unlikely to be universally suitable. Neither is it possible to secure the copyright of recipes; one of the duties of the *Academie Culinaire de France* is to receive new recipes devised by French chefs and if they are considered worthy to put them into the official repertoire. In fact it has never done this so a chef would have to apply for a trademark if he wished his name to go down to posterity as the inventor of a particular dish.

Serving Method

Serving methods can be as important as cooking methods since it is at this stage that the person paying for it first sees the food he has ordered and subconsciously judges it for value for money and quality of cooking, as well as the skill of serving it.

This means that the serving dishes must be in keeping with the standard of the restaurant; if silver dishes are used they should be well-silvered and highly-polished and be covered with lids that fit. The use of earthenware dishes on silver flats is the mark of a high-class establishment while direct plate service is now the most highly sophisticated way of presenting food. An impeccably dressed main dish artistically arranged on an expensive china plate takes time and thought and customers must be prepared to pay for it when dining in a restaurant that can carry it out successfully.

Presentation must be pictographically correct, neat and precise; the emphasis should be on correct combination and blending of ingredients and their embellishment or ornamentation that is pleasing to the perception.

THE AVAILABILITY OF SUPPLIES

Before starting to compile a menu the writer must know what fresh foodstuffs are available and whether he can afford to include them on the menu. With so many once-seasonal commodities now available throughout the year or for far longer and more often than they were, it is tempting to play down the importance of the seasons. Tomatoes used to be available only during summer and none of the many tomato products were then made, thus there were very few recipes that used them. Scientific plant breeding has since made it possible to grow, and for machines to harvest, vast fields of tomatoes in various parts of the world; this and new methods of growing them in hothouses have changed them from being a seasonal luxury to an everyday commodity. New food production techniques have made it possible to produce vast quantities of food at low prices all the year round; the way that eggs, chickens and potatoes are now produced are obvious examples of intensive methods.

Another factor that detracts from the importance of the seasons is that most foods can be deep-frozen at their seasonal peak for use throughout the rest of the year. Manufacturers have developed strains of vegetables which are ideal for freezing purposes and farmers produce whole fields of them for harvesting and freezing at the peak of perfection. But as Louis Szathmary said recently 'The opposite to fresh is not frozen'. Air transport brings fresh luxury foods from other countries where they are in season to add to menus here so making them that much more interesting. Lorry-loads of produce pour into this country from the continent bringing fresh supplies daily thus extending the range of commodities available. Items which not long ago were regarded as being opulent luxuries are now easily obtainable at reasonable prices so finding their way onto the menus of all classes of establishment. A list giving the seasonal availability of all kinds of food is included in Chapter 7.

A restaurateur can go to his local market and actually see the goods before he buys and in our cities even the small trader can go to the fish, meat and fruit and vegetable markets to obtain his supplies fresh daily. Most food suppliers contact caterers to tell them what is available and to take the order. A large-scale caterer will draw up standard purchasing-specification forms for most of the commodities he uses thus facilitating purchasing. No matter how isolated an eating place is, it can be certain of obtaining the supplies it needs to produce a fairly extensive menu, consisting of the items preferred by its customers. It is important not to disappoint them by promising items that are in limited supply even in large towns and rather to take advantage of any local produce that may be available.

CAPABILITIES OF STAFF

A menu must be geared to the capabilities of the staff who will cook and serve the dishes; different kinds of catering establishments require employees capable of coping with the appropriate level as defined by the class of customer and by his requirements. It is tempting to try to set a higher standard of catering by compiling a menu of complicated dishes in the hope that it will spur staff to greater achievements. Such a challenge may not succeed, thus leading to frustration of the staff and customer-dissatisfaction because the food served falls below the expected standard. There is no substitute for experience and although a certain amount of theory is necessary, a head chef will always have to come up through the ranks and have acquired a wide knowledge of his craft and be capable of showing his staff how he wants things done. He sets the standard and bears much of the responsibility for the success of the place where he works.

It has been said that the British do not make such good chefs as those of other nationalities, that they do not have the same feeling for and approach to the job as do the French. This does not mean the British do not possess the same expertise as their continental counterparts but comes in fact, from Great Britain's cookery traditions which are based on very good quality raw materials, plainly served as near as possible in their natural state. There is still a puritanical streak in our nature that does not allow us to become a nation of gourmets like the French but rather regards the pleasures of the table as 'sins of the flesh'! Their island home has insulated the British from many of the extravagances of European culinary practices.

Good dishes deserve good service and the level of skill of the waiting staff has to be considered when compiling the menu. The chef wants his efforts to be appreciated so he dishes the food effectively and expects the waiter to transfer it to the plate in a competent manner, if the waiter does not then his work is spoilt. The inclusion of flambé dishes on the menu can only be justified if there is always a waiter on duty capable of doing them effectively.

124

EQUIPMENT AND UTENSILS

Some account must be taken of the large equipment installed in the kitchen, of the kind of pans in use and of the serving dishes available as they all have a bearing on what dishes can be included on the menu. Obviously a catering department will be equipped to meet the normal range of dishes in the expected number of portions but before any new dishes or revised methods of service can be introduced it has to be ascertained that the existing equipment can cope. This might indicate that the scope and extent of a menu is governed by the way the kitchen is equipped but it is only when there is a drastic change that there is any likelihood of it happening. Most general-purpose kitchens have at least one of each item of conventional equipment to enable both a Table d'Hôte and an à la Carte menu to be served. It is not feasible to use a fast food unit for anything other than a called order menu, indeed it would be impossible to house a conventional kitchen in the space of this unit and neither would the equipment and utensils be suitable.

THE NUTRITIONAL ASPECTS

Every caterer should possess a working knowledge of nutrition and know the food values of the portions he serves so as to be able to assure customers that his food is conducive to good health. It may be thought that this principle is relevant only to caterers employed in the welfare sector but quite apart from the movement of personnel between the two main sectors, the customer in a high-class restaurant would be pleased to know that he will be getting a nutritionally sound meal whatever dishes he chooses from the menu.

Nutrition is applied in practice through the things we eat, drink and digest; dietetics is the science of feeding, and diets are prescribed by doctors and dietitians to remedy various diseases. Recommended nutritional intakes for various groups are published by HMSO and should be consulted by the caterer to keep him aware of possible requirements of his customers. These are likely to be requests from people who want to get slim yet still satisfy a hearty appetite, for a salt-free diet, for a diabetic meal, or from a person suffering from gastritis or an ulcer.

A caterer in the commercial field is unlikely to be able to call upon the services of a dietitian to advise him on any diet food requested and will be responsible for passing the correct and exact instructions to kitchen staff. Recommended Intakes of Nutrients by the Department of Health and Social Security and Recommended Daily Amounts of Food Energy and Some Nutrients for Population Groups in the United Kingdom are the titles of the two reports in use and caterers should learn how to make use of them. Lists of modified diets as used in hospitals are readily obtainable from HMSO.

125

Nowadays many people face the problem of obesity and know they need low-calorie food to keep fit and healthy; this is one reason for the interest shown in *cuisine maigre* and *cuisine nouvelle*. These provide a low-energy but well-balanced diet in the French tradition but without the added richness of cream and butter. This kind of cookery is not something new and revolutionary for as long ago as 1755 Louis Mercier wrote about the lightness and sublety of '*La Cuisine Changée*' saying 'the new cuisine is good for our health and will prolong our lives'.

Nutrition is often regarded as saying which foods are forbidden or should be avoided; this obviously restricts the variety of dishes that can be included on the menu but the aim must be the application of nutritional principles in a professional and attractive way.

As outlined in Chapter 2, macrobiotics or the choosing of a diet in which Yin and Yang represent the negative and positive life forces, when applied to food assist in achieving a balanced diet because every food is either Yin or Yang or in other words, negative or positive. Staple foods play a large part and grains are eaten at every meal; both cooked and raw vegetables, fruits, fish and, very occasionally, meat products are included. Food is chosen according to a set of principles which contribute to making life more adventurous and happy. All this may seem to be more the province of the health food restaurant but in fact is relevant to all forms of catering.

THE LANGUAGE OF THE MENU

The French have studied cookery more than any other nation and it is French chefs who have raised the culinary arts to such great heights. The majority of dishes in the international repertoire are of French origin and it is for this reason that every restaurant of any pretensions has to include these dishes and write the menus in French. This happens in most countries but it is only in England that arguments are raised about its use on menus, probably because English is so widely used throughout the world that there is no need to learn French, or any other language. This country has contributed very many good things to the international list of dishes, mainly straightforward ones without fancy names or literary illusions so that barring a few exceptions such as Welsh Rarebit and Scotch Woodcock, customers know what they are going to get. Surprisingly enough there are few truly ethnic British restaurants in England where the claim is made that the menu is free from foreign influence. Not even on the welfare side of catering, such as school meals or industrial canteens, would caterers dare to say that their everyday menu includes only British dishes. The reason for this is that customers would soon get tired of the wholesome but plainly cooked food and seek more exotic dishes elsewhere. A caterer must not be so chauvinistic in his professional capacity that he excludes everything that is foreign. But there is sense in what that forthright caterer Manny Franks says about

126

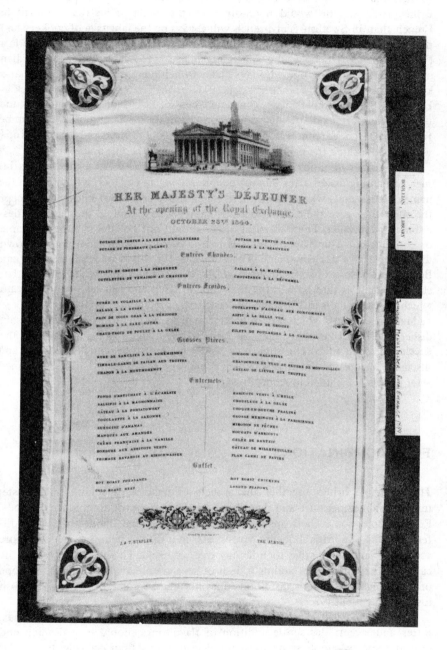

9. Menu for 'Her Majesty's Déjeuner', October 1844

tourists that they come to England to meet British people and eat traditional British food and he would no more print the menu of his establishment in French than in Swedish. Yet French will always be the language of cookery and therefore the language of the kitchen, whether or not the person in charge is a Frenchman. Most people who appreciate music accept and understand Italian musical terms and anyone who lays claim to being a gourmet will agree that a knowledge of culinary French is essential. Over the centuries from as far back as Henry IV, French chefs have concocted new dishes, dedicating them to and naming them after one of their noted contemporaries. The origins of this can be found in De La Varenne's book, *Le Vrai Cuisinier Français*, published in 1651 when he advocated the naming of dishes after famous people and events.

Massialot in his book, *Le Cuisinier Royal et Bourgeois*, also mentioned this idea of naming dishes after famous people as long ago as 1691 and although the names of the chefs who created these classical dishes are not known we accept the titles they gave their dishes because they act as a kind of shorthand in describing the formula. These classical dishes should not be altered either by name or content, but what is permissible is to add or to subtract from a well-known dish and to give it a new name. The authority for this is no less a person than Beauvilliers who says so in his book, *L'Art du Cuisinier*, published in 1814. His claim to fame is that he was the first chef to open and run his own restaurant which he did in Paris in 1782 and he was also a noted author in his day.

Many restaurants which use French terms given an English translation of main dishes but these inevitably take up quite a lot of space as compared with the succinct French titles. This subject of the language of the menu is developed and discussed in greater detail in Chapter 7 and the honours list of dishes named after people is included in Appendix A.

FOOD COMBINATIONS

This principle brings together the aspects of balance of colour, smell, taste, texture and temperature and describes how they affect the acceptance of foods. For example, some chefs are under the impression that the use of several different kinds of spiritis, liqueurs, spices, etc. in a dish is bound to make it more acceptable and distinctive than if only one was used. This is not necessary the case and the gimmick of adding a dash of several unrelated flavours in the hope of titillating a customer's taste buds does not always come off because the dish loses its true identity.

As described in Chapter 2, four basic tastes found in foods are salty, sour, bitter and sweet; the subtle addition of flavourings should help develop and extend these by emphasising the natural taste rather than masking it. There is at present a reaction against the inclusion of heavy sauces which are a legacy from the days before refrigerators when they were useful in disguising food that

128

had lost some of its positive freshness. Simplicity should be the keynote because this does not destroy the true nature and flavour of the commodity; it implies not only uncomplicated cooking processes but also the restricted use of the providers of colour, smell, taste, etc. These organoleptic considerations are discussed more fully in Chapter 2. Most of the well-known garnishes for soup, fish and meat dishes have been devised to complement and adorn, without dominating the main feature. Even these must differ between the courses of a meal and should always be restricted to the limit that can be served without the whole getting cold. It is a very one-sided affair when a chef produces an elaborately garnished main dish only for it to prove too complicated for the waiter to serve; the end result can be that it looks less than appetising after being transferred to the plates.

The problem of serving hot and cold food at the right temperature is a very real one for many caterers who have difficulty in maintaining it correctly throughout a long period of service. Much of the pleasure of a meal can be lost if its temperature is not what the customer expects it to be; it is unpleasant to be served with lukewarm food that should be piping hot and it is equally bad to serve cold dishes that have been allowed to come to room temperature or have been left too long in the freezer and are served frozen solid.

Although it is suggested that the demand nowadays is for natural foods there will still be requests for a spectacular dish for some very special occasion. This could be a flaming *Soufflé Vesuvius* or could be something out of the ordinary such as **Raymond Oliver's Rabbit and Melon and Mustard** or his **Best End of Lamb with Violets**.

PRICING THE MENU

Customers have a certain amount of money to spend each week on meals away from home; some is earmarked for functional meals and they hope there is enough left over for the special occasion. Customers therefore have to choose a restaurant that is within their price range. Prices on the menu of a commercial restaurant have to cover all the costs of providing the meal, including paying for the raw commodities, staff wages, rent, rates, maintenance, laundry and so on, and then to bring in an amount of net profit to repay the entrepreneur for risking his capital in the business and making it flourish.

Caterers try to keep prices unchanged over a period of time as this saves having to alter the prices printed on the menu; they also endeavour to provide customers with value for money rather than to risk losing business. The price charged for a meal is usually determined by the class of establishment, which is reflected in the quality of goods it can afford to buy and the size of portion it can give.

129

In some countries the price of menus in certain restaurants is decided by the government which lays down the standard and the price limitation for a Table d'Hôte 'menu touristique', as in France, which is designed to provide a good meal, at a reasonable price.

In fixing the price of a Table d'Hôte menu it is helpful to divide the total food cost between the courses and work to a percentage formula. Each establishment will have its own ruling on how the total amount is distributed but in general it is from 7.5 to 12 per cent for the first course, 62.5 to 72.5 per cent for the main course including vegetables, 15-20 per cent for the third course plus approximately 5 per cent for the roll, butter and sundries. If the price of the three-course meal is so many pounds plus VAT and the food-cost percentage is 40 per cent this means that two-fifths is allocated for food, leaving three-fifths of the price from each customer to pay for the overheads and net profit. It is these figures that define what the menu is to consist of and the size of portions that can be served.

Portion control is very much a part of menu-pricing as it is impossible to decide on a selling-price that gives the expected amount of profit if there is no knowledge of a definite portion size for every item on the menu. The head chef may take a decision about portion sizes that are out of keeping with customers' desires and expectations by being either over-generous or too mean. The customer-profile goes some way in deciding what should be the ideal size of portion and once this has been established, the kitchen percentage or other control system will ensure that it is being maintained. It is obvious that if the butcher cuts portion-control steaks bigger than they should be – even though it may be only by, say, 10-15 g – then over a period this will amount to a heavy loss of profit. By cutting underweight steaks there is the likelihood of complaints of poor value for money.

Restaurant owners often have to have recourse to a firm of consultants or accountants to investigate the reasons why profits are not up to expectation. These owners are likely to be the amateurs amongst restaurateurs because the professional will immediately look to the kitchen for the source of loss and soon put a stop to it, whatever the cause.

The pleasure of eating a meal should be intense and memorable. The dishes on offer should be those that stimulate the appetite even by the description on the printed list. The words used must tempt the customer to partake of the dishes. This happy state can only be attained by means of the menu and the way it is planned. The planning of a menu is a complex matter that deserves careful thought if the list as presented to the customer is to be faultless. A knowledge of the principles of menu planning will ensure that the level of menu composition is brought as close to perfection as humanly possible.

The menu is the programme that provides a customer with everything he needs to know about his meal plus any entertainment or other facilities that are offered by the establishment.

132

7 Menu and Wine List Composition

Who Writes the Menu? – Suitability of Foods – Special Function Menus – Classical Menu Terminology – Other Entries on Special Function Menus – Composing the Wine List – Cynical Menus – Calendar of Seasons – Menu and Wine List Production – Printing the Menu and Wine List – The Phraseology of Menus and Wine Lists

In Chapter 6 a theoretical explanation of the principles of menu planning was given; in this chapter the practical application of the twelve principles is shown together with details about the actual design and production of menus and wine lists.

WHO WRITES THE MENU?

The first step in the composition of menus is the decision as to whose job it is to write them. In many cases this person is the food and beverage or catering manager, possible in collaboration with another member of his team such as the head chef, head waiter or even the head storeman. Head office may issue menus for use in every one of its branches where these are run on identical lines, leaving no scope for the flair of the individual manager or chef to create his own menus. It should however be the head chef who has the main responsibility of composing the menu.

The person responsible should have sufficient experience to realise the merits of dishes worthy of inclusion, those his customers will appreciate, and what his staff are capable of doing properly. He needs a literary ability to make his menu and wine list interesting to read, and design them so as to sell the goods listed. They must be a sure means of communication between himself and his customers. He needs to know how to spell correctly, should possess a good working know-

133

ledge of the French language, be good at calculating prices and have some original ideas on marketing. His experience will enable him to know the difference between good and bad food combinations, he should have a genuine feeling for good food and wine and have researched the subject of gastronomy. He will realise there is more to menu composition than thumbing through Saulnier's *Repertoire de la Cuisine* or Hering's *Dictionary* to find suitable dishes and will realise the need for a reference library of culinary books. He should have no intense likes or dislikes of food and no prejudices against any form of cuisine. The person who writes the menus must be aware of the subtle differences between luncheon and dinner menu compilation.

SUITABILITY OF FOODS

The following is intended to show how fine the distinction is between lunch and dinner menus as regards dishes that may be suitable for one but not for the other. These distinctions have become accepted by tradition and although not regularised by any authority, professional chefs abide by them instinctively because they know they make good sense gastronomically; they can be disregarded at peril!

DISHES SUITABLE FOR LUNCH	DISHES MORE SUITABLE FOR DINNER
HORS-D'OEUVRE	
Hors-d'oeuvre variés, half grapefruit, grapefruit cocktail, fruit juices, avocados, melon, shellfish cocktails, smoked fish, pâté, salami, parma ham.	Caviar, foie gras, oysters, shellfish cocktails, smoked salmon, avocados, melon, pâté, parma ham.
SOUPS	
All types particularly broths, others not usually garnished.	Consommés, creams, veloutés, and other rich soups with garnishes and accompaniments.
EGGS AND FARINACEOUS	
All types except boiled eggs.	Not considered appropriate for dinner.

134

DISHES SUITABLE FOR LUNCH	DISHES MORE SUITABLE FOR DINNER

FISH

Generally cheaper fish; no elaborate or well-garnished dishes.	All types except cod, haddock, skate, herrings, whiting; more emphasis on shellfish although some people consider it indigestible for this meal.

ENTREES

Stews, meat pies, meat puddings, rechauffé dishes, hot pot, offals, braised steaks, curry, plain boiled meat, vols-au-vent, hamburg steak, pojarski, bitocks, breadcrumbed cutlets and escalopes.	Tournedos, noisettes, suprèmes, sweetbreads, escalopes, quails.

ROASTS AND GRILLS / RELEVES

ROASTS AND GRILLS	RELEVES
Plain roasted meat and poultry with traditional accompaniments, steaks, chops, cutlets, grilled chicken.	These items are poêled or braised – beef: fillet, sirloin veal: saddle, cushion lamb: saddle, boned loin haunch of venison, ham, pheasant, duck, chicken.

VEGETABLES

Cabbage, carrots, parsnips, peas, swede, turnips, runner beans, leeks, onions, Jerusalem artichokes, marrow.	Cauliflower, french beans, endives, asparagus, seakale, spinach, lettuce, courgettes.

SWEETS

Milk puddings, jelly, charlottes, fruit pies, flans, pastries, steam puddings, mousse, fruit salad, compotes, plain ices, coupes.	Cold fruit sweets, ice cream bombes, biscuits glacés, soufflés glacés, hot soufflés, flambé dishes, fruits, pancakes.

Some kinds of potato dishes are more suitable for lunch – these include roast, purée, boulangère, chips, plain boiled and baked.

There is a difference between the composition of a cold buffet for lunch as against dinner, the former having pies and joints whereas chaud-froids and mousses of a more elaborate nature are appropriate for dinner.

Savoury soufflés are more suitable at lunch and savouries are more appropriate for dinner than for lunch.

A similar assortment of cheese is suitable for both lunch and dinner although it is not considered really correct to serve other than a Stilton for dinner. Dessert consisting of fresh fruit can be served for lunch and dinner, but nuts are usually reserved for dinner. Coffee is served at both meals but it is more usual to offer the speciality liqueur coffees at dinner time.

The following points of difference should also be borne in mind when considering the kind of background that is most appropriate for the two main meals of the day:

LUNCH

1. Normally taken at the peak time of man's activity so there is a need to retain mental alertness.
2. Lower room temperature is acceptable.
3. Lighting can be at a high level.
4. There can be a sense of urgency in the tempo and rhythm.
5. Bright colours help to stimulate the senses.
6. Noise is acceptable.
7. Products served may be fairly utilitarian.
8. Customers are confident in their requirements.
9. They are susceptible to alcoholic drinks and these should not be pushed too much.

DINNER

1. Man's metabolic rate is reduced and there is a slowing down after the working day is ended.
2. A reasonably high room temperature is necessary.
3. Diffused lighting helps to create a feeling of relaxation.
4. Subdued colours create an atmosphere of calm.
5. The noise level should be low.
6. There is a greater interest in the products offered and there should be an ample selection.
7. Products should be sophisticated.
8. The pace of service can be slower with pauses between each course, especially before the coffee is served.
9. Partitioning can help to give a feeling of secureness.
10. Consumption of alcohol can be higher than at lunch.

136

SPECIAL FUNCTION MENUS

Special functions can take many different forms, the most common being a **banquet**. A sit-down banquet can be for any number up to the seating capacity of the room but the minimum number before it is worthy of being called a banquet is somewhere about thirty; up to that number it is a **private party** of people. A banquet normally begins with a reception while guests are arriving, they greet their friends while enjoying an aperitif, nuts, crisps and olives, sometimes cocktail canapés and very occasionally tiny, hot hors-d'oeuvre. When dinner is announced, they enter the banquet room, find their table and await the arrival of the important people at the top table. When grace has been said, they sit down and are served with the meal which is a set Table d'Hôte; there are no choices, the portions are all the same size and the courses are usually served in quick succession.

If wine is included in the price it is poured by wine waiters; if extra to the cost it has to be ordered and paid for before guests sit down. A toast is drunk to Her Majesty the Queen just after the sweet has been served, this being the signal that smoking is then allowed. There are usually some more toasts and speeches and the banquet bar stays open until after the last guests have departed.

There are several requirements for a banquet menu; it must contain dishes that are somewhat out of the ordinary but that can be presented really well. It is no good serving foods which can be cooked better at home for small numbers; the days of salmon-trout, saddle of lamb, an ice cream sweet and cheese, all heavy and fairly expensive foods, have gone and organisers now want light but decorative dishes that will fill them sufficiently in the space of four courses.

The hot dishes used for banquet menus must be those that will look good and taste fresh after having been cooked some time in advance and then kept in the hotplate awaiting the commencement of the meal. It is possible to cater for a banquet by using frozen foods, regenerating them according to the manufacturer's instructions, and dishing up on silver, without the customers being aware of the fact, but this is done only at the lower end of the market. Elaborate garnishes make it difficult for staff to serve a dish quickly and neatly, for example the *bouquetière* garnish around a fillet of beef or the veil of spun sugar on top of a pineapple, require speed and dexterity if they are to be served well.

Some banquet managers put the onus of choosing a menu onto the organiser by showing him a printed set of priced menus or a list of priced dishes from which to choose the meal. This may give the organiser some say in what his party will eat for the price they are prepared to pay and it could prevent complaints, but a better way is for the manager to discuss the function in great detail so as to make sure it really is a red letter day for the organiser and his party.

Another kind of special function is that run as a **buffet**, served either cold or hot or with some dishes of each kind, to which the guests help themselves or are assisted by servers and carvers. This help-yourself service is often used for a wedding breakfast in place of the normal sit-down banquet and most guests are

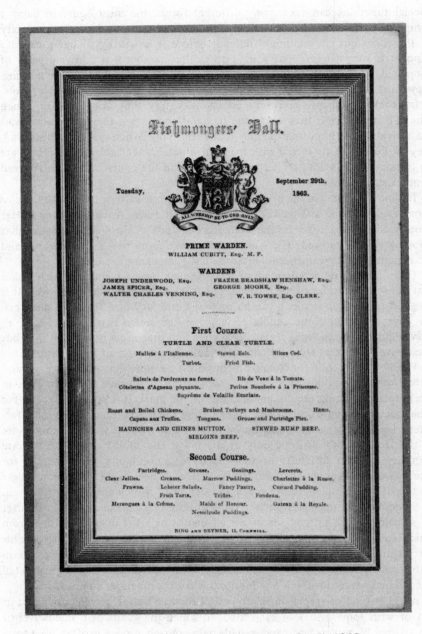

Fishmongers' Hall.

Tuesday,   September 29th,

1863.

ALL WORSHIP BE TO GOD ONLY.

PRIME WARDEN.

WILLIAM CUBITT, Esq. M. P.

WARDENS

JOSEPH UNDERWOOD, Esq.   FRAZER BRADSHAW HENSHAW, Esq.
JAMES SPICER, Esq.   GEORGE MOORE, Esq.
WALTER CHARLES VENNING, Esq.   W. B. TOWSE, Esq. CLERK.

First Course.

TURTLE AND CLEAR TURTLE.

Mullets à l'Italienne.   Stewed Eels.   Slices Cod.

Turbot.   Fried Fish.

Salmis de Perdreaux au fumet.   Ris de Veau à la Tomate.
Côtelettes d'Agneau piquante.   Petites Bouchées à la Princesse.
Suprême de Volaille Ecarlate.

Roast and Boiled Chickens.   Braised Turkeys and Mushrooms.   Hams.
Capons aux Truffes.   Tongues.   Grouse and Partridge Pies.
HAUNCHES AND CHINES MUTTON.   STEWED RUMP BEEF.
SIRLOINS BEEF.

Second Course.

Partridges.   Grouse.   Goslings.   Leverets.
Clear Jellies.   Creams.   Marrow Puddings.   Charlottes à la Russe.
Prawns.   Lobster Salads.   Fancy Pastry,   Custard Pudding.
Fruit Tarts.   Trifles.   Fondeau.
Merengues à la Crème.   Maids of Honour.   Gateau à la Royale.
Nesselrode Puddings.

RING AND BRYMER, 15, CORNHILL.

10. Menu for a banquet at Fishmongers' Hall, 1863

pleased to see a nicely arranged display of well-filled dishes along the length of the buffet table. This kind of function does allow a certain amount of choice since there are usually several different items on each course, for example, York ham, glazed ox tongue and roast turkey, with perhaps half a dozen different salads from which to choose, or to have some of each as the main course.

The following is an example of a menu for a **hunt ball**, before the 1939-45 war:

WEST WESSEX HUNT BALL

Chaud

**Minestrone au Parmesan
Jambon d'York braisé en Croûte
Sauce Madère**

Chaudfroid

**Filets de Sole Jeannette
Mayonnaise de Homard**

**Suprême de Volaille Saint-James
Aiguillette de Caneton Sévillaise
Poulet en Gelée à l'Estragon
Mousse de Jambon aux Pêches
Hûre de Sanglier
Dinde de Norfolk en Bellevue
Langue de Boeuf Ecarlate
Filet de Boeuf Froid Jardinière
Pâté de Gibier**

Salades : Française, Russe, Waldorf

Entremets

**Soufflé de Marrons au Chocolat
Poire Marie-Rose
Macédoine de Fruits au Kirsch
Meringue Chantilly**

Dessert
Café   Thé   Chocolat

Breakfast: **Kippers, Bacon and Egg, Chipolatas.**

A **Commemoration Ball** at a University held during the night towards the end of the summer term could use a similar menu to a hunt ball. Because of the large number of guests present it may be necessary to have several sittings and to avoid long queues, a number of small outlets are set up each offering a different item such as hamburger or frankfurter stalls, ice cream bar, doughnut cafe and so on as well as the main hall or marquee where the full meal is served.

Example of how banquet menus have changed

PRE-WAR (1939) DINNER DANCE	POST-WAR
Hors-d'Oeuvre du Gourmet **Huîtres Natives**	**Hors-d'Oeuvre Louis XIV** **Saumon Fumé**
Coupe aux Nids d'Hirondelle	**Consommé au Fumet de Tortue** **Paillettes d'Or**
Suprême de Saumon Ambassadeur **Pointes Vertes d'Evesham**	**Poussin Rôti Californienne** **Petit Pois à la Française** **Pommes Croquette**
Ris de Veau de Paris Bonne Maman **Mousseline de Jambon de Virginie** **Petits Pois à la Française**	**Vasque de Pêche Andalouse** **Gourmandises**
Sorbet Mandarinette	**Café**
Poulet de Surrey en Cocotte **Salade Viveur**	
Poire de Comice Sultane **Bombe Nougatine** **Excellences**	
Café Moccha	
A Light Refreshment Buffet will be **available from 10.30 until 11.45 p.m.** **to which guests are invited to avail** **themselves.**	

140

Light Refreshment Menu

**Bonne Bouche au Foie Gras, Petits
Pâtés à la Russe, Pains Fourrés –
Carême, Lucullus**

**Sandwiches: Boeuf, Jambon,
Sardines, Oeufs Durs, Saumon Fumé,
Tomate**

**Pâtisseries Françaises: Eclair au Café,
Savarin Chantilly, Puits d'Amour,
Palmiers, Meringue Chantilly,
Tartelettes de Fraises, Gâteau
Mascotte, Gâteau Millefeuille**

**Macédoine de Fruits Rafraîchis
Glaces: Vanille, Chocolat, Fraises**

**Thé Café Chocolat
Consommé en Tasse au depart**

These examples are of very ordinary banquet meals such as for a **Masonic Lodge Ladies Night** but they show how food habits and expectations changed because of the war. They serve to show how much easier it is to be a caterer today because the type of customer is less knowledgeable and less demanding.

A **Reception** is a gathering of people brought together to celebrate an occasion in an informal manner, at which drinks and small items of food are served by waiting staff or obtained from a buffet table and bar. The people may be brought together to meet a celebrity, to learn about a new product, for a fund-raising charitable purpose, to make a presentation or other reason, the main feature being that it is a fairly brief event.

The people attending are supposed to mix and move around the fairly confined space without ever sitting down. Waiting staff circulate with trays of drinks of the various kinds available or to replenish guests' glasses if it is wine. The food is the finer-buffet kind that can be picked up and eaten in one or two bites so that plates are not required. The list can include the usual salted nuts, potato crisps and olives, then, according to the price being paid, some of these following items may be added:

cold: canapés, sandwiches, filled bridge rolls, banquettes of caviar, celery with roquefort;
hot: chipolatas, sausage rolls, small croquettes, small pizzas, quichelettes, small attereaux, allumettes, dartois, jalousies.

Cakes and pastries are not normally served at this kind of event unless requested by the organiser.

141

A **cocktail party** is also a reception, the difference being that mixed drinks based on whisky, gin, vodka and possibly brandy are served. Contrary to the name of the event, a wide variety of cocktails is not served and the choice of drink is fairly restrictive; non-alcoholic drinks must be available.

CLASSICAL MENU TERMINOLOGY

The occasion arises in the life of every caterer when he has to compose a menu in French though many of us have to write all our menus in that language. It is not easy to write a grammatically correct menu in French and only a lot of practice will help to take account of the following observations which are given from the professional viewpoint rather than from that of the linguist.

Full Description

Each entry on the menu should be described in the fullest possible way so as to inform a customer exactly what he is ordering. It should set out to describe the central item, indicate how it is cooked and what garnishes and accompaniments are served with it. This is likely to use quite a lot of words and since the more script there is in a menu the greater the production cost, the use of classical French names that summarise the composition of a dish are of considerable help. The trouble is that even in France, few customers know what many of these names indicate and would need to bring a pocket reference book with them unless the person compiling the menu assists his customers by describing dishes as fully and clearly as possible. By designating fried fish on the menu as being cooked in the Orly style, the writer is adding a certain distinction to it. The same piece of fish can be listed merely as 'deep-fried' but a classical title will ennoble it and bring it to the standard of a high-class restaurant; it becomes more than just 'fish and chips'. Many of the *chef-patrons* of France and to a lesser extent of this country, are eschewing the use of garnish names, not because they are offering new dishes that have not yet been named but because they want to describe the contents of each dish so fully that customers get a very clear idea of it. This might indicate that waiting staff are not capable of giving a verbal description of a dish should a customer request it but the reason is that many customers are reluctant to show their ignorance of menu French by asking what a name means. The result is that these dishes require long descriptive titles such as *Loup en Croûte de la Mediterranée farci de Mousse de Homard et avec Sauce Choron*, **Whole Roast Yorkshire Partridge with Game Chips, Bacon and Compote of Cranberries**, even **Fresh Salmon with a Turbot Mousse in Pastry and Placed on a Caviar, Cucumber and Butter Sauce.**

142

11. Menu for The Royal Wedding Breakfast, July 1885

Source of Origin

From these examples it may be deduced that the origin of the food is of interest to both the menu writer and the customer. Its provenance can be rather vaguely defined as in the first example or as in the second example where it is pinpointed more accurately. The objective is to convince the purchaser of the authenticity of the commodity, to suggest that it comes from the best possible source, that it is good quality produce, and that the customer can identify with the product because he knows a bit about its background – all of which means an association of ideas. This is sometimes taken to extremes as for example in *Filet de Plie de l'Océan frit, Sauce Verte Bon Espoir*; it must be obvious to the customer that all plaice come from the sea so the reference is of little value; the accompanying sauce is more intriguing. In *Timbale de Moules de Roche à la Marinière* it is suggested that the mussels were gathered from the rocks rather than the piles under the pier which perhaps indicates to the customer that these mussels are healthier and fatter but how did the menu-maker trace their place of birth and will the title sell more mussels than if written simply as *Moules Marinière*?

Examples of the importance of place abound in menu terms: will a **braised leg of Aylesbury duck** taste different from one featured as *Cuisse de Caneton du Kent Braisée*? The answer is 'no' because both are the same species. Does the famous Crème Chantilly have a different flavour from Jersey or Devon cream? In this country the cream from any part of the country and from any breed of herd is whipped, sweetened, flavoured and called Chantilly cream and the name is now widely used rather than signifying the double cream as used in most Paris restaurants because Chantilly was the nearby area of production. Baby lamb is written on the menu as Pauillac lamb because that particular part of Bordeaux specialised in producing this fine quality meat.

Dishes Named after Places

Many dishes are named after places not because the ingredient originally came from there but because they are examples of the cookery of the region of even the town or country. *Pièce de Boeuf Salé poché à l'Anglaise aux Légumes* may sound portentous when set against its real name of boiled beef and carrots; this illustrates one of the rules which says it is wrong to translate typical British dish names into French. If the result had turned out to be poor franglais then the rule is a good one but this example proves there can be exceptions to the rules as the title is a true and perfectly acceptable description.

To write *Aloyau de Boeuf rôti aux pudding de Yorkshire* on a menu is likely to cause dismay to the customer so the easy solution is to indicate the 'Yorkshire's' under the general term of *à l'Anglaise*, or to write it all in Enlgish. 'Ragout Irlandaise' and 'L'Irish Stew aux Carottes' are not acceptable menu terms for such a great dish which requires no translation. The great Urbain-Dubois had a go with 'Les Minspais' on a Christman menu but happily this term

144

did not catch on. Yet there are many names like these that are accepted without question, they include Grapefruit Cerisette, Natives Royales, Cocktail de Homard, Steak Diane, Chump Chop grillé, Jambon d'York, Chop d'Agneau, Rumpsteak grillé, Sardines sur Toast, and so on.

The same rule applies when including other national dishes on a French or other country's menus, for example the pasta dishes of Italy do not easily translate so are best left in the original without any corruption; experience in writing such menus and a knowledge of the native language are the best ways to avoid *faux pas*. An outline of some of the most popular dish names is given in Appendix A.

National Menus

When a request is received for a meal consisting of the dishes of a particular country or region the problem is how to represent the country adequately in the space of three or four courses. Recipe books of other countries published in English are likely to be for household rather than professional use and therefore rather domestic. Information on dishes and supply of foods of a particular country are usually obtainable from the Embassy or Foreign Trade representative but the menu can only be planned according to the resources of the caterer and its final form will be the result of trial by tasting.

In a metropolis there is bound to be at least one restaurant where the specialities of a particular foreign country are featured, over and above the usual French, Italian, Indian and Chinese which are to be found in every district. These could include Hungarian, German, Russian, Indonesian, Mexican and many others and in all probability each would be operated by a national of the country. Yet there are many exceptions to this, and there is no reason why anyone else should not do this successfully and fully satisfy even the most critical native of that country.

It might be thought that requests for a banquet consisting of a foreign meal would be mainly for a full dinner but this is not necessarily the case and it could be for any meal from breakfast to supper, including a typical buffet of a country together with the appropriate drinks, not necessarily alcoholic, since there are many places where alcohol is forbidden.

It might also be thought that foreign menus are featured only in good class catering establishments but they are featured widely in the non-commercial sector. An understanding of the food habits of recent immigrants now living permanently in this country is quite important for as they increase in number and strength their particular requirements will have to be met by school, hospital, social service and other branches of welfare catering.

Many colleges of further and higher education have a sizeable number of overseas students who spend three years or more in an academic environment and whilst they are usually happy to eat the same food as everybody else in the college refectory, will welcome the introduction of menus that acknowledges their presence on the campus. It is not simply a matter of writing down the list of dishes, copying out the recipes and telling the cooks to get on with them; there is a need to obtain authentic ingredients of the right quality, to investigate methods of cooking and to check that the result looks and tastes correctly. The gastronomic aspects of countries are described in Chapter 10.

British Menus

Great Britain has contributed many notable dishes to the international repertoire and although some people suggest that the only national dishes the British may fairly claim to have invented are tripe and onions and haggis and black pudding, in fact the many hundreds of items listed in cookery books with titles such as *Good Food From Olde England* are plainly cooked, good quality British dishes. There are not many restaurants in this country that can claim that the menu is authentically British and the cookery is entirely uninfluenced by any outside practices. Is this because the customers of such places, where they exist, would soon tire of traditional British lunch followed by traditional British dinner with not much difference between them, and sigh for some more exotic fare?

There are only two or three Master Cooks still at work who are entitled to wear a low black cap instead of the tall chef's hat. This form of headgear used to be worn in every establishment that served plain British fare and dates from the time when joints were roasted on a spit and carved where cooked; obviously a low, dark-coloured head covering did not show up all the soot and dirt and did not need to be laundered very often.

The places where British food is most likely to be found nowadays, apart from in the home, are boarding houses, boarding schools, old people's retirement homes, hospices, some City pubs and clubs, and prisons. It is only partly to be found in hospitals, colleges and the high tables of universities because other culinary influences have penetrated such establishments. It is necessary to go to the United States, or at least to American-owned hotels in other countries, to get authentic British food in recreated taverns that offer nostalgia with a repast that has been cooked to original tavern recipes. The **Bill of Fare** is likely to include an ample slice of **House of Commons Pie**, a plump farmhouse chicken from the spit, the inevitable chopped beefsteak from the grate and a generous helping of prime Scotch beef in its own natural juices with a real Yorkshire pudding.

The Days of the Calendar

Apart from the seasons of the year, there are many days in the calendar that can be remembered or celebrated by the inclusion of the appropriate food. In addition to national holidays such as May Day and New Year there are religious festival days and anniversaries and notable dates such as Mothering Sunday,

146

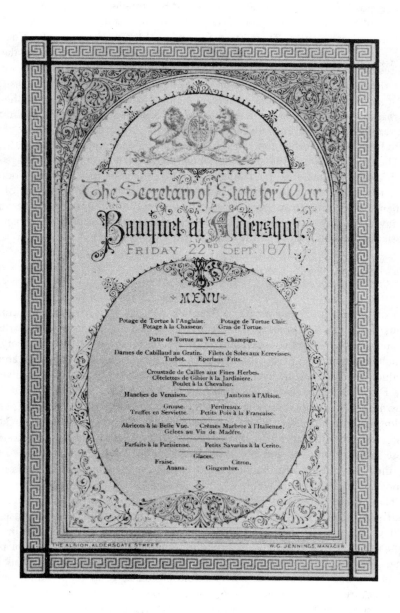

12. Menu for an official banquet at Aldershot, 1871

Father's Day and St George's Day. Each of these special days has traditional dishes associated with it and there is no reason why they should be forgotten.

It is possible to create customer's interest by commemorating famous people or notable events on their anniversary, by the inclusion on the menu of the dish named after them. There are sufficient of these to use some every day of the year on the anniversary of either the birth or death of the person, the day of a discovery or of a victory. It is true that the majority of such classical dishes bear the names of French people or events in French history which means they are mainly suitable for places where the menu is written in French but there is no reason why British rather than Napoleonic victories should not be celebrated. The calendar of anniversaries given in Appendix A shows that there are many more from this and other countries that merit occasional commemoration.

The chef of a West End restaurant much frequented by stars of the stage had the foresight to include dishes named after either the play, its star or its producer on a first night so as to surprise and delight the cast and any member of the audience who came to supper after the show. The chef did not go to the trouble of inventing any new dishes merely using gastronomic licence to rename a classical garnish in honour of the event.

The Literary Turn of Phrase

One of the menu writer's greatest attributes is an ability to transform ordinary terms into ones that sparkle with erudition and at the same time pay tribute to and honour a special occasion. It is not usual to word these openly by actually naming the person or the occasion, but to do it by allusion and to produce an *éloge* on the event by reference to possible similar ones in history. The French language is the one used in diplomatic circles so is ideal for this as shown by the examples later in this chapter which demonstrate how flair and a feeling for the language can conjure up the delights of the table through the written word, without overworking the adjectives. Whilst it may be hard to instil these into daily menus, and in many establishments it would be unsuitable to do so, they may be used for banquets and special events where the desire is more important than the price.

The normal Christmas Day menu includes turkey and Christmas pudding, both good dishes when well-cooked but rather dull-sounding when written so baldey. The titles can be flattered to make them read better, so raising the standard of the meal merely by applying some of the principles of menu planning. The traditional breeding place for good quality turkeys was Norfolk and the use of this could give customers an intimation of good quality, and conjure up a picture of turkeys of long ago when droves of them, each fitted with a pair of shoes for their journey, walked to Smithfield through the snow in time for the Christmas market. The title should also say how the bird was cooked and what garnish goes with it. Writing the Christmas menu in French it would probably be *Le Dindonneau Truffé aux Marrons* but it is not a matter of translating what would have been written in English; the French langauge allows greater scope for literary quotations and for an appropriate theme to be used throughout. For instance, it is possible to include part of the story of Christmas when writing the menu for that day – the first course of a fruit cocktail or soup may become *La Coupe de la Terre-Sainte* or *Le Potage des Trois Mages*, the fish fillets can be rolled to form *Le Berceau de Sole*, the turkey may be distinguished by the title *Le Roi de Norfolk* and the sweet course by presenting it as *Le Pouding de Noël au Feu de Joie* with *Les Délices Feuillettées du Bon Pasteur* (the mince pies) and *Les Mendiants* which means the mendicant friars, the dried fruits.

The use of the definite article, though frowned upon by many pundits, plays a very important part in a menu written in French because it has the effect of exalting each dish to a level befitting the occasion. It is used mainly for special functions when the menu has been composed for just that meal and is therefore unique. Some restaurants use it for the à la Carte menu which is acceptable, but such distinctive titles are incorrect for everyday Table d'Hôte meals. A common fault is to omit the definite article from some of the courses; if used, it must be on *every* entry including the titles which would be *Le Menu* and *Les Vins*, making sure to use the correct genders. This does not work in English except perhaps for the use of **Ye** as in **Ye Bloodie Sire Loin from Ye Spit**, on a medieval menu or **A** or **An** on a traditional menu such as **A Slice of Hazelnut Tart after the fashion of Mistress Rowbottom**.

A farewell dinner can be made more memorable both for the person retiring and his guests if the menu is worded to recognise some of his achievements simply by altering the garnish name. Terms such as *des Adieux, Doyen, Grand Epoque, Ancien Régime, Conquerant, Vainqueur, Triomphant* and *Victorieux* may be used to take the place of the normal dish name because such words convey an idea of the character of the recipient. Further examples of this method of writing menus are given in Chapter 11.

Interpretations

The practice of giving explanations in English of the dishes on a menu written in French should not be necessary in very high-class restaurants because by and large its clientele will be well-educated and much-travelled. In pre-war days the menus in such places did not carry translations and they were not necessary because customers were mostly well-to-do people who had been taught to read menus from an early age. This is not to suggest that regular customers of good class restaurants understand each name on a French menu – nobody has ever been able to confine the whole of the repertoire to the memory and have instant recall of the make up of each of the thousands of different names therein. Certainly the customers of those days knew more about cookery and if they were unsure what any item was on the menu, were not shy about asking the waiter to explain it to them.

This class of people still patronises the élite restaurants around the world but their numbers have been swollen since the war be people from other classes of society who have levelled the standards because they are not perhaps so discerning in their tastes, and because they are not as knowledgeable and therefore not as critical or demanding. For them an interpretation of dish names is necessary even though they may have made gourmet tours to the continent and consider that they have an appreciation of good food.

Writing an English interpretation of a French dish requires an ability with words so that the definition is accurate yet fairly succinct as in *Darne de Saumon Champs-Elysées* which could be explained as **Darne of Salmon braised in Champagne**, served on a layer of mushroom puree, garnished with prawns, coated with white wine sauce and marbled with lobster cullis, or more briefly as **Braised salmon steak in champagne** on duxelles with white wine sauce laced with lobster. While both explanations are perfectly acceptable, the first spells it out in slightly more detail than the second which assumes a culinary knowledge on the part of the customer. It has to be borne in mind that letters and space both cost money in printing menus and wine lists.

The two following examples are a part of an actual à la Carte luncheon menu, without the prices; the first version is couched in a fullsome manner that uses some 140 words for the fifteen items, the same information is imparted in the second version using less than half the original number of words.

A.   LE MENU

Les Zéphyrs de Parfait de Foies de Poularde au Nectar de Dijon

Le Filet de Plie de l'Ocean frit au Sauce Verte Bon Espoir
La Timbale de Moules de Roche à la Marinière
Le Hareng frais de Yarmouth Grillé, Sauce Moutarde
Les Quenelles de Sole Bonne Femme Auguste Escoffier

Le Poussin Grillé aux Tomates Farcies à la Nissarde
Les Bitkis de Poulet à la Chasseur au Porto Vieux doré

La Timbale de Foies de Volaille Grimaldi Monégasque
La Cuisse de Caneton du Kent Braisée Montfermeuil
Le Filet de Boeuf au Poivre Vert à l'Armagnac
Le Civet de Lièvre au Vin Jaune du Moulin Beaujolais
Les Rognons d'Agneau et Chipolatas Sautés au Madère
Le Grenadin de Veau clouté aux Truffes Napoleon
Le Carré de Porc frais Rôti au Chou Rouge à la Polonaise
Le Pièce de Boeuf Salé Poché à l'Anglaise aux Dumplings

B.　　　　　　　　　　　MENU

Mousse de Foies de Poularde

Filet de Plie Frit, Sauce Verte
Moules Marinière
Hareng Grillé, Sauce Moutarde
Quenelles de Sole Bonne Femme

Poussin Grillé Nissarde
Bitkis de Poulet Chasseur
Foies de Volaille Monégasque
Cuisse de Caneton Montfermeuil
Filet steak au Poivre Vert
Civet de Lièvre
Rognons Turbigo
Grenadin de Veau Napoleon
Carré de Porc au Chou Rouge
Boeuf Salé à l'Anglaise

The more detailed the descriptions the vaguer the food often is and what is stated on the menu has the capability of either improving the appetite or killing it stone dead. On the one hand the Carte can be a spacious document designed not so much to accommodate the dishes as the prose. The menu should be for people to eat from rather than to dream about.

Menu Layout and Content

The generally accepted pattern of menu layout as used by most printers is to count the number of words and spaces of each dish and to lay them out from the centre of the page so that they scan according to their length. This gives the neat appearance as shown in many of the examples in this book and since the pattern is used particularly for Table d'Hôte menus, if the prices of the main dishes are different and they have to be included, these figures should be counted in so that the overall balance is maintained. It is not always necessary to include the title of every course on the menu but it is important to keep each one separate by leaving a space so that the distinction is quite clear.

The heading should denote which meal it is, either *Déjeuner* or *Dîner*, what kind of menu it is, Table d'Hôte or à la Carte, and show the overall price and whether service and VAT is included in it. The name or logo of the establishment is usually printed on the card, and if it is in use for one day only, the date is usually added; if in French it should be in lower case. Sometimes the dishes on the menu are numbered which is done to save staff having to write out the full title when taking the order; this is similar to the bin numbers on a wine list.

151

As well as offering a wine list many restaurants use the menu to advertise the wines, usually house wines by the carafe, half carafe and glass and sometimes draught and bottled beers.

On an à la Carte menu it is acceptable to have the names of dishes lined up against the margin because here they constitute a list from which to choose rather than a full list indicating a meal.

When composing the vegetable section of the menu the vegetable should be entered before the potato dishes because the former are the more important of the two.

Menu Wording

Menus printed in French must have the appropriate accents put on those words that need them as to omit or misplace them is very unprofessional. Even capitals should have accents as appropriate but it is permissible to leave them off since many printers would not hold this kind of type.

The use of capitals only or lower case only for printing menus is not recommended as it gives a very uniform look, yet a capital letter for each word, apart from prepositions, conjugations and the definite article, is strictly correct. The practice of using a capital for only the first word of each dish is wrong; just as each word of a chapter heading in a book deserves a capital so does each word of the title of a dish. Some experts suggest that only the name of a person or place should be given the distinction of a capital but the result is that some names in a menu will contain words with capitals while other entries have none. If it is accepted that each item on a menu is a dish in its own right and is quite separate from the others, then it deserves to be treated as a unique entry and to be given the status of a heading. Few people read through a menu line by line as though it was a piece of prose, neither do they go down it as in a telephone directory. They are looking for something they like and when making their selection they are building up a meal in their mind with the expectation of enjoyment. Therefore all the names of dishes on a menu should be printed the same size. A case can be made for using small letters for any verbs within the name and this is often done in describing how the dish is cooked or served such as *accompagné, braisé, farci, grillé, pané, rafraîchi, rissolé* or *rôti,* the past participle being treated as an adjective, either singular or plural, feminine or masculine, depending on the noun it follows. Whether or not these words deserve a capital has never been agreed and opinion and usage appears to be divided equally. Certainly *de* (of) *au* (with) and *en* (in) must always be written in lower case.

The repertoire lists several hundred garnishes ranging from the very complex to the most simple; whatever the name may be it is likely to mean more to the customer than a vague one such as *garni* which many chefs use on the menu, particularly in connection with steak. Terms such as this have no definite meaning and convey very little; it is in effect a loose term used only by chefs who

152

cannot be bothered to define a proper garnish and it is even possible that it could change during the service as its components are used up. Terms to be avoided include 'Maison', 'façon du chef', 'chez soi', unless they can be authenticated. Terms that refer to some of the special dishes of a particular restaurant are acceptable even though they may sometimes be vague. *Chez soi, à la maison* and *du chef* are terms that indicate that the method of making a dish or perhaps the ingredients used as garnish are so distinctive that it is done or used only by that establishment and by no other. The method used may have been invented or perfected by the manager or other member of staff and although not listed under a heading of specialities is something that is not obtainable elsewhere. Such titles give a certain cachet to an establishment therefore the dishes should be of good quality. They should not be confused with the special *flambè* dishes done by the head waiter in the restaurant. These are often given a fancy title such as 'alla Luigi' or 'à la Manuele' indicating them to be the invention of the actual presenter; there is of course a range of classical *flambé* dishes and any innovations are likely to be derived from these.

Some of the people whose job it is to write menus have a habit of putting inverted commas around some of the garnish names they use, for example, Lamb Cutlets 'Italienne'. This gives the impression that the garnish is a quotation borrowed from a particular source, presumably the *Repertoire*. But Gringoire and Saulnier wrote their book of garnishes for all to use and did not ask for recognition as having defined each garnish. Their book has been in use for seventy years, but it is only recently that people have started to put inverted commas around classical garnishes.

In many cases only one of several names are so emphasised on the menu and it must puzzle customers as to why a particular one is so singled out. Inverted commas tend to break up the easy flow of reading and there is no good reason for their use.

Other abbreviated terms sometimes found on menus are 'S.G.' and 'M.P.' entered instead of a price against such items as lobsters, soles and whole birds to indicate to the customer that he will be charged according to the size of the item he is given. *Selon grosseur* or 'S.G.' means according to size; 'M.P.' means market price indicating that the price is geared to what was paid for the item on a fluctuating market.

Time is frequently printed against a dish on an à la Carte menu; this is to inform the customers that the item will be cooked to order and they will have to wait for it. It concerns duck, chicken, best end and so on and is often coupled with the information that the dish is for two or more people; it is usually shown thus: *Canard braisé à l'Orange* (4 cvts, 40 mins) followed by the price.

Diplomatic Aspects

Forethought in composing menus can prevent possible embarrassment and awkward feelings by the thoughtless inclusion of connotations that might cause

153

offence. A possible *faux pas* might be the inclusion of *Lobster Américaine* or *Oeufs Washington* on the menu for a Russian delegation, or *Salade Russe* in that for a USA delegation, in the same way that garnishes such as *Orloff*, *Romanoff* and *Tzarine* might offend, particularly at a time of diplomatic crisis.

Escoffier made an attempt when relations between France and Germany were bad to retitle *Sauce Allemande* as *Sauce Parisienne* but the original name was so well-known that his recommendation for change was not put into practice; the garnishes *Allemande*, *Alsacienne* and *Lorraine* were not affected. A banquet menu for a republican party gathering should avoid garnishes such as *Royale, à la King* or even *Henri IV*. The garnish *Rothschild* and perhaps even *Jerusalem artichokes* would be inappropriate for a gathering of Arabic guests. Members of a Socialist party would not care to sit down to a *Vol-au-Vent Financière*. Tee-totallers must be remembered as they do not like dishes that contain wine, beer or spirits; therefore some liquor-free dishes should be included on all menus.

OTHER ENTRIES ON SPECIAL FUNCTION MENUS

A banquet menu should provide more than just the details of what there is to eat and drink; it can include the grace that is to be said before the meal, the list of toasts, the names of the organisers, any presentations that are to be made, the name of the cabaret, the menu of light refreshments, the dance programme with space for partner's names to be entered, and a seating plan. To include all this information will add to the cost of producing the menu for an annual dinner and dance and for even a small number the cost of a well-produced menu could amount to several pounds apiece. The total cost could be reduced by providing one between two guests or as few as two or three per table of ten people, although it should be remembered that a nicely made menu can be a treasured memento and everyone present will want to take one home.

The practice of embellishing menus and wine lists with apt literary quotations is widespread, particularly for the annual banquet of societies and associations and for those of livery companies. Appropriate passages from the works of well-known writers are placed under the title of each dish and wine on the menu, naming the source. Each entry should be brief and closely associated with the item. The temptation to take them all from Brillat-Savarin's *Physiology of Taste*, the Bible or the works of Shakespeare and Dickens should be avoided and a good cross-section of poets and authors used. They can be used for special events in the calendar such as a Christmas or New Year menu but in a more general way, instead of being connected solely with the food and wine. Phrases relating to gastronomy and with the other arts are suitable providing they deal with the conviviality of the occasion; some of these are given in the section entitled Culinary Sayings in Appendix B.

154

Grace is a fairly brief prayer of thanksgiving said before a meal usually when the family sits down in a formal manner, and nearly always at the start of a banquet before the assembled company take their seats. It is more rarely said at the end of a meal. It can be said by the person in charge of the proceedings or by some-one he has nominated; if a minister of the church is present he may be asked to say a grace. It may be said or sung in Latin, it may be a very simple but serious religious passage or an elaborate or even humorous secular one; many are a mixture but the original idea was to give thanks to God for the food, as expressed in the well known line 'For what we are about to receive may the Lord make us truly thankful'. Charles Lamb said 'that to be thankful for what we grasp exceeding our portion, is to add hypocrisy to injustice. A lurking sense of this truth is what makes the performance (of grace) so cold and spiritless a service at most tables'. To him, 'graces are the sweet preluding strains to the banquets of angels . . . but at the heaped-up boards of the pampered and the luxurious they become of dissonant mood'.

Despite this the **Selkirk Grace** sounds very effective when delivered with an authentic Scottish accent; there are several versions with this the generally accepted one:

> Some hae meat an' canna eat,
> An' some wid eat wha want it
> But we hae meat an' we can eat,
> Sae let the Lord be thankit.

This grace is used at Burns Night celebrations and many think Robert Burns was the author, but in fact it was written long before he was born. It has no con-nection with the town of Selkirk and is actually the **Kirkcudbrightshire Grace**.

More formal is the *Laudi Spirituali* of 1545:

> For these and all Thy mercies given,
> We bless and praise Thy Name O Lord;
> May we receive them with thanksgiving
> Ever trusting in Thy Word;
> To Thee alone be honour, glory,
> Now and henceforth, for evermore. Amen.

This seventeenth century grace is often sung:

> Te Deum Patrim Colimus
> Te laudibus prosequimir
> Qui Corpus cibo reficis
> Caelestis mentem gratia.

155

Oliver Cromwell wrote 'Some people have food but no appetite; others have appetite but no food; I have both. The Lord be praised'.

A well known grace is:

> Bless, O Lord, before we dine
> Each dish of food, each glass of wine;
> And bless our hearts, that we may be,
> Aware of what we owe to thee.

These two are not perhaps used quite so often:

> Here's to us, wha's like us?
> Gaw few, and they're a deid.

> Heavenly Father, bless us,
> And keep us all alive,
> There's ten of us to dinner,
> and not enough for five.

Toasts

To toast a person at a banquet means that the guests wish him or her good health by charging their glasses, rising to attention and echoing the words of the proposer who will have named the person being toasted. A toast is also drunk to honour a person, usually the guest of honour, on an achievement. At any gathering there may be just one toast or a great many; if only one it will be the loyal toast to Her Majesty the Queen. Other toasts will be proposed by one of the senior persons present in an official capacity, and the response given by a distinguished guest. The loyal toast is always very simple and does not require a speech but any others may be made at length and can be the subject of a witty or erudite talk with suitable anecdotes that keep the audience from being bored.

Most Masonic lodges have an annual Ladies Night at which a toast is proposed to them by one of the Worshipful Brothers and their health is drunk by members of the lodge; one of the ladies should make a suitable response. On these occasions it is the custom for the President or Master to take wine with the various groups present, such as guests of lodge members.

The services of a professional after-dinner speaker are often used to round off the meal; this would be someone of note who has the ability to divert and instruct listeners with reminiscences of his career.

156

COMPOSING THE WINE LIST

Nobody has ever considered the possibility of writing a wine list in English and even if more wine was to be produced in this country, customers would still ask for imported wines whose names defy translation into English. The same care devoted to composing a menu must be given to the composition of the wine list, perhaps even more so since some wine lists stay in circulation longer than do menus.

A wine list is equal in value to a menu; indeed wine is usually the source of more profit than the food. The two should be composed to complement each other so that they form a whole by providing a full meal. The wines on the list should match the dishes on the menu by being their equal in quality and value. It would be inappropriate to serve only first growth good vintage wines if the standard of meals was mediocre, or to serve excellent food at high prices with only a very ordinary wine list without any first growths and good vintages.

A wine list should also equal the menu in its variety as in this way it is more likely to suit all customers' tastes. It must include all varieties of wine selected according to colour, taste, countries of origin, sizes of bottle, vintages, and prices. A great deal of expertise is required in composing a wine list that will suit all possible tastes and occasions and that can be maintained without deletions or amendments before coming to the end of its full life.

The Sequence

Wines are not entered on a wine list in the same sequence as are the courses of a menu and it is usually left to the wine waiter to suggest what wines go with various courses and with particular dishes. A wine list is usually composed by country and region, listing the white and red versions of each before going onto the next country. Once it has been decided how many wines constitute the list and which countries are to be represented, the countries or regions are listed in their order of importance as generally accepted by oenologists.

A wine list can consist of only a dozen different wines yet still satisfy customers' demands; it can extend to a dozen or more full pages and several hundred wines. It depends on the establishment and how much wine it aims to serve; the higher the sale the greater the range; the greater the range, the larger the wine cellar.

The generally accepted sequence of countries and wines is France, Germany, Italy and Spain. Other countries whose wines are popular include Australia, Austria, Hungary, South Africa, United States of America and Yugoslavia. Champagne is listed separately and it is usual to put sparkling wine and rosé wines in sections regardless of countries of origin.

The wines of France are divided into the five regions of production of **Bordeaux, Burgundy, Rhône, Loire** and **Alsace** with the possible addition of a section for the lesser wines of **South West France, Provence** and other wine-producing regions; there may be separate headings for the different parts of each region. German wines are sometimes separated into the two kinds – **hock** and **moselle** though the distinction between them is not necessary. In Italy and Spain there are many different wine areas and it would be easy to list these and their products under separate entries.

English wine deserves a place on every good wine list as there are many from which to choose and all are of high quality, despite the difficulties of producing wine in this country.

Other entries on a complete wine list are **Sherry, Port, Madeira, Spirits, Liqueurs** and possibly **Beer. Aperitifs** and **Cocktails** are other possible section headings but if a bar tariff is published they may be included on that. Many people enjoy drinking an aperitif before they start the meal and this opportunity to increase popularity and profit should not be lost.

Entries

Having decided on the format and contents of the wine list, and bearing in mind the importance of ensuring continuity of supplies throughout the life of the list, it is then necessary to allocate a bin number to each entry. A number can prevent the wrong wine being served as it identifies an item even more closely than the name since many wine names are difficult to pronounce because of their length and number of accents. The bin number is followed by the name of the wine, the area, then the name of the shipper, the year of production and the price of the sizes of bottle available, usually halves and full bottles but sometimes also magnums. Any fine clarets could have the growth indicated, these being those that were graded in the official Bordeaux classification of 1855. It is quite important to indicate where the wine was bottled, doing this by using abbreviations such as CB (château-bottled), FB (French-bottled), EB (estate-bottled) etc. It is advisable to include information regarding the authenticity of the wine using the abbreviation:

AOC (*appellation d'origine contrôlee*)
VDQS (*vins délimités de qualité superieure*),
DOC (*denominazione d'origine controllata*)
DOCG (*denominazione d'origine controllata e garantita*)
QbA (*Qualitatswein bestimmer Anbaugebiete*)
QmP (*Qualitatswein mit Pradikat*).

It is of help to some customers in their choice of a white wine to given an indication such as (*d*) dry, (*md*) medium dry, (*s*) sweet, or (*ms*) medium sweet, to assist in their choice.

In the section on brandy the age of the brands offered will be denoted by the various signs used such as:

158

3 star,
VO (very old),
VSO (very superior old),
VSOP (very superior old pale),
XO (extra old)

in order of age but with different standards from one manufacturer to another.

Gastronomic Considerations of the Wine List

Persons dealing with wine require a knowledge of oenogastronomy so as to serve customers well and save them from possible disappointment by choosing the wrong wine. A customer is free to drink chilled chateau-bottled claret with his *Filets de Sole Bonne Femme* if that is his taste but a wine waiter is in the position to give guidance as to the best wine to accompany any dish the customer chooses. Dry white wine precedes red and can then be followed by sweet white; dry white is ideal with fish, shellfish, veal and poultry. Sweet white including **Sauternes** and **Barsac** are excellent with the sweets and dessert.

Rosé wine is treated the same as light white wine and is really only for people who dislike red wine and prefer a pale pink accompaniment with the fish, meat and sweet. **Brut champagne** is a suitable wine to serve with every course of a menu, for those who can afford it; a switch to **demi-sec** or rich is appropriate for the sweet course, and by the end of the meal the result should be euphoric.

Red wine is served with dark meat and with cheese and the savoury; the fresh light wines go with ordinary meat dishes, the medium mature ones with well-flavoured meats and the strong full-flavoured reds with more powerful flavours such as game, venison and salmis. Aged red wine is ideal when served at 15.5° to 18.5°C which is known as *chambré* (or room temperature) though there are some experts who insist on having even a first growth claret served cool at about 13°C and upset the *sommelier* by requesting him to put the bottle in a bucket of ice to chill; they then use a wine thermometer to check the temperature before starting to drink the wine. This probably stems from the days before houses had central heating and *chambré* meant that the red wines were served refreshingly cool rather than lukewarm as nowadays.

Describing the Wines

Some establishments try to make choosing wine easier by including some background information on the wine list. This could be a description of some of their characteristics in terms of body, elegance, finish, etc.; of the area where produced, including its climate, the vines grown, etc., and recommendations as to the foods to be eaten with it. Illustrations could include a map of the area of each section, vignettes of châteaux and districts, labels and bacchic connotations;

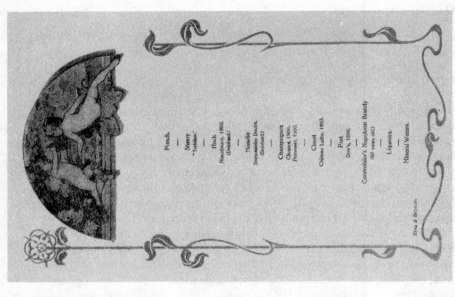

Punch.
—
Sherry
"Tintillas."
—
Hock
Niecebraun, 1902.
(Deinhard.)
—
Moselle
Scurcardelse Doctor.
(Deinhard.)
—
Champagnes
Clicquot, 1906.
Pommery, 1900.
—
Claret
Château Lafite, 1893.
—
Port
Dow's, 1896.
—
Courvoisier's Napoleon Brandy
(60 years old.)
—
Liqueurs.
—
Mineral Waters.

Bleu & Bryner.

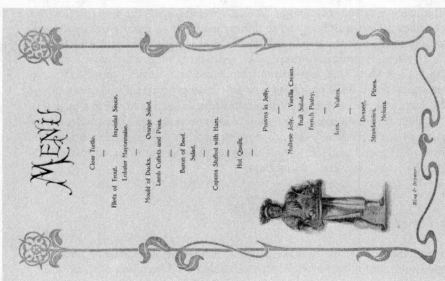

Menu

Clear Turtle.
—
Filets of Trout.   Imperial Sauce.
Lobster Mayonnaise.
—
Mould of Ducks.   Orange Salad.
Lamb Cutlets and Peas.
—
Baron of Beef.
Salad.
—
Capons Stuffed with Ham.
—
Hot Quails.
—
Prawns in Jelly.
—
Maltese Jelly.   Vanilla Cream.
Fruit Salad.
French Pastry.
—
Ices.   Wafers.
—
Dessert.
Strawberries.   Pines.
Melons.

Bleu & Bryner.

160

13. On any menu the wines and dishes should be chosen to complement
one another

14. A menu from the Worshipful Company of Cooks

161

a wine shipper will supply suitable examples. Many wine firms now use a system of numbers to give guidance as to the range from very sweet to extreme dryness of white wines.

There is a large number of wine terms used to describe wines and the condition they are in. They are for use by people in the wine trade and seldom convey much information to the average restaurant customer so should not be used by wine waiters to describe a wine in highly technical terms. Some of them do not make sense and would only confuse would-be purchasers so it is advisable to avoid using such terms as velvety, balanced, flinty, gunflinty, maderised, onion skinned, smoky and so on.

What the customer would find more useful is guidance on, say, the sweetness of a dessert wine and how it would complement a particular kind of sweet. It is not enough to recommend a **Sauternes** or **Barsac** but to be able to say whether one of the wines of a place such as **Rivesaltes** is like cough mixture.

Suggests for increasing the sale of wine could include

1. the use of coloured pages to match the colour of the wines listed on each,
2. grouping wines under the headings of Red, White, Sparkling, etc., and listing all those available under each from whatever region of country,
3. including suggestions of foods each wine is most suitable to accompany,
4. including a brief, to the point, description of each wine,
5. giving a good description of the house wines including those sold by the carafe or glass,
6. using bottle labels to illustrate the wine list.

If fine wines are available they may merit a wine list of their own, possibly done in good handwriting; it is an idea to group them into price ranges rather than of vintage years. More details on the subject of wines are given in Chapter 9.

CALENDAR OF SEASONS

A knowledge of the seasonal availability of foods is necessary when writing menus as this helps to provide topical interest and to introduce changes when they are likely to be effective. It is true that improved means of cultivation and transport have lessened the impact of the seasons since it is now possible to feature a food that is out of season here but has been brought in from another part of the world where it is in season. Yet the real impact of a food in season is not only that it is at the peak of quality and very fresh but that the price is reasonable when compared with the same food if it has to be flown in from another country, or purchased outside its normal season.

Some restaurants have a different menu for each season of the year, thus bringing in new dishes four times annually whilst others find two menus a year enough to introduce new foods in the spring and autumn, which are the times when most changes in supplies come about.

New sources of supply are constantly coming into use so making supplies available here all year around and it is essential to keep up to date with these developments. Such supplies can however be liable to disruption through bad weather or transport problems.

The following lists show, first, the wide variety of foodstuffs now available from both home sources and abroad, all the year round, and a two-monthly breakdown of foods that still follow seasonal trends even though some of the supply comes from abroad.

MENU AND WINE LIST PRODUCTION

After the menu has been composed it has to be put into the final form as the customer will see it. This means having it typed and duplicated, written for mimeographing, or more usually, being set up in type for printing in the required number. A menu is not just a list of dishes and prices but a means of communication between management and customer, a tool of marketing, and a valuable publicity handout.

The *chef-patron* of a small bistro can write the menu on a blackboard with chalk and hang it up where everyone can see and order from it. This costs very little and is quite acceptable at this level; it is flexible in that when a dish is sold out it can be rubbed off the board. The old-fashioned French copperplate writing with its flourishes is good for this and the use of such lettering using green and mauve inks gives a Gallic look to a printed menu for use in a French-style bistro. This indicates that the type used by the printer must be selected to suit the establishment and therefore the ambience of the dining room.

Many establishments still have two menus for each meal: the full à la Carte menu that stays in existence for a period of time and may serve for both lunch and dinner, and the usual Table d'Hôte menu for each meal. The first would probably be printed by a printer but the Table d'Hôte menu, because it is for one specific meal only, is more usually typed and photocopied on the premises.

The customer may be handed both menus to make his choice, at whatever level of expenditure he decides to eat. For this purpose the establishment purchases menu blanks of the appropriate size either with the logo of the establishment and the title of the meal already printed on it, or one on which everything has to be typed, including the name of the establishment, the meal, the date and the price.

Instead of, or sometimes in addition to, a separate Table d'Hôte menu card, some establishments leave space on the à la Carte menu for a list of the special dishes of the day, that can be clipped on, and this may be either handwritten or typed and duplicated. Such a device can serve a useful purpose by featuring

FRESH FOODS THAT ARE IN SEASON ALL THE YEAR

MEAT	FISH	FRUIT	VEGETABLES
Beef, Roebuck, Lamb, Ducks, Mutton, Chickens, Veal, Poussin, Pork, Quail, Rabbits, Turkeys, Pigeons.	Cod (best Oct-Feb.) Crabs, Eel, Haddock, Lobsters, Mussels, Halibut (not May–June), Shrimps, Herrings (not Mar. or Apr.) John Dory, Plaice (best Apr.–Dec.) Soles (Dover), Soles (Lemon) (not so good in summer) Trout, Turbot, Whiting.	Apples, Bananas, Grapefruit Grapes, Lemons, Oranges, Pears, Avocado pears.	Beetroots, Carrots, Cabbage, Celery, Courgettes, Lettuce, Mushrooms, Onions, Potatoes, Parsley, Shallots, Pimentoes, Tomatoes, Watercress.

SEASONAL FOODS WHEN AT THEIR BEST

	MEAT	FISH	FRUIT	VEGETABLES
Jan/ Feb	Geese, Snipe, Hares, Wood-cock, Partridges, Pheasants, Pigeons.	Carp, Sturgeon, Frogs legs, Sprats, Grey mullet, Sparling, Sea bream, Scollops, Skate, Oysters.	Mandarines, Rhubarb (forced).	Brussels Sprouts, Belgian endives, Jerusalem artichokes, Salsify, Swedes, Seakale, Turnips, Parsnips, Leeks.
Mar/ Apr	NZ new seasons' lamb, Snipe, Woodcock, Venison, Guinea fowl, Hare, Wild duck.	Lampreys, Scollops, Salmon, Oysters, Sturgeon, Brill, Whitebait, Mackerel.	Rhubarb.	Asparagus, Leeks, Belgian Endives, Seakale, Broccoli, Spring greens, Cos lettuce, Morels, Jersey new potatoes, Egyptian new potatoes, Spring carrots, turnips.

	Game/Meat	Fish	Fruit	Vegetables
May/June	Plovers, Venison, Guinea fowl.	Hake, Sardines, Mackerel, Dabs, Salmon, Salmon-trout, Mullet, Whitebait.	Apricots, Cherries, Gooseberries, Melons, Nectarines, Peaches, Strawberries.	Asparagus, Aubergines, Baby marrows, Broad beans, Globe artichokes, Mange-tout Peas, Sorrel, Jersey new potatoes.
July/Aug	Guinea fowl, Fallow deer (male 1/8–13/4) Grouse (from 12/8) Leverets, Quail.	Hake, Grayling, Mackerel, Salmon, Red mullet, Tench, Salmon-trout.	Apricots, Blackcurrants, Melons, Nectarines, Redcurrants, Peaches, Raspberries, Strawberries, Plums, Greengages.	Globe artichokes, Broccoli, French beans, Mange-tout peas, Marrow, Aubergines, Peas, Runner beans, Sweetcorn.
Sept/Oct	Grouse, Guinea fowl, Hares, Partridge, Pheasant, Plovers, Snipe, Venison, Woodcock (1/10–31/1)	Dabs, Oysters, John Dory, Herring, Skate, Sparling, Oysters, Hake.	New seasons apples, New seasons pears, Peaches, Melons.	Brussels sprouts, Cepes, Marrow, Parsnips, Pumpkin, Swedes, Turnips, Leeks, Brussels sprouts.
Nov/Dec	Fallow deer, (female 1/11–28/2), Geese, Grouse, Guinea fowl, Hares, Partridge, Pheasant, Plover, Snipe, Woodcock.	Carp, Grey mullet, Hake, John Dory, Skate, Sparling, Sprats.	Rhubarb (forced), Nuts.	Brussels sprouts, Belgian endives, Celeriac, Leeks, Parsnips, Turnips, Swedes.

165

foods in season and local specialities, and to stimulate the sale of a slow-moving perishable item that has been over-ordered. Care should be taken that the clip-on does not obscure any part of the menu to which it is attached.

Before approaching the printer to obtain a quotation it is advisable to have an idea of what the result should look like. The practicalities that have to be decided include:

1. the size and shape of the page that will accommodate all the menu items;
2. the number of pages that will be necessary to contain all the details;
3. how the pages will be bound together;
4. the colour and texture of the paper to be used;
5. the decoration on the cover and whether a heavier paper is needed.
6. the type and size of the print to be used (lower case is easier to read than capitals);
7. the colour or colours of print;
8. whether any art work or colour photographs will be used to enhance it;
9. the way the menu is to be folded, such as gate fold;
10. the length of time the menu will be in operation and whether this will mean having to make it stain-resistant;
11. if French is being used, will each dish be explained in English underneath?

On the other hand, it is possible to send the menu and wine list to an agency such as an advertising agent and ask the agent to design a selection of examples. There are a number of specialist printing firms who have on their staff artists, designers and writers with experience in menu production who will do the entire job. A commercial artist and copywriter could do a paste-up in readiness for the printer or an ordinary printing firm that does short runs of small work will set up what you have decided and print them off. The cost will vary according to the factors already detailed from (1) to (10). It is important to proof-read carefully so as to avoid errors getting into print after which it is too late to alter them.

PRINTING THE MENU AND WINE LIST

It is important to use the house style on the menu and wine list in the same form as on all the other printed material used in the establishment. It is possible to buy printed letters, set them up in the form of the menu and to photocopy the required number. Colour and line-drawings can be reproduced with good definition but there can be a limit as to the weight of the paper. A duplicating machine will produce straightforward typed material but any drawings may not be of sufficiently good quality.

An offset litho machine together with the necessary cutting, collating and binding equipment could be installed which in turn will require a trained person to operate the machine correctly. A computer word-processing system operating from a typewriter keyboard or television screen and a fast printer is an alternative to a conventional copying-maching but the use must be cost-effective, which means it needs a constant flow of work.

A general printer will be doing work for a number of customers so he may not be able completely to satisfy the restaurateur's requirements; the design work may not be as good as is desired and the cost may be uncompetitive.

It is now possible to have printing done in one of the franchised print shops which either sends the work to a central depot or does it on its own machines. To prevent menus and wine lists from becoming dog-eared, dirty and torn it is possible to fit them into clear plastic wallets which are made in various sizes or to have the lists laminated in a wallet or pouch which is heat bonded by machine to seal the contents. For lists printed on one side only it is possible to dry-mount them onto boards and cover the front only with clear plastic.

A photostat machine and a duplicating machine together with the laminating machine will ensure that menus and wine lists have a professional look and last a long time.

It is possible to produce a menu and wine list in Braille for the use of blind people which saves them having to ask their companion or the waiter to read out the menu to them. Such a menu can be produced by computer as a series of raised dots, which can be read by a blind person using the fingertips, although to a sighted customer it appears to be a blank form.

A computer-based information system can have a file of standard recipes in the machine which can be put together in the form of menus suitable for different occasions to conform to a particular cost, or to provide a definite nutritional content. The system keeps the file of recipes and their ingredients and by entering the names of the dishes and number of portions the computer will print out the ingredient list, the requisition and the dish cost per portion. The recipe file can be broken down under the menu composition headings such as colour of dish and cooking method, which assists in producing menus without the usual tension of marrying the several courses into a cohesive whole.

A menu must be easy to read; the dining room may be lit by candles, the customer may be too vain to get out his reading glasses, so it is up to the person producing the menu to make his selection easy by using the right size of type and not having everything too close together.

When different menus are in use for lunch and dinner and a decision has to be made on the use of French it is accepted that the lunch menu be written in English and the dinner menu in French. Some establishments seek to satisfy everybody by having the menu done twice on the same page – one side in French, the other in English.

Language can be used to convey the theme of the restaurant and define the cuisine and service; a friendly atmosphere can be encouraged by the way the menu is worded.

15. What the customer reads on the menu should improve his appetite

168

THE PHRASEOLOGY OF MENUS AND WINE LISTS

What the customer reads on the menu should improve his appetite and get his tastebuds salivating – not kill it; the Carte should accommodate the food not the prose. Menu jargon that gives lyrical descriptions of everyday items usually ends up by defeating its aim because it makes the customer think that the cooking is unimaginably good whereas it is usually the case that the more trilling the description the vaguer the dish actually is when it arrives on his plate in an unidentifiable mass.

Some people like to collect these pieces of prose that usually come from the imagination of pretentious restaurateurs, dilettante owners, or cowboy cooks. Dishes that are over-rich in description serve only to confuse the true gourmet who is capable of deciding for himself whether the 'pan-fried mountain trout' is not a grilled frozen one and the 'morning-gathered baby peas tossed in farmhouse butter' were frozen ones with a dot of blended butter on top! The Trades Description Act can come to his aid but he is usually reluctant to use it and instead vows never to return to the place.

The Americans sell adjectives as part of their merchandising of the menu and wine list; they abhor a blank page, regard it as waste of space and seek to increase sales by several reminders of all the delights the kitchen can offer. Salesmanship lies in describing the dishes in sweet and sour prose and veiling it in a dreamy mist of Lucullan delights and fancies. The following are some examples of menu composition from the States; they are not meant to be amusing but to stir the imagination and the appetite in response to the very articulate appeal.

SAMPLES OF AMERICAN MENU ITEMS

CAESAR SALAD — It's a shame Julius never knew this salad named after him as it's a meal on its own. It's made with iceberg lettuce, golden fried croutons, garlic, anchovy and raw eggs and our chef adds a whisper of aromatic English cheddar to the concoction.

MEDALLION OF LAMB — This is the finest cut off the lamb, taken from the fillet and our chef is so fussy, he insists on choice grade lambs. He cooks it by pan frying and serves it with any of the traditional garnishes that you delight in – *au Marsala, Jardinière* or *Niçoise.*

FRIED RED SNAPPER — Caught not a hundred miles from here in the clear deep water of the Pacific, our red snapper is served with French fries, a bowl of tangy coleslaw, cocktail dressing and a glassful of flavoured Slush.

GROUND STEAK UNDER GLASS Don't ask our chef for the secret of this succulent dish as he won't divulge it – its unique! One order per customer only. (Actually its merely a hamburger tarted up in words only.)

SOUTHERN FRIED CHICKEN Close your eyes and listen when the waiter brings this to table and you'll probably hear the faint strains of a negro spiritual sung to harmonise with the tender milk-fed chicken.

BROILED PORK CHOP This is one of our best-selling dinners because with modern refrigeration pork is in season all the year round. Our product is on the lean side and is broiled well done under our pressure broiler yet stays chock full of juice that it does not fail to stir the taste buds. Served with a panful of shoestring potatoes and a side-serving of spicy apple sauce.

OYSTERS VILLEROY Freshly opened from the cool waters of the Bay these succulents are first dipped in our special batter, then deep-fried to a golden brown as a perfect gift to lovers of seafood.

PHEASANT AU SUC A tender portion of domesticated pheasant sautéed *sec* with *suc* made of oranges and cherries. We serve only male birds from a corn-fed flock of game reared way down South in the Purple Mountain range.

FAST FOOD FARE A whopping (150 g) chopped beef hamburger broiled to your taste, served on a hot toasted sesame seed bun with our own recipe relish, a generous slice of tomato and a crisp leaf of lettuce. Enjoy it with a beaker of our own cola (half cola and the rest ice).

NAMELESS PIE! A delicious light-as-a-breese chiffon pie flavoured with bitter-sweet chocolate fudge and verdant creme de menthe, piled into a mouth-watering crunchy pastry crust and topped with rich thick cream and chocolate shavings. Completely different from anything else you've ever tasted!

APPLE PIE Our famous apple pie made from the greenest apples with dairy butter and barely a pinch of exotic spice so as not to offend the delicate blending of apples and sugar that together produce a symphonic triumph of perfect harmony – served á la mode.

It is perfectly possible to clothe traditional British dishes with this descriptive prose as in the following examples also from America:

ROAST BEEF AND YORKSHIRE	The British are very traditional when it comes to meat and it is with good reason that they insist on prime quality beef that has been properly aged to bring out all the flavour and tenderness. our square-cut Chicago-style roast ribs of beef are cooked exactly to your taste – rare, medium or well-done and served au jus with a Yorkshire popover and tangy horseradish relish.
STEAK AND KIDNEY PIE	Chunks of ox kidney rolled in strips of succulent beef in a deep dish flavoured with Worcestershire sauce and onions, inspired by the traditions of old England to present the perfect pie when topped with light-as-air puff pastry and baked for long hours till tender.

French chefs and copywriters are equally good at gilding the lily in selling food as are the Americans:

Rosettes de Chevreuil aux Champignons Fauves et Foie Gras Persillade
Méli-Mélo de Fromage
Daurade Royale rôtie au Laurier avec sa Fondue d'Orange et de Citron à l'Huile d'Olive
Aiguillettes de Foie de Veau aux Radis et aux Navets
Petite Nage de Queues d'Ecrevisses au Beurre Blanc de Normandie
Figues fraîches refraîchies aux Framboises à la Crème
Pruneaux Confits au Thé de Lotus et à la Crème Fraiche

The wine list can also be given this treatment, no so much in the jargon of the oenologist, as in the phraseology of a copy-writer; it might include a few tips from the supplier who should know the wine better than anyone else. The following are actual examples:

'A fragrant, very delicate wine that tastes like liquid sunshine.'

'Has a wonderful bouquet because made from grapes that grow on the sunny side of the vineyard – fruity yet light on the tongue.'

'Magnificent in its dry lightness, a delicate pink wine from this hitherto unknown vineyard – the best for your money.'

'Lusciously sweet and rich golden in colour; an overpowering aroma and a full, brash body.'

171

Menu planning and menu composition are two consecutive phases of a single operation and of necessity, support and complement each other. The first step is the marshalling of the necessary information about the form of menu to be written, and when this is known, there comes the actual writing. It can be seen that there are many pitfalls but that it is possible to avoid them by a sound knowledge of this complicated but exceedingly interesting subject.

IL
TRINCIANTE
DI
M. VINCENZO
CERVIO,

Ampliato, e ridotto à perfettione dal Caualier Reale
Fusorito da Narni,

TRINCIANTE DELL'ILLVSTRISSIMO,
& Reuerendiss. Sig. Cardinal Farnese.

CON PRIVILEGIO.

IN VENETIA, MDCXXII.
Appresso Alessandro de'Vecchi.

174

8 A History of the Art of the Table and Service

Introduction – China – Middle East – Greece – Rome – Ancient Gaul – Italy – France – Great Britain – Recent Developments – *Nouvelle Cuisine Française*

INTRODUCTION

The art of the table means the creation of a total environment such as is conducive to the complete enjoyment of a gastronomic occasion. 'Environment' includes absolutely everything, from the eating implements and the way in which they are laid on the table to the colour of the furnishings, even to the air-conditioning system. This is the starting-point of gastronomy.

Not that gastronomic events take place only indoors; the setting can be anything from a belevedere in a desert oasis wherein the guests eat while reclining on oriental carpets, to the club-class saloon of a jet plane flying at an altitude of 10 000 m. But in each and every situation, the conditions must create a favourable state of mind that is conducive to the willing acceptance of food and drink; to do this it is necessary to conform to the well-established protocols of etiquette as applicable to the particular culture.

This brief survey of the history of kitchen and table practices and of the eating methods of countries and races is of interest as it shows what changes, if any, have taken place over the centuries.

175

16. 'The Cooks Rout or High Life below stairs'. An eighteenth-century engraving

CHINA

The Chinese have been using chopsticks to convey food to the mouth for at least 2500 years, a fact that shows they ceased to use their fingers as eating implements long before any other civilisation. Eating a meal has always been a serious social occasion for the Chinese and remains so today. The lay-out pattern of dishes in front of the person is dictated by their contents. China was the first country to develop bronze-casting and the throwing of porcelain and china for dishes, so given this knowledge, the eating practices of China were different from any other civilisation until at least the year 1000 AD.

THE MIDDLE EAST

In ancient Egypt, food was served and eaten from baskets placed in front of the diners whilst they sat on the floor. Guests were put at their ease and lulled into a state of mind conducive to the enjoyment of the meal by having hands and feet washed, a garland of flowers put around the neck and given a drink-offering to appease the Gods. Glasses were used as the Egyptians had mastered the method of making glass some 3500 years ago.

Assyria was once the most prosperous and highly civilised country in the Middle East and stone carvings show the inhabitant's approach to eating. It is possible to see King Ashuz-bani-pal who lived from 669–626 B.C. seated on a high backless chair at the low table, sharing a meal with his wife. Although they do not look very comfortable, the table is set with elegant dishes on a beautiful cloth so as to make the meal enjoyable. Later civilisations adopted a reclining position at the dining table, the couches used by the Persians being made of silver and gold, with magnificent dishes for use at the banquets of the wealthy. At the same time the poor were eating and drinking on the move, subsisting on snacks in the form of a *pitta* with all sorts of fillings or on *felafel* made of purée of chick-peas. They ate in a hurry just as we do today in a fast food store where the food is served in a very primitive way as though cutlery and crockery has not yet been invented.

GREECE

Greece is called the cradle of civilisation because of the glories of Greek art, and the advanced state of Greek philosophy and science. Greek artefacts rival

177

in design and style those we make today even with all the advancements of technology on our side.

The art of the table in Greece was expressed through social and religious feasts, with food served in delicate amphora and other kinds of dishes and the wine in gold cups. But – as in other great empires – internal disruption led to the decline of Greek civilisation and the emerging Roman Empire overtook it.

ROME

From the outset, the Romans were a nation of warriors and showed little interest in such effete pursuits as the luxuries of the table. Their great prowess as conquerors brought wealth to the country and so gradually they succumbed to extravagances of gastronomy as have seldom been emulated. Dining became not just the enjoyment of food but the main source of all sensual pleasures.

Some of the sensuality derived from their conquests, as when Cleopatra was invited to Rome; she brought with her a new dimension of exotic flavours and exquisite service that surpassed anything then seen. Naturally the Emperor and his consuls emulated her efforts and squandered fortunes on the purchase of spices to enhance the quality of their meals.

The Romans ate from a reclining position and chose what they wanted from gold salvers presented by slaves, then ate it with their fingers. Much attention was given to the decoration of the *triclinium* or dining room, especially the ceiling since this is what guests saw most. Nero made his architect create a changing scene so that the ceiling was constantly in motion with leaves made of ivory dropping gently from above. Books were kept in the dining room so poems could be recited as part of the proceedings, a habit which eventually became that essential part of a banquet, the after-dinner speech.

So instead of seeking new countries to conquer, succeeding generations of Romans sought the pleasures of an effete life and left the defence of their great Empire to mercenaries. By the fifth century the Roman Empire had been overrun by the so-called Barbarians – Goths, Visigoths, Alemanni and Vandals, and the Roman people returned to the land, leaving their great cities deserted.

ANCIENT GAUL

No other nation attained such heights of gastronomy as the Romans and certainly the table practices of the Ancient Gauls was very simple and functional in comparison. Seating was on tufts of straw and service was from copper with only one goblet of wine to circulate amongst all the diners. A dagger was used to assist the

178

fingers with eating. The dissolution of the Roman Empire left a vacuum throughout Europe that lasted for nearly 300 years until Charlemagne entered Italy in the year 772 and did much to revive the order that had previously existed, albeit with much less ostentation but with greater style, as later adopted by the Kings of France.

ITALY

During the Middle Ages the Crusades brought an exchange of cultures between the Christians of northern Europe and the Mohammedans of the Mediterranean countries. The first crusade took place in 1096 and the seventh in the year 1270. The Crusaders rested awhile in Venice on their journeys East and experienced the luxuries of Venetian civilisation, especially those of the table.

The Venetian Empire occupied a prominent position in world commerce and its wealth helped to advance the art of the table by the use of embroidered linen table cloths and the exquisite Venetian glassware which has been famous since the year 982. Most of the Venetian glass-works were moved to the island of Murano in 1292 to lessen the risk of fire in Venice.

Forks were used for eating fruit that would stain dainty fingers and the table was set in a very elegant fashion, similar to that of today. The Doge of Venice set the fashion throughout Europe for the Baldachino which was a richly adorned canopy in the form of the roof of a tent and supported on pillars to cover the throne or even the entire dining table. It took its name from Baldach, the eastern name for Baghdad and was originally used to protect eastern potentates from the burning sun; in Europe it gave protection to royalty against draughts. During the visit by the Emperor of Germany to King Charles IV of France in 1378 a canopy of cloth of gold was erected to shield them whilst they ate.

Entertainment remained as an integral part of a formal meal and the *entremet* was a pause for a performance by dancers and acrobats, similar to a cabaret act during a dinner today.

Refinement of tableware came when porcelain was first made in Europe, some 700 years after the Chinese had succeeded in making this beautiful translucent form of crockery. The de Medicis of Florence sponsored its manufacture and by 1580 it was in use throughout central Europe.

At the wedding breakfast of the Duke of Mantua in 1581 the table was covered with a delicately embroidered cloth with embossed leather mats to prevent stains. The plates were of porcelain, the carafes and goblets of Murano glassware and table napkins and silver cutlery were placed for each guest. Centrepieces made of forcemeat or marzipan in the form of lion and unicorn, Hercules, castles and fortresses, were arranged along the centre of the table and the function was organised by the Duke's major-domo who was also a nobleman. He was master of the household in charge of all catering and housekeeping arrangements at the

179

palace. Three carvers or *trinciantes*, were on duty in the room as carving the joints was considered a most important task and there were schools of carving all over Italy.

FRANCE

On the richly embroidered, starched and pleated tablecloths used in royal and noble households, were set solid silver and gold figures for show, elegant ewers for wine and water and even more elaborate containers for salt. The *nef* was now used throughout Europe both as an individual salt-cellar and as a place setting to mark the position of important persons at the table. During the eighteenth century the Court of France set the standard of gastronomic excellence for all Europe. There was a system of protocol that commenced with a stately procession to the dining hall with each official in his correct order of precedence. Many of the ceremonial duties were carried out by noblemen or princes of the blood whose title defined the role each played in serving the King. Duties included tasting the food and wine as a precaution against it being poisoned – the duty of food-tasting being a common one in most great households all over Europe.

GREAT BRITAIN FROM THE 16TH CENTURY ONWARD

In England during Tudor times the table was set elegantly with glassware and silverware of fine quality. Food was borne into the room in procession to the sound of music with the carver carrying the joint which he proceeded to slice and taste before serving. Wines from France, Germany and Italy were drunk, their service being supervised by the cup-bearer who was a person of importance in the hierarchy of the domestic staff, often being known as a 'gentleman cup-bearer'.

Carême did not remain long in the service of the Prince Regent but his influence was profound and continued long after he left England after only two years, in 1818. His contribution to gastronomy was in relating architecture to food presentation by the creation of highly elaborate structures around which the food was arranged. The centrepiece was put to practical use instead of being merely to delight the eyes. In Carême's day there were two main courses – or rather *stages* of a meal – each complete in itself and comprises of several different kinds of dishes. The first service of dishes, known as the *entrée*, was laid on the table before the diners entered the room so as to confront them with maximum visual effect. Hot dishes were kept warm by the use of *timbales* which are silver

180

Mr. JOHN FARLEY,

Principal Cook at the London Tavern.

Publish'd Jan.ʳ 1,1783, by I.Fielding, Nᵒ 23, Pater-noster Row, I. Scatcherd & I.Whitaker, Nᵒ 12, Ave Maria Lane.

17. John Farley, principal cook at the London Tavern

containers with an inner liner to hold the food and hot water surrounding it in the outside part, but by the time the first course was consumed (which was likely to take at least an hour) the remainder of the food would be well below the optimum temperature.

When the first service had been removed and preparations finalised for the second or remove course, several *pièces-montées* were brought in, representing famous monuments, ancient cities, pagodas and pediments, made of pastry or pastillage. *Petits fours* were presented in baskets made of pulled or moulded sugar and *entremets* were served even when there was no entertainment, these being dishes that were in complete contrast to the main items of the remove course. A dish of lobsters, pineapple in cream, cooked truffles or an elaborate salad would be offered as an entremet to those whose appetite had become jaded or surfeited. Wine was served throughout the two courses. The roles of the carver and cup-bearer became less significant as that of the head chef increased in importance since it was he who planned the layout of the dishes on the table and supervised their placing in symmetrical order.

The accoutrements of the table became elaborate and much more sophisticated than hitherto. Sauceboats, cloches and réchauds came into use, and fish forks and knives with handles of ivory or mother of pearl, sugar-sifter, cruet stands and fruit baskets made of silver or Sheffield plate, graced the tables of even the lower middle classes. In the mid-nineteenth century eggcup holders, muffiners, tea urns, wine coolers, cheese toasters, brandy burners, marrow scoos and lobster picks made of electro-plated nickel silver (e.p.n.s.) were introduced to add further refinement to the act of eating.

During Victoria's long reign the pleasure of the table were further enhanced not only from within Britain itself but from foods and ideas from the Empire that was being formed, and even more subtly by the arrival of chefs from France. France exported its gifts of gastronomy first to the homes of wealthy Englishmen where they started work in domestic service and in the gentlemen's clubs of London, then as great hotels were built they went to work in them, importing more staff from France to form a brigade. When the chef moved to a new job it was the practice that all the key staff went with him.

RECENT DEVELOPMENTS

One of the greatest French chefs ever to work in England was Felix Urbain-Dubois. He arrived in England after serving at the Court of the Czar of Russia just after the middle of the nineteenth century and he changed the method of service from the French to the Russian style.

Service in this style meant that all food was dressed in the kitchen on silver dishes which were then offered to the guests by waiting staff; guests took hold of the serving spoon and fork to help themselves to as much or little as they wanted. There were no elaborate centrepieces on the table, no joint to carve and each course was served separately in the correct sequence. This method ensured that food would be served at the correct temperature to all at one and the same time and on the kitchen side it permitted fairly straightforward menu planning and closer portion control.

This method of service was in total contrast to that which had existed but was so sound that it was soon adopted throughout the world and has endured until the present day. It had originated in private houses where wealthy people so wished to obtain maximum enjoyment from the meals prepared by their chefs that they were happy to abandon the system that had been in use for hundreds of years. So our thanks go to the Russian nobility, the chefs they brought from France and the waiters from Italy and Germany who all helped to change a long-established practice into a smooth, personal and elegant form of service that was more in keeping with the changing social system and the faster pace of living. The following menu illustrates the trend:

Eight-course dinner held in the Great Hall of the Inner Temple, London on December 1886 in honour of the appointment of Henry Matthews QC, MP, as Home Secretary. (H. Matthews, 1826–1913, became Lord Llandaff in 1895).

DÎNER

HORS-d'OEUVRE	Huîtres au Naturel
POTAGES	Tortue Claire ou Tortue Lié
POISSON	Filet de Sole en Matelote Marinière
ENTRÉES	Petites Casseroles Moscovite Bécassine en Caisse Périgourdine
RELEVÉS	Chapon Troussé aux Légumes Selle de Mouton Rôtie
RÔTS	Faisan Bardé Canard Sauvage
ENTREMETS	Chartreuse de Fruits Bombe Glacée

SAVOUREUX   Croûte d'Anchois aux Olives
                      Biscuit Chaud au Parmesan

Café

VINS

Chablis 1870   St Estéphe   Champagne Ayala 1874
Chartreuse   Port 1858

The building of grand hotels and the provision of food and drink to residents in grill rooms and restaurants meant the transfer of centres of gastronomy from a small number of private houses to a large number of commercial establishments that were open to all comers regardless of title or status. The time-honoured skills of chefs, carvers and cup-bearers could now be enjoyed by others than the highly born. Chefs no longer moved to England to work only in private service and so it was that gastronomy was liberated and popularised. Men such as Ritz and Escoffier expanded the frontiers of gastronomy by exploiting the full extent of the repertoire and popularising classical dishes on their large menus.

The use of service à la Russe permitted a selective Table d'Hôte menu in which the chef could guide customers to the enjoyment of a gastronomic experience, but it obviously had its limitations as to the number of dishes that could be offered.

As hotel restaurants opened their doors to non-residents and as more people began to appreciate the opportunity to eat outside the home so there came the need to cater for a wider spectrum of customers which led to the need to enlarge the menu by adding or adapting to another list of dishes that could be cooked to order – the à la Carte selection.

The introduction of the à la Carte menu was not a sudden fundamental change but an acknowledgement of a new situation, hence not a revolution but a gentle evolution of adapting to new circumstances.

The role of the carver was taken over by the head waiter although those places that specialise in joints still employ a carver as such to practice his skills on hot and cold meats. The function of cup-bearer is done by the *sommelier* who may still bear a cup as signal of his role though tasting a wine for its palatability rather than its purity. To speed up the service to busy customers, waiters then took the initiative and transferred the portion of food from silver dish to plate by spoon and fork. It was this refinement that led to it being called **silver service**.

Acknowledgement of the importance of the *entremet* – the pause for entertainment – was made when it was transformed into the final course of the menu and made spectacular by being partly an entertainment in itself. A *flambé* dessert, a cold one served in an ice carving, or even a combination of hot and

184

cold as in *Cerises Jubilée* or *Soufflé en Surprise* are examples of these presentations that delight the eyes even more than the mouth.

Many new implements were devised and others were improved. Rechauds kept food hotter, and carving and other sorts of trolleys helped to personalise the service. Grape scissors, lobster crackers, asparagus tongs, oyster forks, ice-cream spades and cocktail shakers were introduced to contribute to the better enjoyment of a meal.

Another development worthy of note originated in the United States in the 1920s with the introduction of the 'blue plate special' which was an oval platter with separate compartments for the different parts of a main meal. Its popularity led to the creation of a new form of service which was known as **plate service** and it became firmly established all over the world, even in de luxe restaurants. It was a boon to caterers during the second World War when there was a shortage of skilled waiters and it helped to cut the cost of service because relatively untrained staff could carry it out; also it guaranteed exact portion control. It did however detract from the entertainment value of having a meal in a public restaurant and it remains in operation only in low-star establishments, very often as **plate-cum-silver service** where the main item is put on the plate and the vegetables in a silver dish.

In Germany and Switzerland a form of **family service** is used, mainly because it is the habit in those countries to serve large portions of food. The food is served by the waiter leaving some in reserve and this with the accompaniments and vegetables is placed on a rechaud for customers to take a second helping when they are ready.

In those temples of gastronomy where *cuisine nouvelle* is worshipped as being the ultimate form of cookery, the service is entirely on plates. 'Plating' the meal to make it look like a masterpiece of art is the essential factor so the size, shape and decoration of the plate on which it is displayed and from which it is eaten, has to be carefully selected.

The cost of such a plate is bound to be very expensive and a suitably elegant silver-plated cover would probably be five times as much as the plate so a large capital investment is necessary for this form of service. It is true there is no outlay on silver dishes as they play no part in the performance nor is any *flambé* work done in the restaurant as it is the chef alone who is allowed to do the cooking and presentation. The role of the waiter is not an entirely unskilled one and flair is still needed to lay such an expensive plateful of food in front of a customer.

LA NOUVELLE CUISINE FRANÇAISE

It was Paul Bocuse, the instigator of *cuisine nouvelle*, who criticised some of those who sought to emulate his efforts by remarking that he thought a bargeload

185

of kiwi fruit had hit one loaded with broccoli spears and the salvage operation had flung these rediscovered items widespread through the restaurants of Paris.

Elizabeth David has suggested that *cuisine nouvelle* could not have developed in the way it has done, had it not been for the invention of the modern food-processor machine at about the time that *cuisine nouvelle* was being heralded as the way forward for cooking. There is a lot of truth in both these assertions and M. Bocuse was the first to suggest that too many chefs were carrying out a confidence trick on their customers in the way they were serving dainty portions of these new dishes which were supposed to provide a lighter regimen with the accent on fresh commodities and new combinations of ingredients. *Nouvelle cuisine* was said to be going to reverse the steady evolution that had gone on for 150 years and had resulted in an orderly repertoire that most chefs knew from beginning to end.

The charge against classical French cuisine was that it was too heavy and complicated for today's tastes and led to obesity among its adherents. Sauces and garnishes which had been regarded as the wonders of French culinary art were now charged with being over-seasoned and inappropriate. Jaded tastes had to be revitalised by original combinations of meat or fish with fruits in or out of season, no matter how incongruous these were. Peaches and apricots could be left to rot on the trees but the sorbet had to be made with kiwi fruits or passion fruit – traditional flavours were old hat! This led to the need to import such varieties as caremboles, citronellas, durions, jackfruits and taros at great expense, which in turn led to prohibitive menu prices or else mini-portions.

With vegetables being served separately as though barely related to the main dish, underdone but posed on a side plate so artistically as to make it look full, there was a need for small spring vegetables to be available all the year round. Each carrot was given loving care in cooking with a bit of stem left on, each leek had the green part plaited, other vegetables were subric-ed; with all this beauty treatment it was a wonder they did not become fetid instead of being primeurs! Mousses, farces, pâtés, soufflés, forcemeats, godiveau and other stuffings which had required much hard pounding and difficult sieving were now easy to make, thanks to the new style of food-processor. The use of these mixtures made it possible to offer smooth-textured foods that possessed the commercial advantage of making a little go a long way. A small piece of fish or meat could be bulked out with the preparation, thus keeping the food cost low; these farces could be used in hot as well as cold dishes. Two thin slices of turkey meat sandwiched with appropriate mousseline mixture, garnished with strawberries and sliced kiwi fruit may be initiation rather than tradition but is quickly made and looks good to customers, even though the dish is in bad taste. A long name would help to sell it. Sauces in *nouvelle cuisine* are not based on the traditional *béchamel, demi-glace, jus lié* or *velouté* but are made from the cooking essence or liquid with the addition of stock, wine, spirit and liqueur thickened by reduction rather than by a roux; they are more refined perhaps, but also more expensive.

The *nouvelle cuisine française* was the brainchild of Paul Bocuse in 1975 and was named by Gault et Millau. It has its followers amongst chefs and customers who see it as the ultimate in a system of cookery that demands more thought and feeling than does the blind adherence to the classical repertoire. It has its critics who say that it has disestablished a noble art and opened it to the arrivistes and pretenders who have little respect for the well-being and health of customers. Some want to save cookery from the enemies within and advocate a return from the artistic to the true basics of cookery.

As Escoffier so rightly remarked eighty years ago 'what already existed at the time of Carême, which exists today and which will continue to exist for as long as cooking itself, are the fundamentals'. There is a danger that our inheritance could be lost if chefs allow themselves to be trajected along the road to ephemeral fame by the wrong route and for a misconceived motive.

As John Russell in his *Boke of Nature* said some 300 years ago:-

Cooks with theire newe conceytes, choppynge, stampynge and gryndynge,
Many new recipes alle day they are contryvynge and fyndynge.

9 The Rôle of Alcoholic Beverages

The Names on the Wine Label – France – Germany – Italy – Spain – Portugal – Madeira – Australia – Austria – Bulgaria – Cyprus – Greece – Hungary – Israel – Romania – Russia – South   Africa – Switzerland – United   States – Yugoslavia – British   Wines – Cocktails – Spirits   and Liqueurs – Aromatic Bitters – Cure for a Hangover – Vintage Guides – Wines and Foods – Wine Tasting – Smoking

THE NAMES ON THE WINE LABEL

Before a bottle of wine is opened and tasted it is possible to gain a fairly concise impression of its character and quality from the label. Even a quick glance will reveal quite a lot of information about the wine even though the wording has been kept to the official minimum and set out in a very abbreviated form. It is true that the colour of the wine can be seen through the glass but as red wines are bottled in green glass, the depth of colour cannot be readily discerned. So a knowledge of what is implied by the wording on the label is bound to assist in judging the value of the wine inside. The name of the country of origin, the region, the district and the vineyard all contribute information on the wine, whether it is rough or a good quality wine. The name of the producer, the blender or the shipper also assist in identifying the wine and ensuring that it is authentic.

The sale of wine is estimated to average about 30 per cent of the customers' bill so it is important to merchandise it correctly. The mark-up on wine is sometimes deliberately high because restaurateurs use the extra profit to offset any shortfall of profit on food, but this can lead to consumer resistance so a more positive approach to realistic pricing should encourage more sales at less exorbitant prices. The following information gives an outline of the wines available from the major wine-producing countries of the world that serve to comprise a satisfactory wine list.

FRANCE

There are thirteen wine-producing regions in France of which six are major ones, two that are mainly associated with the production of brandy, and five lesser known ones that nevertheless supply a range of interesting wines, many of which deserve a place on the wine list.

All the good wines have either *Appellation Contrôlée* (AC) or *Vins Délimité de Qualité Superiore* (VDQS) on the label; 'AOC' is also used and means the same as AC. The grade after these is *Vins de Pays* or *Vin de Table* which are both good quality and very drinkable wine suitable for carafe service but nowhere near as good as the first two grades. These *vins de table*, as the name implies, are very ordinary wines of no great distinction but are ideal for everyday drinking. Each region has its own distinctive shape of bottle.

Champagne

The *méthode champenoise* is used in making sparkling wine in many countries but only wine produced by this method in the Champagne region can actually be called champagne. Wine from different vineyards of this region are blended together and then the wines from different years; a quantity of liquor made of old wine and cane sugar is added after the second fermentation and this determines the taste which can be *brut* – extra dry, *sec* – dry, *demi-sec* – medium dry, *doux* –rich or very sweet. There are some twenty major producers whose names are very well known in this country and many smaller firms whose products are not so widely distributed.

Champagne is bottled in quarters, halves, full bottles and can occasionally be obtained in these large size bottles for very special occasions:

magnum	2 bottles	approx	1½ litres
jeroboam	4 bottles	approx	3 litres
rehoboam	6 bottles	approx	4½ litres
methuselah	8 bottles	approx	6 litres
salmanazar	12 bottles	approx	9 litres
balthazar	16 bottles	approx	12 litres
nebuchadnezzar	20 bottles	approx	15 litres

In addition to the ordinary white champagne, pink or rosé champagne is also produced; it tastes the same as ordinary champagne and is made by leaving the black grape stems in contact with the must, or by adding some local red wine before the secondary fermentation. Pink champagne is more expensive than ordinary champagne and is considered to have less acidity. In addition to champagne this region also produces still wines under the name of *Côteaux Champenois* which are AC white wines of very good quality.

The highest quality wines in the world are produced in this region and there are hundreds of different ones, both white and red, as it is the largest wine-producing region in the world. In general these wines are subtle in taste with an elegant flavour, a brilliant colour and a smooth and delicate bouquet, being neither too heavy nor too strong. The areas that produce claret or red wine, include *Médoc, Haut-Médoc, Margaux, Moulis, Saint-Julien, Pauillac, Saint-Estèphe, Saint-Emilion, Pomerol, Côtes de Fronsac* and *Premières Côtes de Bordeaux.* Dry white wines are produced in *Graves, Entre-Deux-Mers, Saint-Macaire, Haut-Benauge* and sweet ones in *Sauternes, Barsac, Cérons, Loupiac* and *St-Croix-du-Mont.*

The wines of *Bordeaux* are bottled in bottles with high shoulders; in addition to half- and normal-size ones it is also possible to purchase magnums. The great wines of Bordeaux are generally château-bottled, the fact being stated both on the label and on the cork as *'Mise en bouteille au Château';* the name of the wine will bear the château name, for example, *Château Calon-Ségur* which is a third growth wine from the Saint-Estèphe area in the Médoc. Many years ago all the notable wines of Bordeaux were classified according to quality and this list still stands, all the wines included in it being the most expensive as they are the most sought after. It is the practice to lay down claret for a number of years after it has been bottled, during which it will improve in quality and increase in value; the year will be stated on the label. These fine wines are classified into the quality of their growths or *crus*, which range from great first growths to fifth growths.

A description of the wines of each area would indicate that it is *Médoc* that produces reds famous for their bouquet and which improve as they age. Although *Graves* produces dry and fruity white wines, the red Graves in a good year have a very smooth flavour and will keep well. There are five great first growths, fourteen second, fourteen third, ten fourth and eighteen fifth growths in this area. These wines are ideal with lamb, veal, pork and poultry and also with cheese.

The *Saint-Emilion* region gives quite strong and dark red wines that seem to have a smell of truffles. They mature gracefully and there are two great first growths, ten first growths, and no fewer than seventy-three classified great growths. These red wines are the right accompaniment with beef, mutton, game and of course, cheese.

Pomerol is a region that produces red wines of great finesse that are rounded and velvety yet full-bodied and deep in colour. Like those from neighbouring areas, these wines improve with keeping.

Bordeaux and *Côtes de Bordeaux* are the areas that produce large quantities of pleasant, fruity red wines, suitable for any wine list because they are above the standard of ordinary table wine. These bear the *appellations* of *Bordeaux Supérieur, Bordeaux Clairet, Premières Côtes de Bordeaux, Côtes de Bourg, Premières Côtes de Blaye, Bordeaux Côtes de Castillon, Saint-Foy Bordeaux, Bordeaux Côtes de Francs* and *Graves de Vayres.*

The dry white wines of *Bordeaux* come from *Graves, Entre-Deux-Mers, Côtes de Bourg* and *Graves de Vayres*; these are fruity wines with a fine bouquet.

Sauternes and *Barsac* are the areas that produce the sweet, heady white wines that have a wonderful bouquet of flowers and honey. There is one great first growth, the incomparable *Château Yquem* and eleven first growths and fourteen second growths.

Burgundy

This region is as important as Bordeaux and produces many wines to match in quality those of that area. The reds do not need to be kept as long as does claret; the bouquet is very distinctive and the colour fine and dark red. It is a soft and velvety wine.

Burgundy is bottled in bottles that have sloping sides; the best will bear the words *'Mise en bouteille par le proprietaire'*, *'Mise à la proprieté'* or *'Mise au domaine'*. White Burgundies and the light reds such as *Beaujolais* should be consumed young. White Burgundies are still nice and fresh up to about two years and are certainly fully matured at six years.

Chablis produces subtle and light white wines with a tinge of green in the pale yellow colour; they are drunk young and fresh. There are a number of *Grand Crus* or **Outstanding Growths** and many *Premiers Crus*.

Côte d'Or

This region is divided into two areas – the *Côte de Nuits* and the *Côte de Beaune*.

The *Côte de Nuits* produces nearly all the great red burgundies of which there are twenty-nine *appellations controlées*; the best known are *Chambertin, Nuits-Saint-Georges, Vosné Romanée, Richebourg, Clos de Vougeot* and *Chambolle-Musigny*.

The *Côte de Beaune* also produces a number of great red wines as well as the greatest white Burgundies. The smooth and velvety red wines include *Corton, Pommard, Volnay, Savigny*, and *Beaune*; the white wines are *Meursault* and *Montrachet*.

The Côte d'Or produces some elegant and distinguished but inexpensive wines such as *Passe-tout-grains* which is made from a mixture of *gamay* and *pinot noir* grapes, and *Bourgogne Aligoté*, a pleasant refreshing white wine which is the appointed one for making the blackcurrant aperitif *Kir*.

The *Mercurey* region produces two predominantly red wines – *Givry* and *Mercurey* – both unpretentious but good, and two whites – *Rully* and *Montagny*.

Mâcon and *Mâcon-Villages* are dry fruity white wines; *Mâcon rouge* and *Mâcon rosé* are also produced in this area, but the greatest of the white wines is *Pouilly-Fuissé* with its greeny-gold colour and nutty flavour; it keeps well for

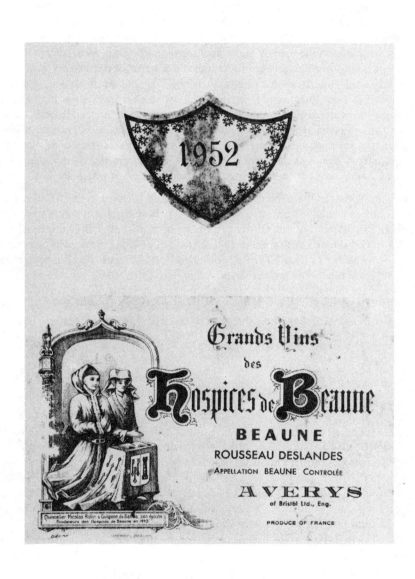

18. *Grands Vins des Hospices de Beaune*

up to five years but is best drunk young. *Saint-Véran* is a newer *appellation* from this district.

Beaujolais is a red wine that can be drunk very young, from three months and for this reason can taste better when served slightly chilled. The name *Beaujolais* alone on a label really only means a wine of carafe quality and the district and commune names such as *Juliénas, Moulin à Vent, Saint-Amour, Fleurie, Chénas, Morgan* and *Brouilly* indicate a much better quality *Beaujolais*.

Nearly half the *Beaujolais* made each year is sold as *Beaujolais Nouveau* which comes onto the market on the 15th November each year immediately following the vintage in September. Three quarters of it is *Appellation Beaujolais* and one quarter *Appellation Beaujolais Villages*. *Beaujolais Primeur* is often seen on the label of these wines but it means the same as *Beaujolais Nouveau*.

Apart from *Beaujolais Nouveau*, and apart from *Beaujolais* being available as red, white and rosé there are four main kinds of Beaujolais which are:

Beaujolais: this can be a blend of wine produced anywhere in the Beaujolais region but is usually from the southern part. It will have a minimum of 9° alcohol, calculated on the OIML system as in use in all EEC countries; it is similar to Gay-Lussac but taken at 20°C instead of at 15°C. *Beaujolais Supérieur*: this is wine having at least 10° of alcohol; *Beaujolais Villages*: this is a better class of wine than the two previous ones. *Beaujolais Crus*: these are the very best wines and are named after the villages where they are made. These are *St Amour, Brouilly, Côte de Brouilly, Chénas, Chiroubles, Fleurie, Juliénas, Morgan* and *Moulin à Vent*. Although the other *Beaujolais* wines are drunk young, these can age well.

Côtes du Rhône

This region produces mainly red wines which are very robust and with a high alcohol content; they age well. The most noble of these is the well-known *Châteauneuf-du-Pape* the other notable red wines being *Gigondas, Côtes Rôtie, Côtes du Rhone*, and *Hermitage*. The white wines are good for up to two years and include white *Côtes du Rhône* and White *Hermitage, Crozes-Hermitage, Saint-Joseph, Saint-Peray* and *Château Grillet*. The well known rosé wines are *Tavel, Livac* and *Chuselan*. Sweet white wines are *Beaumes-de-Venise* and *Rasteau* and sparkling wine is *Saint-Peray*.

Also from this part of France comes a number of AOC wines including *Côtes de Ventoux, Côteaux de Tricastin* and *Châtillon en Diois*; the VDQS wines are *Côtes du Luberon, Côtes de Vivarais* and *Côteaux de Pierrevert*.

Alsace

This region produces six great white and one rosé wine each with its own distinctive character; long green bottles are used and it is all bottled in the region. The wines are distinguished by the name of the grape vine from which it is made – these are *Sylvaner* which is a light, dry fresh and fruity wine; *Riesling* – a very dry wine with a very delicate bouquet and real fruitiness and *Gerwurztraminer* which is a full-bodied dry wine with a subtle bouquet that fills the nose and mouth.

Muscat d'Alsace is a dry, fruity wine with a very distinctive bouquet; *Pinot Blanc*, also known as *Klevner*, is a dry wine with a vigorous character. *Tokay d'Alsace*, also known as *Pinot Gris*, is a dry wine with a heady, full-bodied, even opulent character. *Pinot Noir* is a dry rosé wine with a deliciously fruity bouquet. *Edelzwicker* is a blended wine of this region.

Loire

The dry white wines from this region include the sprightly *Muscadet de Sèvre et Maine, Sancerre, Saumur, Rouilly, Pouilly Fumé* and *Vouvray*; the sweet ones are from *Côteaux du Layon, Aubance, Bonnezeaux, Savennières*, and *Quarts-de-Chaume*.

Rosé wines from Anjou and Touraine are well known and the red wines are light and have an aroma of violets; they include *Chinon, Bourgueil* and *Saint-Nicholas*. Some of the *Vouvray* and *Saumur* are made into sparkling wines.

Provence

This large region produces white, rosé and red wines; those with *Appellation Côntrôlée* labels include *Cassis, Bandol, Bellet de Nice, Palette d'Aix* and *Côtes de Provence* and the VDQS wines are from the *Côteaux d'Aix-en-Provence*. The red wines are powerful and have a big bouquet and the white and rosé wines are light and refreshing.

The South-West

This region produces some AOC wines; the reds are *Bergerac, Côtes de Duras, Madiron, Cahors, Gaillac* and *Côtes du Frontonnais*; the whites are *Montravel, Bergerac, Irouleguy, Jurançon*; the rosés are *Irouleguy, Bergerac* and *Rosés de Béarn*. The sweet white wines are *Monbazillac, Pacherenc du Vic-Bilh* and *Jurançon*.

Jura

This area produces red wines that are good for keeping, rosé wines that acquire a bronze tinge with age and become known as *'pelure d'oignon'*, white wines that are pale gold in colour, fruity and delicate, and the *vins de paille* which are obtained by letting the grapes dry on straw.

Savoy

The wines from this area are mostly AOC; the whites are light, fruity and dry and include *Apremont*, *Abymes*, *Chignin*, *Chantagne*, *Montmelian* and *Cruet*. *Crépy* and *Seyssel* are slightly sparkling and the reds – which are called *Roussetes* – include *Frangy*, *Monthoux* and *Monterminod*.

Languedoc Roussillon

The AOC wines from this region include reds: *Fitou*, *Collioure* and *Côtes du Roussillon*; whites: *Clairette de Languedoc*, *Clairette de Bellegarde* and the well-known sweet sparkling wine *Blanquette de Limoux*. The VDQS wines include – red: *Corbières*, *Minervois*, *Costières du Gard*, *Côteaux du Languedoc* and *St-Chinian*. There are also some very sweet wines called *Vins Doux Naturels* (VDN) the red ones being *Maury* and *Banyuls* and the whites *Muscat de Rivesaltes* – all these are AOC wines.

GERMANY

As compared with France, Germany produces very little wine but what it does produce is always good and it certainly produces the best white wines of any country in the world, the finest of them from Riesling grapes. German wine labels show what grapes the wine is made from.

Riesling grapes ripen late in the year but the wine is not too sweet but very rich, fruity and piquant. *Silvaner* grapes give a big yield of mild and fruity wine. *Müller-Thurgau* is a cross between the *Riesling* and *Silvaner* which ripens early to give a mild fruity wine. *Rulander* grapes give a full-bodied and fruity wine. There are a few German red wines, the best being made from the *Spätburgunder* vine giving a soft, fruity wine. *Trollinger* grapes give a very fresh light red wine. Rosé is called *Weissherbet*.

There are eleven wine regions each having two or more districts comprised of several villages which again are shown on the wine label, thus making identification easy. Although all the regions are close together they produce different kinds of wine because the growing conditions and the weather differ considerably.

There are three grades of German wine: *Deutscher Tafelwein* is ordinary table, *QbA* is quality wine from a specified region and specially graded quality *QmP* wine is the higher category.

The designation *QbA* on the label is the equivalent of *VDQS* and *AOC* of French wines and the *DOC* and *DOCG* of Italian wines. There are five grades of the highest quality wines which are:

1. *Kabinett* – wine made from fully ripened grapes picked at the normal harvesting time;
2. *Spätlese* – a more rounded wine made from late harvested grapes,
3. *Auslese* – wine made from best quality ripe grapes that have sorted from the rest and pressed separately to give elegance and a full bouquet,
4. *Beerenauslese* – wine made from specially selected ripe and over-ripe grapes which give a full, fruity wine with an amber colour,
5. *Trockenbeerenauslese* – made from grapes that have been allowed to stay on the vines until they are shrivelled up, thus giving a very distinctive and expensive wine.

In addition there is *Eiswein* which is made from grapes left on the vines until they become frozen by the first frost of winter; this unique wine is rich in sugar and aroma. There is also *Landwein* which is roughly equivalent to *Vin de Pays*. The German wine regions are as follows:

Ahr: produces excellent red wines that are fiery and powerful yet velvety, and pleasant, steely, fresh white wines and a number of rosé wines.

Baden: produces fresh fragrant aromatic white and some fiery red wines, making for a variety of delicious and full bodied wines.

Franconia: rich and strong white wines that are dry and fruity; they are usually bottled in flagons – *Steigerwald, Maindreieck, Mainviereck* are some of their names.

Hessische Bergstrasse: fruity, elegant and mild wines that have a lovely fragrance.

Middle Rhine: These are dry and fresh wines. The red wines are *Bacharach, Rheinburgenau* and *Siebengebirge*.

Moselle: (includes Saar and Ruwer) white wines which are fresh and delicate and with a fine fruity flavour. The best known are *Bernkastel, Zeltingen, Piesport, Kirchpfad*.

Nahe: these are fragrant wines that have a fruity fragrance and are quite lively. They include *Schloss Boeckelheim, Niederhauser, Rudesheim, Waldboeckelheim*.

Palatinate: over 80 per cent of the production is white wine: these are mild and aromatic wines that are round and strong. *Ruppertsberger, Deidesheim, Koenigsbach, Wachenheim, Duerkbeim, Neustadt, Niederkirchen* and *Forster* are among the best known.

Rheingau: this area produces nearly all white wines that are full of character and elegance with a very fruity nose. Amongst them are *Hockheim, Rauenthal, Erbach, Haltenheim, Mittenheim, Winkel, Schloss Vollrad* and *Johannisberg*.

Rheinhessen: 91 per cent of production is white wine which is smooth and elegant and has fragrance and soft mildness. Some of the best-known are *Oppenheim, Dienheim, Nierstein, Dexheim, Bodenheim, Wonnegau*.

Württemberg: this area produces strong tasting white wines that are not often met in England; they are strikingly fruity and with a distinctive after-taste.

The *sparkling wines* of Germany are known as *Sekt* and are produced in all parts of the wine-growing areas. Ordinary sparkling wine is labelled simply as *Deutscher Sekt* and will be a blend of wines of different origins. The better quality is labelled *Qualitätsschaumweine bestimmter Aubaugebiete* or *Sekt bA* and will be from blends made in the same way as the still wines. It is possible to have a *sekt* made from *Riesling* grapes from the *Moselle* region.

Perlwein is a bubbly wine made by saturating still wine with carbon dioxide; it is a strong rival to the ordinary sparkling wines because of its cheapness and the fact that it is drier than *sekt*. There are also some Euroblend wines that are a mixture of two or more European wines, disguised to look like German wine.

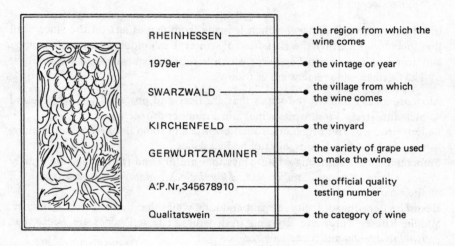

RHEINHESSEN	the region from which the wine comes
1979er	the vintage or year
SWARZWALD	the village from which the wine comes
KIRCHENFELD	the vinyard
GERWURTZRAMINER	the variety of grape used to make the wine
A.P.Nr,345678910	the official quality testing number
Qualitatswein	the category of wine

ITALY

Italy is credited with producing 2000 different kinds of wine made from 700 different varieties of wine grapes. There are only seven principal wine-producing areas of superior quality wines but so as to show the products of all the notable regions this has been expanded to nineteen.

Four fifths of the wine produced is red, the white wines coming mainly from the northern part of the country; there are only a few rosé wines. The quality is defined by the abbreviation DOC (*Denominazione di Origine Controllata*) which is used to denote wine from a clearly defined area, specific grape varieties, method of production and style of wine; there are over 200 of these areas. The other is DOCG (*Denominazione di Origine Controllata e Garantita*) given to certain wines from the finest areas. Italians like their red wines served at temperatures around 16°C and up to 20°C, with the white and sparkling wines at
198

the other extreme of 5°C to 7°C. Amongst the terms used to describe Italian wines are:

abboccato - soft and slightly sweet
amabile - slightly sweet
asciutto - very dry
dolce - very sweet
fiacco - without body or acidity
mattonato - wine that has lost its red colour
morbido - pleasant, well-rounded and velvety
nobile - distinguished, above average
robusto - high in alcohol, good body
sapido - pleasantly rich and with lively acidity.

Generally speaking the wines of Italy have lower acidity than those of France and most of them have a well-rounded but soft and ripe flavour:

Piedmont: there are many full-bodied, dark coloured wines such as *Barolo*, *Barbera* and *Gattinara*, of 12°-12.5° and the *Dolcetto* wines are soft and fragrant reds. *Grignolino* is a lighter red wine while *Moscato* is a delicate sweet white wine. *Asti Spumante* is the well-known sweet sparkling wine. *Vermouth* is produced in this region.

Val d'Aosta: these wines are not generally available in England at present but names like *Donnaz* and *Enfer d'Arvier* for red and *Blanc de Morgex* may become available.

Liguria: only a small quantity is produced so these are not widely available; *Rossese di Dolceaqua* is a soft, aromatic red wine and *Cinque Terre* is the main white one.

Lombardy: the *Valtellina* wines are red wines of character and the *Oltrepo Pevese* are above average table wines. The white wine from this area is *Lugana*, a fruity fragrant wine.

Trentino-Alto Adige: many of the wines from this region bear the name of the area in their title, for instance, *Trentino Riesling*, *Trentino Traminer Aromatico*; the most famous reds are *Trentino Lagrein*, *Trentino Marzemino* and the even more full-bodied *Teroldego Rotaliano*, *Caldaro* and *Santa Maddalena*. Both dry and sweet white wines are produced and some quality sparkling wines.

Veneto: amongst the well-known wines produced in this region are *Soave*, *Valpolicella* and *Bardolino*. *Soave* is a dry white, *Valpolicella* a ruby red, and *Bardolino* a light red wine. Other notable white wines are *Tocai di Piave*, *Verduzzo* and the very sweet *Recioto* wines.

Friuli-Venezia: the red and white *Friulian* wines are named after the grape varieties used in their production including *Merlot*, *Pinot Grigio*, *Riesling*, and *Traminer*.

Emilia Romagna: this is the largest wine-producing region in Italy. The well-known semi-sparkling red *Lambrusco* is produced here, the sweet and dry versions both being popular. *Sangiovese* and *Gutturnio* are quality reds and *Albana* and *Trebbiano* are pleasant whites.

Tuscany: the best-known wine of Italy, *Chianti*, is produced here by two main consortia; *Chianti Classico* is denoted by a black cock on the neck of the bottle and *Chianti Putto* by a cherub. It is a brilliant ruby red wine with the bouquet of wild violets. Other red wines are *Brunello di Montalcino* and *Vino nobile di Montepulciano* and a notable white is *Vernaccia di San Gimignano*.

Umbria: the outstanding wine of this region is *Orvieto* a sweetish straw-coloured, refreshing wine; there is also a dry *Orvieto* that has a slightly bitter taste. A noteworthy red wine is *Torgiano* which is dry and delicate.

Marches: the two main red wines are *Rosso Conero* and *Rosso Piceno*, both pleasant with a nice bouquet. The white wines are labelled as *Verdicchio*.

Latium: the most famous wine is *Frascati*, a dry white wine with a very subtle bouquet; there is also a sweet version of it. The next most famous white is *Est! Est! Est!*, a name that dates from around the year 1100. Other white wines are *Colli Albani* and *Marmo*.

Abruzzo: known as one of the best red wines of Italy, *Montepulciano d'Abruzzo* is a robust wine with a sapid taste that improves with keeping; *Cerasuola d'Abruzzo* is becoming widely known as a fine dry red wine. The superior *Trebbiano d'Abbruzzo* is a good quality white wine.

Campania: from the slopes of Vesuvius come the famous *Lacryma Christi* wines, the red a dry fresh wine that goes equally well with white and red meat, and the white wine with its subtle perfume. *Falerno Rosso* is ruby red in colour, dry and full bodies; the white *Falerno* is also dry and full of flavour.

Apulia: the *Castel del Monte* red, rosé and white wines are good fresh ones as are the *San Severo* ones, in particular the white version. *Primitivo di Manduria* is a full bodied red wine of 14° alcohol on the International Organisation of Legal Metrology system scale as used in the EEC. It is replacing the scale invented by M. Gay-Lussac (1778–1850).

Basilicata: the best-known wine is *Aglianico del Vulture* a vivid red, dry and astringent, full-bodied wine that becomes austere with age.

Calabria: available as red or white, *Cirò* is one of the oldest wines in the world, the red being delicate and the white fruity. *Savuto* is a medium quality red table wine that is drunk whilst young.

Sicily: the vineyards on the slopes of Etna produce a fresh dry white and a big red that keeps well for 15-20 years: both are labelled *Etna*. *Corvo Duca di Salapurata* is on the label of a very good dry white and a delicate red, both of 13° alcohol. *Saturno* can be both a good reliable white and a full bodied red.

Sardinia: the best known white is *Vernaccia di Oristano; Nuragus* and *Vermentino* are whites and *Cannonau* and *Monica* are reds that provide good drinking.

Marsala is made in Sicily and is a dark, sweet, fortified wine that is drunk with the dessert and used in cooking, especially with veal dishes. There is also a version known as *Marsala all'uovo* which is like an egg nog which can be drunk after a meal in place of a liqueur.

SPAIN

Although Spain is known all over the world for its sherry it also exports many good ordinary wines which are taking their deserved place on the wine list. The best quality wines are those from the Rioja area which while they cannot be compared to a good Bordeaux or Burgundy are profound wines in their own right. There are many wine producing regions as follows:

Rioja: this region is divided into three areas. The wines of Rioja Alta are the finer ones being lighter in alcohol than those of the other two areas. The red wines have a wonderful bouquet and a deep rich colour and the whites are soft and smooth. Wines from Rioja Baja have a higher alcohol content than those from Rioja Alta and are more neutral to the taste.

Navarre: there are five main areas in this province all producing good wines, some being very fruity with up to 18° of alcohol; the others of lower alcohol content of around 14° have a higher acidity.

Reuda: this area produces many very good white wines that are fresh and fruity with up to 14° alcohol.

Alella: both white and rosé wines are produced; they are dry and mild.

Priovato: these are full-bodied red wines of 15°-18° alcohol that are very aromatic, dry and somewhat mild to the taste.

Ampurdan: this region produces some deep-coloured rosé wines of very good aroma and freshness that reach 14° alcohol.

Campo di Borja: these are well-rounded rosé and red wines of good alcohol content of 13°-18°.

Ribiero: light white wines are produced here; they are pale in colour and slightly fizzy; the red wines are brilliant in colour and have high acidity.

Valdeorras: this area produces white wines of high sugar content, low acidity and fine aroma. The red wines are rich in colour and have a strong aroma.

Alicante: mainly red and rosé wines having a deep colour and high alcohol content.

Jumilla: mainly red wines with good aroma and high alcohol content.

Yecla: the best-known wines from this production area are the red and rosé ones with a medium to high alcohol content and a clean flavour; also a few whites.

Almansa: dry, light, deep red and robut wines.

Valdepeñas: fresh-tasting white wines that are mildly aromatic and slightly acid; also clarets of delicate flavour and outstanding quality.

La Mancha: the most important wine-growing area of Spain; mostly white wines that are young and fruity, also clarets of ruby red clour and pleasant taste, of 12°-15° alcohol.

Manchuela: produces dry, deep red coloured wines of 11°-15° and rosé and white wines.

Mentrida: only red wines of deep colour and high tannin content are produced here.

Utiel-Requena: red wines of fine flavour and colour.

Valencia: grows dry white wines that are pale in colour and fruity in aroma; some robust ends and some dessert wines. The *rancio* wines for which this area is famous are robust and of high alcohol content.

In addition, two main types of sparkling wines are produced, the *Cava* denomination is given to those produced by the *champenoise* method and the *Granvas* to those produced by fermentation in large tanks.

Sangria is a very popular and refreshing drink that can be purchased ready-made in bottles or made up from red wine, brandy and soda water with sliced oranged, lemons, peaches and plenty of ice. It is a sweet refreshing drink for serving on hot summer days; hotels in this country feature it because so many British people have developed a liking for it whilst holidaying in Spain.

Sherry

Sherry was introduced to England in 1530 and it soon became a popular drink to the extent that more than 70 m bottles are now drunk each year. The name comes from the name the English first gave it, *Sherry Sack*, 'sack' being the Spanish *sacar* meaning wines drawn from casks for export; 'sherry' derives from Jerez de la Frontera the town where all the *bodegas* are. Jerez is *Xérès* in Latin and is the word used in French.

Two kinds of vine are grown on the chalky soil – the *Palomino de Jerez* and the *Pedro Ximénez*. The wine is blended by the *solera* system in which six or more tiers of casks are interconnected, the youngest at the top down to the oldest at ground level. As the sherry is drawn off for bottling the tiers of casks are filled from above.

There are four main kinds of sherry all of them being served as an aperitif to stimulate the appetite; sherry is also very good for adding to foods such as sauces, soups and trifle. The *Sherry Institute of Spain* recommend serving dry sherry at 6°C and adding ice cubes to the sweet ones.

Fino is very pale in colour and is light, dry and crisp on the tongue; when served chilled it is fresh flavoured. *Manzanilla* is the driest and lightest kind of dry sherry. *Amontillado* is a soft amber-coloured sherry that is medium-dry; it is more full-bodied than fino and is the best sherry to serve when using one kind only as it suits people who like their sherry dry as well as those who prefer a slightly sweeter sherry. *Oloroso* is dark golden in colour and has a full-bodied sweetness and a tang of walnuts; it is also possible to obtain dry Oloroso.

Cream sherry is very sweet and smooth to the taste and deep in colour, it is also available as *Pale Cream* and *Brown Sherry*. An *Aperitif Sherry* is also marketed as a medium light blend for mixed drinks, including cocktails. Mixer sherry is designed to be served only as a long drink with ice and tonic water.

Montilla: this wine is similar to sherry and is bottled as *fino, amontillado* and *oloroso* but is cheaper and not fortified, having an alcohol content of

13°-15°C, similar to sherry.

Malaga: this is a very sweet and dark wine which is fortified with brandy; it has a strong bouquet and may be served as a dessert wine.

Tarragona: this wine resembles port because it is very sweet and dark red but is not fortified and is not of particularly good quality.

Palo Cortado: this is a dry sherry that is slightly richer and deeper than amontillado.

Old Bottled Sherry: a few wine merchants are able to offer old bottled sherries of the *amontillado* and *oloroso* types, bearing the date of bottling, which would have improved in keeping; connoisseurs are prepared to pay twice as much as ordinary sherry to obtain a bottle.

PORTUGAL

As well as port and madeira some very good ordinary wines are produced in Portugal. The best known of all is *Mateus Rosé*, a slightly sweet, light and refreshing wine sold in an elegantly rounded bottle; it can be bought as a still wine but is better appreciated and more palatable when carbonated to give the slight sparkle. All Portugal's rosé wines are ready to drink as soon as made so they do not have the year of vintage printed on the label. *Vino verde* means a young wine that can be either white, rosé or red that is bottled soon after it is made whilst still very slightly sparkling; the alcohol content of the first two is low but the red is a much better and stronger wine. *Dâo* wines include some well-aged reds of up to ten years of age and the whites are very smooth and distinguished. *Buccelas* is the region for dry white table wines and *Colares* is a sandy vineyard that produces strong red wines that need to be aged to be enjoyed.

Ordinary table wine is called *vino de mesa* or *vino de consumo*, the better wines bear the insignis UVR which is a guarantee of their genuineness; *riserva* means a vintage wine and *garrafeira* a selected wine of some character.

Port

During the wars with France during the eighteenth century there was a shortage of French wine here so Portugal started to send Port which soon became England's favourite drink.

Port is made from sweet red wine produced in Alto Douro which is matured in oak casks until it mellows and becomes increasingly lighter in colour as it gets older. Nearly all ports are matured in wood until they are ready to drink, *ruby port* being a young one still having its original deep colour and *tawny* being an older, and lighter-coloured port. Cheap tawny port will probably be a blend of ruby and white ports. Port also matures in the bottle; this is genuine vintage port which is the blend of wine of a single year, bottled when two or three years old to be kept to mature for up to twenty years, some being kept 25–50 years before they are at their best. Late bottled vintage port is kept in the wood for six to seven years then bottled and is not rated so highly as real vintage port.

Vintage Character port is one that has been matured in the wood and is ready to drink as soon as bottled, it is similar to ruby port and there is no need to decant it. It keeps well after being opened provided it is kept corked.

Crusted port is a blend of fine young wines kept in wood until five to six years old then bottled so that it matures more quickly; during this time it will throw a crust on the side of the bottle it has been lying on. This happens to vintage ports and it is usual to paint a white splash on the bottle to show which way it has been binned, the crust being on the opposite side to the splash.

By tradition port is drunk at the end of the meal with the nuts or cheese but white port is usually drunk chilled as an aperitif.

MADEIRA

Madeira is produced on the island from which it takes its name; it is a fortified wine which differs from port and the other fortified wines in that it is cooked during the process of ageing. The casks of fortified wine are exposed to the sunshine on the island or stored and gradually heated up to 70°C which gives it a peculiar burnt taste. Madeira does not now carry a vintage year on the label.

There are four main kinds of Madeira: *Sercial* is dry and tangy, light in colour and in body, it is good for cooking: *Verdelho* is medium dry but deeper in colour and body; it is slightly sweeter than sercial. *Bual* is a rich sweet and fruity wine that is often drunk either as an aperitif or as a dessert wine. *Malmsey* is dark and very sweet so is used mainly as an ideal dessert wine and also for cooking. Other kinds include *Southside* which is a rich sweet wine, and *Rainwater* which is slightly drier.

Madeira keeps very well and does not deteriorate when opened; it is usual to serve it at room temperature although the dry kinds may be served slightly chilled.

AUSTRALIA

The soil and climate of Australia are ideal for wine-growing and an abundance of wine of all kinds is produced. Most of it is made by modern machinery which puts it in the average rather than the fine quality range, but it is all of interest.

The names used to describe the wines are the same as those used for French wines of which Australian Burgundy-type is typical.

The red wines are deep in colour and some state on the label which species of grape was used, but most of them are sold under a brand name and as either Bordeaux- or Burgundy-style. The white wines are sold as being Chablis, Mosel or Hock in style. Rosé and sparkling wines are also produced and there are some very good sherry and port wines.

Most of the best wine is drunk by the Australians so that exports, although the range is wide, are not the highest quality but with the advent of co-operatives and the growth of large companies, standards should improve and also the reputation.

New Zealand produces a small quantity of interesting wine that merits a place on the wine list even if it is labelled as claret or burgundy style.

AUSTRIA

Nearly all the wine produced in Austria is delicate and white and is bottled and drunk very young with most of it being consumed by the Austrians. *Schluck* is a well known wine and some of it is bottled under brand names; this wine is comparable with German wines but with nothing like their finesse. The two classifications are *splitzenweine* which is quality wine, and *tischeweine* which is table wine. The finest white is *Gumpoldskirchener* which is fairly heavy and sweet; *Voslauer* is the best red and two others from the Italian Tyrol, *Kalterersee* and *Santa Maddalena* are highly regarded.

BULGARIA

Some pleasant wines are made in Bulgaria and several quite cheap ones are imported, some under brand names. White, rosé, red and sparkling wines are produced and cover a wide range of tastes from light to robust.

CYPRUS

Usually only the fortified wines of Cyprus are seen here and these are mainly the sweet ones of which *Commanderia* is the best known. A lot of sherry-type wine is produced, nearly all sweet and this is the reason why the wines of Cyprus are not often found on wine lists.

GREECE

The best-known wine of Greece is *Retsina*, a dry white or rosé wine flavoured with the sap of the pine tree which gives it an usual flavour which is rather an acquired taste. The wines from the island of Samos are well known, particularly the sweet dessert wine which is used in making sorbet. The other well known dessert wine is *Mavrodaphne*. White, rosé and red wines are produced and the quality is being improved by regulations that guarantee a certain standard.

Ouzo is an aniseed-flavoured spirit that is very popular as an aperitif when mixed with water and ice. *Masticha* is a spirit made with the sap of a local tree which is drunk as a liqueur.

HUNGARY

One of the finest wines in the world is produced in Hungary. This is *Tokay*, a wine that is much prized by oenologists for its excellent quality, particularly the *Eszencia* and *Aszu* type made with five *puttonyos*, for drinking as a dessert wine.

Tokay *Aszu* contains over-ripe grapes measured into *puttonyos* which are buckets holding 13.5 kg; after being squashed the very sweet grapes are mixed with ordinary grapes and the wine is made from them. The label will state the number of *puttonyos* used in making it, the greater the number – up to six – the sweeter and more expensive it will be.

Tokay is also available without any *puttonyos* and some of it is dry but generally it is a golden-coloured dessert wine that needs to be chilled for serving but is quite drinkable at room temperature.

Another well-known Hungarian wine is *Egri Bikavér* sold under the label of *Bull's Blood*; it is a very dark-coloured and robust, dry, red wine that is good for serving with highly-flavoured dishes. Most of the wine produced in Hungary is white and much of it is sold here under brand names whose quality never varies from year to year.

ISRAEL

The standard of wines is very high and compares favourably with those of Italy. This is because they are blended wines of certain types that have consistent quality that make them well-balanced, whether white, rosé or red, sparkling or dessert, dry or sweet. There are some heavy port-type wines much favoured for kosher functions but in general the table wines are very drinkable and there is a range of choice to accompany all kinds of dishes.

ROMANIA

A varied range of wines is produced in Romania; they usually carry the name of the district rather than the grape. As this is a Latin country the wines have a certain affinity with French and Italian styles and are of better quality than those of its immediate neighbours.

RUSSIA

Wine is produced in several parts of Russia and some of the best is exported. These include white wines of varying degrees of dryness, full red wines of high alcohol content, sweet dessert wines, rosé and sparkling wines. The Russians appear to like very sweet sparkling wine and both white and red are made; sweet still red wine is also popular.

SOUTH AFRICA

Wine has been produced in the Cape for more than 300 years and exported for over 250 years. All kinds and types of wines are produced, nearly all of it by the wine-growers co-operative association known as KWV. The wines they export are of excellent quality being made with great care and each year being regarded as a vintage year because of the ideal climate. The good harvest each year means that there is no need to put the year of production on the wine label.

Many of the wines carry the name of the European wine they most resemble and the heavy reds are allowed to improve for a few years in the bottle. Sherry is made in South Africa on the same system as in Spain and is considered to be as good as the genuine Spanish because it goes through the *solera* system for some six years before bottling. Port-style wine is also produced and matured in cask for a number of years according to type and then in bottle, thus it is possible to drink South African vintage port that has had as much as fifteen years in bottle and rivals the same product from Portugal. *Muscatel* is a fortified wine suitable for drinking with any dessert and has the distinction of up to seven years in cask.

Brandy from South Africa is of fine quality, suitable to be drunk on its own; and some good liqueurs are produced perhaps the best known being *Van der Hum* which is made with tangerines and has an orangy-tangerine flavour.

207

SWITZERLAND

Most of the wine produced in Switzerland is drunk there but it is possible to purchase a selection of the better-known wines although they are fairly expensive. Nearly all the production is white wine which is dry and prickly to the palate; the best-known red wines are *Dole* and *Cortaillod*.

Switzerland is a major importer of wine even though a lot of very good wine is produced so only a little is exported. Generally speaking these wines have a clean fresh taste and are drunk whilst young and vigorous.

Neuchâtel: The white wines are made from the *Chasselas* grape and are dry and slightly sparkling when being poured from well above the glass so as to increase the bubbling effect. The best red wines are made from the *Pinot* grapes and are light in colour and quite fragrant. The best rosé wine is *Oeil-de-Perdrix*.

Vaud: this area produces nearly all white wine under the name *Dorin*, some having the name of the village added. Two quite good ones are *Clos des Moines* and *Clos des Abbayes*. Some red wine is produced.

Valais: the best Swiss wines come from this area; *Dole* is the best-known red and *Goron* is nearly as good. *Johannisberg* and *Fendant* are the two really good white wines, the former being very fragrant. *Rosé de Gamay* is a good quality wine.

UNITED STATES

Wine is produced in about ten of the States but only those from California are well known here because it is only from this State that such an abundance of good wine is exported. All kinds of grapes are grown in the region thus all kinds of wine are produced and they have been classified into the five categories as follows:

1. *Aperitif wines* - including all the types of sherry, madeira, marsala and vermouth - also in a variety of styles.
2. *white table wines* - these bear the same names as the European wines but do not attempt to imitate them closely. *Chablis, hock, moselle* and *sauternes* styles are produced and are very good but not of course up to the standard of the genuine ones.
3. *Red table wines* - these also bear the names of the European wines such as *claret, burgundy, chianti*, etc. The label also indicates the grape used in making the wine, often the year and of course, the shipper. These have a higher alcohol content but less acidity than their European namesakes.

4. *Dessert wines* – these are similar to those made in the various countries of Europe and include *malaga, muscatel, port* and *tokay*. The purely American one is *Angelica*, an intensely sweet, light-coloured wine.
5. *Sparkling wines* – some of these are made in the same way as *champagne* while other are carbonated with gas, so there is a wide range of qualities.

As the consumption of American wines increases here so will the names of the producers become better known.

YUGOSLAVIA

Yugoslavia sends us several kinds of white wines that are similar though inferior to German *tafelwein* yet are well-liked because reasonably priced. There is a sufficient variety of them to fill any gaps in a wine list especially as both the region and the grape are used in the title on the label. *Tiger Milk* is a fairly well known name for a sweet *spätlese* type of wine. Some red wines are produced but are rarely exported so the country is renowned for its sound and honest though generally unremarkable white wines, in particular the *Lutomer* and the *Cloberg Laski Rieslings*.

BRITISH WINES

The idea that British wines are inferior to those produced by say, the vignerons of France, is a myth. In fact such has been the improvement brought about in winemaking that home produced wine is excellent and only a discerning gourmet is able to tell the difference.

British wine as made by several firms and by members of wine circles is far removed from those made by our grandparents in the stillroom. This can be accounted for not so much from the use of ready-prepared ingredients, such as grape juice concentrate, as because of a greater knowledge of the chemical processes and the desire to produce top-quality wine. In fact many winemakers look upon convenience wine products rather as good chefs do on packaged soup powder. Certainly it is cheaper to produce wine from ingredients that have been gathered or grown locally. Wine circles have played a big part in bringing about improvements by holding meetings and organising competitions at which members show their wines in the many different sections.

COCKTAILS

The word cocktail is used to denote a chilled mixed drink usually made with a spirit or liqueur as a base and shaken or stirred with other ingredients to produce a short drink made to order as an aperitif. The name is supposed to have originated in New York in 1776 and the story is that the tail feathers of cocks, that used to decorate the bar at Hall's Corner were put into some of the drinks. Then they were used to mix drinks at the Cock's Tail Tavern in Yonkers in 1784 and the name stuck.

The combination of drink to form a cocktail are endless and the United Kingdom Bartenders' Guild has a file of 8000 with new ones constantly being added. Competitions are held to discover new formulas that will please the public. The popularity of the cocktail may rise and fall over the years but they never entirely lose their appeal. The fashions in cocktails change from time to time – those based on gin and vodka are always popular with rum a close runner-up. There are a number of cocktails that never lose their popularity and whose formula every bartender knows by heart; then there are those that come into fashion and are well-known only for a while and the long list of lesser-known ones that can be looked up in the reference books should they ever be requested. The recipe for a cocktail can differ from one bartender to another and from one establishment to another; they also differ in various countries of the world, not only in the ingredients but in the name. The decoration of the cocktail in the glass also varies considerably and there are no hard-and-fast rules so it is a matter of using what is available in the bar. Care must however be taken to ensure that the flavour combinations are harmonious.

SPIRITS AND LIQUEURS

Spirits are alcoholic liquors that can be made from many things such as grain, potatoes, cane syrup, fruits and wine. The liquid is distilled by heating it, so as to increase the alcoholic content and is then flavoured according to kind. Liqueurs are sweetened and flavoured spirits. In France they are usually called *digestifs* or *pousse-cafés*, because in many the soothing properties come from the use of herbs; Americans call them cordials.

Spirits are usually served before a meal, often as a mixed drink whereas liqueurs are normally for after a dinner. Old brandy and mature whisky are also served as a liqueur because they will have gained in smoothness and flavour. The colour, sweetness .and alcoholic content varies considerably between liqueurs and there are thousands of different kinds produced all over the world.

AROMATIC BITTERS

There are a number of aromatic bitters that add flavour, aroma and, to a certain extent, colour, to cocktails and other mixed drinks. A cocktail is meant to stimulate the appetite – the addition of a few drops of bitters helps by giving fragrance and flavour that assist the digestion. Bitters are made to a secret formula from various herbs and some have a basis of alcohol.

CURE FOR A HANGOVER

The true gourmet knows when he has consumed sufficient alcohol and has the willpower to refuse any more; should he inadvertently over-indulge and suffer a hangover, a soluble Vitamin C tablet taken with one or two soluble aspirins followed by a pinch of bicarbonate of soda should prove an effective cure. The old idea of having some of the 'hair of the dog that bit me' which means to carry on drinking the same stuff does not really work. It has been suggested that to avoid the possibility of getting drunk, some fizzy Vitamin C tablets chewed well in advance should help to break down the chemical structure of the alcohol.

A bartender is frequently asked to provide a pick-me-up to relieve a headache caused by over-indulgence by people who do not wish to rely on aspirins or other medicaments. There are a number of such remedies, the best known being the *Prairie Oyster* which is more a psychological than a medical remedy. It is made by putting a few drops of Worcestershire Sauce, some brandy and a tea-spoonful of tomato ketchup into a small glass, dropping a yolk of egg in without breaking it and seasoning with a sprinkling of pepper and two dashes of vinegar. It must be swallowed whole in one gulp; if liked, a few drops of bitters may be added.

VINTAGE GUIDE

Many people choose a wine by the year when it was made, in the knowledge that the weather was good and therefore a good harvest should have produced a better than average wine. The following lists summarise the vintages.

BORDEAUX – RED

1961   An excellent year; still improving and will last a long time
1962   A good year; ready for drinking
1964   Best are the St Emilion and Pomerol; ready for drinking

1966 A large vintage of good wine, and ready but good for many more years
1967 Pleasant medium wines, ready but will keep a few more years
1968 Not a good year, needs drinking
1969 A small vintage; needs drinking
1970 A very good year, keeping well
1971 An uneven vintage, the best need more time but others are ready
1972 Not a good year, and ready as not improving
1973 A large vintage mostly ready for drinking as it has balanced well.
1974 Not a very good year but a large vintage, should be drunk soon
1975 A small vintage but good wines that need storing for another ten years
1976 A large, early vintage; will not keep as well as 1975 vintage
1977 Not a very good year, wines will mature soon
1978 A good, but late vintage; good ones will keep for 10 more years, others are ready
1979 Not a particularly good year, will need to be drunk early
1980 A small vintage of poor quality yielding rather indifferent wine
1981 Some good wine with plenty of colour and finesse but not very consistent, better than the 1976 and 1979 vintages but not up to 1975 or 1978
1982 Excellent wines produced

BURGUNDY – WHITE

1970 A large vintage of good wines; ready for drinking
1971 A small but good vintage, ready but will keep
1972 Not a very good year, should not be kept
1973 A good year, mostly ready but the good wines can still be kept
1974 Not a very good vintage; needs drinking
1975 Not a particularly good year except for *Chablis*
1976 A fairly good year, ready but *Chablis* will keep well
1977 Not a good year; ready for drinking
1978 Good quality wine, the *Chablis* excellent; the clarets are developing well
1979 A fairly good year, nearly ready for drinking but light and thin, variable
1980 A small vintage of wines that will not keep; is cheaper than the 1979's. Not a great year
1981 Is maturing well
1982 A very good year

BURGUNDY – RED

1970 A good vintage which is ready for drinking
1971 A small vintage, ready but will keep well
1972 A large vintage that is good and will keep well
1973 A large but light and thin vintage that is ready for drinking
1974 Not a very good vintage as the wines lack depth and richness

1975 A very bad year
1976 A very good vintage just becoming ready for drinking
1977 Not a very good year; ready to drink
1978 A reasonably good vintage, not as good as 1976 but ready for drinking
1979 A large vintage, but patchy in quality
1980 Not a very good year and most will have to be drunk soon
1981 Better than 1980 but light and is developing well, not yet ready
1982 A very good year though not quite as good as 1983
1983 An outstanding year

ALSACE

1971 Only a small vintage but good; ready to drink
1972 Not a very good year
1973 A very good vintage and in great quantity; ready to drink
1974 Not a particularly good quality or quantity, needs drinking
1975 A very good vintage but not a very great yield
1976 A very good year and remarkable wine; will keep well
1977 Not a particularly good year and wine lack fruitiness
1978 Not a very good year; wine not yet ready
1979 A good year with a large vintage
1980 A fairly good year but not one of the better ones
1981 Nearly as good as the 1979 vintage
1982 A good but not outstandanding year

In general these wines do not improve after five years.

RHONE (RED)

The best years are 1966, 1967, 1969, 1970, 1976, 1978; those that were also good are 1971, 1980.

GERMAN

The best years are 1971, 1975, 1976, 1983

PORT

The best years are 1955, 1963, 1966, 1970, 1977, 1980
Most vintage ports need at least eighteen years to become properly matured, the great years will remain drinkable for at least a hundred years.

WINES AND FOOD

Wine is meant to accompany the food being eaten at a meal and it is useful to know what kinds of wine go with the different courses of the menu, to know the actual regions that produce these, and the names under which they are sold. The following generalisations should help:

Hors-d'oeuvre	ordinary, white, occasionally red according to whether meat or fish predominates
Smoked salmon	moselle, muscadet, alsace
Oysters	chablis, muscadet, sancerre, champagne
Caviar	vodka, champagne
Grapefruit	medium sherry
Melon	oloroso sherry
Pâté	beaujolais, alsace
Soup	dry sherry, dry madeira
Shellfish	white burgundy, alsace, chablis
White fish	moselle, meursault, hock, sancerre
Oily fish	hock, white burgundy
Veal	hock, moselle, vougeot, beaujolais
Beef	médoc, pomerol, red burgundy
Lamb	red burgundy, claret
Poultry	médoc, red burgundy, beaujolais, white rhône
Pork	hock, alsace, beaujolais
Curry	traminer-gewürztraminer
Game	pommard, côtes du rhône
Foie gras	alsace, port, sauternes, barsac, piccolit
Cheese	ruby, tawny and vintage port, st-emilion, pomerol
Sweet	sauternes, barsac, anjou rosé, hock, champagne, oloroso sherry
Dessert	tokay, port, madeira, sauternes, barsac, beumes de venise, monbazillac
Coffee	cognac, armagnac, liquers, grappa

Champagne can be served successfully throughout the meal. Sauternes and Barsac can be served as an aperitif.

Recommended serving temperatures are:

> sweet white 5°-6°C,
> young dry white 8°-10°C
> older white 10°-12°C,
> mature red wines at 17°-18°C,
> Champagne and sparkling wine 6°-8°C.

HOLDING A WINE TASTING

Matching wine with food, or food with wine, is not an easy matter and for very special occasions it is advisable to have a wine-tasting session so as to judge the attributes of a number of possible wines to select the one that best matches a particular course.

A food and beverage manager can develop his tastes and widen his knowledge of wines, and that of his staff concerned with their sale, by holding regular wine-tasting sessions but to do these in a meaningful way it is necessary to abide by a set of rules as follows:

1. Base the tasting on wines of one style but of several vintages
2. Do not taste too many wines at one tasting, certainly not more than ten
3. Do the tasting in the morning but not during a mealtime
4. Carry it out in daylight or under normal lighting
5. Taste only good quality wines
6. Taste dry before sweet, light before full-bodied, young before old wines
7. Cover up the labels so that the bottles are indistinguishable
8. Have tasting sheets available
9. Have the wines at the correct serving temperature
10. Use small capacity glasses with stems
11. Allow approx twenty tastings per bottle
12. Fill glasses less than half-full to allow for rolling it around in the glass
13. Discuss the merits of the wine being tasted with others on the panel
14. Take a good look at the wine in the glass and smell it before tasting
15. Try to name the wine and attempt a full identification
16. Do not swallow the wine; obtain its effect, then spit it out
17. Limit the number of persons at a tasting
18. Have only one bottle of each wine open at a time
19. Eat a little piece of cheese and a dry biscuit after each wine
20. Refrain from smoking whilst tasting as it reduces the effect
21. Do not let anyone with a cold in the head do any tasting

22. Examine the colour of the wine and try to describe it precisely
23. Look at the clarity then taste the bouquet and try to identify the kind of grape from which it is made
24. Take a mouthful and swill it around the teeth and tongue, savouring its acidity, weight, flavour and quality, then spit it out.

SMOKING

A cigar smoked at the end of a meal helps to make it even more of an occasion by adding an extra dimension to the total enjoyment. A good cigar that burns evenly with a long ash helps the smoker to relax after an epicurean meal. A long ash stays on a cigar made from long leaves of tobacco that are well-packed, whereas the ash drops quickly from a cheap one because the short filling disintegrates. A long cigar is usually cooler to smoke than a short one and a Havana is reckoned to be the very best, although some of the well known Cuban firms have relocated to Madeira, Central and South America where they continue to make first-class cigars. The aroma from a cigar can be as satisfying to the persons around him as it is to the smoker and smoking a cigar in female company need not be thought offensive.

It used to be considered good manners to smoke a long clay pipe to round off a meal but a *meerschaum* looks more elegant. A *hookah* which consists of a length of leather pipe connecting a *chauffoir*, tobacco holder and water vase gives a cool smoke that can be made even more exquisite by using rose-water in the vase. However it is not considered good manners to smoke a pipe at dinner. Snuff is still used by many people in place of tobacco and the protocol of snuff-taking can be graceful and act as a friendly gesture towards a stranger at a gathering.

In Victorian times, men used to like to wear a smoking jacket whilst indulging in 'the weed', possibly in order to avoid their normal jacket smelling of tobacco. A smoking jacket should not be confused with the French word *le smoking* which means a dinner jacket or tuxedo.

10 Gastronomic
Practices of Nations
and Sects

Introduction to National Cuisines – Australia – Austria – Belgium and
Benelux – Bulgaria – China – Czechoslovakia – Denmark – Finland –
France – Germany – Great Britain – Greece – Holland – Hungary – India
– Israel – Italy – Japan – Mexico – Russia – Spain – Switzerland – United
States of America – West Indies – Yugoslavia – Soul Food – Rastafarians
– Vegetarians

INTRODUCTION TO NATIONAL CUISINES

This chapter is concerned with the food and drink consumed by the different
nations of the world as part of their normal diet which, to people living outside

217

the country, would mean the speciality dishes and traditional fare of the nation. It deals with individual countries and their own distinctive cuisine or, where more appropriate, with groups of neighbouring countries which have similar dietary habits and use much the same kinds of food. Within some countries there is such great diversity that it is impossible to discuss all the regional variations in the diet and as there are more than 160 countries in the world, it is obviously impossible in the space available in this book to cover all of them, so only those that are recognised as having good culinary traditions which make some international gastronomic contributions, are included.

Each list of dishes of gastronomic note is as comprehensive as possible and an outline of these dishes is also given, but to find the recipes it will be necessary to look through the bibliography at the end of this book.

The number of people taking holidays abroad increases each year and tourism exerts a tremendous influence on every traveller in subjecting him to foreign food and drink and foreign eating habits. What tourists are given to eat and drink plays a large part in the enjoyment of their holiday and part of this enjoyment comes from eating what to them is strange food, even though they may actually be the traditional dishes of the host country. Yet how nice it is when abroad to be offered a meal that reminds one of home! After travelling around for a while seeing the sights some holiday-makers become bored with eating foreign food day after day, and are ready to welcome a change by being offered the food of their own country, always provided it is authentic, and skilfully done. But that should only be after they have savoured the local culinary delights.

The caterer must always be prepared to write a menu for a particular country; it may be at the request of foreign visitors or for a local society which wants to savour the food and wine of another country. At its simplest, it could be breakfast in the Scottish style for football fans coming off the overnight train on their way to a match at Wembley. The caterer needs to know what the menu should consist of, and be able to instruct staff on the preparation of the dishes and know sources of supply of any unusual ingredients.

The national cuisine of any country is made up of a combination of several factors. It will have evolved from the foods produced in that country, including the kind of seasonings and flavourings that most suit the people's tastes, and may have been influenced by any conquerors from abroad and any long association with alien cultures. The climate of a country will have a bearing on the nation's eating habits and on its diet. For example, the inhabitants of a tropical country will normally eat more fresh fruit, vegetables, cereals and farinaceous foods than those who live in a cold climate. The climate will have an effect upon drinking habits; where grapes are grown prolifically the wine will be cheap and the inhabitants can afford to drink it at every meal and young people will be used to it from an early age.

As stated in Chapter 1 the attitude of a country's inhabitants towards the pleasures of the table exerts an influence on its cuisine. For example, the French have devoted much more study to cookery and to the production of wine than any other nation and over the centuries they have built up a repertoire of dishes

218

that is acknowledged throughout the world, and they produce the world's finest wines. As shown later in this chapter, every region of France has its own special dishes but as a country it does not concentrate on traditional national dishes as such and it is more a matter of adapting ingredients to cooking methods and vice versa, and of preparing foods in the special French way with all the flair of a French cook.

Few national cuisines are completely free of all outside influences and any national cuisine takes hundreds of years to develop. It is therefore a slow process of evolvement, with only the occasional upheaval to the steady progress, brought about by possible foreign influences. Some of these foreign ideas may be accepted and gradually become an integral part of the national repertoire; those that are unsuitable will fail and soon be forgotten.

A country that is practically self-sufficient as regards indigenous raw materials such as France or Japan will have a purer culinary pedigree than one that has to depend upon imports of food from many foreign lands. Those few countries that do manage to remain uninfluenced by the cuisine of a neighbouring country may suffer from an impoverished diet; it will be even more stultified if there is little or no exchange of staff from other other countries. When a chef emigrates, he gives his talents to his adopted country.

Ever since the French Revolution it has been the custom for French chefs to work abroad either in the employ of a rich or noble family, in a restaurant, or in their own business. The chef obviously brings with him some of France's culinary heritage which has quite a big impact on the host country since most de luxe hotels and restaurants throughout the world have a French head chef;

Every national cuisine begins in the homes of the people and this somewhat primitive and bourgeois cookery is the basis on which a country's culinary traditions are founded. In turn this leads to the establishment of a more sophisticated class of cookery which is known as *haute cuisine* or high-class cookery.

Every country has at least two levels of cookery, that which is used in the ordinary household to provide cheap and nourishing meals and that which is used on more special occasions when expense is not so restricted. The native language is used at both levels to describe the national dishes although the upper level may use some names adopted from outside influence and which have cosmopolitan reference.

There are over 8000 restaurants, other than British and French, in this country, the largest number being Chinese, with Indian and Italian ones close behind. These are found in towns both large and small throughout the land. In addition there are 500 restaurants which serve Greek food, fifty Kosher restaurants and then the rather more rare ones, mainly in the cities (and even then often only in one of them) such as Lebanese, Thai, Moroccan, Indonesian, Armenian, Persian and a few smaller nationalities. It is possible to gain an idea of the kind of dishes served by these more specialised ethnic restaurants by perusing the menu displayed outside, or by asking or writing for a copy.

A national cuisine embraces the best of its regional dishes and the British cuisine embodies the best dishes of the three provinces that form the United

Kingdom. Not all the regional specialities may be acceptable nationally as cookery in the regions is based on local produce, for local tastes, neither of which may travel well to other regions. A national cuisine draws the best from wherever it is to be found, either accepting dishes in their original form or if necessary, modifying them for the national palate.

It is worth repeating here the important part played by authors of cookery books in a country's culinary heritage. It is their job to chronicle the cuisine of their age, correcting any ambiguities and codifying and refining it in the light of their own generation's tastes, to be handed down to successive ages. This applies very much to books written for domestic use. As that most famous gastronome of all time, **Brillat-Savarin** said so forthrightly, 'The destiny of nations rests upon the food they eat'. More recently **Albert Einstein** insisted that 'An empty stomach is not a good political adviser'.

The following is an outline of the dishes and drinks, mostly common but some uncommon, to be found in a country or group of countries. It does not claim to be comprehensive but seeks to give a résumé of the style of cuisine and details of the various foods, dishes, and alcoholic and non-alcoholic drinks that might be featured in a restaurant where the national food is served. It must be borne in mind that very strict restraints may be imposed on menu composition by the religious and ethnic practices of many countries and sects and that these must be taken into consideration when organising an event featuring a country for which little culinary information is available.

AUSTRALIA

The culinary traditions of Australasia are very similar to those of Great Britain and the pattern of meals and dishes were British in taste. They may have been modified to take account of the difference in climate and to make good use of purely local produce but have since been further changed by the arrival of immigrants from some thirty different countries.

The national repertoire has been extended to include dishes over and above the Britannic-Franco-Italian general range and the international pattern is similar to that of the other industrialised countries.

French chefs have exerted their Gallic influence on Australian menus, particularly in high-class establishments which means that French menu terms are in common use and that Australian gourmets are able to satisfy their demands for gastronomic delights; the standards are equally good whether it be a canteen meal or a recherché meal in an expensive restaurant.

As a meat-producing country Australia is well supplied with quality products and can afford to eat meat frequently, even for breakfast. The oceans surrounding it offer a wide variety of fish, so affording an extensive choice of succulent dishes.

It is a misapprehension to think of beer as the national drink of Australia as it is of England. The fine wines of the country are fully appreciated by the inhabitants.

LOCAL PRODUCE

MEAT	beef, lamb, mutton, pork, veal; offals; corned mutton; chicken, duck, turkey; game birds; rabbit; kangaroo tails,
FISH	barramundi, barracouta, carp, eel, gemfish, hapuku, John Dory, ling, salmon, salmon trout, shark, snapper, trout, tuna
SHELLFISH	crawfish, octopus, prawns, scallops, squid, trevally (caranx georgianus), yabbies (crayfish)
FRUITS	apples, apricots, bananas, cherries, citrus fruits, kiwi-fruit, melons, passion-fruit, paw paws, peaches, pears, plums, quinces, rhubarb, soft fruits
VEGETABLES	asparagus, avocados, beetroot, broad beans, broccoli, Brussels sprouts, carrots, cauliflower, French beans, leeks, marrow, okras, parsnips, pimentos, pumpkin, salad vegetables, spinach, swede, tomatoes, turnips
SPECIALITY DISHES	braised rabbit; rabbit Maryland; rabbit la trobe (stewed marinated pieces of rabbit in sour cream sauce); chicken breasts Bellinger (suprèmes stuffed with salpicon of avocado and banana, sautéed and served with orange segments and shredded zest in a sauce made from avocado and banana purées); yabbie soup (chowder-style containing local crayfish which have a strong and muddy taste); chokos in peanut sauce (peeled and seeded chokos coated with velouté flavoured with peanut butter); Pavlova (dried meringue case filled with cream and fruit); upside-down cake; carpetbag steak (rump steak filled with oysters and baked)
CHEESE	same as for Great Britain including Australian Cheddar; also Dutch, French and Italian varieties made in Australia
WINE	a plentiful selection of all qualities and varieties most of them labelled under prominent European names and having some similarity with them
SPIRITS	Crème de Bananes, Passion Fruit
BEER	Brisbane Bitter, Carlton Draught, Castlemain, Club Lager, Emu Bitter, Fosters, Old Colonial, Swan Lager, Tookey's Club, Tooth's KB

221

AUSTRIA

The culinary heritage of Austria has developed as a very refined cuisine which is mild and even in taste and with soft shades of flavour. It is at once rich and tasty but light, as exampled by the pastries which are exceptionally fine and unequalled by any other country.

For over 600 years Austria, together with Czechoslovakia and Hungary, formed the core of the Hapsburg Empire which encompassed a dozen different nationalities stretching across Europe. The influence of some of these nations is still present in Austrian cookery just as that of Austria is to be found in those of the other countries of the Empire.

Austrian chefs have altered and blended the recipes of these imported dishes to the tastes of their customers, mellowing any pungent flavours but not rendering it too bland. The only really heavy dish is dumplings which play a fairly large part as a garnish with other foods. The capital, Vienna, has exerted its influence on the food of the whole country bringing some sophistication to traditional dishes and sour cream provides a certain distinction to many dishes. Ordinary cream is also used a lot especially in cakes and coffee. Austria is famous for its cafés selling many different kinds of coffee.

LOCAL PRODUCE

MEAT	beef, pork, veal; offals; chicken; venison, wild boar
FISH	carp, eel, pike, trout
FRUIT	apples, apricots, cherries, plums
VEGETABLES	beetroot, cabbage, carrots, cauliflower, cucumber, kohlrabi, marrow, mushrooms, pimentos, red cabbage, sauerkraut
SPECIALITY DISHES	Vienna schnitzel, goulash; bauernschmaus (mixed smoked and roasted pork with sauerkraut and dumplings); beinfleisch (boiled beef); beuschel (minced lights and dumplings); sachertorte; linzertorte; apfelstrudel; marmorgugelhopf (chocolate and vanilla cake); backhendl (chicken cooked as for Vienna Schnitzel)
WINE	sold here under proprietary brand names; whites include Grinzinger, Schluck, and Sievering; reds are Voslauer, Falkensteine and Kaltersee.
BEER	Mundenham, Paracelfus, Senator, Steffl, Weizen Gold, Puntingam, Goesserbrau.

BELGIUM AND BENELUX

Belgian cookery is comprised of two main streams that reflect the two cultures – the Flemish and the French. The national cuisine is the best of both sides with French and Dutch influences contributing to a rich diet with the accent on cream and butter. Good hearty eating habits and an appreciation of good cooking are well catered for and Belgians are discriminating gourmets who enjoy their food and are prepared to devote time to this enjoyment.

There is also some influence from Germany but only those features that enhanced the already high standard have been adopted. The neighbouring countries of Luxembourg and Lichtenstein have similar standards to those of Belgium and the cookery of the Benelux countries is said to be equal to, if not better, than that of France.

LOCAL PRODUCE

MEAT	beef, horsemeat, lamb, mutton, pork, veal; goose; pheasant; rabbit, venison, wild boar
FISH AND SHELLFISH	eels, pike, river trout, sole; crayfish, lobsters, mussels, oysters, shrimps
FRUIT	black grapes (hothouse), cherries, strawberries
VEGETABLES	artichokes, Belgian endives, Brussels sprouts, carrots, celeriac, leeks, Malines asparagus, mushrooms, red cabbage, salsify, turnips
SPECIALITY DISHES	Waterzoi (fish stew similar to bouillabaisse); carbonnade flamande; lapin aux pruneaux; biche à l'Ardennaise; Ardennes smoked ham; sucking pig; pâtés; dishes garnished à la Brabanconne; waterzoi of chicken; café Liègeois (coffee ice cream with coffee syrup and whipped cream)
CHEESE	Concoyotte, Harze, Herve, Limburger, Romodou, Vettekaas
WINE	white wines similar to Moselle and hock, also some sparkling wines
SPIRITS	Elixir d'Anvers, Elixir de Spa, Kirsch, Mirabelle, Prunelle, Quetsch
BEER	Bergenbier, Diest, Gueuze, Jupiter, Kriek-Lambic, Lambic, Louvaine, Rodenbach, Stella Artois Spa water.

BULGARIA

Food is natural, wholesome and abundant so that the people of this small but fertile country are able to eat very well. The food is almost powerfully flavoured. There is a truly native cookery with the influences of neighbouring countries such as Turkey, Greece and the other Slav countries being assimilated.

That the food is wholesome is confirmed by the claim that Bulgarians live to a ripe old age and many of these centenarians suggest it is due to all the ewe's milk yoghurt they eat; this is not actually the case and heredity, sex and environment have more to do with it than diet. In the diet, raw fruit and vegetables are more associated with longevity than is yoghurt.

The Bulgarian government runs a chain of restaurants serving only special diets for people who wish to maintain good health.

LOCAL PRODUCE

MEAT	beef, lamb, mutton, pork, poultry, quails, buffalo.
FISH	carp, sturgeon, turbot, smoked mackerel
FRUIT	Morello cherries, figs, grapes, melon, peaches, strawberries, plums; walnuts are used in cooking
VEGETABLES	pimentos, cucumber, pumpkin, sauerkraut
SPECIALITY DISHES	Tarator (chilled yoghurt and cucumber soup); popara (porridge made of bread, butter, cheese and milk – eaten for breakfast); kyufte (meat balls); poor man's caviar (purée of egg-plant with onion, oil and lemon juice); yahniya ot spanak (stewed lamb and spinach); kartofi sus sirene (baked sliced potato and cheese in milk); banitza sus sirene (baked pie of layers of pastry and egg in cheese and yoghurt mixture); shichcheta (spiced skewered lamb); yoghurt; ghivetch (meat and vegetable stew with egg and yoghurt topping)
PASTRY GOODS	Prazheni filii (French toast flavoured with cinnamon and served with honey), pechena tikva (pieces of pumpkin baked with honey, lemon rind, walnuts and cinnamon)
CHEESE	Sirene (ewe's milk)
WINE	red: Gamza, Cabernet, Mavround, Melnik, Misket. white: mainly of the Riesling type of grape.
SPIRIT	Mastika (anisette), Slivova (plum brandy), Tamyanka, Priska brandy.

CHINA

It is said that the world owes more to China than to any other nation with the exception of France, for its high standard of culinary expertise. Yet the methods and ingredients used in Chinese cookery are fairly simple and lend themselves to quick preparation. The range of traditional ingredients is readily obtainable in England but even so, it is possible to substitute a similar though different item. Nor is it imperative that traditional Chinese methods of preparation be rigidly adhered to. For example a Chinese chef does all the preliminary cutting and chopping with a cleaver, no matter how fine or delicate the ingredient. Ordinary cooks' knives are perfectly suitable for doing this work as is an ordinary pan instead of a *wok*.

An authentic Chinese meal shows the great difference between the way the Chinese live and the English way of life. The eating implements are in accordance with the food as it is easier to pick up chopped or shredded food with a pair of chopsticks than it is with a fork. The lift and shovel action of eating with two long pieces of wood, plastic or ivory makes it possible to do it quite quickly and very satisfactorily.

Vegetables are far more important than meat in chinese cookery. The meat used is mostly pork but may be duck. The menu is composed of a very wide variety of dishes which are combinations of different items; dairy products are not much used and vegetable oil is the usual cooking medium. The sweet section is fairly restricted and canned cumquats and loquats presented plain or in various forms are often the limit.

Soya beans play a large part in many Chinese dishes, either in the form of oil, soya bean milk, bean curd and soya bean sprouts. Soya sauce is used to give flavour to many dishes, including meat. Many different spices besides ginger are used. Pasta is said to have originated in China and taken to Italy by Marco Polo, and many shapes and sizes are used in Chinese cookery.

The Chinese set high quality standards for each traditional dish which must be maintained. The points to consider when preparing a meal are colour, texture, flavour, harmony and variety.

The most popular method of cookery is to **stir-fry** which is to put the food, cut into small pieces, into hot shallow oil and to cook each ingredient separately and evenly by stirring it so as to achieve a crisp but not fatty result. The ingredients are then combined as required. The wok is used to do much of the cooking because it gives even distribution of heat and makes it easy to carry out the stir-fry method. Seasonings are sugar, soy, monosodium glutamate and Chinese sherry, the sugar being used to offset any saltiness in foods.

There are two main systems of service: (i) a succession of courses consisting of appetisers, rice and the various main items served successively and finishing with the soup, and (ii) a pan of hot liquid is heated in the centre of the table and the diner selects from a tray the items he would like, placing them in the simmering liquid on a strainer, each person doing this in turn and getting on with the meal. Finally, the cooking liquid is served out as the soup.

There are four gastronomic regions in China:

1. **Peking**: noodles, pancakes, dumplings and other farinaceous foods are much used; fairly bland taste;
2. **Shanghai**: braised dishes served with thick, pungent soy sauces; mainly fish dishes; much rice; quite highly seasoned dishes;
3. **Szechwan**: hot spicy food using garlic and ginger; rice with everything, mushrooms much used; ham dishes; noodles;
4. **Canton**: this is the cuisine that is used in most Chinese restaurants everywhere; sweet-and-sour dishes; meatballs; dumplings; steamed, lightly seasoned dishes; pork dishes.

It should be borne in mind that ideally meals should be for between six and ten people sitting at the same table, offering a range of small dishes for 'self-service' to create a harmonious whole.

LOCAL PRODUCE

MEAT	lamb, pork; bacon, ham; chicken, duck; pigeon, quail; field mice, lizards
FISH AND SHELLFISH	carp, herring, minnows, perch, red snapper, sea bream, sea bass, shad, sturgeon, tuna; clams, crab, lobster, mussels, oysters, shrimps, squid; shark's fin
FRUIT	cumquats, custard apples, dates, figs, grapes, lily seed, loquats, lychees, mango, papaya, passion fruit, persimmons, watermelon
VEGETABLES	asparagus, bamboo shoots, banana squash, black beans, broccoli, chayote, Chinese leaves, cucumber, egg-plant, ginger root, pimento, lily root, lotus root, mung beans, mushrooms, okra, snow peas, spring onions, tomatoes, water chestnuts, white radish, yams
SPECIAL INGREDIENTS	bean curd, sesame oil, soya beans, pickled vegetables, bird's nests, betal nuts, watermelon seeds, cockroaches, thousand year eggs (duck eggs treated with ashes, salt and lime and buried for several months), egg rolls, dumplings stuffed with various fillings, noodles, pearl balls (pork and water chestnut mixture rolled in rice and steamed), shark's fin soup, bird's nest soup, sweet and sour pork, barbecued spareribs, prawn egg fu yung (egg pancakes containing prawns, bean sprouts and mushrooms served with soy sauce), dim sum (small dumplings with various fillings)
WINE	shao hsingfu (yellow rice wine), kaoliang, shaoshing, liao pan
BEER	Orion

226

CZECHOSLOVAKIA

The food of Czechoslovakia is simply, tasty and very substantial because the people love their food and eat plenty of it. The country is fertile and produces excellent quality foodstuffs which the housewives and cooks know how to use to the full. As part of the old Austro-Hungarian Empire, Czechoslovakia, or Bohemia as it is sometimes known, received some of its culinary traditions from Vienna and this has resulted in a certain sophistication of the household formulas of the Czechs who use sour cream, fresh cream and butter in the finishing of dishes. Dumplings, both savoury and sweet, are a popular feature of the country's food traditions; fish is mostly the fresh-water varieties and is plainly cooked without sauce. Czechoslovakia is not noted as a wine-producing country and does not make enough to export.

LOCAL PRODUCE

MEAT	beef, pork, veal; chickens, geese; game birds, venison
FISH	carp, pike, salmon-trout, trout; crayfish
FRUIT	apricots, apples, blackberries, cherries, plums, strawberries
VEGETABLES	cabbage, carrots, celery, mushrooms, sweetcorn, tomatoes, sauerkraut
SPECIALITY DISHES	Prague ham (eaten raw); parky (Prague frankfurt sausages); smoked ox tongue; goulash; svestkove Knedliky (dumplings with a prune inside); kure po plzensku (chicken cooked in beer with sultanas); rye bread, pickled gherkins, topinky (fried bread with garlic)
CHEESE	bryndza, pivni syr, zlato
WINE	Chateau Melnik, Starovezna, Griotte
BEER	Brodñanka, Budvar, Martinsky, Pilsen Urquell, Prazanka, Tatran
SPIRIT	griotte, slivovice, starovezna, vodka

DENMARK

The Danes eat well and are regarded as being good trenchermen who know how to enjoy the products of their country to the full. Food is plentiful and the diet is rich but bland rather than over-seasoned because the Danes are a conservative race and have not accepted much outside influence. The pleasures of the table include the food, the ambience and the accoutrements and are much stressed in the home, even though the food may be simply cooked and the pattern of living, thrifty. The Danes love to discuss their food with the result that every meal is of note and worthy of discussion with friend or stranger.

Sauces play a big part in Danish cookery and their extent and quality rival those of France. Potatoes are served at every main meal but other vegetables are not so important.

LOCAL PRODUCE

MEAT	beef, pork; chicken, duck, geese, turkey; game birds, venison
FISH	cod, eel, herrings, plaice; dried cod, oysters, shellfish
FRUIT	apples, blueberries, cloudberries, lingenberries
VEGETABLES	beans, carrots, celeriac, leeks, mushrooms, red cabbage, white cabbage
SPECIALITY DISHES	Køldbord (help-yourself hot and cold buffet of up to fifty fishes); smørrebrød (open sandwiches); kroanretning (various hot fillings on rye bread); fruit soups; pickled herrings; smoked eel; smoked salmon; fishballs; frikadellar (pork meat balls); stribet flaesk (belly of pork), stegt gas gylat med svedsker (roast goose stuffed with prunes); salami; Dyrerya (saddle of venison); flavourings used include cumin and horseradish
PASTRY	Danish pastries, pumpernickel, rye bread
CHEESE	Danablu, Esrom, Molbo, Mycella, Samsoe, Danbo, Tybo, Fynbo, Havarti, Danish Camembert and Brie
WINE	Imported
SPIRIT	Aquavit, Cherry Brandy
BEER	Carlsberg Lager, Faze Fad, Nanok, Skibsøl, Tuborg Lager

FINLAND

The Finnish cuisine has been influenced by both Russia and Sweden but still maintains a distinctive flavour of its own. Being a country of lakes and forests, fish and venison feature prominently but perhaps the most distinctive feature is the use of many kinds of berries. These are used in most courses of the menu, often as accompanying compotes and they add a great deal of interest especially

228

to fish and meat dishes; they are also used in soups and sweets. Several liqueurs and spirits are based on these different kinds of soft fruits and they are also made into jams which are often served with main dishes.

LOCAL PRODUCE

MEAT	beef, pork, veal; ham; chicken; bear, elk, reindeer, venison; smoked reindeer tongue
FISH	bream, eel, herrings, lamprey, perch, salmon, trout, white fish
VEGETABLES	beetroot, cabbage, carrots, cauliflower, cucumbers, mushrooms, peas, tomatoes
FRUIT	cloudberries, whortleberries and many other kinds of soft fruit
PASTRY	kera (pancakes with cloudberry sauce), mustikkapürakka (bilberry tart), ohukaisia lakkahillon (cloudberry pancakes), rye bread
SPECIALITY DISHES	voileipia (the Finnish name for smorrebrød); siikas ja munakokkelia (white fish with scrambled egg); roast bear; poronpaisti (reindeer steak); gravelax (marinated salmon); dill, cardamom and juniper are used in flavouring
BEER	Amiraali, Finlandia, Karjala, Olvi, Simnen
WINE	imported
SPIRITS	Advocaat, Aquavit, Jalovino, Lakka (cloudberry), Mesimarja (honeyberry liqueur), Polar liqueur, Schnapps, Suomuurain, Tapio, Vodka

FRANCE

It is generally accepted that the French take a greater interest in food than any other nation and that they enjoy good cooking and possess an educated palate which they constantly try to improve. French people eat out far more often than do most other nationalities, and are prepared to pay out a large proportion of their income on doing so, provided they receive pleasure and satisfaction and get value for money.

The general view of French cookery is that it is rich and elaborate and uses only the finest ingredients and a liberal amount of butter, cream, eggs, wine and spirits in order to achieve a sensuous result. In fact, the secret of French cookery lies in an appreciation and understanding of food and cooking processes so as to obtain the maximum benefit from quite ordinary commodities.

A good French chef has the flair to take full advantage of the intrinsic qualities of everything he uses without recourse to a wide range of flavourings, and
seeks to bring out the essential values contained within the foods. Economy and
ingenuity are used to obtain the best results from the finest products of the
country, whether cultivated under glass or naturally.

Food is therefore one of the major preoccupations of life and the French
repertoire abounds with gastronomic delights, every region having it own special
dishes using mostly local ingredients, dishes that stem from traditional french
domestic cookery. The main repertoire is now used internationally and the
following brief details are given as a guide to the cookery of the important
regions together with an outline of some of the notable wines produced in these
areas. There are thirty-four regions in France, sixteen of which are noted for
their food, but only ten of the areas have been dealt with here in depth. France
is fortunate in that its gourmet clientele realises that it is sometimes necessary to
avoid excesses and to exert restraints when fashion and the pundits so decree.
This has been evidenced by the recent revival of *cuisine nouvelle* and *cuisine
minceur* in which fattening ingredients such as starchy foods and cream have
been deleted and sublimate alternatives used, whilst still adhering to the fundamentals of cookery.

LOCAL PRODUCE

MEAT	beef, goat, lamb, mutton, pork, veal; Bresse chickens, Rouen-naise ducks, goose, guinea fowl, turkey; partridge, pheasant, pigeons, quails, wild ducks; venison, wild boar
CHARCUTERIE	andouilles, andouillettes, boudins, confits, foie gras, quenelles, rillettes, rillons, terrines; pâtés – de campagne (coarse and crumbly), de foie (smooth, made from livers of chicken, duck, beef and pork), of chicken, duck, goose, turkey, etc. (the words pâté and terrine usually mean the same, the word terrine meaning the dish a pâté is cooked in); saucissons – dried sausages (usually eaten raw)
FISH AND SHELLFISH	anchovies, carp, cod, dried cod, eels, hake, herrings, monkfish, perch, pike, salmon, sardines, sea bass, sole, tuna, trout, turbot, whiting; frogs' legs; crab, cockles, crayfish, lobster, mussels, oysters, scollops, shrimps, snails
FRUIT	apples (Golden Delicious, Red Delicious, Granny Smith), apricots, cherries, figs, grapes, kiwi-fruit, lemons, melons (Charentais, Jericho, Ogen), peaches, pears (guyot, William, Beurre hardy, Conference, Comice, passe crassane), plums, raspberries, strawberries (gorella, Cambridge favourite, belrubi, Redgauntlet)

VEGETABLES	artichokes, asparagus, beetroot, broad beans, cabbage, carrots, cauliflowers, celeriac, celery, chard, chicory, courgettes, choucroute, egg-plants, French beans, lamb's lettuce (mache), leeks, marrow, pimentos, pumpkin, sorrel, spinach, tomatoes, turnips; cépes, morels, mushrooms, truffles
APERITIFS	Amer Picon, Byrrh, Dubonnet, Kir, Lillet, Pernod, Ricard, St Raphael, Suze
SPIRITS	Absinthe, Armagnac, Calvados, Cognac, Eaux-de-Vie, Marc, Mirabelle, Negrita Rum
LIQUEURS	Apry, Aurum, Bénédictine, Cassis, Chartreuse, Cointreau, Cordial Médoc, various Crèmes, Curaçao, Grand Marnier, Noyau, Parfait Amour, Prunelle, Ratafia, Triple Sec, Vielle Curé
BEERS	Adelscott, Champigneules, Kanterbrau, Kronenbourg, La Meuse, Pelforth
WATERS	Badoit, Contrex, Evian, Perrier, Vichy, Vittel, Volvic

Cheese

Cheese plays an important part in the menus of France and **Brillat-Savarin** suggested that cheese is the foremost among desserts. This is certinaly the case in France as can be illustrated by the fact that there are 2000 different brands of Camembert alone, made in nearly every region, each with its own label. Yet the very best ones still come from Normandy where it was originally made.

France produces more kinds of cheese than any other country in the world and it is probably for this reason that the range of sweet dishes is rather limited with many being bought in from the local bakery rather than made in the kitchen. For hundreds of years, cheese played a more important part than meat in the diet, a good joint of meat being used only on special occasions. Even today the French eat a total of 12 kg of cheese a year each so the cheese course is an important part of the meal. Fig. 10.1 shows the best known French cheeses with their region of origin. Every region produces other special cheeses which are not exported.

FIGURE 10.1

THE BEST-KNOWN FRENCH CHEESE WITH THEIR REGION OF ORIGIN

Name	*Region of Origin*
Beaufort	Savoy
Bleu d'Auvergne	Auvergne
Bleu de Bresse	Franche-Comte
Brie de Coulommiers	Ile de France

231

Brie de Meaux	Ile de France
Camembert	Normandy
Cantal	Auvergne
Carré de l'Est	Champagne
Comté	Franche-Comté
Fondu aux Raisins	Savoy
Fourme d'Ambert	Auvergne
Livarot	Normandy
Picadon	Languedoc
Pont l'Eveque	Normandy
Reblochon	Savoy
Roquefort	Aquitaine
Saint-Nectaire	Auvergne
Saint-Paulin	in several regions
Tome de Savoie	Savoy

In addition there are the fresh cream cheeses such as Boursin, Demi-Sel, Petit Suisse and Rondelle.

Burgundy

The wines of Burgundy are very distinguished but so is the cookery of this important region which is very opulent. It is natural to expect that wine is used in many regional dishes not only in the well known *Coq au Vin* but in soups, sauces and sweets as well.

The snails of Burgundy feature prominently as an hors-d'oeuvre but according to the local gourmets they are at their best during their time of hibernation from November to April. After three or four hours cooking the snails are ready to be returned to the shells and filled with Burgundy butter. *Gougères* are served before a meal or as a first course, they are small *choux* buns made with diced Gruyére cheese.

Amongst the famous fish stews of France, Burgundian *meurette* is held in high esteem. It requires live fish such as eel, carp and pike cut into pieces and cooked in red Burgundy with the possible addition of some Burgundian *marc*. The *pauchouse* is another fish stew, using white wine.

For a typical Burgundian main course, the *Potée* is a boiled dinner of salt belly of pork with a wide selection of vegetables possibly including haricot beans, cooked with it. *Boeuf Bourguignon* is made of cubes of beef stewed in red wine and *Coq au Vin* is a brown stew of chicken also cooked in red wine which should be thickened with the blood of the chicken. All forms of poultry and game birds and animals can be cooked in the Burgundian style and are very popular.

Cream does not play a big part in Burgundian cookery but mustard does, mainly because Dijon is the centre of its production and there are so many different varieties of such good quality that they deserve a better place than on the edge of the plate.

The *Confrèrie des Chevaliers du Tastevin* was formed in 1934 to promote the wines of France and of Burgundy in particular. A *tastevin* is the wine cup used to sip wines in order to savour their qualities. It is usually made of silver 85 mm in diameter, to be worn around the neck on a ribbon; the small amount of wine is poured in and swilled around to liberate the aroma and show the colour before a mouthful is taken and holding it to bring out the full flavour. It is considered a great honour to be created a *Chevalier*, and to attend the reunions and many great men and women are proud to be members of this *confrèrie*.

Kir originated in Dijon and is named after Canon Kir, the deputy-major of the town, who popularised this refreshing aperitif. It is a mixture of *cassis* which is blackcurrant juice and *Meursault, Mâcon* or *Pouilly-fuissé*, both the juice and the wine being produced locally. *Kir Royale* is made with champagne.

Normandy

The cookery traditions of this fertile region stem from its rich soil, its rivers and streams and from the sea. Normandy is said to be 'the farmyard of France', and milk, cream, cheese, butter and eggs play a dominant part in its simple cookery. Other local products are cider, tripe, *andouilles* and fish from both sea and river, thus there is a rich variety of foods that ensures a wide repertoire of dishes to satisfy the most demanding gourmet.

Among the fish specialities is the *Chaudrée* also known as *Bouillabaisse Normande* and the *Demoiselles de Cherbourg* which may be either small lobsters or very small crayfish; other local fish are brill, conger eel, eel, dab, lemon sole, mackerel, skate, sole, trout, turbot, whiting and John Dory. *Matelote* is very often made with eel, using cider to moisten it and is a *marmite* of fish which, like *bouillabaisse*, can be eaten as a soup and as a main course. Fish cooked in the Normandy style is popular as are those garnished *à la Dieppoise, Havraise* and *Honfleur*.

The lambs of Normandy are reared on pastures near the sea where the aromatic nature of the grass gives a special flavour to the meat. Offals are widely used in Normandy and *Tripe à la Mode de Caen* is a very well-known dish. It is given a long cooking time, at least ten hours in a moderate oven. There are many other local ways of cooking tripe as well as ears, trotters and heads of lamb and veal.

The *andouillettes* and *boudins* of this region are well known, the former deserving of the accolade of the *Association Amicale des Amateurs d'Andouillettes Authentiques*, a society founded in 1958 by Monsieur Francis Amenategui to pronounce on those sausages that are of high quality. *Boudins noirs* and *boudins blancs* are other specialities. A Rouennaise duck is killed by suffocation which leaves the blood inside and is therefore used for *Canard à la Presse* and *Canard au Sang*. Chickens are used in many ways including *Poulet*

233

Vallée d'Auge in which local apples and cider are used. Geese, guinea fowl and game birds and animals are also widely used.

The best Camemberts come from Normandy and are made with fresh rather than pasteurised milk; the other real Normandy cheeses include Livarot, Neufchatel, Petit-Suisse, Pommel and Pont l'Eveque.

The local liqueur is *Calvados*, a spirit made from cider and there are many brands. The 'trou normand' is the name given to a small glass of *calvados* taken midway through the meal, in place of a sorbet; the well known *Bénédictine* is made at Fécamp in this region.

Champagne

Champagne can be used in all kinds of dishes, for marinating, deglazing, in sauces, and in sweets. It might be thought that this applies particularly to the region where this marvellous wine is produced but in fact the cookery of this part of France is as varied as in any other and wine is not a strong feature of it. Apart from the wines, not much other produce is natural to this area so that local chefs have always had to make the best use of limited resources. This means that although the food is very good, the local repertoire is limited in scope so it uses the dishes from its neighbours to extend the menu. As in other regions the true recipes of Champagne are derived from domestic cookery, being upgraded by the chefs to the high standards of today.

As in most other regions, Champagne has its own version of a soup cum main course this being the *Potée Champenoise* of boiled salt belly of pork and ham, with haricot beans and sufficient vegetables to make a full meal. The most famous of all French Soups, *Soupe à l'Oignon*, here assumes a high-class tone by being made with port and champagne.

Champagne, either still or sparkling, can be used in all the shallow-poached fish dishes and it can be used in making a court-bouillon for crayfish and for matelotes. Perch, pike, trout and salmon-trout, bass and sole and of course, nearly all the shellfish and snails are splendid when cooked in champagne.

The most widely-used menu term is *Sainte-Ménéhould* which can be applied to the cooking of pig's trotters equally as to a veal cutlet. **Escoffier** gives the recipe as 'the boned cooked trotters or ears, smeared with mustard, dipped in melted butter then covered in breadcrumbs and grilled'; a spicy sauce and a dish of mashed potatoes are the usual accompaniments but it would appear that the mustard is optional. In some recipes the meat is dipped into the reduced cooking liquid then coated with crumbs and grilled.

Of course, the word *Champenoise* appears against several items on the menu which would indicate that champagne is one of the ingredients. It can be used with all kinds of meat, poultry and game, in fact the *Comité Interprofessionel du Vin de Champagne* which is the controlling body of champagne production, takes on a public relations role in issuing recipes that can be made with their wine. These are of course, very high class such as truffles in champagne – and

234

just think of sauerkraut cooked in it! But it is the sweet dishes made with this most delectable wine are really outstanding.

Alsace Lorraine

This is one of the most outstanding gastronomic regions of the entire country being richly endowed with all manner of good ingredients and wonderful wines. It is almost enough to say that this is the real home of *foie gras*. Cream goes into nearly everything from the soups to the delicious pastries, including the famous *quiche Lorraine*, though it is often made with milk. There is also a *tourte Lorraine* with very thin marinated slices of pork and veal cooked in it, the egg and cream mixture being poured through a hole in the pie crust about fifteen minutes before the *tourte* is done. There is even an **Order of Quiche-Tasters** founded in 1969 to maintain the quality and reputation of the product.

Another great dish of this region is *sauerkraut*, and *Choucroute Alsacienne* is one of the great dishes of the world, yet is easy to prepare and does not cost much to make. The cabbages are grown in a closely defined area and are cultivated solely for making into *choucroute*.

Foie gras is now produced in many other countries but it was in Strasbourg during the mid-eighteenth century that a chef named **Close** first made the enlarged goose livers into a pie, mixing into them some truffles that converted what had been a fairly ordinary commodity into one of the most sought-after dishes all over the world. *Foie gras* is made in many forms and with all kinds of livers but the genuine *pâté de foie gras* is still the best of them all.

The various matelotes of fish and *potées* of meat are features of the region, there being a *Matelote Alsacienne* as well as a *Matelote Lorraine*, both using the same kinds of fish. Needless to say the *potée* is also duplicated but with hardly any difference between the two versions.

The other fish used here are bream, carp, eels, perch, pike, salmon, tench, trout and frogs' legs; crayfish are caught locally. Beer is very popular in Alsace-Lorraine and is used in cooking as with *Carpe à la Bière*. *Carpe à la Juive* is a local dish but must not be confused with Jewish *gefiltefisch* in which the carp is made into a purée. Offals play a large part in the meat section with delectable recipes to transform them into high-class dishes. Many of the game dishes have *sauerkraut* cooked in with them as the garnish; the garniture *Strasbourgeoise* typifies the most popular products being comprised of *sauerkraut*, slices of *foie gras* and pieces of boiled bacon, but as previously stated, cream also plays its part in these fish and meat dishes. There is some German influence on the cooking of this region and some of the names on the menu are still in that language. The pastries are exceptionally good with giant size fruit flans, rich cakes, filled pancakes and the famous *rum baba* which was created by the King of Poland when living in the area. It was based on the recipe for *Kougelhopf* which he remembered from his native town of Lvov in Poland.

The wines of Alsace-Lorraine are produced from the *Sylvaner, Pinot blanc, Auxerrois, Riesling, Muscat, Tokay d'Alsace* and *Gewurztraminer* grapes which are grown along the banks of the Rhine. These are all white wines and only a rosé is produced from the *Pinot noir* grapes. The grapes are left to mature until mid-October and the resultant wines are very distinguished and have a lovely bouquet.

This region is also known for a number of *eaux-de-vie* made from such fruits as raspberries, strawberries, plums, pears and cherries. The liqueurs of this area are based on blackcurrants, mirabelle plums, pears, strawberries, bilberries and raspberries.

The Nord

This is the region north of Paris that lies towards the borders with Belgium and Luxembourg. It is an area of good sound cooking for hearty appetites, while making the best possible use of local produce. The weather here is quite different from that of the south of France and the way of life is therefore more austere but this does not apply to the table and this region is the home of many gastronomic delights. It is an industrial region of mines and factories and of vast fields growing sugar beet but the people who work in these places have a cultivated palate and demand well-cooked and abundant meals even though they wash them down with local beer because no wine is produced hereabouts.

There is a Belgian influence as can be seen in the *hochepots* and *waterzois* and in some of the ingredients in common use on both sides of the border. Fish from the Channel ports of Boulogne and Dunkirk are used in making the soup-cum-main course type of dish known here as *caudrée* or *caudière*. As in most other regions the *potée* acts as a soup then as the main course of meat and vegetables. Cherries cooked in red wine make a soup that is popular in all parts of this area. A speciality is the *flamiche*, a shallow pie of various vegetables in an egg custard mix covered with a pastry lid; there are many versions of it. A *goyère* is the local version of a *quiche*. Local fish of many different kinds are prepared in the styles of Boulogne, Picardy, Abbeville and Dunkirk, with mussels as the main kind of shellfish.

Many of the recipes bear similar names to those of Belgium – *carbonnade* is made in exactly the same way but uses local beer and many other things including rabbit are made as for *carbonnade* and are cooked *à la Flamand*. Instead of *coq au vin* as done in many other regions, here, it becomes *coq à la bière*.

Many items of game, including wild boar, are used but for everyday use it is more likely to be rabbit and the region can be proud of the many ways in which they are prepared, including *gibelotte* which is stewed rabbit, and rabbit with prunes and sultanas. Some of the regional dishes use cream for finishing a stew or a sauce and the *waterzoi* of chicken is finished with it. Garlic is included in many dishes.

Red cabbage, Belgian endives, beetroot, salsify and chicory are the main

236

vegetables; the garnish, *flamand*, consists of carrots, hearts of cabbage, turnips and pieces of boiled bacon. The sweets are mainly flans and *gâteaux*.

Paris

As the capital city and the centre to which young cooks gravitate to complete their training and advance their prospects, Paris is a gastronomes' paradise and its thousands of restaurants embrace the cookery of all regions and nationalities.

There is no true Parisian cookery nor any special regional dishes. Before the spread of urbanisation, the area of the Ile de France around Paris produced all the ingredients needed to supply the restaurants that give Parisian cookery their pre-eminence. Although these districts no longer provide the ingredients, their names will go down to posterity as they were included in the culinary repertoire as meaning a particular item of food. They include *Argenteuil* for asparagus, *Chantilly* for cream, *Clamart* and *Saint-Germain* for peas, *Crécy* for carrots, *Montreuil* for peaches and *Montmorency* for cherries.

Paris is really the melting-pot of culinary expertise whence all that is good has emanated and where most of the classical dishes were created. A dish denoted as being *à la Parisienne* is really one of those names like **Lucullus** or gastronome that can be interpreted as anything that is really high-class. These are the dishes that epitomise the glories of the French culinary art with Paris as the fountain-head from which these marvellous creations flowed. Eating in the restaurants of Paris – no matter of what category – can be a richly rewarding experience; while embracing every conceivable kind of restaurant, it sets its standards of excellence even in the emporiums of '*cuisine express pour gens pressés*' or fast food bar. To try to encapsulate this mainstream of cookery is difficult but can be a very rewarding study.

Brittany

The people of Brittany are supposed to feel themselves to be a race apart by being isolated in this corner of France. The image from a gastronomic viewpoint is that the local repertoire is limited in extent because there are few high-class ingredients and the cooking methods are plain.

But there exists a large number of fine traditional dishes which have been handed down over the centuries; they cover all kinds of ingredients and methods and many are completely different from any other region of France.

Needless to say, fish plays an important part in the diet and the *bouillabaisse* type of soup and stew is exemplified in the *cotriades, daubes, matelotes* and a fish *pot-au-feu*. The liquid is served as a soup onto slices of bread and the fish together with potatoes and a garnish is served as the main course. All the many kinds of shellfish are used in a number of ways with perhaps a dozen different recipes for lobsters, the most famous being *Homard à l'Américaine*, here called *à l'Amoricaine*, because this part of the coast is called *Amorique* and the dish was one used by Breton fishermen. Actually there is hardly any difference between the way both dishes are prepared and the customer would accept either as *Homard Américaine*; even the *Academie Culinaire* has not come to a conclusion as to whether they are the same or different. Many kinds of sea-fish are used, particularly conger eels; the garnish *Bretonne*, is made of shrimps, capers and gherkins when used with fish; when applied to meat dishes it is made of haricot beans. Many of the towns lend their names to local dishes including *Nantes, Quimper, Saint-Malo* and *Brest*.

Sweets consists of filled pancakes, flans, *gâteaux* and doughnut-type fritters.

Lyon

The province of Lyonnais – and in particular its capital the City of Lyon – is considered to be the centre of gastronomy of France as it is here that all that is most delectable in French cookery is to be found, its reputation being higher than that of Paris. As with anywhere else in the country, the standard of cookery stems from the use of local produce and the quality here is high, as it is surrounded by the region of Burgundy. Bresse which is famed for its specie of chicken, and Charolais which gives its name to a famous breed of cattle, are close by. Some of the well-known chefs-patron have their establishments in Lyonnais and their menus show the expert way they deal with local commodities and render them into exquisite dishes, so this area is sought out by gourmets from all over the world as the Mecca of gastronomy.

There are many local specialities, *quenelles* of fish, chicken or veal being very popular because they are made of a rich mixture that makes the basic ingredient go further yet lend themselves to a range of sauces and garnishes and are very easy to eat. The range of charcuterie items is probably wider here than anywhere else in France and this includes local hams, some raw and smoked and others cooked; the *rosette de Lyon* is a salami-type sausage, one of many that make a great contribution to the local cuisine.

Amongst the better known dishes are *Gratinée Lyonnaise* which is a thickly garnished soup of onions, *gougères* which are cheese profiteroles, *pochouse* – a fish stew, *coq au vin, boeuf bourguignon* and *boeuf à la mode*.

Provence

The Provencaux eat modestly and are content to eat little, even a crust of bread dipped in olive oil being considered acceptable. Even the aromatic smell of a traditional meal of this region makes it different from one prepared anywhere else yet this is brought about only by the use of olive oil, garlic and a few herbs.

The recipes used are straightforward and are intended to make the best possible use of the ingredients of the dish rather than seeking to disguise them; a harmonious result is the aim.

These basic flavours are combined in *aioli*, a sauce widely used in Provençale recipes with garlic replacing the ubiquitous onion as used elsewhere. It is made by pounding garlic from which the germ has been removed, adding egg yolks and salt then olive oil, drop by drop, so that it develops the consistency of a sauce. If it becomes too thick a little warm water or lemon juice should be added. It is meant to be eaten with any kind of freshly cooked vegetable or pulse, hard-boiled eggs or salt cod.

Most Mediterranean countries use olive oil but it plays a more important part in Provence than anywhere else. For example, it is said that a good soup can be made simply by adding oil to boiling water but the famous *aigo boulido* is even easier – some crushed cloves of garlic, sage, thyme, bayleaf and seasoning are added to hot water and this liquid is poured over slices of bread sprinkled with oil to constitute a soup. The three flavours – of herbs, garlic and oil – serve to enhance the main items and there is an exact herb to match each kind – fennel for fish, juniper for game and beef, cloves for fish and beef, rosemary for lamb and mutton, saffron for fish and tripe, savory for dishes with tomatoes in them, and sage for pork and, of course, for *aigo boulido*. Thyme is used for rabbit, fresh basil with tomatoes and dried orange rind for certain sauces and fish dishes.

Olives are used in cooking with both fish and meat; *poutargue* made from the roes of the grey mullet is much appreciated and anchovies play an important part mainly as *anchouiada* which is added to stews and grills of meat and chicken. To make *anchouiada*, anchovy fillets are crushed with a little garlic, shallot and thyme into warm olive oil, then a few drops of vinegar and the sauce is made. *Bagna Cauda* is used as a dip for various crudités at the start of a meal and is a feature of this coastline, right into Italy as far as Genoa. Here it is almost the same as the *anchouiada*.

Provence is the region for *bouillabaisse* which is a speciality of Marseilles because to make it authentically requires the various kinds of fish landed there. *bourride* is a similar soup-cum-fish dish.

Daube de boeuf, carbonnade of mutton made with white wine rather than beer, *oiseaux-sans-tête* and stuffed maws, from which haggis is descended, are specialities of Provence and help to make this a very distinctive cuisine.

Bordeaux

This region is second only to Lyon in its love and appreciation of good food and wine and it is not the fact that the region produces the finest wine in the world that has brought the food of the region to a similar high standard. An abundance of good food is available. The sea, the rivers and the fertile land yield a wide variety of fish and shellfish including local oysters. There are sheep from the salt marshes near the coast, as well as poultry and game and many kinds of small birds, and a plentiful supply of butter and cheese plus the truffles from nearby Perigord and local *foie gras*. Not far away lie the Cognac and Armagnac areas which produce the best brandies in the world. Many dishes bear the designation *à la Bordelaise* which indicates that claret is used in the cooking; it is applied to many fish and shellfish dishes, to chicken, duck and wild duck, and to meat, particularly grilled or shallow-fried sirloin steaks. Pauillac in Bordeaux is well-known for its fine wines including three that are *Crus hors Classe* but also gives its name to a small milk-fed lamb that is featured on the menu as *Agneau de Pauillac*, and usually plainly roasted.

The oysters of Marennes, near Bordeaux are the well known *Portugaises*, perhaps not as large and full of flavour as the English natives or as *belons* which are the best French oysters, but are very juicy and quite acceptable. Bordeaux has its own *chaudrée* of fish, served with fried croutons rubbed with garlic and also a stew of local mussels, flavoured with saffron.

The black truffles of Perigord are famous above all others for their deep colour and exquisite aroma and are the most expensive commodity used in catering. The jet-black colour adds a distinctive finishing touch to very many dishes and the taste and aroma they impart to any dish that demands their inclusion, is superb. Truffles are in season in the region from November to March and the freshly dug ones are served 'sous la cendre' in which they are wrapped and baked in charcoal.

GERMANY

Germany is made up of several different regions which were once countries in their own right; this means that there are distinctive regional methods of cookery and eating patterns from one part of the Republic to another.

The general image of German cookery is that it is heavy and well-seasoned, that portion sizes are large and the taste overpowering. This is no longer completely true and the obese German is an out-of-date character for although Germans are still hearty eaters who thoroughly enjoy their food, they are health-conscious and know when to put a curb on their appetite. The flavouring of German food is stimulating, the presentation orderly, the combinations innovatory and the whole meal proclaims its nationality. German chefs take great price in their calling and rank themselves second only to the French, as evidenced by the fact that many of the top jobs all over the world are filled by them.

As the wealthiest country in Europe, West Germany has been able to afford to widen its national diet with imports of everything it does not produce itself, thus bringing an international look to its menus. Sausages of all kinds, raw, smoked or cooked, are perhaps the most typical aspect of German food and with such a wide selection their inclusion can never pall and they are acceptable at every meal. Dumplings feature fairly prominently, *Leberknodel* being a variety made with minced liver, but both sweet and savoury ones are made.

240

The Germans are very fond of game, especially venison and it is featured in many quite imaginative ways on menus in all hotels and restaurants.

LOCAL PRODUCE

MEAT	beef, pork, veal; sausage products; chicken, goose; game birds, hare, rabbit, venison
FISH	carp, cod, eels, haddock, halibut, herrings, oysters, pike, salmon, trout
FRUIT	apples, apricots, cherries, blackberries, ligonberries, pears, plums
VEGETABLES	beetroot, Brussels sprouts, carrots, cauliflower, cucumber, celeriac, kale, kohlrabi, leeks, runner beans; sauerkraut
SPECIALITY DISHES	Sauerbrauten (braised marinated beef with sour-sweet raisin sauce), Holsteiner schnitzel (breadcrumbed veal escalope with a fried egg and anchovies); dampfnudeln (steamed dumplings covered with breadcrumbs and nutbrown butter); geselchtes (salted and smoked pork); Westphalia ham (considered to be the best in Europe); spatzle; rippchen mit sauerkraut (spareribs with sauerkraut); himmel und erde (potato, apple, black pudding and onions with bread)
PASTRIES	strudels, torten, schwarzewalde gâteau, käsekuchen
CHEESE	Altenburger, Backstein, Bierkäse, Harzer, Limburger, Rahmatour, Weisslaker, also German Brie and Camembert. Quark is used in cooking
WINES	the two main types are hock and moselle, also sparkling wine and some red wine.
SPIRITS	Baerenfang, Brandy, Branntwein, Citronen-eis-Likor, Dixtiner, Enzian, Kirsch, Kümmel, Schnapps
BEERS	Beck, Berliner Pils, Bayrische G'frorne, Heldenbrau, Holstein, Lowenbrau, Dortmunder Union

GREAT BRITAIN

This country has a pure culinary pedigree that is based on good quality ingredients prepared in a plain and simple way so as to enhance rather than disguise them.

The range of dishes is comprised of the traditional specialites of each county which put together provide an inexhaustible supply of menus. Although in general the food is served ungarnished and in a fairly straightforward manner,

241

19. A nineteenth-century certificate of admission to the freedom of the
Worshipful Company of Cooks

it can be elaborated to look spectacular even though the item is a plain roasted joint.

The climate decrees that the British diet be a fairly heavy one and certainly no other country can boast so many good pies and puddings, both sweet and savoury, hot and cold, in its repertoire. The sweet puddings, both steamed and baked and whether suet or sponge, are some of the glories of British cookery and can be made light and airy. They need not be stodgy and heavy as traditionally imagined.

Other generalisations – that vegetables are served overcooked and watery, gravy is lumpy, coffee is weak, that there are only half a dozen sauces in the repertoire as compared with the hundreds in the French repertoire as well as other similar allegations – are erroneous and no longer valid.

The visitor from overseas who wants to sample British cookery does not find it easy as there are few truly national restaurants that serve nothing but traditional dishes. The majority of restaurants serve an international menu which is usually a mixture of French, Italian and British dishes and even school, hospital and industrial canteens use a wider repertoire than solely traditional British dishes. As **P. Morton Shand** said, we are in danger of losing our own good cookery and have not acquired really good French cookery in its place – merely a deplorable international compromise.

When correctly done, British cookery is amongst the best in the world and is certainly the most welcome because amongst the most simple, and the fine flavour of the excellent ingredients is maintained; such is their quality that no camouflaging such as with thick sauces, is needed.

SOME REGIONAL SPECIALITIES

BEDFORDSHIRE	apple Florentine pie, spiced ale, Catherine cakes
BERKSHIRE	bacon pudding, faggots, poor knights of Windsor (pain perdu)
BUCKINGHAMSHIRE	Stokenchurch pie (minced meat with macaroni baked in a pie), pancakes
CAMBRIDGESHIRE	sausages
CHESHIRE	flummery, Chester pudding (steamed, containing blackcurrant jam)
CORNWALL	Cornish pasty, hoggan (a Cornish pasty closed at the top, star-gazy pie (whole herrings, pilchards or mackerel in a custard, their heads sticking out through the pastry covering)
CUMBERLAND	currant pasty (filled with brown sugar, currants, spices, apple and scratchings), rum butter, sausages, Cumberland ham, potted char

DERBYSHIRE	Bakewell tart, steamed batter pudding, Buxton pudding, Derby round of beef
DEVON	Sally Lunns, squab and apple pie
DORSET	Portland pudding (rich steamed fruit pudding)
DURHAM	pikelet (same as a crumpet), whig (caraway-flavoured yeast bun), pot pie
ESSEX	whitebait, oysters, raised mutton pies
GLOUCESTERSHIRE	royal pie (made with lampreys)
HAMPSHIRE	friars' omelette (baked apple egg custard)
HEREFORDSHIRE	love in disguise (baked stuffed heart coated with vermicelli), whortleberry pudding
HERTFORDSHIRE	pope lady cake (very light sponge)
HUNTINGDONSHIRE	Huntingdon pudding (steamed gooseberry pudding)
KENT	lamb's tail pie, oast cakes (deep fried currant scones), twice laid (deep-fried codfish balls), oysters, huffkin (yeast tea cake), chicken pudding
LANCASHIRE	black pudding, brawn, Eccles cakes, Lancashire hot pot, parkin, potted shrimps, barmcakes, tripe, sheeps' trotters, Hindle Wakes (boiling fowl poached for several hours)
LEICESTERSHIRE	frumenty, Melton Mowbray pie, medley pie (cooked beef and bacon with apples and beer made as a pie), curd cheesecakes
LINCOLNSHIRE	mock goose (stuffed boned shoulder of pork shaped and roasted)
LONDON	Chelsea buns, jellied eels, pease pudding
NORFOLK	dumplings, stuffed marrow
NORTHAMPTONSHIRE	venison pie
NORTHUMBERLAND	pan haggerty (layers of sliced potato, onion and cheese cooked in a pan(, singing hinnies (hot girdle cakes)
NOTTINGHAMSHIRE	swan pie, rook pie
OXFORDSHIRE	Oxford sausages (pork, veal, suet, rusk, sage and thyme), Deddington Pudding Pie (cooked ground rice and currant filling baked as a pie)
SHROPSHIRE	fidget pie (bacon, apples, potatoes and onions in a pie), Shrewsbury biscuits

SOMERSET	Bath buns, elvers cakes, Sally Lunns
SUFFOLK	pork and onion dumplings, chitterling turnovers
SURREY	maids of honour, eel pie
SUSSEX	partridge pudding, stewed lambs' ears, pumpkin pie
WARWICKSHIRE	Coventry godcakes
WESTMORELAND	herb pudding, rum butter, parkins, lobscouse
WILTSHIRE	Bath chaps, Devizes pie (calf's head, brain, tongue and bacon in a pie), Bradenham ham, Salisbury steak
WORCESTERSHIRE	jugged pigeons, Worcester sauce, potted lampreys
YORKSHIRE	Yorkshire pudding, savoury pudding (soaked bread with herbs and spices, onion and oatmeal baked as a pudding), bilberry pie, pikelets (thick pancakes), hams, Barnsley chop
WALES	Snowdon pudding, Welsh rarebit, lava bread
NORTHERN IRELAND	Irish stew, colcannon (as for bubble and squeak), hunters' pie (lamb chops baked inside a mashed potato pie), boxty, carrageen (seaweed)
SCOTLAND	Cock-a-leekie, Scotch broth, Bawd Bree (hare soup), Arbroath smokies, porridge, venison roll, Scotch eggs, Forfar bridies, Colcannon (as for bubble and squeak), haggis, potted head, mutton pies, minced collops, stovies (stewed sliced potato and onions) Dundee cake, petticoat tails, bannocks, dropped scones, cream crowdie
CHANNEL ISLANDS	conger soup, ormers, limpets, conger eel pie, Jersey steaks (hamburger mixture), fliottes (batter dumplings), Jersey wonders (bun mixture made with baking powder, threaded through and deep fried)

OTHER LOCAL FOODS AND TRADITIONAL DISHES

FISH	cod, dabs, haddock, hake, herrings, mackerel, plaice skate, salmon, smelts, sole, trout, turbot, whiting, whitebait
SMOKED FISH	Arbroath smokies, bloaters, eel, finnan haddock, kippers, mackerel, salmon, sprats
SHELLFISH	cockles, crabs, crayfish, Dublin Bay prawns, lobsters, mussels, oysters, scallops, whelks, winkles

245

FISH DISHES	kedgeree, dressed crab, fried fish and chips, fried cods' roe, fried scallops and bacon, potted char, potted shrimps, fish cakes, angels on horseback
MEAT ITEMS	shepherd's pie, cottage pie, sea pie, raised pies, steak and kidney pie, steak and kidney pudding (can also contain oysters and mushrooms), Irish stew, boiled salt beef, boiled leg of mutton and caper sauce, curried meat, mixed grill, marrow bone, baron of beef, roast beef and Yorkshire pudding, sucking pig, grilled gammon rasher, crown of lamb; toad in the hole, polony, saveloys, black pudding, brawn, tripe and onions, bath chaps, potted beef, potted game, sausages, jugged hare, grouse, partridge, pheasant, pigeon, snipe, wild duck, woodcock, club sandwich, bookmaker's sandwich, ploughman's lunch, chicken pie, spatchcocked chicken; veal, ham and egg pie
VEGETABLES	bubble and squeak, pease pudding, cauliflower cheese
BREAD, CAKES AND BISCUITS	baps, crumpets, manchets (rich bread rolls), muffins, oatcakes, potato scones, girdle scones, wholemeal scones, tea cakes, soda bread, currant loaf, malt loaf, Victoria sandwich, parkin, gingerbread, Scotch pancakes, Madeira cake, Simnel cake, Chelsea buns, hot cross buns, Bath buns, doughnuts, Bath Oliver biscuits, Abernethy biscuits, Swiss roll
SWEETS	junket, blancmange, fools, caudle, syllabub, Christmas pudding, mince pies, lemon meringue pie, suet puddings with various fillings and flavours, steamed and baked sponge puddings, fruit pies, milk puddings, apple amber, baked apple dumpling, Eve's pudding, cabinet pudding, summer pudding, lemon curd tart, crumbles, queen of puddings, syrup tart
CHEESE	Caboe, Caerphilly, Cheddar, Cheshire, Derby, Double Gloucester, Dunlop, Melbury, Lancashire, Leicester, Lymeswold, Stilton, White Stilton, Wensleydale and occasionally Sage Derby and Blue Vinny. There are many others that can only be obtained from such specialists as Peter Rance at Goring-on-Thames.
DRINKS	cider, perry, mead, lambswool (beer and wine sweetened and flavoured with nutmeg and baked crab apples in it), ginger wine, Scotsmac, apple juice

246

BEERS	barley wine, bitter, brown ale, mild ale, milk stout, nut-brown ale, pale ale, stout, strong ale, lager
WINE	Although nearly all the wine produced in England comes from German stock, and there are some 200 vineyards, English wines have their own particular flavour, quite distinct from any other country. English wines are generally light, dry and slightly green in colour and they have a clean, fruity flavour. A great deal of care goes into their production and each one merits its place on the wine list. Some of the producers are Adgetstone, Abbey Knight, Felstar and Lamberhurst Priory
SPIRITS	gin, Plymouth gin, sloe gin, whisky (blended, malt)
LIQUEURS	Atholl Brose, Bronte, Glayva, Glen Mist, Heather Cream, Irish Mist, Drambuie, Lindisfarne, Pimm's, Royal Tara (orange cream)
OTHER DRINKS	Black Velvet (half stout and half champagne), Pink gin, Pimm's Royal (made with champagne), mulled wine, Negus, hot toddy
WATERS	Ashbourne, Ashe Park, Buxton, Malvern, Highland Spring

GREECE

As eaten in the home, Greek food is rather dull and plain and the cookery methods in general use are straightforward. Olive oil is used both for cooking and for pouring over cooked foods. Herbs are widely used to enhance the flavour of the foods and spices are added to give a certain oriental touch. Lemon juice is used in many dishes and provides a refreshing flavour as do black and green olives and yoghurt, all of which are used a lot. The basic ingredients are generally inexpensive and the cooking cannot be said to be complicated or high class but the natural bold flavours of food are brought out by it and by the use of good quality olive oil.

LOCAL PRODUCE

MEAT	beef, goat, lamb, pork, sucking pig, veal; rabbit; chicken, duck, turkey
FISH AND SHELLFISH	anchovies, red mullet, salt cod, swordfish, trout; crayfish, cuttle fish, octopus, prawns, squid

247

FRUIT	apricots, cherries, figs, grapes, lemons, oranges, peaches, pears, quinces, water melons
VEGETABLES	artichoke, beans, celeriac, egg-plant, okra, peas, pimentos, spinach, tomatoes, vine leaves
SPECIALITY DISHES	taramasalata (smoked cod or mullet roe with oil and lemon juice); moussaka; tamara (carp caviar); dolmas (stuffed vine leaves); keftedes (meat balls); avgolemono (chicken and rice soup with hard-boiled egg and lemon juice); loucoums (turkish delight); baklava (very thin layers of puff paste with nuts, soaked in honey syrup); halvas (semolina dumpling with syrup and almonds); Turkish coffee
CHEESE	Feta, Kasseri, Kefalotir, Kyatolyri, Lemnio, Manouri, Myzythra, Parnassou
WINE	Retsina (resin-flavoured type of white wine), Brousko (red dry), Thasso (red dry), Verdea (rosé), Robola (dry white), Samos (sweet), Mavrodaphne (fortified sweet), Kokkineli (dry red)
SPIRITS	Ouzo (aniseed), raki (strong ouzo), brandy

HOLLAND

The cookery of Holland can be described as being more substantial than refined but it makes up for this by the quality of its excellent produce. The standard of living is high and the population is happy to spend on eating out as this brings them into contact with international dishes; foods in their season are given prominence. Dutch food has much in common with its close neighbour Germany as they share a common heritage. The day's meals are the same as in England except that breakfast includes Dutch cheese and processed cold meat. It is a simple cookery that makes the best use of the country's natural products.

The *rijstaffel* is a separate culinary aspect of Holland which came from Indonesia, once a colony belonging to the Dutch. It consists of a large selection of side dishes to be served with ample *Nassi Goreng* together with prawn crackers, sauces and *sambals*. Sufficient time needs to be allowed to appreciate it to the full. *Nasi Goreng* is cooked rice fried in oil with garlic and chili pepper, until brown; diced fish, shellfish or meat is added and it is served with strips of flat omelette on top.

248

MEAT	beef, pork, veal; ham, smoked tongue; offals; chicken, duck; game birds; hare, texel lamb (like pré-salé)
FISH	bloaters, cod, eels, haddock, halibut, pike, soles
FRUIT	apples, apricots, pears, rhubarb
VEGETABLES	asparagus, beetroot, Belgian endive; black, green, red, white and yellow pimentos; Brussels sprouts, cabbage, carrots, cauliflower, egg-plant, kale, leeks, lettuce, potatoes, radish, red cabbage, sorrel, spinach, tomatoes; sauerkraut
SPECIALITIES	Hutspot met klapstuck (hot pot), zurkool met spek (sauerkraut and bacon); uitsmijter (fried egg on bread and ham with gherkin); hazepepper (jugged hare); waterzoi (fish stew)
CHEESE	clove, Edam, Friesian, Gouda, Leiden, Massdam
WINE	imported
SPIRITS	Genever (gin), Citroen brandwein, Advocaat, Curaçao, Crèmes
BEER	Amstel, Heineken, Oranjeboom, Breda, Skol, Leeuw

HUNGARY

The culinary traditions of Hungary have some similarity to those of its near neighbours such as Bulgaria and Rumania but Hungary was closely associated with Austria as part of the Austro-Hungarian Empire and it too has been influenced by other countries of that Empire, notably Turkey. Of the countries of this part of Europe, Hungarian cookery is the richest and spiciest and it is of course, the home of paprika made from the red pimentos that are grown there. paprika is very pungent and some is quite sweet and mild, but it plays a big part several names and qualities with *kulonleges* being the very special quality. Some paprika is very pungent and some is quite sweet and mil, but it plays a big part in many national dishes such as goulash.

Hungarians love the food of their country and are proud of its elaborateness which approaches that of French cookery. Certainly meals in Hungary are of a better quality than those of neighbouring countries. Sour milk and sour cream are much used, fresh curds, dill and caraway give flavour to all kinds of dishes; lard is used instead of butter.

MEAT	pork is the most widely used meat; beef, lamb, mutton, veal; bacon; offals, geese, turkey; hare, wild boar
FISH AND SHELLFISH	carp, catfish, fogas, frog's legs, perch, pike, salmon trout, sturgeon, trout; crayfish
FRUIT	dried fruits; soft fruits; apples, cherries, chestnuts, rhubarb
VEGETABLES	cabbage, cauliflower, cucumbers, kohlrabi, mushrooms, peppers, sorrel
SPECIALITIES	goulash, salami, Porkolt (braised beef with galuskas which are dumplings), Toltott borjuhus (veal stuffed with foie gras), Eszterhazy rostelyos (braised steaks in sour cream sauce), Fatanyeros (several pieces of either pork, beef or veal with bacon rashers, arranged on a plank and garnished with pickled vegetables), Lecso (chopped bacon, pimento and tomato stew), Toltott paprika (stuffed pimentos), soured cabbage, csirke paprikàs (sauté of chicken with paprika and cream)
PASTRY ITEMS	dobosh, strudels, tortens
WINE	Tokay (with 3, 4 or 5 puttonyos), Egri Bikaver (Bull's blood), Mori Ezerjó, Szekszardi Kadarka, Pécsi Olaszrizling, Villány-Siklos
SPIRITS	Apricot Brandy, Barackpalinka, Kirsch, Szatmari Szilva (plum brandy
BEER	Kinizsi, Matyas-Sor, Siraly

INDIA

The whole essence of Indian cookery, and this includes all the countries of the sub-continent, lies in the use of spices. We tend to regard Indian food as consisting of a wide variety of curries yet strangely enough, curry is not even an Indian word. Many dishes are in fact curries but each one is made with a different mixture of the thirty or so different seeds, fruits, berries and leaves that are used to enhance but never to overpower a dish.

Indian food is never so highly seasoned as to camouflage the basic ingredient and nothing is over-elaborated. The cooking techniques are simple, the native ingredients are very ordinary but the use of all the seasonings makes them come alive in a very appetising and digestible way.

Although the English usually accept a blend of various items called curry powder, the Indian cook will select and blend his own elements knowing what effect a slight variation of each will have on the finished dish. He wants his concoction to enhance and enrich the basic commodity but not to dominate it. It must give a smooth and mellow result but it cannot of course, be bland; it must have a pronounced fragrance that is full of character and complexity. The changes are made by varying the amounts of the robust and pungent and the softer aromatic ingredients of the seasoning mix, blending and milling them to a distinctive harmonious mixture.

Curry is an anglicised Indian word that means any kind of dish. Indians in the different regions use different mixtures and each region has its own style of curry. *Masala* is the name given to a particular mixture of from ten to thirty ingredients; *Garam Masala* is stronger but more fragrant; the addition of tumeric makes the various blends of herbs and spices into a curry powder and when mixed with *ghee*, into curry paste. *Vindaloo* is a special curry from Goa; *tandoori* is from the Punjab where the food is marinated in spices and yoghurt then cooked over charcoal or wood. Tamarind is used in making curries and is usually an ingredient in commercial chutneys. Plain yoghurt is used instead of stock in making curry, and *ghee* which can be clarified butter or vegetable oil, is used for frying the ingredients.

INDIAN SPECIALITIES

Tandoori Murgha (a tandoor is a clay oven – the meat or chicken is marinated in vinegar, oil, lime juice, yoghurt and tomato puree with spices; the spices are then ground and rubbed into the commodity and left for 12 hours covered with the marinade which turns red; the meat is then roasted); kebabs are also cooked in the tandoori style; Brinjal (aubergines stuffed, stewed or curried), Patra (vine leaves stuffed with a spicy mixture); Pork Vindaloo (a fiery flavoured sweet and sour stew); Alu Keema Tikki (spicy cooked minced meat wrapped in potato pastry and deep fried); Kamargah (chops cooked in spiced milk); Chawal (soak rice, then fry in hot ghee, add water and stir and cook until dry); Chawal Pullao (rice cooked with onion, garlic, garam masala, ginger and cumin); Safed Korma (spicy stewed mutton with cashew nuts and poppy seeds); Puri (bread dough made as thin discs and deep fried); Pami (Indian cream cheese cut into pieces, deep fried and served with spiced sauce); Rasgulla (cream cheese balls in syrup); Chaat (small highly spiced titbits for eating with the fingers).

Because of the dense land mass, fish has never been a commonly used ingredient in the interior of the country. Local species of fish include *hilsah, mahsir, mango-fish, beckt*, and *rohu*.

251

ISRAEL

The population of Israel includes the two ethnic groups of Jews and Arabs who live in close proximity but usually in separate towns; for example, Bethlehem and Nazareth and the old City of Jerusalem are populated by Arabs and in Haifa Jews and Arabs live right across the town. The two kinds of Jews are the Ashkenazi who are from Eastern Europe and the Sephardim who come from Spain, Portugal and the countries of north Africa; needless to say, both races have their own ways of cooking, but methods are governed by the laws of their religious beliefs.

The orthodox Jewish dietary laws have to be kept by Jewish people of all sects and ethnic origin, not only in Israel but wherever they may be living. These laws are religious by nature and are implemented by officials of a Kashruth commission whenever Jewish people hold a catering function in a public hall or restaurant. Foods for these functions are the generally permitted foodstuffs including all fruits and vegetables, grains, tea, coffee; or foods that have been processed in the kosher method including meat that has been ritually slaughtered, poultry that has been bled, and certain kinds of fish. Foods that Jews are not permitted to eat include pork, ham, bacon, shellfish and game. More details are given in Chapter 1.

The religious laws go even further and lay down that (i) dairy products and meat products may not be cooked together in any recipe; (ii) meat and milk must not be eaten during a single meal; (iii) separate utensils, dishes, cutlery and crockery must be kept for cooking a milk meal and a meat meal and may not be interchanged. (This means having two separate and completely equipped kitchens for an orthodox Jewish hospital, nursing home, etc.).

The reform movement has gone some way to eliminate these dietary laws but of some 365 000 Jewish people living in Great Britain no fewer than 260 000 are orthodox and abide by their religion. Many of these are professional people.

Although the Jewish race has been dispersed into many different countries since the *dispora* and have adjusted their way of living to their adopted country, when they come together to live in Israel they bring with them not just the habits of the place in which they live but also a pool of dishes of Jewish origin.

The standard of living in Israel is good and the Israelis have made what was a desert land, bloom and bring forth fruit, vegetables, cereals, and flowers in abundance, mainly in the hundreds of kibbutz or communal settlements and co-operatives. Consequently the traditional diet of the ghetto has been greatly enriched and the Israelis enjoy a wide selection of ingredients cooked by methods that originated in many countries (including Arab ones) that make for a very interesting repertoire.

The phrase 'with milk and honey blessed' is true not only of Jerusalem but of the entire country.

LOCAL PRODUCE

MEAT beef (forequarter), lamb, mutton, veal; chicken, duck, goose, turkey.

FISH anchovies, bass, bream, carp, cod, halibut, herring, pike, salmon, trout, tuna

FRUITS apple, avocado pears, cherries, dates, grapes, grapefruit, oranges peaches, pears, prickly pears, plums, raspberries, strawberries, melons

VEGETABLES asparagus, beetroot, broccoli, cabbage, carrots, cauliflower, celery, Chinese leaves, egg-plant, beans, artichokes, okras, sorrel, spinach, tomatoes, courgettes

SPECIALITIES Chopped liver (purée of sautéed chicken livers and onion mixed with sieved hard boiled egg white); gefilltefisch (carp stuffed with matzo meal and onion stuffing, poached in court-bouillon); felafels (spiced purée of chick-peas, rolled into balls and deep fried); kreplachs (like raviolis with various savoury or sweet fillings); blintzes (pancakes filled with spiced mixture of cottage cheese and cream, fried in butter); knedles (bread or potato dumplings); schaleth (pudding of apple purée, dried fruit and eggs baked inside a noodle crust); schav (sorrel soup made similarly in Germany); bagels (rings of yeast dough poached, drained, sprinkled with poppy seeds and baked); latkes (spoonfuls of grated raw potato with eggs and flour, shallow fried); Chola (plaited sweet bread dough with poppy seeds); Houmos (purée of chick peas); Matzos are the dry, saltless and unleavened biscuits eaten especially during the Passover in place of ordinary bread, and at any other time of the year

WINES all kinds of good quality table wines are sold under brand names, some red wines are sweetened with grape juice; many sparkling and fortified wines such as vermouths and sherries

SPIRITS brandy; Israeli versions of most well-known spirits and liqueurs, Sabra Liqueur (cactus)

253

ITALY

The general view that Italian cookery is coarse and heavy and a poor relation of French cookery is entirely mistaken as is the impression that it is limited to pasta and rice dishes. The fact is that Italian cookery is very varied and there is a big difference between that of the Northern part as against that of the South.

Italian cookery is so varied because the country was formed from a number of independent states, each with its own traditional foods and cooking methods and regional produce. Thus there is a wide range of diets and food habits and it is easier to describe the cooking of each region and its specialities than to generalise about the food of the entire country. Italian cooking can be fine and subtle or cheap and heavy, according to the region and to the standard of the establishment. Certainly pasta products can provide cheap, filling meals, but equally they lend themselves to refined dishes of a high gastronomic standard. The overall standard is not perhaps as exquisite as that of French cookery but it should be remembered that some of their prowess stemmed from the culinary traditions of Italy and there is now no comparison between the two because they are completely different. Some of the dishes of Italy may hark back to 'the glory that was Rome' in for example, the sweet-and-sour preparations, the use of small birds, and the use of spices and herbs.

The Italian people are dedicated to the art of good eating and drinking and will go into raptures over the merits of a particular dish or wine and use glowing terms to describe the subtle nuances of a dish. Eye appeal is generally colourful.

Cheese plays a fairly important part in the menu and for pasta dishes; few are served without it, yet milk dishes are not a feature. Tomatoes and tomato sauce are used to a great extent as is olive oil and garlic.

LOCAL PRODUCE

MEAT	beef, goat, lamb, pork, veal; chicken, duck; game birds; chamois, hare
FISH AND SHELLFISH	anchovies, carp, eel, mullet, pike, sardines, tuna; dried cod; calamarii, clams, crab, crayfish, mussels, octopus, scampi, squid
FRUIT	apricots, cherries, grapes, lemons, mandarins, melons, nectarines, peaches, pears, plums, pomegranates
VEGETABLES	artichokes (globe), asparagus, beetroot, broad beans, broccoli, cabbage, carrots, cauliflower, celery, celeriac, chicory, Jerusalem artichokes, leeks, mushrooms, peas, pimentos, pumpkin, radicchio, spinach, tomatoes
SPECIALITIES	brodo, zuppa and minestra are some of the various kinds of soup; antipasto means hors-d'oeuvre; Pastasciutta is the general term for the one hundred or more different shapes and sizes of

254

Italian pasta; risotto; salami; grissini; bagna caôda (oil, garlic, anchovies and truffle used as a dip or sauce); polenta (corn meal paste); prosciutto (cured ham served raw); pizza; gnocchi (potato dumplings); vitello tonnelato (braised veal served cold with tuna and anchovy sauce); maiale in porchetta (roast sucking pig); pollo alla cacciatora (chicken chasseur); cuscinetti di vitello (veal cordon bleu); zampino or zampone – the lower part of a leg of pork, boned, stuffed and boiled; coppa – a type of raw ham made in the form of a large sausage; Italian truffles are light golden brown in colour and are often grated on a silver grater over a pasta or rice dish, the flavour is delightful

PASTRY	A maretti (macaroons); Bonét (chocolate bavarois); Cassata
CHEESE	belpaese, caciocavallo, dolcelatte, dolceverde, gorgonzola, mozzarella, parmesan, pecorino, provolone, ricotta
SPIRITS	Aurum, Cerasella, Fiori d'Alpi, Galliano, Grappa, Strega, Sambuca, Maraschino, Noretta
WINES	Dolcetto d'Alba, Grignolino, Barbera, Barbaresco, Barolo, Chianti, Pinot del Poggio, Spumante, Lambrusco, Lacryma Christi, Soave, Valpolicella, Marsala
BEER	Dreher Trieste, Poretti, Whurer, Nastro Azzuro

There are seventeen main regions of Italy each with its own characteristic form of cookery and its own recipes, most of which date from medieval if not Roman or Etruscan times. As it is not possible to deal with each of the regions in the available space, the following have been selected to show some of the typical gastronomic delights of this lovely country.

Piedmont

The *cucina* of this region is quite high class as compared with that of many of the other regions of Italy and this distinction is probably due to the influence of the neighbouring country of France. In fact there are similarities in the cookery traditions of the whole coastline from Provence to Piedmont. It is a distinctive, delicate and sober cuisine that is tasty but not over-pungent; at the same time hearty and healthy and without excessive seasoning. That great treasure of the table, the white truffle abounds in this region and in autumn it is used in abundance by being grated over many savoury dishes.

Piedmont produces some of the finest wines of any region of Italy and many of them are too well-known to warrant description. Among them are Barolo, Barbaresco, Grignolino, Dolcetto, Barbera and Malvasia. The sparkling wines are

255

Asti Spumante and Moscato d'Asti and all the great vermouths are produced here.

Among the most typical culinary delights are *bagna caoda* (a hot dipping sauce of anchovies, garlic and oil); *bollito misto* (boiled joints of beef and veal with vegetables), *lumache alla Piemontaise* (snails in herb butter); *vitello tonnelato* (boiled veal with a cold sauce of anchovy, lemon juice and olive oil); *zampetti di maiale* (pigs' trotters coated with crumbs and shallow fried); *cafe valdostano* (black coffee, red wine, grappa, sugar and lemon rind); *spumone* (like *zabaglione*).

Veneto

The antiquity of Venice shows in its cookery traditions which are very refined and gentle stemming from medieval and Renaissance times when Venice was a very important city. The finesse is due to the wealth of its citizens in bygone times who cultivated a cookery quite difference from the other States.

As a seaport, Venice used all the different kinds of fish found in the Adriatic and cooked them in superior rather than simple ways. The Venetian hinterland reaches to the border with Austria and although mountainous in the north, it has an abundance of products for a very rich and varied repertoire.

Despite this abundance the cookery of the region is based on two staple commodites – rice and brown beans – and these play an important part in everyday cookery. Soup or *minestra* as it is called, includes either or both of these and they appear in dishes in their own right – rice as *risotto* with hundreds of different recipes for garnishing it and the beans as a very sustaining meal when cooked for hours on end. The importance of *fagioli* or kidney beans is that they were issued during Mussolini's regime as a social security hand-out to assist families in need.

The great dishes of the region include *pate di fegato* (cooked calf's liver mixed with butter); *salsa peverada* (chicken liver, anchovy, garlic, lemon juice, oil and vinegar as a cold sauce dip); *risi e bisi* (rice and fresh pea broth); *polenta*; *risotto nero* (*risotto* made with the ink from squid); *bacala* (dried salted cod); *radicchio* as a salad or a vegetable; *fegato in agrodolce* (calf's liver in sweet-sour sauce); *crema fritta* (fried breadcrumbed pieces of pastry cream). The wines of this region include the well-known Bardolino, Soave and Valpolicella. Custoza is a dry white wine that is becoming very popular.

Tuscany

The cookery of this fascinating region is very basic, showing its rustic and domestic origins without refinements and has more flavour than eye-appeal. It

256

consists of good wholesome ingredients plainly cooked by grilling or spit-roasting preferably over a wood fire. Food is therefore mainly cooked quickly and fiercely but there are some dishes that require long slow-cooking; either way it has to be done to perfection before it will satisfy a Tuscan. The region is a hilly one and in many parts the only things that can be grown are olives and grapes. Even the grape harvest is lean but many superb red wines and a few fine white ones are produced, the best known being Chianti.

Chianti is a brilliant ruby-red wine with an intense aroma; it is dry and slightly tannic but becomes velvety as it ages. It can be drunk young or left to mature, the word *Riserva* being used to indicate wine that has been aged for at least three years. The island of Elba is a part of this province and produces both red and white wines of 10°-11° of alcohol. Other wines include Parrino and Montescudaio in both white and red versions. The specialities of Tuscany include *gnocchi di ricotta* (small dumplings made of ricotta cheese); *pastasciutta alla toscana* (any pasta in thick tomato and oil sauce); *bistecca alla cacciatore* (sauté veal or beef steak covered with chasseur sauce); *fegato alla toscana* (calf's liver sauté with sage and lemon); *involtini in umido* (thin slices of veal rolled up with ham and sage and braised in white wine and tomato); *maiale ubriaco* (pork chop cooked in Chianti with fennel seeds and garlic); *panforte di Siena* (spiced almond cake); *torta di riso* (rich Condé rice mixture baked).

Rome

The cookery of Rome and the province is simple, healthy and smooth yet with a forceful distinction that sets it high amongst other regions. Whereas other areas make full use of olive oil, in Rome lard is more generally used and oil is only used for deep frying. The ingredients are fresh and genuine but they are cooked simply and complicated methods and garnishes have no place. But it is not a frugal diet and the population is happy to pay to acquire good quality ingredients which are grown in abundance in the region.

There is still a Roman Empire influence in the way that spices are used but at the Renaissance, cookery was modified to become less complicated. Sauces or *ragu* were very much a feature of cookery but today the only one in general use is tomato which goes on spaghetti, fish and meat indiscriminately. It is said that it is impossible to find a bad eating place in this region and even the most humble *osteria* or *taverna* serves cheap but good meals.

Among the notable dishes are *calzone* (salami and cheese mixture in bread dough as a deep fried or baked turnover); *pizza* (with tomato, basil, garlic and oregano); *pizzette fritte* (small deep-fried pizza rounds topped with tomato and *mozzarella* mixture); *lasagne di carnevale* (pie of *lasagne* with cheese and bacon); *spaghetti aglio e oglio* (tossed in oil and garlic); *agnello pasquale* (hotpot with onion, potato and herbs); *costata alla pizzaiola* (sauté steak covered with rich tomato, garlic and olive mixture); *pizza dolce* (sweetened round of dough covered with sweetened cream cheese and egg mixture with almonds).

257

The wines of this area include those of the area Castelli Romani, Frascati, Alto Lazio, the Torre Ercolana Montefiascone where the famous Est! Est!! originates and Falerno.

JAPAN

Japanese cookery is unique in that it has resisted any outside influences and only slightly resembles that of its neighbours China and Korea. It is an entirely oriental cuisine and the typical meal is composed of rice and vegetable dishes with the food cut into bite-size pieces before cooking. The entire meal experience is of quality foods and aesthetic service as a form of ritual. Thus, the decoration and display of the whole meal is of equal importance to the actual cooking and together with the selection and arrangement of the table appointments, must create a harmonious whole. Japanese cookery is sophisticated and the cooks train throughout their careers to become expert in *Sushi* (rice cookery) or *Sashimi* (raw fish dishes) qualifications, and absolute quality standards are presented for each traditional dish.

By tradition the Japanese kneel down to eat; food is eaten with chopsticks which is why most items are cut small and why it is possible to serve it in tiny bowls, thus conveying the feeling of delicateness. The principles that have to be considered include colour, texture, flavour and overall harmony, with some contrasting emphasis in the combinations and from the serving utensils.

The methods of cooking are rapid and precise, based on the staggered approach, with great care taken to add the ingredients at exactly the right time and with the individual characteristics of each ingredient being prized. Food is prepared in these groups:

1. *suimono* – the clear soups
2. *yakinomo* – grilled foods
3. *nimono* – boiled foods
4. *mushimono* – steamed foods
5. *agimono* – fried foods
6. *sashimi* – sliced raw fish
7. *namasu* – pickled raw fish and vegetables
8. *hitashimono* – boiled green vegetables in shoyu
9. *tsukemono* – pickles
10. *sukiyaki* – cooking in a chafing dish at the table.

There are three systems of presentation which go to make an ordinary everyday meal in Japan a thing of beauty:

1. a succession of courses starting with appetisers and soup followed by a succession of well-thought out combinations of rice with the main fish or meat and accompaniments, all artistically arranged;

258

2. the appetiser and soup followed by an assortment of seafoods and vegetables deep-fried in batter and served with various dips;
3. the appetiser is served and whilst it is being consumed, a beautiful dish of raw and parcooked fish, meat and vegetables is presented and cooked at table on a griddle or hot rocks. Small portions of each are served, then more is cooked.

Japanese food and the way it is prepared are deeply rooted in Japan's different religions, cultures and history which means that national and imported foodstuffs are never mixed and that the true cuisine is as authentic today as it was during the Middle Ages.

LOCAL PRODUCE

MEAT	beef, lamb, pork, veal, venison; dog; game birds; chicken, duck, turkey
FISH AND SHELLFISH	bonito, bream, carp, eel, mackerel, salmon, shark, swordfish, whalemeat; cuttlefish, octopus
VEGETABLES	aster leaves, bamboo shoots, bean sprouts, bracken fern, broccoli, burdock, Chinese leaves, chrysanthemum leaves, egg-plant, Japanese horseradish, lotus root, mushrooms, okra, peas, radishes, stachys, various kinds of seaweed, water chestnuts, yams
OTHER SPECIAL INGREDIENTS	sesame oil. tofu (soya bean curd), black beans, lima beans, yingko nuts, miso (soya-bean paste), dashi (fish stock made from bonito and seaweed
SPECIALITIES	shoyu (soy sauce); sashimi (thin slices or cubes of raw fish with horseradish soy sauce); aji-no-moto (monosodium glutamate); nigiri zushi (rice balls with green horseradish paste, covered with a slice of raw fish or thin omelette); tsukimono (pickled vegetables); tempura (fritto misto of fish, shellfish and vegetables dipped in egg-batter and fried, served with soy sauce dip); sukiyaki (onions, cabbage, spinach, bamboo shoots and leeks cooked in front of the customer with thin slices of raw beef dipped in egg and served with rice)
WINE	Mirin (sweet saké for cooking)
SPIRITS	saké, whisky, Midori (melon liqueur), seishu is a highly refined saké, toso is a sweet saké
BEER	Sapporo, Yebisu, Kirin

MEXICO

The culinary traditions of Mexico embrace the best of Spanish, Mayan Indian and Negro cookery and the ancient cooking techniques of the Aztec and Inca civilisations. In common with that of other Latin races, the flavour of the food is spicy and hot but the very hot chillies play a big part in many basic dishes and even those that are not hot in themselves are served with piquant chilli sauces and relishes.

Maize or sweetcorn is a staple in the diet and in the form of *tortillas*, for example, it helps to tone down the pungent tastes. Corn is boiled in lime water, hashed then reboiled to yield *hominy* which is ground and used for making *tortillas* and *tamales*.

Meat is eaten only in moderation because it is not generally of very good quality. Beans – red kidney, black, pinto and many other kinds – are served with every meal, usually after the meat.

There are more than sixty different kinds of chillies and it can be said that the basics of the Mexican diet are maize, beans (*frijoles*) and chillies. Rice is used and is sometimes served as a garnish with soup.

LOCAL PRODUCE

MEAT	beef, goat, lamb, pork; chicken; turkey
FISH	abalone, dried shrimps
FRUIT	bananas, cassava, coconuts, grapes, mangoes, oranges, papayas, peaches, pineapples, plums
VEGETABLES	avocados, beans (green), cactus, chayotes, chillies, onion, peas, potatoes, pumpkin, squash, green tomatoes
SPECIALITIES	tortillas (thinly-rolled maize dough cooked as a pancake on a griddle and served hot as bread); burrito (a hot tortilla sandwich filled with chicken, beans, cheese, chili con carne, folded, fastened and shallow fried); tacos (a tortilla filled with fish, cheese, meat or beans, rolled up and usually deep fried); toastado (a fried flat tortilla filled with beans, chicken, cheese, avocado, etc., with hot tomato sauce); tamales (minced cheese, chicken or meat with thick chilli and tomato paste inside a steamed maize pancake); empanadas (fried meat rissoles); refritos (purée of beans fried as a breakfast dish); enchilada (a tortilla filled with spiced shredded pork or chicken and fried); chili con carne (stewed meat with chili powder, tomato and red kidney beans); posole (soup made with ground maize); guacamole (mashed avocado, onion, tomato, chillies, coriander and lime juice – used as a dip); mole poblano de guajalote (turkey in chocolate and chili pepper sauce)

CHEESE	guajaqueno, quesillo, queso blanco
WINE	not used very much
SPIRITS	Aguardiente (distilled from sugar cane), Mescal or Tequila (from magney cactus), Kahlua
BEER	Pulque (like tequila made from magney cactus), chicha de manzana (cyder)

THE MIDDLE EAST COUNTRIES

This title covers the countries of Europe and Asia inhabited by people of Arabian culture and includes Turkey, Egypt, Iran, Iraq, Jordan, Lebanon and Syria but not Israel. There is a great similarity between the cuisines of these countries and any distinctions between them are mainly concerned with levels and combinations of seasonings. The staple commodites are the same in all these countries and cooking methods are fairly primitive. The influences of Greece and Rome have left their marks and the religions practised by the inhabitants have a bearing on the diet. There is still a wide difference between the diet of the rich and that of the poor people, the rich consuming many imported foods to supplement the local produce which tends to be stereotyped because so much of the area is desert. In countries that export oil, the standard of living is constantly improving and the diet of all classes is becoming less monotonous. The climate, as well as the mainly Muslim religion, affects the pattern and substance of meals; many foods and all alcohol are forbidden and other items do not stay fresh in the intense heat so are not used. Thus the consumption of meat and fish in some of these countries is very low, even where communications and storage facilities are good. Rosewater and bergamot are favoured essences.

Dried pulses, in particular lentils and chick peas are used in many dishes and to some extent replace meat in a stew. Rice cooked as for pilaff is used, particularly with mutton and goat.

LOCAL PRODUCE

MEAT	beef, camel, goat, mutton, offals; chicken, duck, goose; (meat must be halal or ritually slaughtered)
FISH	sturgeon
FRUIT	apricots, dates, figs, grapes, guavas, melons, oranges, peaches, pomegranates, also dried fruits, pistachios and other nuts
VEGETABLES	broad beans, cabbage, courgettes, cucumber, egg-plant, okras, pimentos, radishes, sorghum, squash, tomatoes

SPECIALITIES	ashe mast va khiar (cold yoghurt and cucumber soup); yalanci dolma (stuffed vine leaves); alabalick izgarasi (charcoal grilled trout with almonds); barbunya izgara (grilled red mullet); jujah kebab (spit roasted poussin with rice pilaff); bakhlava (layers of pastry and butter soaked in honey syrup); falafel (chick pea rissoles); betingan meshwi or poor man's caviar (purée of egg-plant with oil and lemon juice); yakni (stewed lamb with fresh and dried vegetables); kousa mahshi (courgettes stuffed with rice and meat filling); koumiss (mare's milk yoghurt); kefir (as koumiss, used by invalids)
CHEESE	Labna

SWEDEN AND NORWAY

In common with the other two Scandinavian countries as well as that of Finland, the culinary pattern of the Swedish people is of peasant-style food with fresh fish as the mainstay of the diet. Swedish food is not highly spiced but some of the accompanying sauces are, which equates with the tastes of the other two Scandinavian countries. However, being a rich country there are many imported foodstuffs and the cooking can be very sophisticated, a typical *smörgåsbord* having as many as sixty different dishes on it both cold and hot, a bewildering array that is for the first course at lunch only.

The food of the Norwegians is very similar to that of the Swedes except that in Norway it is mostly fish and dairy products. The meat in use is beef, lamb, venison, capercailzie, duck, goose, ptarmigan, snipe and seagull; smoked lamb is commonly used. All kinds of fish are a staple in the diet with cod, eel, halibut, herring, mackerel, mussels, salmon and whale meat. Some good cheeses are made including Cheddar, Gammelost, Geitost, Nøkkelost and Primula.

The Koltbord or Smörgåsbord selection is served mainly at lunchtime.

Aquavit is made in many different flavours and is drunk very cold.

LOCAL PRODUCE

MEAT	beef, goat, lamb, mutton, pork, reindeer, veal; chicken, goose, turkey; game birds; venison
FISH AND SHELLFISH	bass, buckling, carp, cod, salt cod, haddock, halibut, herring, kilkis, klipfish, ling, salmon, smelt, trout; crayfish
FRUIT	apples, blueberries, cloudberries, lingonberries, pears, plums
VEGETABLES	beetroot, cabbage, carrots, cauliflower, celery, horseradish, kohlrabi, mushrooms, parsnips, swedes

SPECIALITES	smörgåsbord (a buffet selection including hot and cold fish and meat with bread); fruit soups; kjottkaker med bytlebaer (meat balls with cranberries, apples and pears); far-i-kal (mutton stew); gravlax (raw cured salmon flavoured with dill); rokt lax (smoked salmon); kaldolmar (stuffed cabbages with beef, pork, and rice); plommonspackad flaskkarre (loin of pork and prunes); kott-bullar (beef meatballs fried then poached); bruna boner (baked brown beans); bockling herring
PASTRY	knackebrod, saffron bread, spritz rings, rye biscuits
CHEESE	nikklelost, gjetost
WINES	imported
SPIRITS	aquavit (with many flavourings) brannevin, schnapps
BEER	Falcon, Brygghusöl, Mellanol Tib, Three Towns

POLAND

This is a very good cuisine that stems from the fertile land and thousands of lakes that make up this country and the thrifty hard-working population knows how to make the best possible use of Nature's gifts. Several other countries have contributed to the repertoire, not just near neighbours such as Germany, Hungary and Russia but also Italy; the Jewish people who were invited to live in Poland contributed many of their ethnic dishes to the Polish repertoire. As in Russia there is the use of sour cream for finishing dishes and pickled cucumbers are used in cooking. The quality of Polish cakes and pastries is very good and there is a wide selection of them; babas are Polish by origin.

LOCAL PRODUCE

MEAT	beef, pork; bacon, ham; ducks, geese, turkey; game birds; rabbit, wild boar; venison
FISH AND SHELLFISH	carp, eel, herrings, perch, pike, salmon, tench, trout; crayfish, snails
FRUIT	apples, blackberries, cherries, hawthorn berries, pears, plums, prunes, raspberries
VEGETABLES	beetroot, cabbage, chard, cucumber, gherkins; horseradish, kohlrabi, mushrooms, pumpkin, sorrel, turnips, wild mushrooms

263

SPECIALITIES	zrazy wolowe z kasza gryczana (mushroom soup); cold fruit soups; bortsch; tripe; salami; sauerkraut; bigos (sauerkraut cooked with pork, beef, bacon, game, garlic sausage, tomato purée and red wine); pierozki or pierogi (dumplings made with various fillings – ham, mushroom, fruit, etc. and poached); krupnik (barley and vegatable broth); chlodnick (cold soup of beetroot, radish, cucumber, prawns, hardboiled egg and cream); babka (yeast cake similar to babas); sernik (cream cheese cake)
WINE	Mead
SPIRITS	Vodka, zubrowka, pejsachowka, wyborowa, goldwasser (vodka sweetened and flavoured containing specks of gold leaf)
BEER	Zywiec

PORTUGAL

The cookery of Portugal is best described as being a simple peasant style that is straightforward rather than elaborate. It is spicier than that of Spain but the seasoning is not overdone and by being finished with cream and butter, is smoother. Portugal's former colonies have contributed to the culinary heritage, mainly from the items imported, including the popularity of curry. Madeira and port are used in cooking and lemon juice is used to finish dishes. Fish is used a lot, often as a *bouillabaisse*. Although not a very large country, each region of Portugal has its own specialities thus making it possible to feature the menu of a particular province.

LOCAL PRODUCE

MEAT	beef, goat, lamb, pork, veal; tripe, duck; pheasant; hare, quail
FISH AND SHELLFISH	cod, bacalhau (dried salt cod), bass, hake, horse mackerel, red mullet, soles, sardines, tuna; clams, crayfish, lobster, prawns, squid
FRUIT	figs, grapefruit, grapes, lemons, oranges, peaches, pears, quince
VEGETABLES	kale, pimentos, pumpkin, sweetcorn, tomatoes, turnip tops
SPECIALITIES	presunto (smoked ham); caldo verde (broth using kale); canja (chicken broth); caldeirada (fish soup-stew); escabeche (pieces of fish, meat or poultry fried, then pickled and served cold); cozido (boiled dinner of beef, chicken, sausage with vegetables, chick peas and rice); iscas (marinated liver fried, with bacon); pudim (baked egg custard served with a sauce)

CHEESE	alcohaca, castelo branco, flamengo, queijo da Serra, ranacal, serpa
WINES	vinho verde, Dão red and white, vila reals, pinhel, alenquer, cadaval, bucelas, setubal moscatel, port, Madeira
SPIRITS	Bagaco, Brandy

ROMANIA

This is a rich and cultured cuisine that is closely related to that of Bulgaria and though both were part of the Turkish empire, Romania kept its sovereignty and the influence was less marked. It was part of the Austro-Hungarian Empire which also left its mark and as in Hungary, a lot of different kinds of pimentos, both fiery and mild, are used. Romania is the seventh largest wine-producing country in the world and the quality is good.

LOCAL PRODUCE

MEAT	beef, mutton, pork; chicken, duck; wild boar, chamois
FISH AND SHELLFISH	carp, sturgeon; crayfish, mussels, snails
FRUIT	apples, apricots, cherries, peaches, plums, soft fruits
VEGETABLES	cabbage, carrots, leeks, lettuce, pimentos, sauerkraut, tomatoes
SPECIALITIES	ratza cu varza acra (braised sauerkraut and duck); pui gatit cu vin si masline (sauté of chicken in wine and yoghurt sauce with black olives); ciorba de praz (cold soup of sauerkraut juice); pastrama (spiced, salted and smoked meat, served grilled); ghiveciu (stewed meat and vegetables); musaca (moussaka finished with a layer of eggs and cream); sarmale (stuffed brined cabbage leaves)
CHEESE	Brynza (ewe's milk), Kashkaval
WINES	white: Perla, Riesling red: Nicoresti Babeasca, mustarii (unfermented grape juice), turberil (grape juice starting to ferment)
SPIRITS	Tzvica (plum and almond)

RUSSIA

It would seem impossible to condense the cookery practices of a nation of 230 million people composed of 170 different nationalities into a short résumé but in fact the culinary traditions are not profound as there are very few truly Russian dishes, those in general use being French versions of Russian ones, or French dishes with Russian names.

The international repertoire contains a large number of Russian dishes, practically all from Czarist times, which were the creations of French chefs who were then working in the houses of rich and noble families. In those days, train-loads of food arrived daily from France to add to the variety of dishes demanded by the Russian aristocracy. Many dishes were named after the family or the location of their house.

Russian people like eating and drinking on a large scale and the climate in winter is such that a high kilocalorie intake is necessary. Thus the main culinary tradition is for ample-size portions of a wide variety of foods. The problem encountered by travellers on being invited into the homes of Russians has been well recorded, many having assumed that the lavish display of *zakouski*, or cocktail canapés, was the actual meal, whereas it was simply the appetiser and having eaten his fill the poor guest was then led into the dining room to start eating a gargantuan meal!

Russian cookery became more widely known after the Revolution in 1917 when many wealthy emigrés settled in the West and opened restaurants. The people of Russia have a natural buoyancy of character which is easily stimulated by a well-prepared meal; they enjoy the pleasures of the table even if the tenor of their traditional dishes is that of the sourness that comes from the use of salted cucumbers, dill, horseradish and sour cream. Each region or country of the URSS has some culinary traditions with sufficient dishes to produce a good selection of menus but to arrive at a typical national menu, it would be necessary to draw from all over.

LOCAL PRODUCE

MEAT	lamb, mutton, pork; offals; chicken, duck, goose; rabbit, hare, game birds; sucking pig
FISH AND SHELLFISH	bream, carp, cod, grey mullet, herring, red mullet, pike, salmon, sprats, sturgeon; prawns, crayfish
FRUIT	apples, cherries, cranberries, plums, grapes, whortleberries; soft fruits
VEGETABLES	asparagus, beetroot, cabbage (green and red), cucumbers, egg-plant, Jerusalem artichokes, kohlrabi, marrow, dried mushrooms, potatoes, pumpkins, radishes, sauerkraut

266

A French version of a Russian menu could be as follows:

MENU

Caviar d'Astrakan aux Blinis

Bortsh Ukrainien

Suprême d'Esturgeon Czarine

Cotelette de Volaille Kievsky
Subrics d'Oseille
Pommes Impératrice

Soufflé Glacé Siberien

Café

SPECIALITIES chicken kiev; boeuf strogonoff; blinis; coulibiac of salmon;
bortsch; stschy (broth type cabbage soup); batwinia (cold
sorrel and beetroot soup); vareniki (cheese dumplings); kashe
(buckwheat flour paste baked as a loaf, the inside crumb removed,
mixed with butter and baked); pirochki or piroguis (minced
cooked beef and hard boiled egg wrapped in a pancake and
deep-fried); sernic (pancake filled with cottage cheese and
raisins, served with cream on top); kapoostmak (braised cabbage
with prunes and sour cream); sigui (a Baltic fish), kilkis (smoked
Baltic sprats); smetana (sour cream); caviar; pojarskis; bitkis
Caviar: beluga, either black or grey, is the best quality; osetrova
has smaller grains and is second best; sevruga has the smallest
grains; malossol is fresh, slightly salted sevruga caviar; pressed
caviar is a mixture of broken grains of osetrova and sevruga,
lumpfish caviare is the dyed roe of the fish of that name; there
is also red caviar from the salmon. There are a number of recipes
for zakouskis in the hors-d'oeuvre section in Escoffier's *Complete Guide to the Art of Modern Cookery*

PASTRY rye bread, poppy seed bread, buckwheat loaves, Kulich (Easter
cake)

267

CHEESE	brynza, kurt, medynsky, rossisky, tushiri
WINE	mukazani (Georgian red), tsinandali (Georgian white)
SPIRITS	Vodka: krasnaia golovka (the best); zubrowka (with buffalo grass); rubinovaia (orange); smarodinouka (red, with black-currants); Chachis Araki, brandy; Nastoika (sweet brandy); Gorny Doubnyak

SPAIN

The food of Spain is rich and distinctive and reflects the wide range of commodities and the seasonings used rather than from the use of cream and butter as in other cuisines and although olive oil is used in many dishes, the real Spanish dishes are not greasy. The cooking is not sophisticated and stems from the household rather than that of the court so it is not a refined one. The influence of Greeks and Romans followed by the Moors from North Africa has been absorbed.

The use of dried peas and beans is to be noted; rice is used in the form of paella which is designed to make a little fish or meat go a long way. Pastry, pudding and cake as the dessert is replaced by fresh fruit but bread is a mainstay of the diet.

LOCAL PRODUCE

MEAT	beef, lamb, mutton, pork, veal; chicken, duck, turkey; pigeon, game birds, rabbit
FISH	anchovies, dried salt cod, sardines, red mullet, skate, trout, tuna; crab, crayfish, prawns, lobster, mussels, octopus, oysters, squid
FRUIT	bananas, figs, grapes, medlars, melons, oranges, peaches, pomegranates
VEGETABLES	beans, courgettes, egg-plant, globe artichokes, pimentos, tomatoes
SPECIALITIES	gazpacho (ice-cold tomato, cucumber and pimento soup); piperada vasca (Basque flat omelette); tortilla (Spanish omelette); olla podrida (similar to pot au feu); cocido (stewed vegetables with pork and dumplings); paella (chicken, squid, prawns, crayfish, mussels, lobster and crabmeat cooked with pilaff of rice flavoured with garlic and saffron); jambon di serrano (cured ham eaten raw); bacalao (dried salted cod); sangria (red wine fruit cup); escabeche (fried fish, meat or chicken, marinated and eaten cold)

CHEESE	cabrales, manchego, nata
WINE	Rioja, Vega Sicilia, Malaga (sweet), Montilla (like sherry but not fortified), Valdepeñas
SPIRIT	brandy, Aguardiente (grappa), Anis de Mono, Cuaranta-y-Tres, Izarra, Sapinder
BEER	Cergal, Coral, Sagres, San Miguel

SWITZERLAND

The high standard of living of the Swiss people means they enjoy a rich and generous way of living with ample-size portions and second helpings of good quality food. The Swiss have successfully combined French, German and Italian cookery into a classical cuisine in keeping with their high standard of living with more emphasis perhaps on the Teutonic influence than on that of France.

Having four languages and being divided into regional Cantons means that there is wide variation in the people's diet but overall there are not many truly native dishes and the diet is an international one. Being very mountainous, it is not possible to grow very much produce so the emphasis is on dairy products. The quality of the sweet dishes is very high and many pastry cooks go to Switzerland to learn their craft.

LOCAL PRODUCE

MEAT	lamb, pork, veal, offals, chicken, goose; pigeon, game; venison; goat, chamois
FISH AND SHELLFISH	eels, bondelles, perch, pike, salmon, salmon trout, trout, snails, fera, lavarot, lot
FRUIT	apples, apricots, cherries, chestnuts, peaches, pears; raspberries, redcurrants
VEGETABLES	asparagus, beans, cabbage, (green and red), celery, leeks, mushrooms, spinach, tomatoes
SPECIALITIES	fondue (Gruyère and Emmenthal cheese melted with white wine and kirsch, eaten by dipping cubes of bread into it); raclette (the melted part of cheese scraped warm onto a plate, eaten with jacket potatoes and pickled onion); fondue rapperswil (deep poached strips of steak dipped into various sauces with glacé fruits; Béarnaise, curry, ketchup); fondue bourguignonne (deep fried small cubes of steak dipped in various hot or cold

269

sauces); gnocchi; rosti (sliced cooked potatoes shallow fried with onion pressed into a cake); spaetzli; bunderlfeisch (dried beef eaten raw in slices); rohschinken (smoked ham); kalbssteak humpelmayer (veal escalope with banana, apple and curry sauce); quiches; Berner platte (smoked loin of pork, brisket or beef, bacon, sausage, potato and beans)

PASTRY	basler leckerlei (cinnamon biscuits); fritters; cheesecake; streusel (coffee cake), guggelhof
CHEESE	Emmenthaller, Gruyere, tomme vaudoise, vacherin, bratkase, appenzeller
WINES	white: Fendant, Heidenwein, Mondemont, Lutry, Yvorne red: Thurgau, Merlot, Dole, Cortaillod, Herrschaft, Valais, Château Rolland
SPIRITS	Kirsch, Marc, Prune, Williams
BEER	Labani, Apenbrau, Calanda Festbier, Driekonigs Bier, Sternbrau, Cardinal, Henninger Meisterbock, Pic
SAUSER	new season's wine
NON-ALCOHOLIC WINE	grapillon (white)

UNITED STATES OF AMERICA

To try to encapsulate the culinary traditions of the whole of the United States into a brief summary is obviously impossible because there are so many different national and ethnic cuisines to deal with. There are the Red Indian, Dutch, French and English contributions which were further enhanced by the culinary traditions brought to America by immigrants from many other countries. It would be nice to say that all these different food habits have blended together to form the American national cuisine but in fact there are no truly authentic American restaurants but plenty of culinary traditions so that they are regional rather than national.

The wealth of produce has had a tremendous effect upon food habits and modern means of transport have made goods readily available everywhere so that it is possible to describe the culinary traditions from the national foods and to say that regions divide on ethnic lines where immigrants, no matter how long settled in the New World, still keep alive the culinary traditions of their homeland.

270

As the world's greatest food-producers the Americans lack nothing in their diet thus making it possible to say that all foods are obtainable as well as some that are peculiar to particular areas and not grown elsewhere. Thus only these special products are listed, together with the few dishes that can be said to have originated in the United States though they may be based on some other country's foodway.

LOCAL PRODUCE

MEAT	wild turkey, buffalo, wild boar, wild goose, cornish game hen, reindeer, raccoon, opossum, muskrat; corned beef
FISH AND SHELLFISH	bluefish, butterfish, cusk, pickerel, pomfret, pompano, red snapper, shad roe, striped bass, swordfish, tilefish, tomcod, whitefish; abalone, little neck clams, terrapin
FRUIT	bing cherries, cranberry, huckleberries, pecan nuts, persimmons, quince
VEGETABLES	black-eyed peas, chayotes (squash), lima beans, snap beans, squash, sweet potatoes, yams
SPECIALITIES	apple pandowdy (apple pie made in a deep dish with biscuit type pastry); New England boiled dinner (salt beef with carrots, onions, potatoes, cabbage and small beetroots); jambalaya (meat, chicken, shellfish with rice, like paella); hominy (dried corn, soaked and boiled); hominy grits (hominy cooked in water as for porridge); corn pone (maize flour dough, baked then shallow-fried); succotash (sweetcorn kernels with salt pork and lima beans, kidney beans or broad beans); ambrosia (sliced oranges with sugar and freshly grated coconut); hamburgers; hot dogs; Boston baked beans; clam chowder; saratoga chips; corned beef hash; salad Waldorf; chop suey; cecils (beef croquettes); Southern fried chicken; chicken Maryland; hashed brown potatoes; O'Brien potatoes; chicken à la King; Philadelphia pepperpot (broth soup with tripe); Vichyssoise
PASTRY	Parker House rolls, Graham crackers, pumpkin pie, angels' food cake, devil's food cake, blueberry pie, waffles, banana bread, Boston cream pie, chiffon pie, pecan pie, flapjacks
CHEESE	Brick (Cheddar type, elastic, with small holes); Herkimer (sharp, aged Cheddar); Pineapple (cheddar in the shape of a pineapple); Siederkrauz (like Limburger); most varieties of European cheeses are made in America
WINES	Wine is produced in half of the States but 90 per cent is made in California in six main regions and it is mainly from there that it is exported

SPIRITS	Bourbon (maize whisky), Rye, Cayo Verde, Coffee Sport, Forbidden Fruit, Rock and Rye, Southern Comfort
BEER	Budweiser, Falls City, Genesee, Hudephol, Muller High Life, Pabst, Rainier, Schlitz, Schmidts, Simon, Straub

WEST INDIES

The Caribbean is composed of nineteen different countries that stretch from Florida to Venezuela, discovered by Columbus in 1492. Many of them have been ruled variously by Dutch, English, French and Spanish over the centuries. This created a combination of cooking styles to which can be added that of the slaves sent there from Africa, the native Indian races, and the Chinese who went to work there. Differences between the foods of the different countries are influenced mainly by foods grown locally because especially in the smaller islands, imported foods can still be scarce. Some foods that grow well in one place may not be part of the culture of another.

The dishes of the West Indies are highly flavoured and pungent and many burn the mouth. Spices are mainly allspice and cinnamon; garlic, bay leaves, chillies and lime juice are used as flavourings with any other herbs and spices available. Coconut milk is used in cooking, but not much dairy produce is so used.

The cookery of the Caribbean area is simple and only the use of spices provides the exotic distinction. Most meat is cooked slowly so as to render it tender. The stockpot is still widely used in the household and is greatly prized. Lime juice plays a big part in cookery, in drinks, and limes are used as a decoration. As with many holiday resorts, what the tourists eat is very different from what local people – white or black – eat and hotels serve international dishes with only local overtones.

LOCAL PRODUCE

MEAT	beef, lamb, goat, pork, sucking pig; chickens, turkey; manacou (a small marsupial)
FISH	flying fish, grunt, grouper, hayfish, jackfish, knogfish, mackerel, mollusk, red snapper, salmon, tobalo, tunny fish; crabs, land crabs, crawfish, crayfish, turtle, frogs; dried salt cod
FRUIT	avocados, bananas, citrus fruits, coconuts, guavas, limes, melons, mangoes, paw paws, peanuts, plantains, pineapples, sugar apples, star apples

272

VEGETABLES	achee, breadfruit, calabash, cassava root, dasheen, eddo, egg-plant, malangas, okras, pimentos, pumpkin, sorrel, sweet potatoes, tanya, taros, yams
SPECIALITES	Callilu soup, Coo-Coo (type of polenta containing slices of okra, served cut into slices to serve with meat or fish); Coco Quemada (a sweet made with coconut syrup, eggs and sherry); stuffed breadfruit; peas and rice; plantanos fritos (shallow fried plantain); guava cheese; souse (pigs' head and trotters served cold with lime juice sauce); bird pepper sherry (sherry bottled with small chilli peppers); ginger beer
SPIRITS	rum (many different kinds); Curaçao; Tia Maria. Chococo (coconut and chocolate liqueur); Pimento Dram (allspice flavour spirit); rum punch (dark rum, lime juice, sugar and ice); planters' punch (rum and fruit juice); daiquiri (rum, lime juice and sugar) Angostura bitters
BEER	Allsopps lager, Dragon, Ebony, Red Stripe

YUGOSLAVIA

Several different nationalities each with its own culinary traditions go to make modern Yugoslavia. Four main religions and three languages are shared amongst the population. It is a rugged land and the cookery is equally so and is as varied as the different cultures.In addition, the neighbouring countries have left their influence on the food and there are Austrian, Hungarian, Italian, Turkish and Greek contributions to the national diet, their impact being left in the various provinces. As a part of the Turkish empire which included many Middle Eastern countries, there is also an Arabic influence.

Fish is more widely used than meat, the meat being cut into cubes for kebabs or in minced form. Mutton is more likely to appear in a stew than as a roast, a whole spit-roasted sheep being a celebration meal. Herbs play a large part in all kinds of dishes, more so than spices.

LOCAL PRODUCE

MEAT	beef, lamb, mutton, pork, veal, offals, goat, quails, chicken
FISH AND SHELLFISH	carp, John Dory, mackerel, perch, pike, sardines, sprats; squid, trout
FRUIT	apricots, cherries, medlars, melons, mulberries, peaches, plums, quinces

273

VEGETABLES	cabbage, carrots, celeriac, egg-plant, pimentos, potatoes, pumpkin, sauerkraut, tomatoes
SPECIALITIES	hladna zakuske (assorted dried sausages); prsut (smoked hams); gibanica (baked pie of layers of pastry and egg, cheese and yoghurt filling); cufle (fried meat balls); bosanski lonac (several different kinds of meat and vegetables cooked in white wine); sogan dolma (onions stuffed with meat and rice); bosanska kalja od kapusa (pork or mutton stewed with Dutch cabbage and tomatoes); salata od praziluka (leeks cooked in oil and vinegar, served as a salad); hajducki cevap (grilled steak)
PASTRY	ratluk (Turkish Delight); caraway bread
CHEESE	sir (ewe's milk)
WINE	white: Pinot Blanc, Riesling, Sauvignon, Ilocki, Zilavka red: Teran, Cabernet, Dingac, Crmica, Prokupac, Blatina
SPIRITS	Slijivovica (plum brandy), Travarica, Vlahov, Pelinkovac Kruskovac (pear)
BEER	Slovenia, Istria-Union, Karlovac, Niksio, Ztatovoc, Tomislav

SOUL FOOD

The term 'sould food' may not be as well known as 'sould music' but is an aspect of catering that assumes a major role in certain parts of the world. The word 'soul' is used by coloured people to describe the sense of ancestral pride they have in their roots, as it governs the way they live. The use of the term 'soul food' demonstrates their feeling for traditions in the eating style of their their ancestors who through circumstances not of their own making, were forced to live frugally on cheap foodstuffs that required simple cooking methods.

'Soul food' restaurants are in effect, a public expression of the culture of a suppressed and long-suffering people. This does not mean that they are to be found only in the ghettos nor that they are run-down eating places that offer no amenities. Although they are found mainly in disttricts where there is a coloured population this does not mean that they are patronised only by the very poor.

The ingredients used for Soul Food menus are of a cheap kind but this does not prevent them from being made into attractive dishes.

In the section on the islands of the West Indies it is shown that simple indigenous ingredients are cooked by elementary methods and an iron pot on a charcoal brazier will produce as good a result as in an oven. Soul food is fairly highly seasoned to suit the traditional tastes of its partakers. The ingredients used include:

MEAT	salt pork; pig's feet, ears, tails and hocks; tripe; spare ribs; chitterlings; squirrel; chicken, canned meat
VEGETABLES	dandelion, black-eyed peas, luna beans, kale, okras, squashes, sweet potatoes, tomatoes, yams
OTHER ITEMS	buttermilk, cake, cold tea, cornmeal, corn bread, hominy grits, peanut butter, canned pork and beans.

RASTAFARIANS

This movement was started in Jamaica some fifty years ago and now has adherents throughout the West Indies, the United States and England. Its members let their hair grow in long locks, and study the Bible diligently.

When it comes to diet, rastafarians follow a strict code of conduct as derived from the Mosaic laws which express their spiritual and political feelings. Orthodox rastafarians do not eat fish, flesh, fowl, milk or eggs and do not take alcohol or use salt. Functional rastafarians will eat meat slaughtered according to Kosher rites but prefer plant foods. Real rastafarians are few in number and most are people who copy them as fashion. Some of the genuine ones live like hermits in the mountains in caves or hand-made huts and live off what they can grow.

VEGETARIAN MEALS

Many ordinary people have stopped eating meat and adopted a vegetarian diet, not so much because of the cost of meat, their dislike of it nor that they have changed their religious beliefs, but because they feel that animals suffer violence in going through the slaughtering procedure and therefore they will not eat the flesh. In some countries a vegetarian diet is traditional, in others meat has been made taboo by a leader of a religious sect; in times of famine or poverty a populace may have found it unobtainable or too expensive and therefore eliminated it from the normal diet.

There is a danger of shortage of protein when changing from a diet which includes meat to a fairly strict vegetarian diet and this can cause malnutrition. Before devising this sort of menu it is necessary to know whether the meal will be, (i) lacto-vegetarian, (ii) lacto-ovo-vegetarian, (iii) moderate vegetarian, or (iv) vegan which is very strict vegetarian. There are also moderate and strict fruitarian diets, all with different requirements. To add to this there are food faddists such as those who follow a macrobiotic regime, eat only organic foods, do not eat cooked foods, or will not accept foods imported from a particular

275

country where they consider the government is oppressive, and so on. Where some members of all these sects are gathered together, the caterer has a real problem to solve.

11 The Creation of a Gastronomic Occasion

The Requirements – Preparing for the Occasion – Some Aphorisms on Dining – The Theme – The Menu Content and Menu Card – Matching the Menu to the Occasion and to the Person – Historical Occasions – Burns' Night Bill of Fare – Stage Management of the Occasion – Spectacular Occasions – Medieval Banquets – The Role of the Toastmaster – Gastronomic Occasions – Unconventional Meals – Guidance for Gastronomic Themes – The Environment and Function Management – Service – Superstitition – Etiquette – Table Manners

20. The Banqueting Room at the Royal Pavilion, Brighton

The creation of a gastronomic occasion has more to it than the mere provision of good food and efficient service and there are many other factors which contribute towards the total enjoyment; their importance is discussed in this chapter.

THE REQUIREMENTS

In music the value of the clarity of each individual note does not of itself provide a sense of balance and harmony but each makes a contribution towards the pleasure of listening. One of the best analogies to be used in the context of a gastronomic occasion is a classical opera. When mounting an opera, a number of interrelated factors are paramount to its success – the plot, the libretto and the music score. When the opera is presented to the public, the theatre in which it is produced, the stage setting, the visual effects and illumination, the orchestra and its conductor and probably most important of all, the ability of its principal singer as well as its chorus, will all contribute to its success.

Similarly, the comfort which is provided in terms of accommodation as well as the integrated environmental effects such as the visual, thermal and auditory environment will all contribute to the enjoyment. The better the environment created the more likely it is that the experience will be a memorable one.

278

PREPARING FOR THE OCCASION

The planning of a gastronomic occasion requires just such an overall perspective in its approach. It must be recognised that any one single factor taken in isolation cannot create a gastronomic experience, but when all the contributing factors are brought together and evaluated as a whole then the occasion should transcend the satisfaction of a simple physiological need and elevate the partaker to a state of sensual delight in both physiological and psychological terms.

To achieve this it is not only the palate that must be maintained in a state of continuous stimulation and expectations, but the whole state of mind should be prepared to a progression of pleasurable moments. This is achieved through pre-planned experiences in food offering, presentation impact, good service, a thematic entertainment – all carefully introduced within an harmonious crescendo.

A gastronomic occasion should therefore be comprised of a theme, a fitting menu with appropriate beverages and a suitable sequence of entertaining activities such as musical diversion, cabaret, speeches or an environment where relaxed conversation can take place. It requires the support of a skilled kitchen staff under an efficient *chef de cuisine* and the dedicated involvement of the waiting brigade under the supervision of a *maître d'hôtel* who controls with a logistic approach, the various sequences outfront.

The Contributing Factors

The list of these factors is fairly extensive but not all of them necessarily apply to each occasion; the organiser must know which are more apt in a particular situation than in another. Some are of a permanent nature and are therefore given for possible consideration; it may only be possible to implement others at a time when renovations are being carried out.

PERMANENT FIXTURES

The exterior of the building in which the event is to take place is the first form of contact that the visitor has with the establishment and the impression obtained at this stage is of importance in projecting what the establishment may be like inside. The name of the establishment, the elegance of the lettering in which it is displayed, the canopy, lighting, size of pot plants, all contribute to the impression the establishment makes upon persons entering the premises.

THE SIZE AND SHAPE OF THE DINING AREA

The size and shape of the dining room have an immediate effect upon the customer as he enters. In any situation the visitor must be provided with a

279

feeling of well-being and security. A large dining room will permit many guests to be accommodated, yet its layout must be such that an intimate atmosphere has been created so as to enhance the sense of security and of belonging.

The most restful and peaceful ambience is obtained by means of a round or an oval dining room where perusing eyes can scrutinise the surroundings without encountering sharp features. Another advantage of this shape of dining room is that it provides an ideal situation for positioning table arrangements towards a focal point where the presentation of the various features of the evening take place. This focus may be the orchestra, the cabaret or the entrance used by waiters when presenting the sequence of dishes.

Relief features may be obtained within the room with elegant pillars, symmetrical plaster work and arched windows or alcoves with concealed lighting.

SOME APHORISMS ON DINING

Man's knowledge of consumer behaviour within an enclosed space can be used to convey the feeling of an harmonious theme specially created for the occasion and providing the right atmosphere. **Brillat-Savarin** himself propounded a number of considerations which ought to be taken into account when contemplating the promotion of a perfect dinner; the rules still hold good for the creation of a gastronomic occasion though some of his points may have to be modified in relation to commercial practices, but they are still extremely valid.

Among his aphorisms in *The Physiology of Taste* are the following:

'**Let the number of guests not exceed twelve, so that the conversation may be constantly general.**' Savarin may be referring not only to the classic order of the *triclinium* but also to the need of containing the party within an optimum number for the perfect provision of food and an informed exchange of ideas.

'**Let them (the guests) be so chosen that their occupations are various, their tastes analogue, and with such points of contact that one need not have recourse to that odious formality of introductions.**' The variety of interests will preclude conversation from falling into the specific although similar tastes will facilitate enjoyment of the food offered and permit the commensals to focus their attention on the main reason for their reunion which is the food. The reference to the practice of introductions is an obvious one. In situations where the individuals need to be introduced to strangers a state of alertness of the mind needs to be maintained and this will prevent relaxation which is one of the main contributors to good digestion.

'**Let the dining-room be brilliantly lighted, the cloth as white as snow, and the temperature of the room be from 16° to 20°C.**' The environmental considera-

280

tions are ranked very high in Savarin's pronouncements, indeed he places them before the food itself; this aspect will be pursued as a separate topic.

'Let the men be witty and not pedantic, and the women amiable without being too coquettish.' The desirability of maintaining a sense of alertness through good conversation and feminine gracefulness is expressed here.

'Let the dishes be exquisitely chosen, but small in number, and the wine of the first quality, each in its degree.' It must be noted that at the time he wrote these pronouncements the prevailing method of food presentation was still the classic French style of service as inherited from the Renaissance period in which dishes were placed in large numbers directly onto the table. Savarin in fact pointed in the direction that of necessity had to follow much later; that the wines chosen should be of quality in their respective place is now an accepted maxim for these occasions.

'Let the dishes be served from the more substantial to the lighter, and from the simpler wines to those of finer bouquet.' This pronouncement ought to be considered in the context of time with regard to food; it is generally agreed that the dishes that conclude a meal should be light and refreshing so as to permit guests to leave the table with a feeling of well-being. It is generally accepted that dishes should be presented in order of intensity up until the service of the main dish and the move towards lightness from the next course. Savarin's pronouncement on wine is still the most apt for any occasion.

'Let the eating proceed slowly, the dinner being the last business of the day, and let the guests look upon themselves as travellers who journey together towards a common object.' The necessary for a pause in between courses is important and is emphasised here. The main objective of gastronomy is not just the pleasure derived from food, but as Savarin also points out, 'Its object is to watch over the preservation of men by means of the best nourishment possible.' Thus it is hoped that the occasion will help to extend his journey through his span of life.

'Let the coffee be hot and the liqueurs be specially chosen.' It may be that Savarin is indicating that the chosen liqueur should fit the occasion, rather than offering a choice of several liqueurs as is modern practice.

'Let the guests be detained by social attraction and animated with the expectation that before the evening is over there will be some further enjoyment.' Entertainment has been associated with gastronomic occasions from the very beginning and the role of entertainment is to maintain a convivial mood and create a sense of excitement.

281

'If any man has ever been a guest at a repast uniting all these conditions, he can boast of having been present at his own apotheosis; and he would have enjoyed it less in proportion had these conditions been forgotten or neglected.' These are Brillat-Savarin's conditions and there are only few minor exclusions which are not totally relevant to the commercial context. He indicates that Man could reach his own deification through this experience provided these maxims were followed. In principle, if good judgement, love and care are exercised, and prime materials are placed at the disposal of a keen and informed chef working in a well-equipped kitchen with adequate assistance; if the décor of the dining room is appropriate, if choice tableware is available and if a good head waiter with informed assistants is to serve the meal, then this experience could be created.

The following points are mainly for the guidance of and consideration by the commercial entrepreneur; the success of the occasion will be due to the feelings of love, care and pride he has for his fellow men and for the great traditions of the art of gastronomy.

THE THEME

The theme for a gastronomic occasion must be decided only after serious and involved research on the part of the organiser and of the caterer who will implement the concept in a manner fitting for the occasion. He must satisfy himself that he is in the position to meet the request through the resources made available. The theme is his 'plot' which must be carried through to a desirable conclusion. The menu will be his libretto, which will unfold at various stages the gastronomic plot. The prime food materials to be transformed by his chefs into finished dishes which are a credit to the culinary art, are his musical score. His chefs and his waiters will be the artists who will ensure that his ideas are converted into a successful gastronomic experience.

Stages and Considerations in the Implementation of a Gastronomic Theme

It has to be appreciated that a variety of experiences serve to enrich man's life and that in modern times these may be much sought after by the community who like to attend social gatherings.

The theme should comprise a historical, national, contemporary or geographical reference, a suitable menu and an appeal to the senses which reinforces the thematic approach. In selecting the theme, it must be remembered that for maximum effect it is necessary to attempt to re-create a situation or an effect which is clearly evocative of what is intended. For this purpose stage settings may be rented from local theatres to provide the desired background; plants, flowers and even portable fountains can be used to enhance the concept.

282

Visual Environment

Both colour and illumination can be modified to enhance the concept. Spot-lights and light filters of various colours make an excellent contribution, although the selection of colours must be such that it does not interfere with customer's well-being, nor with food presentation. For these reasons primary colours should be used sparingly, and diffused colours should be in the cold spectrum so as to induce relaxation. Candles may be used to good effect to create an intimate atmosphere and they help to bring down the height of the ceiling, but air-circulation needs to be mechanically assisted so as to prevent the smell of burning wick from interfering with the aroma of food.

Music

Noise, and in particular excessive noise, can be a source of irritation. Melodic harmonies can be a contributory asset by providing a sense of security and by acting as a form of welcome to the guests. Certain kinds of music are imme-diately associated with a particular occasion of even with a certain place. The sound of an accordian conjures up the atmosphere of a Parisien bistro, and so on.

THE MENU CONTENT AND MENU CARD

The contents of the menu must reflect the principles of menu planning and menu composition as indicated in Chapters 6 and 7. It is necessary to reiterate the importance of ensuring that the dishes selected are presented in the correct sequence in ascending order of intensity as for the main course, then descending to a finale which is appropriately light. The card should reflect the theme of the occasion and include full details of the proceedings.

The dishes should be prepared and garnished according to conventional rules. As indicated in Chapter 1, man is normally suspicious of new foods and modern forms of food preparation. When these need to be introduced extreme care and sensitivity should be exercised, in keeping with the consumer's culture and knowledge. In what follows, guidance is offered on fitting the menu to a specific occasion, ideas about suitable terminology, and the historical occasion outlined will, it is hoped, provide thought for the planning of future events.

MATCHING THE MENU TO THE OCCASION AND THE PERSON

One of the most challenging aspects of menu composition is to word the menu so that it reflects the nature of the occasion by using synonyms in place of the classical garnish names. Occasions which call for this kind of menu composition are certain special days in the calendar such as Christmas, and special functions held for a particular group or for a particular purpose.

For example, a booking may be received for a party of people who are celebrating some special event yet there are not enough of them to warrant a private room nor do they wish to order a special menu, but there is a well-known person amongst them. Given sufficient notice the chef could rename one of the main dishes or a sweet on the menu after the VIP who would take it as a compliment that he or she was sufficiently important to be honoured by having a dish designated in his or her name. The length of notice required to put this into operation would be determined by the printer rather than by the caterer because only some slight modification to the original dish is necessary. Customers attending a special function usually delight in trying to elucidate the meaning of any novel although entirely traditional titles given to the dishes. Instead of writing the menu for Christmas Day in the usual way it is possible to present it with appropriate literary allusions as in Chapter 7.

When paying tribute to a person who is retiring from his post after giving valued service over a long number of years the menu could allude to his career as in the following:

MENU

Le Consommé Couronner
Les Paillettes du Doyen

–

Le Zéphyr de Sole des Adieux

–

Le Tournedos de Boeuf Grande Epoque
Les Haricots Verts Héritage
Les Pommes de Terre Rissolées du Patriache

–

Les Fraises Ancien Régime
Les Mignardises Bel Esprit

–

Le Café Hommage

It is difficult but perfectly possible to compose a menu that exactly suits any particular occasion, from a meeting of the *Ancien Association des Amis d'Andouilles d'Angers* to, say *Zygologists of Zanzibar*.

The menu for New Year's Eve is a fairly traditional one but it can be so worded that it is made even more worthy of the occasion merely by altering the classical garnishes to take account of the date. The price charged often allows for offering a choice of first course from oysters, smoked salmon and foie gras; this is followed by a choice of rich soups including consommé, turtle, or bisque with appropriate accompaniments, a fish course of sole or salmon then the main course of a good quality cut of beef, chicken or veal with a fine garnish and served with quality vegetables, then the sweet which is usually a superb ice-cream concoction followed by fresh fruit and a basket of petits fours. The words suitable to convey the sense of occasion include *Nouvel An, Bonne Année, Saint-Sylvestre, Bon Augure, Anniversaire, Porte-Bonheur, Espérance, Nouveauté.*

For a truly gastronomic occasion where the participants know what they are eating and can understand and interpret the usual menu shorthand there are several methods of approach, the one most frequently used being the very effusive style as in the following example:

21. Preparation for a banquet at the Guildhall, London, at the beginning of this century

LE MENU

**Les Zéphyrs de Parfait de Foie à la Gelée au Oporto accompagnés
de Petits Brioches Chaudes**

–

**La Tassette des Bon Viveurs d'après une Recette Originale escortée de
Paillettes Dorées au Chester**

–

**La Timbale de Homard et Sole Presentée à la Vauclusienne et servie avec
quelques cuillerées de Riz Sauvage**

–

Les Cailles fourrées et envelopées à la Façon de l'Amphitryon

–

La Marquise Givrée au Chartreuse

–

**Le Contre filet de Boeuf Poêlé et entouré d'une Belle Garniture
La Bouquetière de Primeurs
Le Panier de Pommes de Terre Croquant**

–

Le Coffret de Frivolités de Lacam

–

L'Infusion de Mocca

———

The wines served at this function should by rights receive the same elegant descriptions but there is no need to give any details other than the full name, the vintage and the shipper; anything more would complicate the issue, for example, *Sancerre Clos et Caves de la Perrière*, 1972, *Domaine* bottled by *Archimbault, Pommard Cuvée de Dames de la Charité, Hospice de Beaune* 1978, *Château Rieussec* 1970 1ère *Cru Sauternes*, etc.

There is nothing pretentious about a menu written in this style, indeed it demonstrates not only the ability of the chefs who would produce it but also the professionalism of the person who composed it. A great deal of thought would need to have been given to the selection of dishes and the wines so that they merged into a well-rounded whole rather than remaining as a series of dishes. This method of dish projection is much favoured by French *chefs-patrons* who tend to go into laudatory descriptions of their specialities, mentioning every ingredient and method used in making them, even though there could well be a single word that would encompass the whole.

The other main way of writing a gastronomic menu is to do it in rather matter-of-fact terms which state plainly that there is no need to gild the lily as the food is perfect and any extraneous or extravagant phraseology would be out of place, as follows:

LE MENU

Le Saumon d'Ecosse Fumé

–

Le Germiny aux Paillettes

–

Le Délice de Fletan Cléopâtre

La Tourte de Ris d'Agneau Lucullus

–

Le Sorbet au Champagne

–

La Selle de Chevreuil Diane de Châteaumorand
Les Fleurs de Brocolis Hollandaise
Les Pommes Hérisson en Buisson

–

Le Soufflé Glacé Edouard VII
Les Biscuits Perlés

–

Le Demi-tasse Moccha
Les Mignardises

———

The accompanying wines would be listed as briefly as are the dishes, for example *Pouilly Blanc Fumé 1978* with the smoked salmon, *Meursault 1976* with the halibut, *Beaune du Château Blanc* with the tourte, *Château Meyney 1972* with the venison, *Champagne* with the sweet and brandy with the coffee.

The main differences between these two menus, apart from the actual dishes, printing costs and the demands they make upon the knowledge of the partici-

287

pants and the prowess of the chefs, are that the first makes the meal more of an occasion and is written in a literary style designed to stimulate the appetite whereas the second menu could be criticised for having too many geographical and other associations. The use of the indefinite article is entirely appropriate in both menus since they are for a special party of gastronomes in which formality and uniqueness are absolute requirements.

The following example shows how the same menu can be reworded to suit any particular occasion.

LE MENU

Les Cornets de Saumon fumé Renaissance

-

La Tasse des Fondateurs

-

Le Délice de Sole Alma Mater

-

L'Escalope de Ris de Veau Palmarès

-

Le Sorbet au Cliquot

-

La Selle de Pré-Salé Cérémonial

-

Les Fleurs Verts des Eminences
Le Nid de Pommes Amandines

-

L'Ananas Voilé Emérité
Les Frivolités Academique

-

La Tassette Honorer

———

LA CARTE DE VINS	LA CARTE DES METS
Chablis ler cru	Les Cornets du Roi d'Ecossé Lucullus
Sercial-Eduardo Henriques	L'Elixir Double des Amphitryons

Sylvaner Reserve 1979 P. Sparr	**Le Zéphyr de Sole Grand Vatel**
Fleury Les Moriers 1979	**Le Medaillon de Ris de Veau des Maîtres-Queux**
	La Neige au Champagne
Château de Lisse 1975 Saint-Emilion	**La Selle de Pré-Salé Prince des Gastronomes**
	Les Fleurs de Brocolis au Beurre
	Les Pommes Amandines
Blanc Foussy Brut – Touraine	**L'Ananas Voilé Collegium Coquorem**
	La Caissette de Frivolités Culinaires
Crusted Port	**La Demi-Tasse des Gastronomes**

The first version is for the centenary celebration of an academic foundation as indicated by the dish titles and the second shows the same dishes renamed to suit the banquet for a chefs' association. By changing only the last word of each dish it is possible for the same basic menu to be used for almost any group of people belonging to a particular society.

In the second example the headings of the two sides of the menu have been added. There is no rule which says on which side each should be, although it is usual to put the food on the right and the drink on the left hand side.

HISTORICAL OCCASIONS

The following are accounts of one or two events which are felt suitable to illustrate the points made about matching the menu to the occasion.

A banquet was held on 25 October 1850 in honour of the Lord Mayor of London on the occasion of the Great Exhibition of 1851. It was offered by the Mayors of Great Britain and Ireland at the Guildhall, York, in the presence of HRH Prince Albert.

There were two menus, one for the top table of eighteen, the other for the remaining 248 guests. As was the pattern of those times there were two courses, each consisting of many dishes. The first course for the top table consisted of three soups, three fish dishes, three relevés and six entrées plus six side dishes.

289

The second course was of two soups, three roasts, six relevés, various vegetables including asparagus, five entrements and desserts. For the other guests the first course consisted of four soups, four fish dishes, six relevés, ten entrées and the second course was six roasts, four cold dishes, various vegetables and six sweets.

The dishes of each course were all brought out together and arranged on the tables artistically, it was not the intention that each guest would necessarily have some of everything as there were many more portions than guests, for example in the second course for the general guests there were no fewer than one hundred and sixty dishes of food.

One of **Alexis Soyer's** best known creations was the *Hundred Guinea Dish* he devised for the top table only of this banquet. For this he purchased 180 chickens, capons, turkeys, pigeons, pheasants, partridges and grouse and used just the two small pieces of meat found against the backbone of each, known as the *sot l'y laisse*. These were supplemented with several flights of small birds including stuffed larks, buntings, plovers, quails, snipe and woodcocks and a garnish that consisted of cockscombs, truffles, mushrooms, crayfish, olives, asparagus, sweetbreads, quenelles, green mangoes and pieces of turtle flesh.

The total cost of all these ingredients came to £105, but it must be remembered what a huge sum £105 was in those days. Eighteen people shared this dish which was just one of fifteen entrées on the first course. An engraving of this banquet depicts these distinguished guests seated at the top table almost hidden behind some enormous and most elaborate centrepieces representing fruit and flowers.

Soyer entitled this dish on the menu as *L'Extravagance Culinaire d'Alderman* and it really was rather a reckless and frivolous invention to use only the two small pieces from each bird and to discard the remainder. These small pieces are not sufficiently delicate or succulent to warrant such extravagance and the whole dish is exaggerated nonsense. We remember Soyer for many less eccentric creations such as his *Lamb Cutlets à la Reforme.*

Delmonico's Restaurant in New York was the best-known high-class establishment for almost a hundred years from the time it opened in its original premises as a smart cafe in 1827 until its demise in 1923. It succeeded because it was the first restaurant to introduce French dishes to New Yorkers and to serve them extremely well and in an atmosphere that was tranquil but extremely elegant. For thirty-four years from about 1862 the chef was **Charles Ranhofer**, A Frenchman who was a true creative artist and who succeeded in blending the traditions of French food to the tastes and produce of America so as to set a standard which other restaurants found it difficult to attain.

Most of the dishes served at Delmonico's are to be found in Ranhofer's book, *The Epicurean*, which was published in 1893, and also in a book called *The Table* by **Alessandro Filippini**, who worked at Delmonico's as a head waiter for nearly twenty-five years. Two of Ranhofer's creations are **Chicken à la King** and **Lobster Newburg** both named after customers of the Restaurant. **Oscar Tschirky** (1868–1950) who afterwards achieved everlasting fame as **Oscar of the Waldorf**

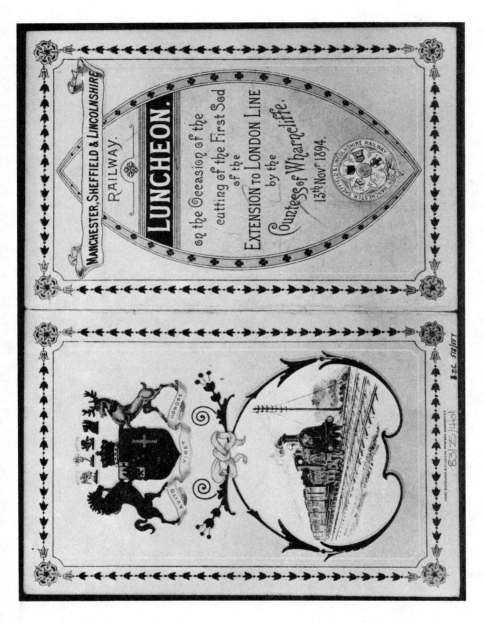

22. The opening of a new railway line not infrequently provided the excuse for a lavish luncheon in the nineteenth century. This menu was served on the occasion of the cutting of the first sod of what was to become the Great Central Railway's ill-fated main line to London

* Menu. *

Oysters

SOUPS

Thick and Clear Turtle

FISH

Salmon Estragon Sauce and Cucumber
Fillet of Sole à la Portugaise

ENTRÉES

Bonne Bouchées de Foie Gras
Sweetbreads à la Toulouse
Chaufroid de Côtelette d'Agneau Renaissance
Punch à la Romaine

REMOVES

Saddle of Mutton Duchesse
Boiled Turkey, Celery Sauce, and York Ham
Mayonnaise of Lobster

ROAST

Pheasant Bardé Sur Croustade and Golden Plover
Chipped Potatoes

Braised Celery à l'Espagnole

SWEETS

Apricot Meringues   Charlotte Russe
Parisienne Jelly   Ice Pudding

Cheese   Salad

DESSERT

Café Noir

---

* Toasts. *

Proposed by

"The Queen" ... ... The Chairman

"The Prince and Princess of } The Chairman
Wales"

"Success to the New London { The Right Hon.
Line" } Lord George
Hamilton

"The Countess of Wharncliffe" { Sir
Edward Watkin,
Bart., M.P.

"The Chairman" ... ... { R. D. M
Littler, Esq.,
C.B., Q.C.

originally worked as a waiter at Delmonico's and went on to make the restaurant at the **Waldorf-Astoria Hotel** the most important one in New York whilst at the same time, educating his customers in the subject of gastronomy, as exemplified in these two menus.

Buffet Dinner at Delmonico's given in honour of the visit of His Royal Highness Edward, Prince of Wales, on 12 October 1860.

MENU

Consommé de Volaille

—

Huîtres à la Poulette

—

Saumon et Truite au Beurre de Montpelier

Filet de Boeuf en Bellevue	: Galantine de Dinde à la Royale
Pâte de Gibier Moderne	: Cochon de Lait à la Parisienne
Pains de Lièvre Historiés	: Terrine de Nerac aux Truffes
Jambon de Westphalie à la Gendarme	: Langue de Boeuf à l'Ecarlate
Mayonnaise de Volaille	: Salade de Homard à la Russe
Grouse : Bécassines	: Faisan : Bécasses
Gelée au Madère	: Macédoine de Fruits
Crème Française	: Glace à la Vanille
Petits Fours	: Charlotte Russe

—

Pièces Montés

———

Sixty years later another Prince of Wales was in New York, but times and menus had changed:

Dinner in honour of His Royal Highness, Edward, Prince of Wales, on Wednesday 19 November 1919 at the Waldorf-Astoria Hotel

MENU

Tortue Verte à la Waldorf

—

Crabes d'Huîtres à la Newburg

—

Poitrine de Pintade Farcie, Sauce Diablée
Pommes Douces à la Dixie : Coeurs de Laitue à la Française

—

Pouding au Riz à l'Américaine

White Hock   **Café**
Cigars
Cigarettes

———

   Probably the largest number of people ever to sit down together was at the banquet given by President Loubet and members of his government for every mayor and mayoress of France in September 1900. No fewer than 22 695 people were served with a sumptuous seven-course repast as follows:

Délice de Saumon froid, Sauce Mayonnaise

—

Ballotine de Faisan Saint-Hubert

—

Pains de Caneton de Rouen

—

Poularde de Bresse Rôtie

—

Filet de Boeuf en Bellevue
Salade Potel

—

Glace Succès Condé

—

Dessert

———

The outdoor catering firm of Potel et Chabot used 2000 kg of fresh salmon and made 1200 litres of mayonnaise; they boned out 2400 pheasants for the ballotines and cooked 2400 kg of beef for glazing. 50 000 bottles of wine were consumed and there were a quarter of a million plates to wash up afterwards!
294

A famous menu of recent times was the one provided by **Paul Bocuse** – the guru of French chefs – and members of staff from his restaurant at *Collonges au Mont d'Or* in Lyons, for President Giscard d'Estang at the Elysée Palace after Monsieur Bocuse had been awarded the *Légion d'Honneur* for the outstanding contribution that he has made to the art of French cookery.

The dinner at the Elysée Palace consisted of:

Leacock's Fine Old Madeira	**La Soupe de Truffes Valérie** **Giscard d'Estaing**
	–
Meursault Poruzot 1975	**L'Escalope de Saumon à l'Oseille**
	–
Moulin-à-Vent 1967	**Le Canard Claude Jolly** **Les Petites Salades du Moulin**
	–
Château Mouton Baron Philippe 1969	**Les Fromages**
	–
Laurent Perrier Champagne	**Les Desserts**

The consommé was presented with a julienne of vegetables and truffles, covered with a dome of puff pastry and baked; the breasts of duck were whole and coated with aspic jelly.

BURNS' NIGHT BILL OF FARE

Every 25 January for the past 180 years Scottish people all over the world have sat down to celebrate the birthday of Robert Burns the poet. They celebrate this most famous Scotsman with what is called a Burns Supper, which is actually an anniversary dinner, either formal or friendly, at which the bill of fare is fairly straightforward, but the entertainment takes up most of the time.

Many caterers have long experience of organising Burns Supper and use the same menu year after year because this is what the organiser wishes and what tradition demands.

The bill of fare must include haggis, the only problem being that it is equally suitable as the entrée and the relevé, but once its place is established the remaining courses can be built around it. It is customary to have soup – either Cock-a-leekie or Scotch Broth – as the first course, then according to the price being charged, the haggis or a fish, especially salmon. Whether served as the main

295

course or as a subsidiary, the haggis is always served with mashed potato and purée of swede (or sometimes turnips) and optionally with whisky sauce which is made of seasoned double-cream well-flavoured with neat whisky. If haggis is the first meat course it is normally followed by roast turkey with the traditional garnish and vegetables; occasionally roast beef is served. The favoured sweet is Scotch Trifle, but Apple Tart or an ice cream is often featured; the last course is a selection of Scottish cheeses with bannocks, oatcakes and the accompaniments.

Equally as important as the meal are the speeches, recitations and songs, and details of these should appear on the bill of fare in the form of a programme together with the names of the speakers. To start with, the chairman welcomes those assembled, grace is said, and the first course served; then – whether the main course or not – the haggis comes as the focal point of the meal so the chairman rises and calls upon the company to stand and receive it. The 'great dish' is carried on high by the chef preceded by a piper and followed by the head waiter carrying two bottles of whisky. They bring the haggis to the Chairman who rewards them with a glass of whisky each and proceeds to address it with the poem of Robert Burns which runs to eight verses and lauds it in terms of 'Great Cheiftain of the Pudding Race'. When he comes to the line in the third verse 'And cut you up with ready slight' the chairman has to slash a cross in the haggis. Once the address is finished, the haggis and vegatables are served to everyone together with a glass of whisky and the dinner proceeds to its conclusion; there is an intermission and then the speeches begin. The first toast is to the Immortal Memory of Robert Burns, a speech of some twenty-five minutes about the poet's life and times, possibly with quotations from his writings. Then follow other speeches, the 'Toast to the Lassies', the response to this toast and an 'Appreciation of the Immortal Memory' which is a fairly serious one about the poet, in contrast to the Toast to the Lassies which can be lighthearted. Other toasts may be included, such as one to Scotland, to the town where the occasion takes place, or to the guests.

Then comes the entertainment with music, recitations and Burns' songs with everyone joining in the chorus; this can go on for as long as the programme allows, being brought to a close by the singing of Auld Lang Syne. The bill of fare can be written in the sort of dialect used by Burns, or in Gaelic, according to the kind of people attending the function; the menu is usually printed in blue and bound with a tartan ribbon.

The Faring

–

Cock-a-Leekie

–

Chieftain o' the Puddin' Race

–

Neeps and Nips

—

Roastit Bubblyjock
wi' a' the trimmings

—

Tipsy Land

—

Kebbuck o' Cheese
an' Oatcakes

—

Coffee

———

The proceedings usually end with the entire company being served a **doch-and-doris** which is the name given to the parting drink, a generous measure of whisky, before leaving for home.

STAGE MANAGEMENT OF THE OCCASION

As has been noted the ideal of gastronomy according to **Brillat-Savarin** and other food-lovers requires a small selected party who share a common interest in their love of food, convivial conversation and exchange of ideas. Yet since ancient times, spectacular entertainment has been a major feature of banquets, and the word *entremets* or intermission was derived from it.

Commercial catering has at present to deal with a wide spectrum of people whose interests are general and who frequently derive their pleasure from a composite product, that is, both food and entertainment. To this end the caterer needs to cultivate both his flair and imagination to cope with the management of such occasions; indeed he is required to talk knowledgeably and with confidence on such matters. There may be some who regard these aspects as being the role of a professional stage or theatre manager. The caterer may decide to seek the advice of such experts.

What follows is designed to provide guidance on aspects of stage management and to provide the background for an informed approach to entertainment at functions, from spectacular occasions to stage-managed specific period or theme evenings; or simply presenting various courses in an entertaining manner.

SPECTACULAR OCCASIONS

The lights are dimmed, there is an expectant hush as into the room comes a long line of waiters each bearing a dish of flaming *Soufflé Vésuvius*. It is the climax of a special function, a theatrical finale to a memorable meal that should bring the assembled company to their feet, clapping madly. The mood and the occasion have demanded something spectacular to round off the evening. Special effects and out-of-the-ordinary presentations are an integral part of banqueting and head chefs and waiters are happy for the opportunity to demonstrate their showmanship even though this may only reach the dubious height of sticking a sparkler into a Christmas pudding and lighting as it goes in! Most of the effects are brought about by igniting warmed spirit or liqueur in the same way as *flamber* work is done in the restaurant; the alcohol burns with a bright flame and there is little danger of the waiters getting burnt or the room catching fire. Another way is to make hollow moulds of coloured ice with a dry battery and torch bulb switched on inside; the cold sweet is placed on top, probably veiled in spun sugar.

Solid carbon dioxide known as **dry ice** is sometimes used to create the illusion of serving a dish with clouds of steam pouring from it. A small piece placed in a portion of fruit salad gives the impression that it is very hot whereas it is the opposite and in fact, too well-chilled. Interesting effects can be created by using it but care must be taken as its temperature is very low indeed and can cause burns if handled.

The practice of wheeling in a large celebration cake out of which steps a young lady, or – as seen in gangster films – a bunch of hoodlums with guns blazing, is an old one yet it still furnishes ideas which might include the four-and-twenty blackbirds in a pie, should the demand ever arise for such a spectacle, but it is more likely to be a flock of doves.

Perhaps equally well-known is the famous **Gondola Dinner** held at the **Savoy Hotel** in 1905 when the forecourt was flooded and the surroundings made to look like the Grand Canal in Venice with waiters dressed as gondoliers, **Caruso** singing Venetian songs and an elephant in one of the gondolas carrying a birthday cake on its howdah. On another occasion, **Krupp** the German armaments manufacturer had champagne flowing from a fountain in the forecourt. For fancy dress balls, guests commissioned eminent stage and ballet designers to produce original costumes for them.

A ballroom can be transformed into any kind of setting, from the simplest with flowers and pot plants hired from the local parks department, to a very elaborate theme, say Dracula's Castle or a circus ring, made specially and installed by a firm of scenery designers, with real performers. The menu should echo the theme and the service should spring suitable surprises.

A simpler way of honouring a particular occasion is to fashion a Genoeise sponge in various shapes, for example, as a book with the covers made to look like leather and a suitable title and author's name written in royal icing. This is a personal way of paying respect to the guest of honour and it comes appropriately at the conclusion of the meal; it can be made from any suitable material – gum paste, pulled sugar, poured sugar, nougat, marzipan, chocolate, or ice-cream. As well as a book, baskets of fruit or flowers, shields or plaques, a crown or garland, a picture, a monument or a bust may be suitably inscribed. A child is thrilled to see its name written on a birthday cake or have the cake made to the design of something that is a favourite of the child at the time, such as a train, football pitch, or even 'E.T.'! It is usual to present petits fours in these specialities if they resemble a receptacle, or, if not, around the dish on which the commemorative piece is set.

Earlier in the meal it is possible to add distinction to a special occasion by setting up a table in the reception area for the canapés, salted almonds, olives, etc. and to have, perhaps, an ice carving on display, illuminated from beneath or by remote spot light. It should be a carving that is appropriate for the occasion, say, a large crown and sceptre if royalty are attending, or a sailor or guardsman for a naval or regimental occasion. It is possible to make ice models in moulds but at present the range is limited and the resultant pieces are not very large.

The presentation of *caviar* or *foie gras* set in an ice socle on a trolley can be carried out successfully for a small gathering of people but otherwise socles are not now used during a hot meal. Potatoes to accompany a relevé can be served from a potato basket made by weaving strands of raw potato around a frame or from a nest made of *pommes pailles* fried between two round frying baskets.

It is perfectly in order to use socles for cold buffet work as they have the effect of raising small items from the dish so adding boldness. Some of the things on a buffet are purely for display although they are made of food – these include works carved from a block of salt or any kind of fat, centre-pieces made of pastillage, chocolate, marzipan or nougat; these can be made as working models or illuminated. At some buffets dummies are used to enlarge the display and whole salmons, hams and galantines made of polystyrene or plaster of paris are coated and glazed.

At a buffet wedding breakfast, the wedding cake is the centre of attraction; for an Elizabethan feast a magnificent boars' head could be the centrepoint or the chefs could carry a roasted baron of beef shoulder high around the room before commencing to carve it.

A cold buffet display is traditional in hotels at Christmas and Easter where it may serve as one of the meals on the programme or as an alternative to the traditional festive ones. Some restaurants feature a display of produce in the restaurant, sited so as to attract attention as customers enter the room; it could include baskets of fruit, floral displays, selected bottles from the wine list, a display of unusual vegetables and possibly items of raw fish and meat, set in crushed ice, being featured as *plats du jour*. A suitable background of velvet or fishnet can help to make the display realistic and assist in selling the goods.

The practice of emphasising the contents of a cooked dish by displaying the raw product alongside must be done with due regard to the regulations concerning hygiene. For centuries it has been the practice to present, say, a game pie with the raw head of the bird used and some of the tail feathers adorning it. The peacock used to be valued for the table perhaps more for display purposes than for its actual taste, but this is now frowned upon as being unhygienic and ought not to be done.

MEDIEVAL BANQUETS

A study of Elizabethan foods and the eating habits of that period is necessary in order to offer customers an evening of authentic fantasy of the way our forefathers passed an evening at home. Living as they did in an age where there were no distractions, people made the last meal of the day into an event by sitting down for several hours and separating the courses with entertainment from songsters, minstrels and jesters. It is as well to be as authentic as possible whilst still making the meal acceptable to present-day tastes. Not everyone will appreciate roast peacock or swan since the meat is likely to be tough and acrid. A boar's head would be unobtainable, so a pig's head made as a brawn and decorated to look authentic has to suffice. A hare in a coffin, baked sturgeon, a suckling pig, salamagundy, artichoke pie, syllabub with King Harry's shoestrings, would be more popular but they must be put onto the menu in the language of the time. The other way is to rewrite a more modern menu as given below, thus making sure that everyone gets a good meal.

The Elizabethans were good trenchermen so they usually had as many as nine 'removes' the name for the wooden platter which they filled with food from all the dishes available. Nowadays two main courses are sufficient.

The meal should be served on great refectory tables using wooden or pewter platters, mead cups and bifurcated daggers. The room should be oak-panelled and the floor strewn with rushes; stained glass windows, an open fireplace, a minstrels' gallery and authentic antiques are necessary to provide the right atmosphere. The serving wenches should be sufficiently buxom in their décolleté attire and be sufficiently rollicking yet not bawdy. The minstrels should also be attired in costumes of the period and play medieval music on authentic instruments.

Suitable drinks are claret, ale and mead, this last being the basis of the word 'honeymoon' because at that time newly-married couples were advised to drink mead (made from fermented honey) for a month so as to be healthy and virile. This menu shows the way to word a menu of the period.

Order of Ye Dyshes

—

Ye Liquorish Slurpe Translucente

—

300

An Fynaceous Denizen of Ye Oceanes
Served with ye sauce of ye Lowlands

—

Several Pancreas of ye lyttle Sheepes in ye Pattyes

—

Ye frostyd Liqueur wythe Master Raleigh his Fragrant Weede

—

Ye bloodie Sire Loin from ye Spit
Seethee Colewurtes wythe Chesten Nuttes

—

Ye Earthe Apple of ye Endies

—

Ye Cake made Typsy after ye fashyone
of Mistress Mary Fforde

—

Byvalves wrapt in ye Pygg Fleshe set on Toste

—

Ye Wonderous Potion brewed from ye
ground Benes of ye Braziliaane Shrubbe

—

Divers headie wynes yravished from ye Varlets
Henrie of Fraunce
Philipe of Spayne
ye Duc of Burgundie
ye Pretender of Portugalte

———

THE ROLE OF THE TOASTMASTER

A formal banquet would use the services of a professional toastmaster whose duties are to assume control of the conventional part of the proceedings from announcing the names of guests as they arrive and making the announcement that dinner is served, through to the toasts and speeches by giving the necessary commands and ensuring that speakers are properly introduced, until the end of the proceedings. A **Master of Ceremonies** is required when investitures or similar customs or events, above that of introducing speakers, are to take place.

The loving cup is part of the ritual of toasts and is much used by the City of London livery companies and in some countries as part of the ceremony of a wedding feast. The cup itself is a richly emblazoned work of art made of gold or silver with several handles and sometimes a cover. Newly-weds entwine their hands and drink from it simultaneously but at a company dinner the cup is filled with spiced wine for the master and wardens to drink a welcome to the visitors. It is then passed round the table for each guest to drink from, wiping the rim before passing the cup to the next person. Sometimes the person stands up and bows to his neighbour who also stands to take off the lid, holding it whilst the other person drinks, a practice said to have originated as long ago as 978 AD when King Edward the Martyr was slain at Corfe Castle whilst drinking from the loving cup.

A possible concoction for a loving cup is a mixture of sherry, madeira, port and claret with sugar and spice which indicate that it was the custom for only a few sips to be taken by each guest; occasionally beer was used as the basis of a loving cup.

GASTRONOMIC OCCASIONS

Caterers can attract good business by organising a special gastronomic experience or occasion either as a single meal or for the whole or part of a week. There can be a lot of extra business from obtaining the services of the chef and possibly some of his brigade from a well-known establishment in another country to come and produce special meals for the event here. The arrangements can be for a mutual exchange whereby the 'home-team' will go to the visiting chefs' establishment and present 'a taste of Britain' in return for which he will come to them, or it is possible to obtain the services of a well-known *chef patron* from home or abroad; the fee will naturally be in keeping with his standing.

Such an event is rather like getting a world-renowned prima donna to deign to give her services at a celebrity concert not in a great opera house but in the village hall. As the star attraction it is only to be expected that the protagonist will be rather temperamental and very demanding; the slightest upset is likely to cause him to fly off the handle because of the difficulties of working in someone else's kitchen.

By tradition French chefs are highly strung and proud as peacocks of themselves and their culinary prowess; they are strict disciplinarians who brook no nonsense in their kitchens. Very often the visiting chef prefers to bring most of his own ingredients and equipment in case certain things are unobtainable in the exact form to which he is accustomed.

Such occasions are much sought after by true gastronomes who welcome the opportunity to partake of the food of a well-known place without having to make the long journey to it.

UNCONVENTIONAL MEALS

The old saying 'One man's meat is another man's poison' is borne out by the wide differences between the food habits of nations and the taboos and prejudices that are entertained by one nation or sect against certain foods which are perfectly acceptable to others. Necessity and hunger are frequently the reasons for a change from the ordinary diet as evidenced by the acceptance of elephant meat during the siege of Paris in 1870. Because of the shortage of fodder the two young elephants of the *Jardin d'Acclimatation* were shot and sold as meat for human consumption. Every household and restaurant in Paris seemed to have an endless supply of elephant black pudding, elephant sausages and elephant steaks as though the miracle of the loaves and fishes had been repeated. Cats and dogs and horses had already been tried and the citizens of Paris lived mainly on wine, coffee and bread during the two years of the siege.

During the second world war when meat was strictly rationed, restaurants were ready to try out any kind of unrationed meat they were offered. Reluctantly, they had to resort to contriving dishes from unrationed viands such as badgers, goats, pigeons, rooks, venison and whalemeat, or as some did, to serve rabbit under the guise of chicken.

The nutritional value of other animals is the same as that of the domestic animals we are accustomed to eating and it should not make us shudder to think of, say, the people of South Korea eating dogs and worms as normal everyday foods. It is no more revolting to eat worms, slugs, locusts, even chocolate-covered ants, as people of the Far East do, than for us to eat oysters, frogs, snails and prawns. The difference between horsemeat and kangaroo meat cannot be very marked yet we were prepared to accept canned kangaroo tail soup from Australia whilst deploring the export of horses to the Continent to satisfy the demand of those hippophagists who like the sweet taste of horseflesh.

That the rest of the kangaroo is perfectly good to eat is vouched for by the **New York Explorers Club**, whose recent annual banquet included hippopotamus liver pâté, roast haunch of kangaroo, bear meatballs in gravy, lionburgers in sesame seed buns and mousse of moose; the drink was an African admixture of mud and blood. The British are as reserved about trying out unusual ingredients as they are in character and our flair as pioneers and explorers does not extend to the table.

Just as we prefer to use a real vanilla pod to flavour a sweet dish so we should endeavour to use genuine rather than artificial cochineal. Yet real cochineal is produced from an insect of South America which feeds upon cacti and is then brushed off and baked to yield the well-known scarlet dye; this makes it quite expensive. In Roman times each rich household had its own dormouse farm to breed these little animals which were highly esteemed as table delicacies. They were fed on acorns and fattened on nuts before being cooked when they probably looked like quails. Present-day examples of esoteric esculents are new-born mice dipped into treacle and eaten raw by the Chinese, stewed or grilled snake in several countries including France, Australia and Hong Kong; the fruit bat in

303

Malaysia; whale-blubber in Alaska, jellyfish in Japan and lizards in Central America.

It is doubtful if even the most carefully researched recreation of a Roman banquet would be acceptable to many people nowadays and rather than inflict outlandish combinations of food, no matter how authentic they may be, it is advisable first to try out the chosen dishes and if necessary, to alter the composition in the light of modern tastes.

GUIDANCE FOR GASTRONOMIC THEMES

The following list of some eighty themes shows but a few of the very many possibilities of putting on an entertainment or diversion for a gastronomic function. Each title can be interpreted in a number of ways according to the available resources and to its appropriateness to the occasion.

OCCASION IN THE CALENDAR

Dickensian Christmas Party
St Valentine's Day Dinner
Burns' Night
Midsummer Night's Dream
Harvest Home
Grape Harvest
St George's Day
Shakespeare's Birthday
Halloween
May Day
Walpurgis Night

GEOGRAPHICAL

Vienna
French Regional
Creole
Vie Parisienne
Cockney
Roman
Grecian
Persian
Medieval
Hollywood
Montmartre
Chinatown
Desert Oasis
Deep South

PAST EVENTS

Gay Nineties
Naughty Nineties
Fin de Siècle
Edwardian
Victorian
Elizabethan
Renaissance
Roaring Twenties

PERSONAGES

Cinderella's Ball
Cleopatra's Palace
Louis XV's Court
Madame Pompadour
Countess Marie Waleska
Dame Nellie Melba
The Court of Russia
Rossini, the composer

Coronation   Dean Swift
Golden Jubilee
Good Old Days (music hall)
Harlequinade
Great Gatsby

NATIONS	GENERAL
Egyptian	Palm Court
Romany	Monastery or Nunnery
Israeli	Barracks
Italian	Cossack
Spanish	Foreign Legion
French	It should be remembered that there are over 160
Portuguese	countries in the world, each one offering possi-
Germany	bilities of a theme event. In addition there are
Indian	regions, cities and even villages that can provide
	suitable subject matter.

MISCELLANEOUS	OPERATIC
Zodiac	La Bohème – Paris Student 19th Century
Nautical	Carmen – Spanish Gypsies
Saturnalian	Rigoletto – Mantuan Rennaissance Court
Equatorial	La Traviata – French High Society
Tundra Regions	Faust – German Villagers
Bacchanalian	Mary Stuart – Scottish High Society
Dîner aux Chandelles	Don Giovanni – Spanish High Society
United Nations	The Beggar's Opera
Scheherazade	

THE ENVIRONMENT AND FUNCTION MANAGEMENT

The Dining Room must provide for maximum comfort and visual effect.

Thermal Environment

The temperature to be maintained in the dining room at the time of the guests' arrival should be between 17 and 20°C. It may be noted that if (i) a large number of people are assembled, (ii) hotplates and spirit lamps are used, and (iii) flaming takes place within the dining area, the temperature will inevitably rise and this

305

will cause discomfort and promote excessive perspiration which for various reasons is most undesirable.

Visual Environment and Food Display

Visual impact stems from the colour scheme of the room and its contents. Table layout and food display interfere with this. When colour contrast is desirable to highlight those features which may require attention on special occasions, it must be done in such a way that it does not interfere with the accepted norm of colour combination and aestheticism.

Table Layout

The table layout must conform with the organiser's requirements and the total theme. The seating arrangements must be such as to provide a comfortable stay, which means a chair with arms and a soft cushion, so that people can linger for several hours without any need to get up to stretch their legs during the proceedings. Chairs should be positioned so that guests find themselves seated directly opposite another person and the seating plan requires much thought and planning in order to accommodate like with like so that conversation is encouraged.

Table Setting and Floral Decorations

The way that the table is laid has a great impact on the enjoyment of a meal, and it is advisable to plan it to the last detail. The tablecloth should normally be in white damask; the crockery, glassware and cutlery should be completely suitable for the event and special cutlery ought to be provided for the service of special dishes. The care taken in laying the table is as important as that taken in the preparation of the meal; chairs, plates, napkins, and glasses should reflect symmetry as well as aesthetic appearance. Place cards should be nicely lettered and the menu printed on stiff card to stand straight.

Table and floral decorations should not be such as to prevent social exchange. A display of elegant trophies or centrepieces made of food together with flowers and an épergne add a touch of graceful living and finesse to the table layout; the trophies are a reminder of the continuity of life and of the history of an association or institute. Floral arrangements for table use must be carefully chosen not only for the colour scheme of the occasion, but for their scent and for their meaning, as some have connotations of evil, even of death, whilst others denote happiness and life. The height and abundance of the display should be calculated so that it does not interfere with the flow of conversation across the table, but this of course depends upon the width of the table. Smilax and ferns can be used

306

along the centre of a dining table or pinned to the front of a buffet table to add colour. Artificial flowers have the advantage of having no scent but are usually regarded as being inferior to the real thing, no matter how realistic they look. Flowers are sometimes used to decorate a dish of food and these may be fresh, made of wax or carved from vegetables but they are *not* intended to be eaten.

Staff Uniforms

Staff uniforms for these occasions may either be the conventional one in black and white or tail-coats. On very special occasions waiting staff wear white gloves and wine-waiters will wear a leather apron and carry a silver tastevin around the neck; they will probably hold bottles only by the punt even if serving wine from magnums. **André Simon** used to say that the food of a gastronomic occasion should flatter and assist in cajoling a performance from the wines but then he was a wine man: the happy medium is where neither the food nor the drink is the greater but each complements the other and is indispensible.

For some people, a good meal is possibly the only pleasure they have in their otherwise unhappy lives so the entire occasion must be intense and memorable with the surroundings playing a large part in the experience.

SERVICE

Once the company of people has assembled and the announcement is made that dinner is served, guests move to their places and seat themselves in readiness for the first course. Announcements and grace may be said but all too often, customers at a gastronomic occasion, find the first course already set out on the table. This is bad practice not only because the temperature of the food is likely to be altered but its hygienic state becomes doubtful according to how long it has been lying on the table in readiness. Not even bread or rolls should be put out in advance.

The service should be carried out in an orderly style, waiters taking their cue from the head waiter who should signal every move. The top table is accorded precedence and all others wait for the chief guest to commence and finish each course. The length of pause between each course should be regulated throughout the meal so that no hint of hurriedness or of delay is communicated to the customers. There should be a slightly longer pause before the coffee is served towards the end of the meal, and smoking is not usually permitted at formal meals until coffee has been served and the loyal toast drunk.

It used to be the practice to offer cigarettes with the sorbet at the halfway stage of the meal but this practice was discarded long before people began to give up the habit of smoking. Where no toasts are to be drunk, and in countries where there is no royal head of state and the president is not held in much esteem, smoking is acceptable throughout the meal, often whilst partaking of the food.

Like many other art forms, gastronomy has had to move with the times and now more than ever, it has been put on a commercial basis with emphasis placed on it becoming a profitable operation. Apart from the question of what people are prepared to pay for a gourmet meal there is the problem on the production side of what is the upper limit of numbers that can be served, without allowing the slightest fall in standards.

SUPERSTITION

Many caterers are superstitious about catering for parties of thirteen guests and guests themselves may not care to sit thirteen to a table. In some establishments the head waiter overcomes this by placing a lucky black toy cat on a fourteenth chair removing the cover in time with those of the actual guests. Other notable forms of superstition in this country are a combination of red and white, which has connotations of death, and serving the wine anti-clockwise, particularly on Naval occasions.

ETIQUETTE

Etiquette is defined as 'the conventional rules of personal behaviour in polite society', a definition which immediately indicates that etiquette is almost culture-specific and that its principles vary in different continents and at different periods. Many of the basics of table etiquette have been inherited from the ancient Romans, amongst others the ritual of washing hands, offering thanks to the gods, the seating arrangements for the host, hostess and other dignitaries, bowing in deference to other guests and staff bowing to guests. In medieval times manners receded to an extent, and it was considered acceptable for guests to help themselves with their fingers out of the communal pot. They were told not to clear their nose with the tablecloth and to refrain from breaking wind. In modern days our table manners are much more sophisticated which imposes a certain control on the partaker as well as on the server.

Points for consideration include politeness in dealing with others, courtesy, grace of manner and dignity, following the correct form of serving food with appropriate implements, not interrupting conversation, not serving food from the incorrect side or in such a way as to cause embarrassment to guests, serving the food according to the guests' status and sex, serving the food in large amounts on the plate, filling wine glasses more than three quarters full, raising pitch of voice above that used by customers. Receiving without thanking, forcing the pace of eating, use of the correct form of address for each guest, being informed of cultural differences when dealing with guests from other countries, and many other small but important details.

TABLE MANNERS

Patterns of behaviour at the table used to be so atrocious that many ecclesiastics found it necessary to set down precepts for better table manners. Eating and drinking has always occupied such a very central position in the social life of people especially in the Middle Ages that it was felt necessary to impress on them what was and what was not good etiquette in society, especially at the table.

In attempting to impose some discipline upon people at table and in trying to raise the standards of polite behaviour, writers had to point out all the bad things people were doing, such as slurping the soup, dunking bread in the common dish, picking the nose at table, loosening the belt, blowing on food to cool it, using a knife as a toothpick, and so on. **Erasmus** warned those who had the bad habit of searching through the whole dish to find the most succulent pieces, to be satisfied with what was immediately in front of them. Another writer had to point out that it was impolite to smell the portion of fish or meat then to return it to the common dish as being unsatisfactory. When they were first introduced it was felt necessary to explain the correct use of serviettes or table napkins; it was pointed out that it is all right to use them to wipe soiled cutlery rather than using the tablecloth, but the habit of tucking the serviette into the collar or a buttonhole was decried as being vulgar. The writers were keen to advance the civilising process of table manners and also that of general behaviour and forms of conversation. It might be thought that these books stemmed from court circles in France but there are books written in English, French, German and Latin, many of them especially for children to ensure they grew up with some knowledge of table maners.

12 Gastronomy and Gastronomes

What is Gastronomy? - What is a Gastronome? - Pierre Androuet -
Paul Bocuse - X. Marcel Boúlestin - Brillat-Savarin - Carême - Robert
Courtine - Fanny Cradock - Curnonsky - Elizabeth David - Escoffier
- Mario Gallati - Michel Guérard - Philip Harben - Ambrose Heath -
E. Herbodeau - Roger Lallemand - Rosa Lewis - E. Longue - Lucien
Ogier - Raymond Oliver - Marguerite Patten - H.-P. Pelleprat -
Pomiane - Raymond Postgate - Mme Prunier - Ritz - Albert and
Michel Roux - André Simon - Soyer - Toulemon - Jean and Pierre
Troisgros - Vatel - Roger Vergé and others

310

WHAT IS GASTRONOMY?

Gastronomy means a love and true appreciation of good food and wine, two of the pleasures of life which when supported by good service and jovial company help to create a truly great meal experience.

A gastronome should be fastidious about everything concerned with the preparation and presentation of the meal and never allow anything that is not perfect to be served or eaten. He should concern himself with such minor details as the feel and balance of the cutlery, the thinness of the glasses, the lay of the tablecloth and the comfort of the chairs.

The company must be congenial so that the flow of conversation is continuous and does not start only when the second wine has been served. The gastronome must not be an impetuous person but someone who has patience to sit in his chair for several hours at a stretch whilst partaking of a meal. A gastronome is not a pretentious person and will abhor any pretentious comments that are passed about the food and wine. He will show equal appreciation of an ordinary table wine as of a first growth claret when served in its right place, knowing that even the simplest things of life can convey a meaning of quality and an expression of hospitality. A properly cooked steak and kidney pie will give as much pleasure as, for example, a much more elaborate and expensive dish such as *Timbale de Chapon Maréchal Foch*; the gastronome will regard each as an epicurean delight in its particular context.

The setting for a gastronomic meal does not have to be the Salon of a palace nor does the number of guests have to run into hundreds to make it a worthwhile gathering. However the cooking must have been carried out with great skill and loving care with the sole thought of satisfying all those who are to partake of it.

The true gastronome needs not only to have studied the cultural role that eating plays in societies but to have acquired an understanding of how such topics as archaeology, art, geography, history, mythology and religion hinge upon the subject of gastronomy.

Gastronomy can act as a catalyst to unite men of many persuasions. **Brillat-Savarin** thought it would be possible to tell a true gastronome by submitting him to what he called a gastronomic trial or test. This involved eating his way through a portion of poêled veal, a portion of turkey stuffed with chestnuts, a roasted fat pigeon, a dish of well-garnished sauerkraut, followed by a good helping of *Oeufs à la Neige*. But this is really a test of a gourmand and the true gastronome would want to pause and dilate upon the subtleties of one of the courses before proceeding to savour the next.

The true gastronome, whilst showing his appreciation of the most refined yet elaborate dishes of a meal will partake only in moderation and normally be well-satisfied with some everyday dishes which though simple, are often the most difficult to produce to perfection. Without perhaps ever having done any cooking, a gastronome is able to sum up the way a dish has been prepared, detect the ingredients and pass a judgement on its quality.

311

23. Charles Elmé Francatelli

A bogus gastronome is one who is proud of his *embonpoint*, who believes that only dishes that are lengthy and involved in their preparation are worth eating, the only good recipes are those passed secretly from mother to daughter, and that it is necessary to devote lots of time to getting a dish exactly right. Furthermore, he considers plenty of advance warning is necessary if a meal is to be exactly right – all ideas which are completely at odds with present-day practices.

Gastronomy is a much misused word and the true gastronome knows that it should be used to describe the art and culture of civilisation only when participation is honoured by truly stimulating repasts. The love of good food and wine comes perilously close to sheer gluttony if the sole interest of the diner is the well-being of his belly and not his civilised senses.

WHAT IS A GASTRONOME?

Gastronomy can only come into being when one person or a number of people, sit down to a meal wherein the science and art of good eating and drinking have been combined. The scientific aspect is that the meal be nutritionally sound and that thought has been given to the health of the recipients so that their bodily requirements will be met. For the restaurateur or hotelier the other scientific fact is the need to make the meal commercially viable. The useful flow of publicity that can come from a gourmet event must be matched by a financially sound level of profit, which means finding *fins becs* who not only appreciate good cookery but are able to afford to eat out frequently. The art lies in the way the room has been made ready and the table laid. The person doing the cooking should be an artiste.

Gastronomic events make good publicity material for any kind of commercial establishment because many of the general public see themselves as gourmets, given the money and the opportunity. A gastronome must have a deep interest in the subject of food and drink and be constantly making a study of it: by reading books, patronising gourmet restaurants, or by belonging to a dining club or an association of gastronomes.

The true gourmet who already has a deep knowledge of good food and drink is a fairly rare person so it is not easy to gather together a number of gastronomes to form the nucleus of a such a society. It needs persons with the ability to discourse on any topic appertaining to food and drink and who have a fund of relevant anecdotes and stories with which to divert fellow-members and at the same time instruct those who are seeking to acquire knowledge of the wide ramifications of the study that constitutes gastronomy. **Brillat-Savarin** suggested that the four professions that provided notable numbers of gastronomes were finance, medicine, the cloth (meaning the church) and men of letters; nowadays gastronomes can be recruited from a much wider circle of occupations.

313

It has been said that the first gastronome was **Esau** who, according to the Old Testament sold his birthright for a mess of potage which was probably a portion of pease pudding, that well-known accompaniment to faggots. This may serve to show that it is not always necessary to have a high income in order to be a gastronome; provided the yellow split peas are from the last harvest, are properly cooked with the addition of, onion, carrot, clove and then finely puréed, seasoned and buttered, the mess of potage will attain to *haute cuisine* standard and be a delight to eat. It is perfectly possible to judge an establishment's gastronomic standard by, say, its cheese board; it is sufficient to glance at the range on display, note the countries of origin, whether from farmyard or factory, how fresh it looks and what accompaniments are offered. From such small details of perfection is gastronomy born.

Among those who have spent time meditating about gastrology was **Archestratus** who originally went to Greece from Syracuse in Sicily. He presented a treatise on gastronomy that discussed the functions, anomalies and resources of the stomach and the laws that govern it. **Philoxemus** accustomed himself to eating extremely hot food by constantly drinking boiling water until his gullet became exceptionally conditioned to anything served very hot. This was not perhaps so much for the furtherance of gastronomy as to enable him to get in first when the hot dishes were brought in from the kitchen.

The following profiles are of people who can be said to have exerted a fairly profound influence on gastronomy. Some are more well-known than others, possibly because the spotlight fell on them more vividly, or that they were more influential in their day than the others. All have made a notable contribution to the study of food and drink but the list is elective and a thousand other names could have been added.

PIERRE ANDROUET

M. Androuet is well known as the author of the *Guide de Fromage*, the most authoritative book on the subject of cheese. He is a wholesaler of fine cheese and runs a restaurant in Paris that specialises in dishes using cheese. In addition he is archivist to the **International Association of Food Writers** and is well-known throughout Europe as a judge at culinary competitions, and as a gastronome.

Pierre Androuet has been in the cheese business all his life so his writings are the result of his own experience rather than being purely theoretical. His knowledge of food and wine is unsurpassed and he is in the tradition of that special breed of Frenchmen whose love of gastronomy outweighs their problem of *embonpoint*.

He does not proclaim the merits of French cheese to the detriment of all others, in fact one of his favourite dishes is **Welsh Rarebit** made with red Cheshire cheese and he praises Stilton as being one of the noblest cheeses in the world. Whichever of the many hundreds of different cheeses is being served he

314

insists that (i) it should be served at exactly the right temperature so that the full flavour and aroma can be enjoyed; (ii) it should be cut into wedges for serving and the crust removed if necessary, and (iii) it should served with exactly the right kind of wine that will marry with the particular cheese. To say that red wine should be served with cheese is inexact; a true gastronome such as M. Androuet will be able to suggest the most appropriate one.

BOCUSE – LE MEILLEUR OUVRIER DE FRANCE

Paul Bocuse owns his own restaurant at Collonges-au-Mont-d'-Or near Lyon where customers can see straight into the kitchen on arrival before entering the restaurant which seats 140 on two floors. The lower floor is decorated with antiques and artefacts but this is simply a background to the showmanship of the owner, a characteristic that stems from his inspired attitude to food, his flair as a chef and his hearty appetite. The menu is in accordance with his views on letting the produce decide the method and dictate the finished dish. His approach to *cuisine moderne* is not that of over-elaboration of the plate with inconsistant garnish of kiwi fruit and broccolis, but to ensure that the customer is satisfied with a generous size portion of the actual food.

Monsieur Bocuse is both a *chef-patron* and an entrepreneur with many business interests including restaurants overseas, consultancy, manufacture of preserves and chocolates, the sale of kitchenware badged with the Bocuse logo, and many other activities.

His main contribution to the advancement of catering is as the innovator of *cuisine nouvelle*. He is the man who stood French culinary practice on its head by showing that there was no need for all the heavy basic sauces and cream, eggs and butter with which to finish dishes with. He toned down some of the excesses of French classical cookery without losing any of its panache, but giving it greater finesse and a healthier result. His disciples are to be found in kitchens both great and small, throughout the world.

X. MARCEL BOULESTIN

Marcel Boulestin's fame stems from the restaurant of his name that is still in existence in London's West End. He was first a journalist who came to England to learn the language but stayed to spend his life in his adopted country. He was born in 1878 and wrote his first book on cookery solely from his experience of eating out; this he did so well that it was an immediate success and he was asked to write another as well as articles for the press.

This fame prompted him to open his own restaurant which he did in a modest way with some financial backing. He was not a *chef-patron* but rather a friendly restaurant owner who looked after his customers well, without worrying whether he made any money out of his efforts.

He wrote several books in an attempt to interpret French classical cookery as practised in his restaurant, to the British housewife. He appeared on television doing simple demonstrations of this sort of cooking and was the first person ever to do so in 1938. He was on the advisory council of the Wine and Food Society and contributed many articles to its magazine.

His contribution to gastronomy was considerable as he not only wrote about the fine art of cooking but saw that it was carried out in practice in his own establishment; there he maintained a high standard that eventually ensured his reputation both as a businessman and a gastronome. He died in 1943 but the restaurant still prospers and it recently held an exhibition of its founders works.

JEAN-ANTHELME BRILLAT-SAVARIN

Brillat-Savarin enjoys renown as the most famous gastronome of all time and his book serves to epitomise the abiding interest that French people have in food. He was born on 2 May 1755 at Belley in the Ain district, the son of Marc-Anthelme Brillat; he added the Savarin from his great aunt, Mlle Savarin who left him a legacy provided he adopted her name.

The area in which he grew up is one that is rich in local produce with crayfish, pike and trout, mutton, game and a breed of small turkeys. The local hams were cured in a paste of sandalwood, spices and wine.

As a man he worked as a lawyer. He was tall but ugly and dressed carelessly. He gave the appearance of being absent-minded but was a better listener than a talker. It was only after a good meal that he became loquacious and then he bubbled over with good conversation. In 1793 Brillat-Savarin was elected Mayor of Belley but soon after was denounced as a republican, arrested and sentenced to be shot. He managed to escape from prison, went to Switzerland and then to the United Stated where he kept himself by teaching the violin and French language.

On his return to France three years later he took up life as before, being made a *Chevalier de l'Empire* in 1808. He just managed to finish writing his book, *The Physiology of Taste*, before his death on 2 February 1826. He was buried in the *Père Lachaise cemetery* in Paris. One of his brothers and a nephew were named as his executors and they let a publisher have the manuscript for the sum of 1500 francs; they got twice as much for his Stradivarius violin.

The Physiology of Taste is in two parts. Part 1 is a series of meditations on the Senses, Taste, Gastronomy, Food, the Theory of Frying, Thirst, Drinks, Gourmandism, Gourmands, Gastronomic Tests, the Pleasures of the Table and

316

24. Brillat-Savarin

many other topics concerning the art of good eating. Part 2 consists of anecdotes about foods and meals, receipts for restoratives, and about the French emigré who was in such demand for dressing salads at dinners that he made and sold hundreds of cases containing the necessary ingredients to prepare the different kinds of salads. The book is available from several publishers and various translators have rendered it into English.

ANTONIN CARÊME

Carême was one of the few pastrycooks to become a head chef, or perhaps more precisely, he was a chef who was equally at home in the pastry as in the kitchen. His claim to fame is that he brought together the widespread methods of cookery and classified them in his books so that chefs would have a code of practice instead of there being many different ways of doing any particular dish.

Carême was born in poverty in Paris in 1784 and at the age of twelve was apprenticed as a pastrycook in a small cake shop. He was appointed pastry chef to Talleyrand, the diplomat and statesman and during the twelve years he worked for him, became equally accomplished in the work of the main kitchen.

On the 8th and 9th of June 1984 a gala banquet was held in the Banqueting Hall and Great Kitchen of the Royal Pavilion to mark the bicentenary of the birth of Antonin Carême. It was here that Carême worked as head chef to the Prince Regent during the year 1817 and served several large banquets in the style of the one given below.

Over 180 guests from all walks of life came on each of the two nights and willingly paid £200 each for the privilege of paying respect to the memory of one of the greatest chefs.

Twenty-five well-known chefs came to work under the direction of Michel and Albert Roux to produce a wonderful display of centrepieces in the style of Carême and to prepare the following menu:-

DÎNER

Oeuf Froid Carême

Coquillages, Crustacés et Quenelles de Poisson Prince Regent

Turbotin en Aspic Vincent La Chapelle

Salmis de Cailles Grimod de la Reynière

Sorbet au Thé Amer

Selle d'Agneau Prince Talleyrand

Fromage Bavarois aux Fraises

Petits Fours

Café

The event helped to raise money to pay for the restoration work being carried out at the Royal Pavilion and to support research into culinary history in the name of the Carême Fund at the University of Oxford History Faculty Board.

CARÊME
Bicentennial Programme
ROYAL PAVILION, BRIGHTON
8th. June 1984

25. Antonin Carême

"The fine arts are five in number, to wit: *painting,
sculpture, poetry, music, architecture -- whose main
branch is confectionery.*"

Anatole France, quoting Carême.

Oeuf froid Carême

Michel Roux
Maître Chef, Waterside Inn

Albert Roux
Maître Chef, Le Gavroche

•

*Coquillages, Crustacés et
Quenelles de Poisson Prince Regent*

Peter Kromberg
Maître Chef, Hotel Intercontinental

•

*Chablis
Grand Cru les Preuses
1981
Domaine de la Maladière*

*Selle d'Agneau
Prince de Talleyrand*

Bernard Gaume
Maître Chef, Hyatt Carlton Tower

•

*Château Giscours
1976
3me Grand Cru Margaux*

"Carême," said the Prince Regent one day, "You will kill me with a surfeit of food. I have a fancy for everything you put before me. The temptation is really too great." "Your Highness," replied Carême, "my duty is to tempt your appetite; yours to control it."

From the preamble of Carême's *Cuisinier parisien*.

Fromage Bavarois aux Fraises
Recette originale de Carême

John Huber
Senior Lecturer, Slough College

.

Champagne Mumm Cordon Vert

.

Café et Petits Fours

.

Eau de Vie de Framboise Massenez
Armagnac de Montal 1960
Port Sandeman 1960

Honoured Guest Chefs

Georges Blanc
La Mère Blanc, Vonnas

André Mathevon
Moulin de la Galette, Moulin

Gerard Boyer
Restaurant Boyer, Reims

Paul Louis Meissonnier
Président,
Société des Maîtres Cuisiniers de France

Jean Gallas
Président,
Société des Cuisiniers français

Louis Outhier
Restaurant L'Oasis, La Napoule

Daniel Giraud
M.O.F.

Gerard Pangaud
Paris

Paul Haeberlin
L'Auberge de l'Ill, Illhaeusern

Alain Senderens
L'Archestrate, Paris

Michel Malapris
Président, Académie Culinaire

Roger Vergé
Le Moulin de Mougins, Mougins

Main Speaker

Lord Briggs
Provost, Worcester College, Oxford

Speakers

Hugh Johnson
Author

Michel Budin
Director G. H. Mumm

When the Czar of Russia visited Paris in 1814. Carême was seconded to his staff and as his name became more widely known, many wealthy people tried to get him to work for them. He was eventually asked to come to England as chef to the Prince Regent who had just had the Royal Pavilion in Brighton built as his home and wanted someone capable of cooking vast meals of highly decorative food for a large number of guests. Carême was famous as a designer and decorator of elaborate centre pieces on which to present food and had studied architecture in order to increase his skill in design.

He remained at Brighton for only a short while and it was the same in Russia when he was chef to the Czar. He then spent seven years working as head chef to the Rothschild family at their Paris home but for the last ten years of his life his health deteriorated and he spent much of his time writing. He died in 1834 in poor circumstances. A list of his books is given in Chapter 4.

ROBERT COURTINE

Possibly the most feared and revered man in Paris catering circles is Robert Courtine, food critic of *Le Monde* and a prolific author of books on food and gastronomy. With more than fifty years of experience behind him there cannot possibly be anybody more knowledgeable than he in every conceivable aspect of food and drink.

Yet Robert Courtine is an ascetic-looking man who is completely unlike the popular image of a food critic as a jovial and rotund man who dines out several times a week with no expense spared. If the standard of restaurants in the capital and beyond has been maintained since the Second World War, it is largely because of M. Courtine's insistence on high quality and good value. His integrity of purpose is such that he would rather hurt a person and decry an establishment than damn it with faint praise. He has never pulled punches in anything he has written or spoken on the subject which he knows better than any other man in France.

M. Courtine also writes under the pen names *Le Reynière* and *Savarin*; his books, many of which have been translated into English, include *La France par Votre Table*, *Grand Livre de la France à Table*; he was the editor of *Larousse Gastronomique* and often appears on French television on which he has a reputation for being forthright in any discussion about food.

FANNY CRADOCK

Fanny and Johnnie Cradock have made a very great contribution to the cause of gastronomy both here and abroad, by means of their articles and their books but above all, by their demonstrations both on television and in such places as the Royal Albert Hall. Their influence has been aimed at housewives whom they have taught to produce better meals on slender budgets and to do them with aplomb. Fanny and Johnnie made their reputation by appearing before the public dressed elegantly as though ready to go to a party, then proceeding to produce fabulous dishes without making a mess of their clothes. Their demonstrations are always well thought-out and they have introduced many new ideas using new gadgets and innovatory methods. Their love of food and wine is very evident and they are extremely effective in putting over the message that cooking can be fun. They are well respected abroad and have been honoured by many important associations connected with food and wine, particularly in France.

Fanny Cradock gained her love of cookery from her grandmother who brought her up; she loved doing special dishes even though she had her own cook. It was her grandmother who showed Fanny the importance of correct table lay-up and how everything should match when preparing a meal, but apart from this, she is entirely self-taught and has mastered the subject by her own studies and experimentation.

She started to write when still quite young and produced several novels and children's books in quick succession but was persuaded that a book on cookery would sell even better and her first book, *The Practical Cook*, was published in 1949. This led to requests from several newspapers to write their woman's columns, then under the pseudonym *Bon Viveur*, she and Johnnie wrote on food, wine and travel for the *Daily Telegraph*. This meant visiting hotels and writing articles on their joint experience as to the way staff looked after them as ordinary customers; thus they became hotel and restaurant inspectors and their reports were well respected. Unfortunately the law did not permit them to name those establishments that did not measure up to their standards.

Fanny and Johnnie Cradock also toured the country doing cookery shows and then came their series of television programmes with Johnnie doing the wines. They may be theatrical in their approach, the techniques they use may be glossy but all is done in good taste with great dexterity born of experience and a recognition of what their audience want to learn from them.

CURNONSKY

Maurice-Edmond Sailland (1872–1956) was a writer and boulevardier who changed his name to 'Prince Curnonsky' and was dubbed *Prince de Gastronomes* as a result of an election organised by two Parisian newspapers, who formed a jury and invited readers to vote for several candidates. He was a well-known character and so won the contest with a large majority. He wrote novels and short stories before confining his writing to food and drink which was appropriate since he loved eating and drinking. As a columnist he was influential and as a cookery writer he wrote dozens of books, including one on French gastronomy in thirty-two volumes. He founded the *Académie des Gastronomes* in 1927 to encourage the art of cookery and the furtherance of gastronomic standards.

ELIZABETH DAVID

With only a handful of books to her name, Elizabeth David nevertheless enjoys an outstanding position as a cookery writer and most other writers give her the accolade. She possesses a large library of very old cookery books and from her love of reading them stems her work as a scholar and researcher of culinary matters. Her knowledge of France and its language stems from the time she studied at the Sorbonne. She became an actress, then after the war started writing a cookery column in *Harper's Bazaar*; her first book, *Mediterrean Cooking*, was almost the first book on cookery to be published after the war. She is highly critical of her own work and of English food especially when it is badly cooked.

GEORGES AUGUSTE ESCOFFIER

It is usual to couple the name of Escoffier with that of Ritz and it has been said that they were indispensible to each other. But this does a disservice to them both as each had an interesting career before they met and, in Escoffier's case, after Ritz had retired.

Escoffier was born in 1846 in Villeneuve-Loubet near Nice, in the house which is now the *Museum of Culinary Art* and contains a wonderful collection of ephemera concerned with cookery. He started work at his uncle's restaurant in Nice and at the age of nineteen went to Paris where he worked as *commis rôtisseur* at the *Petit Moulin Rouge* restaurant. He was there for four years until he was called up for military service during the Franco-Prussian war. In 1871 he went to work at the Hotel Luxemburg in Nice, then returned to the *Petit Moulin Rouge* this time as head chef. In 1879 he became a director of an outdoor catering firm which he ran for five years; in the meantime he helped to form the *Societé Culinaire Française* and started to write for *L'Art Culinaire*, a journal which he had founded with Phileas Gilbert.

Escoffier did go into business on his own when he opened a small restaurant in Cannes in 1878, but he preferred the bustle and noise of a large kitchen and later in 1883, began working as head chef at the **Grand Hotel** in **Monte Carlo** which was being managed by César Ritz. At the end of the Riviera Season they both transferred to the **Grand National Hotel** in **Lucerne**. They were separated for a while when Ritz bought and ran his own hotels, one in Baden-Baden and

324

the other in Cannes, but by the end of 1889 they were back together again, this time at the **Savoy Hotel** in London.

Richard D'Oyly Carte had been in America for performances of the Gilbert and Sullivan operas of which he was the impresario, and had built the **Savoy** to the same standard of luxury that he had seen in hotels there. It opened on 6 August 1889 as the *hotel de luxe* of the world but it was soon running at a loss. It needed someone who could attract persons of note to patronise its restaurants and to return again and again and to recommend them to others. Ritz revolution-ised the way the hotel was run and Escoffier ran the kitchen and secured such a reputation for good food that people flocked to it.

They left the **Savoy** together in 1898, went to the newly-opened **Ritz Hotel** in Paris then returned to London for the opening of the **Carlton Hotel** where Escoffier remained until 1919, Ritz having had to retire in 1903 because of a nervous breakdown. Escoffier carried on working as an adviser and a demonstra-tor and journeyed throughout Europe and the United States in the cause of culinary affairs.

In 1928 he was made an officer of the *Légion d Honneur,* France's most honoured award. During his years in England he was a founder-member of the *Association Culinaire Française de Grande Bretagne* and in 1911 was on the advisory board of Westminster College, the first college set up to prepare young people for a career in catering.

Escoffier died at Monte Carlo in 1935, a well-known international person-ality, but as with many great men and women, his achievements were not fully appreciated until long after his death. First, Escoffier re-organised the work of the kitchen brigade so as to make it operate more efficiently and economically, second he added many new dishes to the repertoire; third, he modified and up-dated cooking procedures and finally, he codified and simplified cookery practices. His name will never be forgotten.

MARIO GALLATI

Head waiters who find time to write their memoirs are scarce and most of them live out their lives and are then forgotten, both by their customers and their colleagues. This is a pity because the chef is only as good as the waiter who serves the food and there must be a strong understanding between them if the customer is to be satisfied. Just as there are *chef-patrons* so do head-waiters set up their own restaurant in a small way; some become extremely successful and make a good name and a lot of money for themselves.

Mario Gallati was born in a small village near Milan in 1889, the son of a shoemaker. At the age of ten he got a job in a restaurant in Milan as a general assistant and two years later left for Nice, then went to Germany before landing in this country at fourteen years of age. He worked first at the **Savoy Hotel**, then at the **Hotel Cecil**, then the **Russell** and for a long time he was at the **Queen's Restaurant** in Leicester Square, a favourite rendezvous of stage stars.

He learned how to run a restaurant whilst working at Romano's Restaurant in the Strand, one of the most popular restaurants of its day where guests had to wear evening dress and where royalty were frequent customers. In 1918 he returned from war service in Italy to open the **Ivy Restaurant** and built its reputation to its present high level, particularly amongst theatrical personalities whom Mario got to know well, and also amongst publishers and writers.

After running the **Ivy** for twenty-eight years he left; he was then 57, but at this age he opened his own restaurant, the **Caprice** in Arlington Street, with the financial support of many of his previous customers and friends. Within a short time of its opening, gossip writers were mentioning the **Caprice** in their columns and it was not long before business was booming. People knew that Mario was very knowledgeable on good food and wine and set the highest possible standard of cooking and service; moreover they knew they could arrive and stay late and feel relaxed. He employed two shifts of staff so as to ensure that his waiters did not hurry customers by yawning, looking at their watches or piling chairs on the tables. He chose his staff very carefully and paid them well with the result that they stayed with him and became known to customers, many of whom were also regulars. He also chose his chef well with the result that he had no worries on the kitchen side and the food was always up to his demanding standards. Mario Gallati's story is typical of many head waiters'; he fostered friendship with his customers who when called upon were willing to provide the financial backing for him to open a restaurant where they would receive excellent personal attention from their partner and friend, Mario Gallati.

He died in 1975 on the very day the **Caprice** went out of business. It was in decline because it was no longer fashionable; it had catered for a minority section of the public and the comment was made that the day Hollywood died, the Caprice started to die with it.

MICHEL GUÉRARD

Michel Guérard is one of the leading chefs in France and is responsible for an advancement of cookery practices that has had a great influence on cookery throughout the world. He was responsible for the introduction of an entirely new way of cooking known as *cuisine minceur* which combined with the *nouvelle cuisine* of Paul Bocuse to create a system of cooking and serving that revolutionised classical practices and caused a major upheaval of culinary traditions.

Michael Guérard runs his own restaurant at Eugènie-les-Bains and is recognised as one of the leading chef-patrons. His influence stemmed from the book he wrote in 1976 entitled *La Grande Cuisine Minceur*. In this book he showed the need to render classical French cookery into a lighter and less fattening form with a lower intake of calories but without losing any of its succulence.

In 1978 Monsieur Guérard published another book, *La Cuisine Gourmande*, a title which would seem to imply that he had turned his back on the simple style he had been advocating. In fact the two books are complementary and show that he never abandoned French culinary heritage in favour of a restrictive diet, but that the two forms are entirely compatible.

Michel Guérard, Paul Bocuse and the brothers Troisgros were the innovators of *cuisine moderne* which embraces the controversial subject of *cuisine nouvelle*, whose demise has been continuously forecast but is still firmly established in the majority of first-class establishments. A great deal of thought and experiment is required to render the masterpieces of *la cuisine moderne* into their ultimate form and only such mentors as Guérard and Bocuse could have initiated this.

Michael Guérard spent some of his formative years as *chef saucier* at the *Hotel Crillon* in Paris and as a chef in charge in private service to form an ideal background of experience before centuring into business on his own. The two books by Monsieur Guérard have been translated into English by Caroline Conran. They have helped to spread his fame and are in constant use by those go-ahead chefs who see the need to follow fashions in food.

PHILIP HARBEN

Philip Harben came to fame by means of television. He was the tubby-looking man with a beard who showed viewers how to cook. He was more of an actor than a cook as was evidenced by the wearing of a butcher's apron but he exerted a great deal of influence on British cooking not only through his television performances but also through his twelve interesting books on cooking.

He started work as the manager of a small restaurant in Hampstead then during the war years worked as canteen manager for British Overseas Airways. He worked in other canteens and made his debut on television in 1946 after being recommended by André Simon, and soon became a star. His programmes did not go down well with professional chefs and he received many unkind remarks from them. At this time he started his own catering contract business, then set up a company to produce non-stick pans which were sold under his brand name.

AMBROSE HEATH

The first of Ambrose Heath's books appeared more than fifty years ago and he wrote more than seventy others after that. He did not study cooking but devel-

327

oped a taste for food and wine and was a co-founder with André Simon of the *Wine and Food Society* in 1933.

He started writing articles for newspapers and magazines and this led to the books which in general were on individual subjects rather than comprehensive treatises. They are modest and unpretentious in content yet he was an erudite writer with an ability ro present the most pretentious and sophisticated recipe in a very simple way. He was born in 1891 and died in 1970.

EUGENE HERBODEAU

Eugene Herbodeau 1888-1982 worked in many parts of France before moving to the **Carlton Hotel** under Escoffier in 1913, where he stayed until 1921. He then worked as chef at the **Metropole Hotel** in **Brighton**, the **Ritz** in London and again at the **Carlton** from 1928 to 1937. He then ran the **Ecu de France** in Jermyn Street until his retirement in 1957. He was awarded the *Légion d'Honneur*.

ROGER LALLEMAND

Monsieur Lallemand is the author of a long list of cookery books, a lecturer at the main practical catering college in Paris, a member of the *Académie Culinaire de France*, of the *Société des Cuisiniers de Paris*, and also a member of the *Club des Cent* and of the *Club Prosper-Montagné*. He is a very practical man with a profound knowledge of his subject and an ability to sort out the wheat from the chaff when revising old recipes. He is not afraid to argue a point with those more dilettante writers who seek to impose their views on the public as against the highly professional approach which he brings to bear on the topic.

His series on *La Cuisine de Chez Nous* runs to twenty-five books, each covering an entire region of France, giving recipes for the dishes that originated there and listing the oenogastronomic associations of each region. Monsieur Lallemande is also preparing a four-volume book on cookery and a gastronomic bibliography.

He is a true gastronome who has played a major part in maintaining the high standards of French cookery and in reviving the historical masterpieces of the regions.

328

ROSA LEWIS

Although a legend in her lifetime, Rosa Lewis' reputation as a hotelier has increased as more people have heard about her since her death in 1952. She was born Rose Ovenden in 1867 and went into service as a maid-of-all-work in the house of a city clerk. After six years of this she decided that being a cook would be a better paid job than being an ordinary domestic so she got a job in the kitchen of the *Duc d'Orleans* in his London suburb house; there she watched the chef at work and quickly learnt all she could about cookery. It was not long before she was working as a cook-in-charge in private service. This led to her coming to the attention of the Prince of Wales who was a frequent guest in the houses of the nobility and was so pleased with a meal he had eaten that he asked to see the chef – it was Rosa. She was in the service of Lady Randolph Churchill and of many others but always within the royal circle in which the Prince of Wales moved. With her husband, she set up as a boarding-house keeper in Belgravia and also became a freelance cook, taking over the kitchen from the chef in private houses to produce dinners for special occasions – doing no fewer than twenty-nine in six weeks in Coronation year! She became a friend of Escoffier who presented her with a photograph of himself and invited her to attend a meeting of the *Ligne des Gourmands* a professional association. Rosa became chef at Whites' Club and in 1902 she took over the lease of the Cavendish Hotel in Jermyn Street

26. Miss Rosa Lewis and her staff, at the Cavendish Hotel, Jermyn Street, W1, in May 1938

and made it one of the most famous hotels in London. She did everything, greeted the guests, did the shopping, cooking and serving, decided on the furnishings and redecoration, put in bathrooms and other amenities that made the hotel a success and brought her even more fame and notoriety.

The press of that time called her 'England's greatest woman chef'; she set up a tutorial scheme to encourage other women to emulate her and was generous to the impecunious but hard on the foolish and perverse.

In 1941 the Cavendish was badly damaged by bombs and she was injured but carried on working until she reached the age of 85 before giving up her career. Her memory is kept alive in the new hotel which now stands on the site where there are some interesting relics on display for customers of the new Cavendish.

EDOUARD LONGUE

There are thousands of well-known gastronomes in France who earn their living by writing articles on all aspects of food and drink, but only a few ever achieve international renown for their profound knowledge of the subject.

The best-known of these professional gastronomes is Edouard Longue who has devoted the past twenty-five years of his life to writing on the subjects of nutrition, cookery and tourism. He is founder-president of the *Association Française de la Presse Gastronomique et Touristique* and vice-president of the international federation of gastronomic writers known as *Fiprega*, founded in 1933. He is the secretary of the gastronomic society *Les Amis de Curnonsky*, and a member of the *Comité National de Gastronomie*.

In addition to the five hundred or so articles that have appeared above his name on the subject of foods, their preparation and digestion, he is author and editor of a wide range of books including *La Cuisine du Bonheur* written in collaboration with **Raymond Oliver**. His book, *Le Livre de la Cuisine Juive*, is the authoritative work on kosher cookery because it not only gives an appreciation of Jewish gastronomy but also devotes one third of its pages to an explanation of the rules governing the pattern of food and meals for orthodox Jews.

Monsieur Longue was educated at the *Faculté de Medicin* and the *Faculté des Sciences* in Paris and was a teacher for some twenty-five years before becoming a food writer and author. He is active as a judge at culinary competitions and salons and travels widely in his pursuit of perfection in all things gastronomic.

LUCIEN OGIER

At 80 years of age and sixty-four years after he first started working as a commis chef, Lucien Ogier still plays an active part in the kitchen of his restaurant

L'Aubergarde at Pontchartrain which he opened fifty years ago.

After his apprenticeship in Grenoble, M. Ogier moved to Paris to work in leading establishments including the *Ritz* Hotel, the *Larue* and *Lucas-Carton Restaurants*. He once worked a season at the *Casino* in **Dieppe** under the direction of Escoffier. Lucien Ogier has taken the lead in the training of young people and has served on several advisory bodies including the *Concours du Meilleur Apprenti*, the *Prix Pierre Taittinger* and of the *Lycée Hôtelier Jean-Drouant* in Paris.

For twelve years he was President of the *Association des Maîtres Cuisiniers* and has held many other honorary positions both at home and overseas. His knowledge and love of food and drink is profound, which is why he continues to make his unique contribution to the furtherance of the industry he serves so well.

RAYMOND OLIVER b. 1910

Raymond Oliver is the doyen of *chefs-patrons* and has exercised a marked influence on the progress of gastronomy in France, through his own restaurant, his writings and his appearances on French television. His 300-year old restaurant *Le Grand Vefour* in Paris has consistently held its place as one of the very best in France and has constantly achieved top rating in many good food guides. *Le Grand Vefour* was destroyed by a bomb at Christmas 1983 and has been re-opened by Oliver's chef **Yves Labrousse**. Oliver's son already has his own restaurant in Paris and teaches at a cookery school.

It is generally agreed amongst chefs that it was M. Oliver who was responsible for the rebirth of fine French cookery after the end of the Second World War.

M. Oliver's work has always been innovatory; although a traditional chef by training he is not afraid to use his remarkable talents to broaden the frontiers of cookery by remarkable combinations of foods. Two examples of his ideas are rabbit with melon in which the meat is cooked in melon juice and cream, flavoured with Dijon mustard and garnished with melon balls; another is best end of lamb *poêlé* and served on an oval pad of set creamed spinach on a layer of *duxelles* with an arrangement of crystallised violets on the meat. Dishes such as these are indicative of Raymond Oliver's freshness of approach which although different from that of his fellow chefs-patron, has been equally revolutionary. Although his chef has taken over the running of his restaurant Raymond is still active and keeps remarkably busy in his study of the state of gastronomy.

MARGUERITE PATTEN

Marguerite Patten is the best known and most prolific of all cookery writers writing for housewives. Her books are big, brightly illustrated and carefully

331

written so as to make the results successful. She wanted to be an actress but in between plays, took a job as a demonstrator, becoming senior demonstrator during the War for the Government, then for several food and detergent firms.

Her books from Hamlyn and other publishers sell something like one million a year, proof enough of the enormous influence she exerts over the standard of cookery in the homes in this country. She has written several hundred cookery books, most of them still in print and also a very useful bibliography of culinary books.

HENRI-P. PELLEPRAT

Henri-P. Pelleprat, (1869–1949) worked at the *Café de la Paix* and at the *Maison Dorée* in Paris before becoming a lecturer at the *Cordon Bleu School*. On his retirement in 1932 he devoted his time to writing books, mainly on pastrywork, his first having been published as early as 1913.

POMIANE

Dr Edouard de Pomiane was one of rare breed of men – a scientist with a deep love for food who was able to explain the chemistry of cooking in simple terms that all who heard him could easily understand.

He was a professor at the *Institut Pasteur* in Paris with a medical background which he applied to the study of nutrition. He allied his deep knowledge of this to his hobby of cooking and was then able to give answers to the problems met by chefs and food technologists. He gained a wealth of knowledge of cookery and was a keen gastronome who later achieved popularity from his role as a food expert on French radio and through his several books on cookery.

Born of Polish parents, he studied at the school for Polish emigrés in Paris. He is like Brillat-Savarin in the way he describes the chemical, social and culinary reasons for doing things in a certain way and by his reminiscences. He said that no two human digestive systems work alike and that the same diet which can make one person put on weight will not have any effect upon another. His understanding of cookery is profound even though his approach to it is lighthearted and he can make even a fairly complicated dish seem easy. His books are a delight to read whether in the original or translation.

332

RAYMOND POSTGATE

Raymond Postgate was the founder of, and for seventeen years, the editor of *The Good Food Guide*. He had long been a connoisseur of food and wine and his desire to improve British culinary standards led him to recruit volunteers to visit and report on catering establishments. These visits and reports were published, and put chefs and waiters on their mettle so that their places of work would receive a good report in subsequent issues of this much respected guide.

Most of the investigators were well-known gourmets but their visits were entirely spontaneous and they went incognito. They received no expenses or fees for their investigations and no free meals from establishments. No advertisements appeared in the guide and reporters were free to express their unbiased judgement of the meal experience.

Before long, Raymond Postgate became a public figure and a person with much influence in catering circles. In 1962 *The Good Food Guide* was taken over by The Consumers' Association but he remained as editor and then as adviser until 1969, shortly before his death.

He was a very cultured man of strong left wing views. Before achieving fame as editor of the GFG, he had achieved distinction as an elegant writer of detective novels, as a journalist on the *Daily Herald*, as a social historian and as a classical scholar and translator of latin texts. With G.D.H. Cole he wrote the best selling *The Common People* and several books on wine that he wrote showed his ability to present the subject to the man in the street in an easily understandable way.

He was a Grand Chancelier d'Ambassade de St. Emilion.

Mme S. B. PRUNIER

The firm of Pruniers was founded in 1872 in the *rue d'Antin* in Paris by Mme Prunier's grandfather Alfred, and was taken over by his son Emile in 1898. The restaurant specialised in oysters and customers then had no choice but to eat them raw until one day an American customer asked for some cooked oysters; two years later, fish of all kinds, was the mainstay of the menu.

Mme Prunier started working in the firm as secretary to her father and helped to open another restaurant for the firm, the *Traktir* also in Paris, then took over the entire business when her father died. *Maison Prunier* in St James Street, London, was opened in 1934 and was a success from then until it closed more than forty years later. Mme Prunier was awarded the *Légion d'Honneur* in 1954 and was the only woman ever to be admitted to the otherwise all-male *Association of French Chefs in Great Britain*.

CÉSAR RITZ

César Ritz, the man whose name is used as an adjective to describe anything that is of the highest class - a place that is luxurious, a repast that is sumptuous and plenteous, and something that is highly priced - was born in Niederwald in Switzerland in 1850. His birthplace could not have been more primitive or remote and his family was of poor peasant stock. He was sacked from his first job as wine *commis* in a hotel in Brieg so left for Paris where he was more successful and eventually got a job at the famous *Voisin Restaurant* where he learned about attention to detail and the minute intricacies of first-class food service, doing so at the lowly level of *commis* waiter.

It was in Vienna in 1873 that Ritz first came into contact with the noble, princely and powerful people of Europe. Here were emperors, kings and princes, including the Prince of Wales, and he stored away in his mind details of their habits, their wants and their dislikes which was afterwards to bring him valuable patronage. At the age of 24 Ritz met them again, this time in Nice which was the fashionable place in which to be seen from December to April each year.

After two seasons as manager of hotels in San Remo he was sought out by the owner of the *Grand Hotel Nationale* in *Lucerne*, recently opened as the most luxurious hotel in Switzerland but running at a loss. Ritz used his friendship with the important people he had met in Vienna, Nice and San Remo, to fill the hotel to capacity. The *Grand Hotel Nationale* became not only the most luxurious but also the best-run hotel in Europe and its fame spread so widely that even crowned heads had to book well in advance in order to secure accommodation.

The *Nationale* was seasonal and for the ten years he worked there Ritz spent the winter season at hotels in Menton and Trouville until he was offered the post of manager of the *Grand Hotel* in *Monte Carlo* which was where he met **Auguste Escoffier** and formed the perfect team that was to last until Ritz's forced retirement in 1903, caused by a mental breakdown.

Between them, the two men put the *Grand Hotel* at *Monte Carlo* firmly on the map as being the place to stay, which together with the *National* at *Lucerne*, made Ritz and Escoffier world renowned.

Richard D'Oyly Carte heard of them and travelled to meet and talk business in the hope of getting them to do for his newly opened hotel, the Savoy, what they had done for the Grand and the National. The **Savoy Hotel** had just been built and badly needed a manager capable of filling it with rich people, and of satisfying their demands. Ritz turned down the offer but after paying a visit to London and recognising the hotel's potential, he accepted the job and started there in 1889, bringing Escoffier and several other key members of his staff to help him. Within a few months they had put the Savoy firmly in the front rank of luxury hotels and at the same time they had revolutionised London society's habits, it was success all the way until 1897 when they suddenly and inexplicably, left the hotel.

Ritz had many other interests; he was acting as consultant in planning and redeveloping hotels in many countries; he was also director of several hotels and set up his own company to build grand hotels around the world, the results being the **Ritz Hotels** in **Paris** and **London**, opened in 1898 and 1905 respectively.

The **Carlton Hotel** was being built at that time with Ritz involved in it, and in 1899 Ritz and Escoffier came back to England to open it; together they hoped to make it a rival to the Savoy and all the other luxury hotels in London. It was the first to have a private bathroom with every apartment and it kept its reputation both for food and accommodation until it was bombed during the Second World War.

It was precisely at the time of the Coronation of Edward VII that Ritz felt the effect of his years of working under extreme pressure and suffered a complete nervous breakdown. The King had to postpone his Coronation because of an operation for appendicitis but soon recovered and the delay lasted only a couple of months. César Ritz' illness was much more serious and although he returned to work for a short time, from mid-1903 he was no longer able to cope. He died in October 1918 at the age of 68, but such had been his devotion to his job of satisfying the most difficult and demanding customer and the improvement of hotel food and accommodation, that in the forty years of his working life he achieved more than any other hotelier has ever done.

ALBERT AND MICHEL ROUX

The two Roux brothers have spent seventeen years of their lives teaching the British people how to appreciate good food and in doing so have exerted a very significant influence on gastronomy. The first restaurant they opened in 1967 after spending nearly nine years in private service was *La Gavroche* the only restaurant in Britain to earn three stars in the **Michelin Guide**. The brothers own four other well-known restaurants plus a pastry commissary, a charcuterie factory, a butchery business and an outdoor catering section; they are in business in Britain in a very big and highly successful way. As well as their own restaurant interests they have assisted several of their staff to set up good-class restaurants of their making, by funding 50 per cent of the capital in the same way that the brothers themselves had been assisted when they first started in business. In this way their influence is becoming even more widespread and with the help of their book, *New Classic Cuisine*, they are pointing the way forward so that many more may participate in their success. There is a two-year waiting list to be apprenticed to them.

Both Roux brothers began as pastrycooks and as such were the organisers of an extraordinary course put on for the *Societé des Pâtissiers de Paris* at Aston Clinton, which culminated in a fantastic and never-to-be-forgotton display of the many branches of the art of the pastrycook. The value of their early training is well demonstrated by the extent and elegance of the sweet course on their menus.

Both brothers were in private service - Albert with Lady Astor and with Mr and Mrs Peter Cazalet, and Michel with the Rothschilds in Paris - excellent training grounds for all branches of cookery for they are equally at home cooking at the stove as in the pastry department. This makes them rarities amongst chefs and again explains their success story for they know what standards to set.

ANDRÉ SIMON

M. Simon has probably exerted more influence than any other person on the advancement of catering in this country, and if his emphasis has been more on wine than on food this is to be expected since he spent thirty-three years as British sales manager for **Pommery**, the champagne firm.

He was born in 1877 in Paris, moved to England in 1894 remaining there until his death in 1970. He wrote over a hundred books, mostly concerned with wine but including the *Concise Encyclopedia of Gastronomy* which appeared in nine sections between 1939 and 1946, later being published in one volume.

With A. J. A. Symons he founded the *Wine and Food Society* 'to bring together and to serve all who took an intelligent interest in the problems and pleasures of the table'. The first meeting was held in 1933 and 500 members joined within the first three months, each paying one guinea subscription. The Society publishes its own magazine, *Wine and Food Quarterly*, which is very popular and is sold world-wide. The Society is still strong and has branches throughout this country and in many countries overseas. The Wine and Food Society is not an élitist body of rich gastronomes and the titled people on its Council were appointed because of their knowledge of food rather than because of their wealth or distinction.

One of the endearing features of the Society's magazine was its regular feature, *Memorable Meals*, which showed the food and wine for a meal given by a host for a few friends either at home or in a public restaurant, where everything was presented in the finest manner even though the dishes themselves may have been simple, but perfectly cooked, thus showing that to be a gastronome demands a thorough understanding of all levels of cookery and the ability to fit dishes into a suitable menu, rather than having a bottomless purse. Simon's name may not yet be very widely known amongst the general public but prophets seldom receive due recognition during their lifetime. The day will come when this man's life-long devotion to the furtherance of good food and wine in Britain will become more widely known and due honour will be paid to his memory.

ALEXIS SOYER

Alexis Soyer was a man who was larger than life, a flamboyant yet profound person whose life-story makes fascinating reading and whose contribution to the well-being of the British, both poor and rich, is immeasurable. He was born near Paris in October 1809 and his first job was as an apprentice cook. He moved to England in 1831 and worked for five years in private service during which time he gained a reputation for his advanced views on cookery and on the need for reforms in the way people ate.

This made him a well-known person who kept himself in the public eye and eventually led to his appointment as head chef at the **Reform Club** in **Pall Mall**, for which he made an excellent public relations man during the fourteen years he worked there. He dressed very smartly both in uniform and in ordinary clothes and transformed the kitchen at the **Reform Club** into a showplace to welcome visitors. His chef's uniform included a red velvet hat with a tassel, worn over one ear.

With the publication of his first book in 1845, Soyer's name became even more of a household word and he continued to produce many other books, each of which ran to many editions. They were written for all classes, including the very poor. At the same time he invented many gadgets and produced bottled sauces which were marketed under his name which was a guarantee of good sales. In the hungry 1840s when bad harvests brought famine to England and Ireland he volunteered to run soup kitchens to provide nutritious broths, on one occasion for 26,000 people who would otherwise have had nothing to eat.

During the Crimean War it was found that more troops were dying in hospital than on the battlefield, their deaths being caused by poor nursing and badly cooked food that brought disease and malnutrition. Alex Soyer offered his services to try to improve the dreadful situation and together with Florence Nightingale reorganised the feeding arrangements, so saving the lives of many soldiers who would otherwise have died from sheer maladministration; Soyer was in effect, the first-ever hospital catering adviser. He went on to redesign the kitchens at Wellington Barracks and to suggest improvements in the iron rations issued to troops.

Soyer was of the school of Carême by which is meant that he carried on using ornate set pieces and elaborate presentations when ever the occasion called for them. He was an innovator and the creator of many new dishes, and also improved and renamed some of the classics of his time. He was a man who loved the limelight and lost no opportunity to publicise himself and his business activities; the cult of the chef can perhaps be said to have started with him.

Soyer became ill whilst serving in the Crimea and the last years of his life were spent suffering from the effects of overwork. He died in 1859 at the early age of 50, sadly missed by an adoring public who admired him not only for his flamboyancy of character and as a man-about-town, but also as one who had constantly sought to do good to his fellow-men.

27. Alexis Benoit Soyer, from the original by Emma Soyer

PIERRE TOULEMON

Pierre Toulemon, (1894 - 1980) came from a family of chefs and was apprenticed to a pastrycook in Périgeux. After working at the *Elysée Palace* and *Les Ambassadeurs* in *Paris* he moved to the **Carlton** in **London** and worked under Escoffier. After working at the **Metropole Hotel** in **London** and at **Kettner's Restaurant** he was head chef for twenty years at the **Ladies Carlton Club** followed by another twenty years at the **Connaught Hotel**.

JEAN AND PIERRE TROISGROS

The two brothers have run their own restaurant at Roanne, near Beaujolais since 1953 and had constantly maintained its high standard during these years. Both brothers worked under **Fernand Point** at his restaurant *La Pyramide* at *Vienne* and also at several places in Paris before coming together to run the family business of restaurant and wine merchant. They are followers of *cuisine nouvelle* and use reduced stock instead of traditional sauces but flavour the reduction with meat or fish glaze to provide full taste. They do however, favour the highest calorie sauces of all, those made with eggs and butter or oil such as *sauce Costelloise* which is like *hollandaise* but uses olive, peanut and walnut oils. Classical garnishes are replaced by appropriate items that complement the main article.

Jean Troisgros died at the early age of 57 years in 1983 but his brother Pierre is carrying on the family traditions.

VATEL

The story of how Vatel committed suicide because the fish did not arrive is well-known, based on facts recorded by **Mme de Sévigné**. There is obviously more to the story as no head waiter of sound mind would kill himself with his own sword just because the fishmonger was late with deliveries that morning.

Although described as being head waiter to the **Prince de Condé**, it is more likely that Vatel was his equerry or manciple and thus the person in charge of the entire catering arrangements. The visit by Louis XIV and most of his Court in 1671, was an important occasion which Vatel had so organised that the King was bound to be favourably impressed by the high standard of hospitality and of everything that was being done to make his visit a memorable one.

But the arrangements did not go as smoothly as expected and some of the things that still cause nervous breakdowns to caterers happened to Vatel - more people arrived than expected with the result that there was not enough room nor

339

enough food for everyone. Next day the fish that had been freshly landed that morning did not arrive from the port in time and this must have been the last straw. Rather than make excuses to the royal visitor or substitute another dish, Vatel chose to end his life by his own hand.

ROGER VERGÉ

Roger Vergé is one of the best known chef-patrons of France and runs *Moulin des Mougins*. He is one of the small group of chefs who created *la nouvelle cuisine* and his book, *Cuisine of the Sun*, shows how he creates fresh, light and imaginative dishes of what he calls 'joyful cooking'. In addition to recipes, Monsieur Vergé includes many anecdotes that make the book more personal, from his experience of working at the celebrated *Tour d'Argent Restaurant* and the *Plaza-Athenée Hotel* in Paris. The book was translated by **Caroline Conran** and is pleasingly laid out so as to make it clear and easy to follow. Not that he expects his readers to follow his instructions slavishly for he advocates the need to adapt, invent and improvise when working in the kitchen. His cooking has the brilliant richness of Provence as it stems from uncomplicated methods and simple ingredients but used in an imaginative way and treated with respect. It is this philosophy that has helped him to gain the highest awards from the food guides.

Other notable gastronomes include:

Appollinaire, Guillaume	1880–1918	Wrote novels, essays and plays
Beebe, Lucius	1902–66	Journalist and author who reported the New York social scene during the Naughty Nineties and the doings of the greatest gourmands of all time – Diamond Jim Brady and Lilian Russell, the singer
Brisse, Baron	1813–76	Served as Minister of Forests under Louis Philippe; editor of *Liberte*; culinary writer
Cambacères, J. J. , Duc de	1753–1824	Statesman and friend of Napoleon
Dumas, Alexandre	1802–70	Novelist and playwright
Grimod de la Reynière	1758–1838	Wrote the annual *Almanach des Gourmets* from 1803 to 1812, and the *Manuel des Amphitryons* in 1807 – gastronomic notes

Johnson, Samuel	1709-84	Lexicographer and critic, with his constant companion Boswell, the diarist
Monselet, C.	1825-88	Author of the *Almanac des Gourmets*
Montagné, Prosper	1865-1948	Wrote twelve books, including one in collaboration with Escoffier; edited *Larousse Gastronomique*
Murat, J.	1767-1815	Officer under Napoleon; Marshal of France, later King of Naples
Nignon, E.	1865-1935	Writer who was also chef to the Czar of Russia; worked at Claridges then opened his own place in Paris
Root, W.	d. 1982	Foreign correspondent for USA newspapers and author of books on Italian and French cooking
Saintsbury, G.	1845-1933	Professor of Rhetoric at Edinburgh University
Thackeray, W. M.	1811-63	Novelist, poet, gastronome, editor
Sala, G. A.	1828-95	Journalist and novelist
White, Florence	1860-1934	Founder of the *English Folk Cookery Association*; was a headmistress, trained at *Cordon Bleu School* in Paris

13 Places of Entertainment

AN OUTLINE OF THE FUNCTION OF ESTABLISHMENTS

'Its purpose is to watch over his conservation by suggesting the best possible
practices has been solely in the realm of the great houses and grand hotels of
Europe. **Brillat-Savarin** in his **Meditation on Gastronomy** suggested that 'Gastronomy is the intelligent knowledge of whatever concerns man's nourishment' and
'Its purpose is to watch over his conservation by suggesting the best possible
sustenance for him .

THE HOLBORN RESTAURANT

AND

KING'S + HALL,

LONDON.

BY its architectural beauty, and the variety of its manifold departments—offering, as they do, unsurpassed accommodation to every section of the public—this Restaurant is pronounced, by many widely-travelled connoisseurs, to be the finest in Europe. It is certain that, to the conscientious and unremitting efforts of the management to administer faultlessly to their comfort and luxury, the public have responded by an extent of custom which, large and elaborate as the institution already was, has now necessitated the addition of the Western Annexe, where parties of even greater magnitude than hitherto can be accommodated. It need only be said that, whereas, at its inauguration twenty years ago, the Holborn Restaurant could only seat three hundred guests, it now entertains upwards of two thousand five hundred.

A BRIEF comprehensive glance at the resources of this Restaurant will here suffice. Banquets on a grand scale, for parties numbering five or six hundred, are served in the magnificent new King's Hall, which is also available for Cinderellas, Balls, Concerts, &c. The numerous other banqueting salons—such as the Royal Venetian Chamber, the Council Chamber, the Queen's, Prince's, Duke's, Commodore's, Colonel's, Captain's, Phœnix, Caledonian, Japanese and Chinese Salons, &c.,—are of varied dimensions, adapted to parties ranging from 25 to 250 guests.

28. The Holborn Restaurant, part of the Frederick Gordon empire

Many of the practices that exist and many of the great strides that have improved the nourishment of mankind have come from a variety of quarters and from a number of contributors, some working in the most humble situations but who had the interest of their fellow-men at heart. **Nicholas Appert** gained an understanding of the principles of preservation of foodstuffs whilst working as a bottle washer for a Champagne firm. His discovery permitted people to have a supply of food even in the most inhospitable environments. Deep-freezing as a means of preserving food had been established in the polar regions for a considerable length of time before Clarence Birdseye developed it commercially in the 1920s. Many of the dishes which found their way on to the tables of the rich and famous had their origins in equally unlikely places, where either necessity or availability of materials encouraged the local cook to make use of certain ingredients and thus to introduce them to the world.

In this context it is of benefit to both the professional caterer and the student of gastronomy to become fully acquainted with the *raison d'être* of the various types of establishment in which catering is carried out, their scope, purpose and operational characteristics, so that they can objectively evaluate what contribution can be made to improve or maintain the established standard in any operation where his knowledge or skills are required.

An awareness of the evolution of these establishments is also of primary importance, since a knowledge of the past inevitably assists in foretelling future patterns and prepares the individual to accept necessary changes. The example of the Sun Inn makes this explicit. The understanding of many of the other establishments' activities should provide further thought on the gastronomic perspective because, although their requirements vary considerably, all have a common purpose, that is to provide man with the best and most agreeable nourishment so as to make his journey on earth a pleasant one. If the humble supply of nourishment is carried out in this spirit in every establishment then Voltaire's expression *'Qu'un cuisinier est un mortal divin'* can be equally applied in any circumstance and the contributor becomes a worthy disciple of gastronomy.

This chapter lists the many different categories of eating places that exist, it categorises them into two main groups then gives a description of each, an outline of its aims and operation and shows how each functions.

The two main sectors of the industry are the **Profit Sector** which includes restaurants, cafes, snack bars, coffee shops, coffee bars, member's clubs, bistros, estaminets, brasseries, grill rooms, chop houses, trattories, taverns, pizzerias, butteries, public houses, night-clubs, fast food outlets, holiday camps, fish and chip shops, departmental store restaurants, oil rigs, ships' catering, railway catering, airline catering and others. The **Cost Sector** includes industrial catering, hospitals, schools, colleges, universities, social services homes, the armed forces, prisons and so on.

PROFIT SECTOR EATING AND ENTERTAINING PLACES

This includes more than 150 000 outlets and constitutes approximately 60 per cent of the total market; the Cost Sector has some 45 000 outlets and constitutes approximately 40 per cent of the market. The total turnover of the entire catering market of food and drink is some £4 000 million per annum.

The forerunners of hotels and restaurants were the inns, taverns and alehouses. The distinction between them is not absolutely clear, but an inn offered food, drink and accommodation for travellers who were generally well-to-do people whilst a tavern offered food and drink only, including wine rather as does a wine bar of today. A tavern offered entertainment and refreshments but catered mainly for the local population. An alehouse was not so grand as either an inn or a tavern and sold only ale and various other kinds of beer; music and games were the forms of entertainment it offered.

Neither a tavern nor an alehouse could offer any accommodation and inns, taverns and alehouses all held different forms of licences. Various Acts were passed to govern the conduct of all these and licences were required as long ago as 1552. In 1553 an Act was passed that controlled the number and in 1604 another Act further increased the level of control over their operation. *The Innholders' Company* was formed in 1437 as a guild to bring professionalism to the vocation of innkeeping. The first brewery company was opened in 1542 and by 1686 there were a number of tied houses. By the beginning of the nineteenth century there were dozens of brewery companies and over half the alehouses were 'tied', which meant that the landlord worked for the brewery company rather than for himself. From 1830 alehouses and taverns began to be known as public houses; some were called gin palaces and concentrated on selling that innocent-looking spirit because of its cheapness.

Licensing Justices were appointed from 1834 and by 1869 the number of public houses had been limited by the Wine and Beer House Act. Taverns gradually lost their separate identity and eventually became coffee houses and restaurants.

Inns started as hostels to provide shelter and food for pilgrims and other travellers journeying to the shrines of the saints or on the King's business. The hostels were buildings attached to the abbeys, where possible, outside the town so that late arrivals could enter without having to worry that the town gates were shut. Hostels offered very austere accommodation, homely food and ale as brewed by the monks for themselves. By the fifteenth century the number of hostels had been increased by the opening of commercially-run inns where the accommodation, food and drink was better than at the hostels. Each inn distinguished its identity by erecting a sign outside so as to imprint itself in the minds of travellers.

The status of being the keeper of the most important inn of a town has always been a privileged one because much of the official business of the town was centred on the inn and the innkeeper was expected to be a man of many parts who knew how to satisfy all ranks of customers with appropriate food, drink and accommodation. The following account of the history of an imaginary inn illustrates its changing fortunes over the years.

The Sun Inn

The Sun Inn was built early in the sixteenth century on land belonging to the fellows of a college of some importance. It was leased to the local Lord of the manor and run by a landlord and his wife. The quality of the beer he brewed and the excellence of the meals cooked by his wife soon made the place popular with both the local inhabitants and the county officials. The size of its public rooms made it possible to cater for civic dinners in grand style and for use as the local courtroom.

During the Civil War the Sun Inn served as the headquarters of the Parliamentary army and was where the Council of War held their meetings. The King was defeated so the good business continued but when the King's son was enthroned, his men and the Cavaliers took their business to a rival establishment.

Happily a new source of business soon came with the inauguration of the coaching era and the landlord branched out as a coach operator early in the eighteenth century. By 1740 he was running three coaches to London each week and fifty years later there were fifteen coaches a day stopping at the inn, as well as stage wagons and local carriers.

The ground landlords were happy to finance the improvements necessary to cater for the increased business by extending the front, building a new Assembly Room and later adding a third story of bedrooms. The yard was glassed in for the convenience of travellers.

At this time the price of the Ordinary or table d'hôte lunch, was one shilling and sixpence (the equivalent of 7½p today) the beer or wine being charged extra. The food was plainly cooked but abundant and the innkeeper stood at the head of one of the communal tables and did the carving and serving, with an assistant doing the same for another group of travellers. It is customary to depict the innkeeper as a jovial character with an ability to make all guests feel at home whilst in his care. He is deferential to the local aristocracy but can joke and drink with the casual tipplers.

Innkeeping in those days meant far more than just supplying meals and accommodation and a large number of ancillary workers were employed to carry out such jobs as grooming and shoeing horses, cleaning stables, and loading and unloading the coaches. It was usual to grow vegetables and fruit in the garden behind the inn; pigs. cattle, chickens, ducks and geese were reared for the table; the innkeeper brewed his own beer, and his wife made the bread as well as cooking the meals.

Landlords and landladies came and went during the long history of the inn; some grew wealthy from the way they ran it whilst others added little lustre to the glory of the Sun, or to themselves. Often it was while there was a woman in charge that its reputation as an eating-house increased and she did all the local

347

banqueting business such as Hunt Balls and dinners for local associations; she put on lectures, staged plays by strolling players, arranged auction sales and markets, and many other events.

The opening of the railway through the town hit the Sun hard and as passengers and goods left the roads the inn had only its local trade to cater for. This state of affairs was the cause of the closure and demolition of many inns, especially those outside the towns. The hard times on which these inns had fallen caused **Earl Grey**, a former Governor - General of Canada to propose the founding of a company to rescue and preserve these fine old places and in 1903, **Trust Houses** was formed.

The Sun Inn had already changed its name to the Sun Hotel and its size and reputation made it an ideal establishment to take under Trust Houses' wing and to nurse back to health. The company put in a manager who was paid commission on the amount he took for food and accommodation but with less emphasis on the sale of drink, which was to pacify the temperance movement which was very active at that time. Although it was a private enterprise company with philanthropic shareholders, it kept its dividend at 5 per cent and used the profits to purchase more hotels and refurbish existing ones, but in the case of the Sun, its position on a prime site in the centre of the town made it a target for redevelopment and in the early 1960s the Sun was demolished to make way for the type of shopping arcade with offices over as seen in so many provincial towns and cities. After nearly 400 years of fine service to the people of the town and country and to travellers whose route went through it, the Sun was eclipsed, and ghosts of former landlords will have to be content to roam the aisles of the chain stores that now occupy their former home.

Mine Host

Perhaps untypical of his breed but a noteworthy if rather wayward innkeeper was **John Fothergill** of the **Spread Eagle** at **Thame**. He was not typical because although he could be a charming host, if he took a dislike to a customer's face he delighted in behaving in a deliberately rude manner hoping thus to make him to leave the inn, without too much fuss.

He transformed the Spread Eagle during the nineteen twenties and thirties from being a farmers' public house that only did business on market day, into a hotel that attracted gastronomes from London, Oxford and elsewhere to dine and wine and sometimes stay there. He left an account of all the hard work he put into trying to make the hotel a success in two books, *An Innkeeper's Diary* and *My Three Inns*, in which is shown how his eccentric and sometimes very awkward nature often destroyed his earnest attempt to bring splendour and renown to his inns.

His efforts to attract a sufficient number of connoisseurs of good food and wine came to naught and he was forced to sell the Spread Eagle. Then after a brief interlude at a hotel at Ascot he took over the **Three Swans** at **Market**

348

Harborough and tried to wean the locals from steak and chips and beer to more sophisticated food and drink. Although not trained as a caterer he had learned a great deal about food and wine and was capable of concocting great meals out of simple ingredients.

His story can serve as an example that it is necessary to put on an act and behave as 'mine host' even if it is alien to the innkeeper's character. It is inadvisable to be rude or condescending to customers and it is necessary to give them what they want, not what the host thinks they should have.

Restaurants

This name comes from the word restorative and restaurants began as quiet, respectable places that served healthy food in the form of distilled broths that were meant to revitalise the partakers and sustain good health as their name promised. From simple soups, the menus of these establishments were enlarged to offer other dishes considered suitable for invalids, including eggs, calves' feet and chicken but this led to protests from the caterers who under the name of *traiteurs* sold cooked foods for home consumption.

The first restaurant in France was opened by a M. Boulanger in 1765 or 1766 and its success led to many others being opened but the first real restaurant as we recognise them today was the *Grande Taverne de Londres* run by **Antoine Beauvilliers** who had been chef to the **Comte de Provence**. The *Tour d'Argent* in *Paris* claims to be 400 years old, which would date its foundation from 1582 but it was then an auberge rather than the very high-class restaurant it is today. In the City of London, Crosby Hall had been an eating-house since it was built in 1466 and was restored and run by Frederick Gordon. In 1910 it was dismantled stone by stone and re-erected in Chelsea and is now the headquarters of the British Federation of University Women. A Bill of 1786 decreed that the *traiteurs* must stay open until 11 p.m. during the Winter and until midnight in Summer, thus peace was made between the two forms of catering as the restauranteurs stayed open until the early hours.

The restaurants of France were not all high-class and most of them catered for ordinary people who were pleased to be able to eat healthily and well without having to cook for themselves; this practice has since become a way of life for the French who are happy to spend a high proportion of their income on meals in restaurants. Examples of small, unsophisticated establishments are the *buchons* of Lyon.

By 1830 Paris had become a city of restaurants and cafés but only a handful were in the de luxe class. In the ordinary restaurants and cafés the menu was strictly Table d'Hôte and the customer had to take the set meal that had been prepared. It was only in de luxe restaurants that customers had any choice and could select what they wanted from the Carte which listed the dishes that would be cooked to order. It was to one of these select restaurants that Georges Escoffier brought his talents in 1865, coming as a young *commis* to work under **Ulysse**

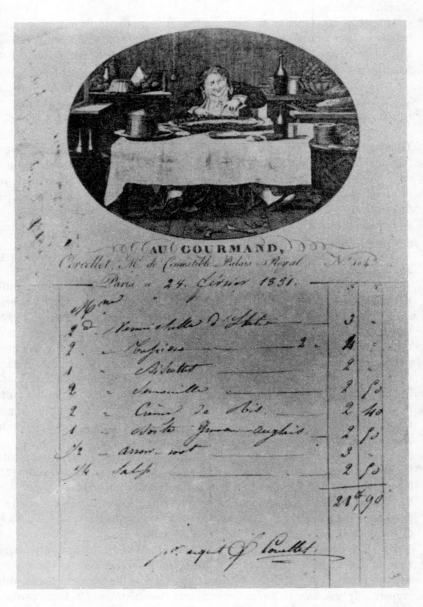

29. An early nineteenth-century Parisian restaurant bill

350

Rohan the fiery head chef of the *Petit Moulin Rouge* which was just off the *Champs Elysées*.

The French Revolution of 1789 brought a temporary halt to the increase in the number of restaurants and caused redundancies amongst chefs employed in the houses of the aristocracy. Many decided to come to this country and enter private service where they were less likely to lose their patrons; then in much the same way as the Roux brothers did more recently, they set themselves up in business by opening their own restaurants, working very hard and long in order to achieve a good reputation.

COFFEE SHOPS

Coffee was first used in this country in 1648 being introduced from Turkey, having first been cultivated in Arabia. From 1642 there had been a puritanical influence that advocated temperance and so led to the opening of coffee houses, much to the disgust of the alehouse keepers.

The first coffee shop in England is supposed to be the one that opened in Oxford in 1650; it was followed two years later by **Lloyd's Coffee House** in the **City of London** where many of its customers were people connected with shipping insurance. Many other coffee houses were opened and some of them became meeting places for people with a common interest or in a particular job such as the law, politics, the stage or artists, while others were patronised by fashionable beaux. They were places where customers went to read, talk or gossip, to lay plans or plot against their enemies as well as to drink coffee.

By 1660 the consumption of coffee had increased to such an extent that the Government found it worthwhile to tax coffee and make it necessary to apply for a licence to operate a coffee house. People spent so long over a cup of coffee that it was felt that idleness was being encouraged so a proclamation for the suppression of coffee houses was passed but rescinded after only eleven days; the number increased until 1683 when it is estimated that there were 3000 coffee houses in London alone.

Innkeepers decided to follow the fashion by converting one of their public rooms into a coffee lounge as an alternative to the bar and many hotels now operate what are called coffee shops but are really informal restaurants that serve a limited menu throughout the day for people who have not the time for a full meal. Some of them are open day and night serving the same menu all the time.

Cafes

Coffee came into use in France at about the same time as here and the coffee houses that were set up to serve it became the meeting places of similar groups

351

as in this country. They were called *cafés* and served only a limited range of drinks but gradually some of them changed and became restaurants so as to be able to offer a wide range of dishes. In France many cafés and restaurants were able to extend the serving area onto the pavement outside where customers could eat and drink while watching the world pass by. Coffee mixed with chicory is the national beverage of France as tea is of this country.

Coffee Bars

In the early 1950s there was a renewed interest in coffee houses in England but this time for good coffee made on Italian coffee machines and served in a young and gay, snack-bar type of environment. These places filled a demand for **espresso** and other kinds of coffee and a snack meal for those who could not afford the price of a full meal or whose pride prevented them from frequenting tea shops or snack bars.

From 1954 onwards, hundreds of such coffee bars were opened in nearly every town and city; many offered live entertainment and stayed open late at night serving sandwiches, salads, omelettes, gâteaux and pastries to accompany a variety of coffee drinks. These trendy coffee bars were a long way from the coffee houses of the seventeenth and eighteenth centuries and further still from the coffee stalls that filled a need for people doing the town from the beginning of this century until the 1950s when they were swept away by the all-night opening of more congenial establishments that maintained a better standard of hygiene and offered a wider choice of goods.

Clubs

Some of the bigger and better-known coffee houses changed their pattern of operation and became drinking or gambling clubs, open only to members. Then they moved to premises where it was possible to provide accommodation for members thus making them a home-from-home for persons of a similar social background who could spend their leisure time being looked after in the manner they were accustomed to at home. Thus they became gentlemen's clubs and every town of any note had its membership club housed in sedate premises with comfortable masculine accommodation. There were also other clubs that held regular meetings and dinners but did not own their own premises. Most of them had a good library.

Although the first members' club opened in 1693 it was during the first half of the nineteenth century that most of them were formed. In London the area of St James became clubland with the **Athenaeum** which opened in 1815, the **Reform** in 1836, the **Carlton** Club, **Crockford's**, **Whites'**, **Brook's** and **Boodles**, the **Royal Automobile Club** and many others. The clubs were run by a committee of members and the power of election of club members was vested in them; the use of the 'blackball' ensured a very select membership. **Crockford**, a fishmonger, made enough money to build a magnificent club-house in St James' Street; **Ude** was appointed as head chef and the club quickly gained a reputation for its kitchen and cellar as well as for its gambling tables. Crockford was able to retire in 1840 as a millionaire. This was in complete contrast to, say, the **Athenaeum** where the members lived more simply as is evidenced by the kitchen accounts for 1832 which show a total of 17 322 dinners served at an average price of 2s $9\frac{3}{4}$d each or approximately 14p in decimal currency; the quantity of wine drunk by members and their guests during the year came to only half a bottle apiece. But the clubs' dining rooms today serve food of a very high standard and their cellars rival those of the most ancient of our colleges in the Universities.

Bistros

This name is usually given to an informal kind of restaurant but without signify-ing any particular national or ethnic connection. Unlike a snack bar, a bistro serves proper meals and, usually, the wines to go with them. Although it would appear to be an Italian word, in fact *bistro* derives from the Russian word *bystro* meaning quickly and in France it means a place where a customer can go to eat as little or as much as he wishes from a menu consisting of individual items, rather than taking a whole menu.

Estaminets

An estaminet is a café selling simple things to eat and drink. The drink includes coffee, beer, wine, fruit drinks, aperitifs and spirits; the food includes simple items such as sandwiches, croissants, pieces of quiche and perhaps some pastries. Service is at the bar but there is usually some seating inside and outside, an additional charge being made for bringing anything to the table. These are unpre-tentious places that are purely functional in providing a quick drink and, if needed, a bite to eat, and there are thousands of them all over France.

Brasseries

This category means a catering outlet that serves only beer and suitable food to accompany it. If it is a free house it will sell various kinds of beer brewed by several different breweries, indeed some brasseries pride themselves on a range of beers imported from most of the beer-producing countries of the world, in addition to all the native ones in cask, keg and bottle. The food is more varied than that normally found in a public house and would consist of meals that taste good with beer rather than merely bar snacks. Brasseries were first introduced in

353

France in the mid-nineteenth century: they are much more common in Germany where they are known as *bierhallen* or *bierkeller*.

Grill Rooms

A grill room was the restaurant in an hotel provided for the use of residents who did not want to dress for dinner or who wanted a fairly straightforward meal rather than the more elaborate one served in the main restaurant. Originally grilled foods were cooked in this room on a silver grill but the remainder of the menu was a scaled-down version of that served in the restaurant and was very often produced in the same kitchen but sold at a lower price. The service was formal and without frills; the amenities of the room were satisfactory but little attempt was made to provide other than an absolutely neutral atmosphere or possibly an Olde English one. This is not to suggest that the food and service were second-rate or that only guests who did not possess evening dress frequented it, neither was it a room for men only; quite simply, it was the second-best restaurant in an hotel where there was more than one. A grill room would also be open for lunch.

In the days when many restaurants regularly featured a cabaret as part of the evening s entertainment there might be two shows interspersed by dancing in the main restaurant but just one show and no dancing in the grill room.

Chop houses

A chop house was the restaurant part of a tavern and was sometimes called the chop-room. Hard wooden benches, high-backed wooden settles with the walls half-panelled and the floor strewn with sawdust or sand, convey the atmosphere. It would be staffed mainly by grey-haired, dignified waiters who appeared to have worked there for years. The bill of fare included grilled chops and cutlets but as the cooking is strictly English, steak, kidney and oyster pudding would often make its appearance as would oysters by the dozen, a plain cold table of joints and pies, stolid English puddings and savouries such as Welsh Rarebit. The most suitable and popular drink would be beer served in tankards. The emphasis was on hearty eating and drinking in a noisy crowded place where the atmosphere might be stuffy but was not starchy.

Trattorie

The name is Italian for any kind of eating place and in this country is likely to be a somewhat hybrid restaurant which combines the popular dishes of Italy with some Italian versions of French classical dishes. The menu is usually extensive with a good mixture of Italian and French dishes and some emphasis on lamp

354

cookery. The menu will probably be entitled *Lista delle Vivande* and the wine list would feature a good selection of Italian wines. The service is usually easy-going and friendly so that customers are put at ease by the lack of obsequiousness, indeed the waiters might even be considered too cheeky.

Tavernas

These are eating places that are a few grades below a trattoria; in Italy the main feature is the bar counter where customers can stand and drink if they do not have time to sit and talk and drink. Food is served from a fairly limited menu consisting of individual dishes rather than meals. The service is competent but without any frills at all and the atmosphere is reasonably calm. The decorations are sometimes designed to give the effect of a medieval tavern with the appropriate lighting, furniture and crockery and cutlery.

Osterie

These are a very basic kind of establishment which serve only alcholic drinks to customers mainly contadini, who need a reviver to refresh them and keep them going. The amenities are very lowly and the pattern is to drink up quickly and go. They are found in the back streets and market places of most towns in Italy.

Pizzerie

These are really snack bars that are equipped to serve a limited menu with pizzas as the main item. Each region and city of Italy appears to have its own version of a pizza which makes it possible to list a lot of different ones at various prices but with only some slight variation in ingredients and quantities necessary to distinguish between them.

The dough for the pizzas may be made on the premises which would give the *pizzaiolo* the opportunity to show off his skills in front of the customers, moulding the base by flinging it into the air then deftly adding the various toppings and putting it into the pizza oven to bake. Pizzas can be made to order or prepared in advance behind the scenes; to make money in such an establishment requires a fast service and quick turnover by customers therefore the atmosphere should be smart and colourful.

Butteries

This name implies high-class snack-bars which serves individual dishes, prepared to order on a back-bar cooking-unit possibly by a chef, or by the person who also serves. The service should be quick with customers being seated on high stools at the counter or at tables around the room. The decoration is usually smart and light in colour, in keeping with the name; it should help show off the dresses worn by the ladies. The menu would include original snack dishes and a selection of drinks, to *cordon bleu* standard, artistically served on nice china. The actual meaning of 'a buttery' was a store from which victuals were issued to undergraduates at university.

Public Houses

These are now an integral part of the hotel and catering industry because, public houses now not only sell drinks, but invariably offer food to accompany it, the standard ranging from what is colloquially known as 'pub grub' to full Table d'Hôte meals in the style of the old 'Ordinary'. In addition there are the chains owned by the brewers or by catering companies where each branch serves the same limited menu in identical surroundings. The environment may be olde worlde even though the food is regenerated in a microwave oven; many breweries are reintroducing the beers they stopped brewing years ago in the hope that these will satisfy the demand for real ale; they also hope that the food will bring in the customers. More emphasis is being placed on catering in pubs and with over 65 000 of them in this country they are now a major section of the industry.

Night-Clubs

There is a wide difference between the sedate members' club as previously described and the swinging club in the cellar for those people who want to disco the night away in bubbling abandon.

In this kind of clubland which is usually housed in cramped basement quarters in city centres, clubs are launched possibly with a good membership and though some may endure, few go on for long unless they have something exclusive to offer members for their fees.

The good night-clubs become successful by being exclusive as regards membership, allowing only friends of friends to join. But since a really good night-club may have 5 – 6000 members and a long waiting list it means that the right balance of young, middle-aged and old, aristocrats and playboys, British and foreign has been achieved. There might be about 100 members on the premises at any one time. An important job is that of the bouncer on the door to ensure that no harlots, *papparazzi* or gossip columnists are allowed in to ply their trade or to pry on notable customers.

A decent night-club will be able to demand high annual membership fee but may compensate for this by charging realistic rather than ridiculous prices at the bars and in the restaurant. Nevertheless the bill for one night at such a club is

356

likely to come to £100 per person, without counting losses or gains at the gambling tables.

It might be assumed that apart from the entrance hall and cloakrooms, the decoration does not matter as these other rooms will be in semi-darkness with only the dim table lights and the flashing coloured laser beams of the disco gadgetry, but in fact the dance floor will take up a very small space, not necessarily because there is a shortage of area but so as to make the dancing intimate.

No night-club can expect to succeed without a fairly *recherché* menu and a renowned kitchen to back it up. The most appropriate dishes are those usually associated with supper, high tea and breakfast. *Croque Monsieur*, which is a cooked sandwich is often featured on the menu as it is reckoned to be an ideal dish for this style of catering and many of the other savouries are also suitable. Food will be available on a high class à la Carte service until approximately 2.30 a.m. and afterwards there will be a more limited menu of hot and cold snacks for members still playing at the gaming tables.

Fast Food Outlets

The fast food business covers a fairly wide spectrum of catering and includes some very well-known names; it is also the fastest growing section of the Profit Sector and the one with the most intense competition. The well-known names have branches in every town of any size, many of them operating on a worldwide basis. They include **Berni Inns, Burger-King, Kentucky Fried Chicken, McDonalds, Wimpy, Spud-U-Like** and there are many others that go under trade names; there will undoubtedly be others to join these. It might be said that these places contribute nothing to the study of gastronomy, but the consistency of quality and the standardisation of a formula that brings the customer back again and again surely indicates that he is being satisfied and that is what gastronomy means. By concentrating their efforts on a straightforward menu that is easy to produce at a price the customer is happy to pay, the company has ample proof that the system is satisfactory. The customer never feels let down by being served with a less than perfect item of its kind no matter how simple it is; he accepts the requirement of clearing away after he has eaten his meal.

The menus of fast food outlets are uncomplicated and the customer is able to make up his mind quickly because of the limited selection. Prices charged are usually less than in traditional restaurants because there is no need to pay highly skilled staff and with every item being cooked to order there is no over-production.

The firms engaged in the fast food business have invested a lot of time and money looking into every aspect of the operation including product testing, personnel training, equipment evaluation, hygiene, purchasing, market research and cash taking; all these have their effect upon the finished items so ensuring that the establishment is always up to standard and always enjoyable of its kind. As **Brillat-Savarin** said, a gastronome does not always want to eat elaborate dishes and will happily settle for a simple dish provided it is cooked to perfection.

357

30. A pioneer of fast food – 'Le Marchand de Macaroni à Naples'

Take-Aways

These operate at all levels from ethnic restaurants and fast food emporiums to the very high-class restaurant which is happy to prepare dishes for delivery to customers' homes. Some operate solely as take-aways but the majority offer it as a sideline to the main business of operating a restaurant.

Holiday Camps

Although there were holiday camps in operation early on in this century, the first of the kind that are so well-known today opened at Skegness in 1934; there are now some forty-four camps providing more than 100 000 bed spaces. Many of these camps are situated on the coast so the business is seasonal; this means that the profit has to be made during the short summer season although some camps do open early or after the end of the season to accommodate large conferences.

Where customers book for full board they expect meals to be sufficiently substantial to satisfy their appetites, thus generous portion sizes should be provided. The food has to be cooked by large-scale methods, using convenience foods wherever they will assist in keeping food costs low. The food is usually plated to standard portion control and with maximum eye-appeal. All dishes included in the menu must have the widest possible appeal as there is little oppor-

358

tunity of giving customers a choice; alternatives such as omelette, chipsteak, burger or cold meat must not be over-popular so as to divert too many people away from the main dish.

In addition to the amusements and entertainment there are such catering outlets as licensed bars, coffee bars, seafood stall, ice cream and hamburger counters, the idea being that the customer's every wish is catered for in the camp and there is no need for him to go off the site during his stay, unless it be for an organised excursion or to such activities as are not catered for on the site.

Working-class holidaymakers like good old-fashioned holiday-camp holidays where Babycham, keg beer and tea rather than cocktails and wine are served. They prefer chips with everything from such exotic dishes as moussaka to angels on horseback; but provided the portion size is adequate and the food reasonably well cooked the holiday will be a gastronomic treat.

Catering for Leisure

As the length of the working week decreases and job-sharing and early retirement are encouraged. so people have more time to spend on leisure pursuits. These comprise many different activities held in many different places but nearly always include provision for refreshment facilities. Some of the leisure centres belong to local authorities who may decide to let a contractor do the catering whilst others have their own catering services to run it, they hope, at a profit. Many leisure centres belong to private firms who not only cater for the normal daily activities but are able to use the facilities for private functions such as banquets and receptions.

Ships Catering

The two branches of catering at sea are that of the luxury cruise liners, and that carried out on ferries linking different countries.

Passengers choose a cruise holiday not only for the ports of call but also for the ship's reputation for its food as expressed in the company's brochures, or from a friend's recommendation. Each day's events contribute to the enjoyment of the cruise but the meals are the most important part of the entire voyage. The menus are Table d'Hôte with a wide variety of choices for each course. If time permits, a passenger may have a five-course lunch, and a seven-course dinner though the restrictions of service may prevent its full enjoyment because people on the second sitting are waiting to come in, or the staff are anxious to go off duty.

Three main meals plus mid-morning coffee, afternoon tea and late night sandwiches are served in pleasant surroundings by competent staff. According to the price paid, there may be different classes of restaurant, even though it may be a one-class boat. Caviar, smoked salmon and very many other fine foods are

359

included on the menu but the portion size and quality will not be that of à la Carte restaurant ashore where such items are seldom included in a set price meal.

With a very large number of passengers to cater for at one and the same time it is necessary to use large-scale cooking methods and then to attempt some personal finishing touches at the point of service. There is usually a comprehensive wine list with a few top quality ones for the delectation of the holidaying gastronome but the overall experience cannot be expected to rise to Lucullan heights, no matter how calm the voyage.

The ships that link various countries, carrying passengers as well as goods, usually have a large catering commitment in the restaurants, snack bars and public bars which, depending on sailing times and duration, serve appropriate food and drink to travellers.

Unless the sea is rough, such a voyage can be passed very pleasurably by eating in one of the dining areas, chosen according to price. The menu will be that of the home port of the ship with Table d'Hôte and à la Carte sides to it, thus giving a fairly wide choice; the wine list may not be a lengthy one of fine wines but is bound to contain some of superior quality that match the quality of the food.

A gourmet could do worse than make a trip on a cross-channel ferry without even landing on the other side but eating much of the time away, a pleasure which could be further enhanced by a tasting at a nearby château or distillery.

Railway Catering

Railway catering is complementary to the business of conveying passengers across a country and is an important part of the transit business. Each day in Great Britain some 300 restaurant cars and 500 buffet cars are in service on main routes serving meals or snacks, according to the running schedule. Changes to this traditional pattern are taking place and the style of meals for first-class passengers will be similar to those served aboard airplanes. It will be cooked at railway depots and loaded aboard for reheating from chilled, in a microwave oven before being served to passengers in their seats. Second-class passengers have a choice of buffet car or trolley service.

On express trains in France, a four-course meal is served from heated trolleys wheeled through the dining car; it is plate service by an hostess at something more than 100 French francs, without wine. The buffet car would be a high-speed fast food operation of hand-held food such as French stick sandwiches, filled croissants or slices of pizza – no hot meat pies or cold pork pies as served in England!

It is still possible to recapture some of the magic of train journeys of the Edwardian era by taking the Orient Express from Victoria to Italy and enjoying

31. William Towle, General Manager of the London Midland and
    Scottish Railway Company at the Adelphi Hotel, Liverpool,
    1912

a gastronomic menu. The golden age of rail travel has been recaptured by the owners of the Orient Express who pamper passengers as they head across France and Switzerland to Venice or Florence. Dinner is served in the Wagon Restaurant in impeccable style in the ambience of the days of Pullman Car Travel with French chefs providing a gourmet meal on the lines of this menu:

DÎNER

Le Feuilletée de Lotte au Beurre de Nage

Le Filet de Boeuf Poêlé Hercule Poirot au Vin de Bordeaux

La Seléction du Maître Fromager

L'Alcazar au Chocolat

Les Mignardises

Le Café

———

Continental breakfast and late night supper are served in the *wagons-lits*. The standard set for meals on this train are simply that each course is plated so that it looks attractive and is delicious to eat but that it is not too rich or filling. Some à la Carte items such as caviar, foie gras and smoked salmon are available.

Coach Catering

Travellers on long-distance luxury motor coaches can now obtain a snack meal with hostess service, and look at a video film instead of merely reading the newspaper or going to sleep. To compete with the railway, coach operators have felt it necessary to speed up the journey and to offer in-coach catering facilities such as snack items and a selection of hot and cold beverages either from a vending machine or from a properly equipped counter. The food is prepared at base and packaged attractively so as to compare favourable with the snacks offered at motorway service stops.

The affinity between transport and catering has endured for centuries - a factor which has led some caterers to use historical forms of transport as the setting for an eating-place by buying an obsolete bus, railway coach or barge and fitting it out as a thematic restaurant. The alternative is to buy ephemera of a particular means of transport and use it to decorate the room. This could mean

362

laying out the restaurant in the form of, say, a railway carriage, using wooden rail sleepers as divisions, or even using vintage cars in which customers sit and eat. A restaurant can be made mobile by driving it to where it is wanted, as for an outdoor catering function, a mobile fish and chip shop or a snack bar in a roadway lay-by.

Motorway Catering

Although the prime reason for setting up service areas on motorways was to get motorists to break their journey and so relieve the fatigue of driving long distances, it is not unknown for people to drive to a motorway restaurant to enjoy a gourmet meal. Most large service areas have several different eating-places, each offering a different kind of menu at different price levels; the type of service depends on the standard of each. At all levels the quality of the food served is satisfactory while at the top end it may be so good as to attract people to use the restaurant as something more than a caravanserai. The drawback is that a motorway caterer in England cannot apply for a licence to serve intoxicating liquor, thus making any gourmet occasion a dry rather than a bucolic one. On the continent, service area restaurants serve alcohol.

Airway and Airport Catering

The various airlines pride themselves on the standard of food they serve to passengers travelling with them. At the top end of the market the meals are very expensive ones, the cost being reflected in the price of the air ticket. At the other end the people on a package tour will receive a very simple cold snack meal but in between these two an airline will have a hundred or more levels of catering, some of these being meals taken aboard at foreign airports.

Certainly the menus for first-class passengers rival those of any high-class restaurant and meet the expectations of the most discerning gastronomes. Meals are prepared individually at the commissariat for reheating in the airflow ovens on the aircraft and they still look fresh and taste good thousands of miles from home. Fresh salmon, lobster, game in season, baskets of fresh fruit, champagne and fine wines – even though in quarter-size bottles – are served from silver on to good quality glass and china to be eaten with silver-plated cutlery. There is even *gueridon* service with whole hot joints and a classical garnish being carved to order by hostesses whilst flying high across the world.

Depending on the particular airline, the destinations served and the expected nationalities of passengers, menus are devised to satisfy ethnic requirements and printed in the language that would be understood. The significance of meals served to airline passengers can be gauged from the fact that the food cost of a meal in the first class cabin equals some 5 per cent of an airline's operating costs.

Some of the contractors at London Airport produce upwards of 20 000 meals

363

per day but only 5 per cent are for first-class passengers. 30 per cent are for club class and the remainder for economy or tourist class.

Catering at airports for passengers and the general public is usually done by a firm of caterers who tender for the right to operate the various sites on behalf of the airport authority. As probably the first and last place to be seen by overseas visitors, airport restaurants should exemplify all that is good of the nation's eating places and of the food and service that is available.

A large airport is like a small city that bustles with life throughout the whole day and night and where facilities for eating and drinking are constantly available every day of the year at what should be a consistently high standard.

Departmental Stores Catering

There are two sorts of catering carried out in departmental stores which run a public restaurant – one for the customers and one behind the scenes for the staff employed in the building. The public restaurant is really for customers in the shop who feel the need for refreshment and to sit down for a rest, although of course it may also be patronised by people who come in for the meal only.

The type of menu used should suit the expected customer which in most instances means catering for women shoppers who want a light meal they can choose from an attractively-worded array and that is not very fattening. Some stores achieve such a high reputation for the food they serve that customers queue to get in and the restaurant is busy all day rather than just at meal-times. Research shows that customers of a big store or a shopping precinct like to eat there and a food counter or restaurant can do very good business.

Fish and Chip Shops and Restaurants

These are so well-known that there is little need to explain the operation of either the take-away or eat-in establishment, yet there could be a lively discussion as to the best type of potato for making chips, the ideal frying medium and is the best kind of batter to use. According to the **Potato Marketing Board**, Desiree, Kind Edward and Maris Piper are the best maincrop varieties for chips, but it is the size of the chip that gives the quality and they should be from 1.0 – 1.5cm thick rather than being of the shoestring variety as favoured by some fast-food emporiums. Ideally they should be very crisp, but when eaten away from the fish and chip shop they are bound to get soft and soggy so it is as well to douse them with vinegar as an aid to digestion. There are dozens of good quality frying oils and fats and the best batter is made like a Yorkshire pudding mixture.

Many people insist that fish and chips are the national dish of Britain no matter what kind of fish is fried and the fact that there are more than 10 000 take-away fish and chip shops in this country, several hundred mobile ones and
364

many rather more splendid fried fish saloons or restaurants serving only this meal, would appear to indicate that this is true.

Outdoor Catering

This branch of catering embraces all kinds and levels of special occasions, from operating an ice cream van, hamburger stall or drink tent at a county show to a small dinner party in a private house or a government reception for a foreign delegation. Whatever the occasion, it involves sending food, staff and equipment from the firm's depot to the venue and setting-up, serving and clearing away in a thoroughly efficient manner. This means that the organisation must be foolproof so that any untoward eventuality can be quickly overcome and that nothing mars the quality and service of the meal.

Depending upon the menu and cooking facilities, the food is either partly prepared or fully cooked at the depot but however the operation is carried out, and whatever the problems caused by lack of facilities, the resultant meal should be as outstanding as any banquet being held under ideal conditions.

The problems associated with providing food for an unknown number of people with the vagaries of the weather and traffic to contend with, often means that a mixture of fresh and convenience foods is the only way to do the job efficiently.

Cost Sector Eating Places

The Cost Sector is also referred to as the Welfare Sector because it provides a service designed to meet certain social requirements as well as some special nutritional ones. A large part of this side of the catering industry is a public service run by local or central government agencies, although few of these agencies write the menus for those who will receive them.

As with the Profit Sector this is made up of a large number of different operations. In the main these establishments are not run on commercial lines in that they do not have to make a profit, but they do have to work to a budget. Most of them have to cater for people of all ages, both sexes and of various occupations and economic classes, ethnic groups and nationalities. In many of the fields of operation the 'customers' are there on a long-term basis.

In amongst these non-profit operations are an increasing number of establishments where the catering is being handled by contract. These include government and local authority establishments such as hospitals and educational units where the catering contract has been awarded to a firm of contractors. The growth of private hospitals and clinics where patients may pay £100 or more per day and consequently the standard of food is very good, puts them in a completely different category from National Health Service hospitals. In fact the establishments that cater for private patients belong to the Profit Sector of catering even though they are carrying our work that is almost identical to that being done in the Cost Sector.

Catering in Hospitals

The food served to patients in NHS hospitals varies enormously from one to another because each hospital caterer has freedom to prepare his own menus, subject to approval at regional level. The system in use has some influence on the kinds of dishes served. For example, either a cook-freeze or cook-chill system may be in use; it may be a menu totally composed by convenience foods or the food may be cooked conventionally and served by one of the individual tray systems. Because of the numbers to be catered for, food has to be cooked in bulk for all those on normal diets and only the modified diets can be given individual attention. Whether the food is sent to the wards in bulk or in portions, the problem lies in getting it ot the patient nicely served and still hot and appetising. Food in hospital is meant to be an essential part of the patient's recovery by tempting him to eat a meal that is both attractive in appearance and nutritionally sound. To do this on a food cost of only about £1.30 per day per patient for three main meals including additional beverages and special dietary needs is a task to tax the most professional of caterers and to do it for people whose appetites are liable to fluctuate from hour to hour and still keep food costs to an acceptable minimum, is a tough job. To keep within the food budget it is necessary to prevent over-production and the way some hospitals do this is to get patients to choose what meals they want twenty-four hours in advance. Menu choices can then be totalled and only the exact number of portions of every dish selected are cooked.

The Department of Health and Social Security publishes a book for use in catering departments under the title *Manual of Health Service Catering*. Copies are obtainable from HMSO.

Industrial Catering

This branch of the catering industry only really came into being after the Second World War immediately after the end of hostilities, although some enlightened employers offered meals in pre-war days. It was given low priority and did not gain importance until the 1960s when there was a resurgence of interest by employers concerned about the provision of welfare facilities for their workers. Many employers recognise that a substantial and nutritious midday meal has a bearing on the mental and physical alertness of staff and therefore take an interest in what goes on in the canteen. The aim of industrial catering is to provide a substantial meal at a reasonable cost in pleasant surroundings, and as a fringe benefit. Where hard physical work is entailed there is a need for a large kilocalorie intake but with much of the work in industry now being done by mech-

366

anisation and even by robots, the recipes and menus can be changed to provide a lighter diet which means serving dishes with lower carbohydrate and fat content.

By tradition the canteen meal had a high content of meat which meant that there was also a lot of fat because cheap cuts – used to keep prices down – contained a large proportion of fat. The ever-increasing cost of meat gives rise to the problem of providing good value for money as regards portion size, without the need to resort to a lot of made-up or minced dishes. This makes menu planning in industrial catering very different because there is bound to be customer-resistence to dishes that are not recognisable.

There is a demand for more sophisticated fare with a choice of menu, served in small quiet lounge areas rather than in the usual hangar-like canteen. The canteen itself should be capable of playing a second role of leisure centre by combining sports facilities with restaurant and bar.

The small proportion of employees eating a cooked meal in canteens which is the reason for the enormous annual subsidy of several hundred million pounds (despite the consumer's contribution) needs to be reversed because it makes staff feeding too significant a cost centre as a business within a business. As with other branches of the Cost Sector there is a wide range of operations under the heading of staff feeding. It includes the head office and branches of all kinds of businesses and industries.

Catering on Oil Rigs and in Camps

Looking after the staff employed on an oil rig or oilfield is a demanding job for a tough guy, whether he be employed by the actual firm or by a specialist catering contractor.

The caterer is in charge of the whole welfare aspect including the feeding arrangements, accommodation, entertainment, bars and duty-free supplies, but with food as the most important aspect. Staff on a rig are usually on duty for two weeks at a time doing arduous and potentially dangerous work and employers realise that meals must afford some compensation. The accommodation and off-duty facilities are restricted; the personnel to be fed will be of several nationalities and there are several grades of supervisors, scientists and management to be catered for, thus making big demands on the catering staff. The hotel side employs chefs, bakers, stewards, men's room attendants, gallery porters and house-keeping staff who also have to be provided with accommodation.

The catering manager has to provide interesting menus that will satisfy the cosmopolitan crew; big steaks topped with fried eggs may be the favourite fare but a choice of several hot courses together with a cold buffet at main meals must be offered, usually on à la Carte lines.

An *oil rig* will carry a supply of victuals for a minimum of twenty-one days but the supply vessel or helicopter can bring fresh goods more frequently thus avoiding the chance of menu habituation, though weather conditions may cause delayed supplies. No alcohol is allowed on an oil rig.

An *oil camp* is likely to have a corps of indigenous workers amounting to several thousands, possibly of several different nationalities and religions, with each group needing to be fed according to its tenets. In addition there will be the supervisory and management staff, also of several different nationalities, with messes for each grade.

Camps are often sited in remote parts of the world far from civilisation which means overcoming problems of supply and making working and living conditions as pleasant as possible. Tropical or arctic conditions may have to be contended with and these extremes are reflected in the diet. Sources of supply, means of transport and storage are reflected in the food on the menu; as with an oil rig, the importance of the quality of the food and its contribution to the welfare and health of staff is enormous.

Educational Establishment Catering

The eating facilities provided for persons attending centres of education cover many aspects, from the local authority school meals service, public schools, colleges of further and higher education, to universities and special kinds of schools. Each has its own method of operation, level of costs, and attitudes towards gastronomic standards.

Local authorities are in charge of nearly all these establishments and employ all the staff needed to run them, from the county catering officer or school meals organiser to counterhands and cleaners. In schools the local authority decides on the kind of operation, if any, and how it may be done with the maximum uptake by pupils and minimum subsidy.

The pattern of providing a two-course family-service meal that helped children to learn table manners and adopt social graces came to an end in 1980 when the government made local authorities consider the need for new methods which would save money. The pattern of school meals is now a help-yourself service of portion-control snack items that can be cooked quickly and require little or no skill. The ideal that school lunch should be a well-balanced one that supplied one third of the child's daily nutritional needs has had to be abandoned since it is difficult to reconcile the child's needs and what the parent is prepared to pay, with the government's decision to cut the subsidy.

It is said that our food habits are engendered in the early part of our life and are influenced by both the meals and surroundings at home and the school dining room. If one third of a child's weekly meals are the snack-bar type as served by the authority, or the contents of a lunch-box as put in by the mother, the future health of the people of this country is at risk since it is unavoidable that for the sake of convenience, as one headmaster recently said, junk foods will be used.

This is a situation that needs to be corrected; more importance must be given to meals in school and teachers should realise the need to take an interest in what children eat at the lunch break. A healthy appreciation of food is a practical matter rather than a purely theoretical one and should be encouraged. The school

368

meal should be part of the curriculum and given equal importance with the other subjects on the timetable.

Catering in boarding schools is more important than catering for day schools since apart from the occasional tuck-box, pupils' feeding is solely in the hands of the school caterer or bursar. He must have a very good knowledge of practical nutrition and ensure that pupils acquire good eating habits and etiquette. The menu is likely to be a set one and choices available only if the dining hall is run on cafeteria lines.

Catering in Colleges

Students attending a college or university have many demands on their limited income and face the problem of what their priorities are after allowing for rent, fares, clothing, textbooks and visits. What is then available has to be spent on meals in the refectory and drinks in the students' union bar since there should be something to be gained from patronising both from the point of view of socialising. Local authorities pay the salaries of the people employed in student and staff refectories and although the college caterer may keep a profit-and-loss account of his operation, the balance sheet is usually made out at County-Hall and there the demand is that the operation breaks even, to include administrative costs.

It would be nice to think that students in college are given the opportunity to cultivate an appreciation of good food and to develop a discerning taste and gastronomic tendencies. In fact although the opportunity is there, the prospects are nullified by the constant cry for cutbacks in expenditure and meals in colleges cannot but be so mundane that they do nothing to encourage an interest in gastronomy.

Those colleges which have an academic department of catering usually offer student and staff of the Faculties a valuable opportunity of acquiring gastronomic attributes by eating in the public restaurant which operates as part of the curriculum. In addition to lunch and dinner, some departments hold gastronomic events of the kind outlined in Chapter 11 of this book, which are of a very high standard despite the nominal price charged.

University Catering

For centuries the best place for a young man who wanted to become a cook, was in the kitchen of one of the colleges of our older universities. There he would be taught the highest standard of cookery by a master craftsman who would have respect for college traditions and British culinary heritage. The dons of the college liked to live well, they knew a lot about food and drink and took a keen interest in it, especially French dishes and wines; colleges had a reputation for the quality of their table and the job of college chef was a coveted one.

369

High Table is for the dons of a college and, on occasion, for their guests; the standard of food is very high and the wines from the college's own cellar are the best to be found in any kind of establishment. For the undergraduates of the college the quality of their meals is related to their grant and they do not want to have to pay out too much of it for battels which are the charges for board and lodging. This means that their meals are geared to the lowest possible cost rather than to a gastronomic standard; lunch is probably of help-yourself snacks with a choice of hot dishes, and dinner, a waiter-service three-course meal with no choices. It is possible for undergraduates to order a private dinner party to be prepared and served by college staff to the same standard as High Table but at a commercial price. During vacations most universities cater for conferences and private dinners and for these the standard of food and drink will be according to the fee charged. The college servants add tone to the proceedings and work in the finest traditions of service, whether the venue be Oxbridge or Redbrick.

Catering for the Social Services

This aspect of welfare catering comes under the direction of the county catering adviser or a social services catering officer who will liaise with the director of social services of the local authority. The three areas are (i) luncheon clubs in day centres, (ii) meals-on-wheels, (iii) old people's homes and (iv) children's homes. Some authorities operate a central kitchen which supplies meals to all their units, including nurseries and special schools; if the capacity was sufficient it could also cater for the school meals service. Other authorities use conventional kitchens at numerous sites and others buy in frozen individual or bulk meals and have them delivered to each site. Some authorities such as an inner city borough will serve as many as 2000 meals in day centres and 1500 meals-on-wheels daily. The catering officer will ensure that the nutritional needs of all the classes of people being served are met and that meals look appetising and are hygienically safe.

Catering in HM Forces

The food service system of the army in camp is based on multi-choice self-service main meals with daily menu changes. Numbers at base camps are usually fairly static, varying only when units are posted away or on manoeuvres. The Army Catering Corps (ACC) has an excellent manual that gives recipes for a wide range of meals at all levels, not all in large-scale quantities. Each unit is largely self-accounting and can enjoy a degree of autonomy as regards the meals it serves, providing it does not exceed the daily allowance. The ACC provides the skilled staff for all units; it has its own school of cookery and does its own grading of personnel by examination and experience.

370

The Royal Navy sets a high standard of catering both at sea and at its shore bases and the quality of meals plays a vital role in the morale of the sailors especially when they are away from home for months at a time. A ship's galley is necessarily small and low-ceilinged, the equipment is fuelled by electricity and steam and the stoves have guards to prevent pans sliding off when the sea is rough. All food is cooked in traditional ways and the use of convenience packs in canned and de-hydrated form is kept for emergencies. Imaginative menus, usually on a fairly long cycle, are designed to make the meals the high spots of the day and to help prevent boredom. When home supplies become low, fresh foods are taken on at ports of call and from supply vessels of the Royal Fleet Auxiliary. All the bread ˙ is baked on board by the cooks.

The dining areas are also limited in space which means having sittings, the ratings mess being run from a servery that offers several choices. Senior ratings have their own dining area and the officers' wardroom is separate, but all three are grouped around the galley.

The Royal Navy has a School of Catering, with its own examination system for cooks and stewards which leads to promotion through the ranks to com-missioned officer level.

AIRFORCE

Catering in the Royal Air Force is of a very high standard, equal to that of the other services but as with the other branches of Her Majesty's Forces, the food-cost allowance, the way the catering officer uses it and the skill of the cooks, determines the standard of catering at any camp, be it a small outpost or a base depot with thousands of airmen to be fed. The RAF School of Catering provides the training of cooks and stewards and not only sets a high standard for each unit but ensures that after he has served his time, an airman is qualified to fill almost any catering job in civilian life, and will be much sought after. Although the formation of this branch of the forces goes back only to 1918 the standard of catering is on par with that of the others and airmen are as well-fed as are soldiers and sailors.

The schools of catering for all three services are centred at St Omer Barracks at Aldershot.

NAAFI

The Navy, Army and Air Force Institute (NAAFI) operates the leisure-time facilities for all three of the services by providing bars, restaurants, entertain-ment and shopping facilities at most base camps in all parts of the world where British forces are operating. A large number of catering managers and chefs are employed by NAAFI and the standard of food and amenities offered is very good. The Ministry of Defence operates a large number of officer's messes for all branches of the services including staff colleges, headquarters, training centres and unit messes. Posts as civilian mess-managers in this field of catering are similar to those of the food and beverage manager in other branches of the industry. The manager has to have sufficient knowledge and experience to be able to organise such special events as the regular mess dinner, an anniversary, a posting or promotion, any of which has to be carried out in accordance with protocol and in the traditions of the service and the unit. These are very special gastronomic occasions where an extremely good menu, fine wines and impeccable service combine to realise a very pleasant affair that is unsurpassed by any other branch of catering, including the High Table at university or the banqueting hall of an hotel.

Appendixes

A The Naming of Dishes

NAMING DISHES AFTER PEOPLE

This Appendix lists some of the notable persons who have had dishes named after them. In some cases the dishes were named during the person's lifetime but in many instances the name was awarded long after the person's death, being given in honour of their achievements and to keep their memory alive.

While it is true that most of these dishes are named after French people there are several from other nations; it was not necessary to have been a noted gastronome in order to be honoured by the naming of a new dish.

As an example of how dishes get their names, **Lobster Newburg** is said to have been conceived by the chef of **Delmonico's Restaurant** in **New York** in honour of a Mr Wenburg who was a regular customer. Ben Wenburg was a wealthy fruit importer who often took large parties of friends to the restaurant where he was sometimes allowed to show off in front of his friends by doing *flambé* work. When Pascal the head waiter finished the lobster dish in the restaurant he announced that henceforth it would be known as Lobster Wenburg and the customer agreed. However, some time later, Ben Wenburg had a disagreement with Lorenzo Delmonico the owner, who retaliated by changing the name of the dish around and using 'u' instead of 'ew', thus creating *Homard Nuberg*. However, in practice it has been changed to *Newburg* or as sometimes written, *Newburgh*.

FAMOUS PEOPLE AFTER WHOM DISHES HAVE BEEN NAMED

Agnes Sorel	1409–1450	Mistress of Charles VIII of France
Alexandra, Queen	1844–1925	Wife of Edward VII
Arenberg, Prince	1753–1834	Member of an old Belgian family
Artois, Comte d'	–1836	Grandson of Louis XIV
Aumale, Duc d'	1822–97	Fourth son of Louis Philippe
Bagration	1765–1812	Russian general

373

Balzac, Honoré de	1799–1850	poet and novelist, noted gastronome
Brisse, Baron Léon	1813–76	gastronome, edited *La Liberte* in which he published a menu every day and a book called *365 Menus*
Bart, Jean	1650–1702	French admiral
Beauharnais, E.	1781–1842	French Prince
Béchamel, Marquis de	1630–1705	Louis XIV's finance minister
Bennett, Arnold	1867–1931	English novelist
Bernhardt, Sarah	1844–1923	Famous dramatic actress
Bismarck, Prince Otto	1815–98	Chancellor of the German Empire, 1861–90
Boiéldieu, Francois-Adrien	1775–1834	Composer and professor of music, wrote *La Dame Blanche*
Cambacérès, Jean Jacques, Duc de Parme	1753–1824	Grand Chancellor under Napoleon
Caruso, E.	1873–1921	Italian opera singer
Casanova, G.	1725–98	Italian adventurer and writer
Chambord, Comte de	1820–83	grandson of Charles X of France
Chartres, Duc-de	b. 1840	member of the d'Orléans family
Chateaubriand, Vicomte de	1768–1848	writer and statesman
Chimay, Princesse (née Miss Clara Ward) married Prince Chimay of Belgium	d.1906	U.S. musical comedy star
Choiseul, E.	1719–85	French statesman and minister to Louis XV
Choron, A.	1772–1834	composer and musicologist
Cleopatra	69–30 BC	Queen of Egypt
Clermont, Marquis de	1777–1865	Politician
Colbert, Jean Baptiste	1619–83	Statesman
Condé, Prince de	1621–86	General, married the niece of Cardinal Richelieu
Condorcet, M.	1743–94	French philosopher
Conti, Prince de	1629–66	Brother of Prince de Condé; married the niece of Mazarin

Cumberland, Duke of	1721–65	Son of George II, British military commander
D'Arblay, Madame (nee Miss Frances Burney)	1752–1840	lady-in-waiting to the Queen; married General D'Arblay; novelist
Déjarzet, Virginie	1797–1875	French singer and actress
Demidoff, Nicholas	1774–1828	Member of a noble Russian family
Diane		Mythological daughter of Jupiter and Latrone, sister of Apollo; goddess of hunting
Doria, Andréa	1466–1560	Commander of the Fleet of Francis I
Du Barry, Comtesse	1741–93	Mistress of Louis XV, founder of Cordon Bleu school in Paris
Edna May	1878–1948	American actress and singer in musical comedies; created the Belle of New York
Edward VII	1841–1910	Eldest son of Queen Victoria; Married Princess Alexandra of Denmark. King of England from 1901–1910.
Epicurus	341–270 BC	Greek philosopher
Esau		Son of Isaac and Rebecca
Francis I	1494–1547	King of France
Garden, Mary	1874–1970	Famous scottish singer who created the leading role in Debussys opera, *Péleas et Mélisande* in 1902
Gavarni P.	1804–66	French humorous artist
George Sand (Amantine-Lucile-Aurore Dupin)	1804–76	Novelist, friend of Chopin
Godard, Benjamin	1849–95	Composer
Gounod, Charles	1818–93	Composer
Héloïse,	1101–64	Abbesse du Paraclet, lover of Peter Abelard
Henri IV	1553–1610	King of France married i) Marguerite de Valois, ii) Marie de' Medici

Holstein, F.	1837-1909	German statesman
Ibraham Pasha	1789-1848	Viceroy of Egypt
Jackson, Andrew	1767-1845	President of the United States, 1829-33
Joinville, Prince de	1818-44	Third son of Louis Philippe
Judic, Anna	1850-1911	Celebrated French actress
de Jussieu, Antoine-Laurent	1748-1836	Botanist
La Vallière, Duchess de	1644-1710	Mistress of Louis XIV
Lamballe, Princess de	1748-92	Friend of Marie Antoinette
Louis XIV	1638-1715	Crowned King of France, at 5 years of age, reigned 1643-1715
Louis XV	1710-74	Also crowned King of France at age of 5; reigned 1715-74
Lucullus	110- 57 BC	Roman general
Maintenon, Marquise de	1635-1719	Second wife of Louis XIV
Malakoff, Duc de	1794-1864	Marshall of France
Marguery		Owner of the restaurant in Paris named after himself; originally the plongeur at the Restaurant Champeaux
Marie-Louise	1791-1847	Daughter of Francis I, married Napoleon in 1810, became Duchesse de Parme
Marie-Thérèse	1638-83	Daughter of Philippe IV of Spain, married to Louis XIV
Mary Stuart	1542-87	Daughter of James I of Scotland, married the Dauphin and became Queen of France
Marigny, Abel F.	1727-81	Brother of Mme Pompadour, built the Louvre and Les Gobelins
Marigny, Anguerrand de	1260-1315	Minister to Philippe IV
Masséna, André	1758-1817	Marshal of France under Napoleon
Medicis		Members of a famous Florentine family
Melba, Dame Nellie	1861-1931	Famous Australian prima donna

376

Menelik	c.1300	Emperor of Ethiopia, son of Solomon and Sheba
Mercedes, Maria de las	d. 1883	Wife of Alfonso XII of Spain
Metternich, Prince von	1829-95	Austrian Ambassador to France
Meyerbeer, Giacomo	1794-1864	German opera composer
Mirabeau, Comte de	1749-91	French political writer
Mirepoix, Duc Charles de	1699-1757	Statesman
Monselet, Charles	1828-88	Gastronome and poet
Montespan, Marquis de	1641-1707	Mistress of Louis XIV
Montglas, Marquis de	1607-75	Writer
Montgolfier, Joseph Michel	1740-1810	
Montgolfier Jacques-Etienne	1745-99	brothers, hot-air balloonists
Montholon, Comte de	1782-1853	General under Napoleon
Montmorency		A noble French family descended from Bourchard
Montpensier, Duc de	1824-90	Son of Louis Philippe, became Prince Louis d'Orléans and took Spanish nationality
Mornay, Philippe Duplessis	1549-1623	Friend of Henry IV of France
Murat, Prince Joachim	1767-1815	General, afterwards King of Naples
Nelson, Horatio Lord	1758-1805	Admiral
Nemours, Duc de	1814-96	Second son of Louis Philippe; became King of Belgium
Nesselrode, Comte de	1780-1862	Russian nobleman and diplomat
Omar Pasha	1806-71	Turkish general and statesman
Orloff, Comte Alexis	1787-1862	Russian General and diplomat
Otero, Carolina	last part of 19th and early 20th Century	World-renowned Spanish dancer
Parmentier, Baron Antoine	1737-1817	Pharmacist, popularised potatoes in France
Patti, Adelina	1843-1919	Spanish prima donna
Pierre le Grand	1672-1725	Czar of Russia 1689-1725, married Catherine
Pojarski	1578-1642	Russian patriot of the Romanoff family

Polignac, Princesse de	1749–93	Friend of Marie Antionette
Polignac, J.	1780–1847	Prince, diplomat and statesman
Pompadour, Marquise de	1721–64	Mistress of Louis XV
Rachel, Mlle Elisa	1821–68	Famous Swiss actress
Réjane, Gabrielle	1857–1920	Famous actress
Richelieu, Cardinal	1585–1642	Statesman under Louis XIII; Foreign Minister; made Cardinal in 1622
Romanoff		Family name of Czars of Russia
Rossini, Gioacchino	1792–1868	Italian composer, mainly of operas; gastronome
Rothschild		name of a family of bankers with world wide connections
Saint-Germain, Comte de	1707–78	War Minister to Louis XVI
Sévigné, Marquise de	1626–96	French writer
Soubise, Prince de	1715–87	Marshall of France
Souvaroff	1729–1800	Russian General
Talleyrand, C. M.	1754–1838	Statesman and diplomat under Louis XVIII
Tetrazzini, Luisa	1871–1946	Famous prima donna
Toulouse, Comte de	1678–1737	Illegitimate son of Louis XIV; Grand-Admiral of France
Vatel, François	d.1671	Major-domo to the Prince of Condé
Verdi, Giuseppe	1813–1901	Composer of operas
Villeroi, Duc de	1644–1730	Marshall of France
Voisin	19th century	Proprietor of a famous restaurant in Paris
Walewska, Maria	1810–68	Wife of French minister
Xavier, Comte de	1730–1806	Prince of Poland and Councillor at the Court of Louis XVIII

There are many lesser - known and therefore less frequently used garnishes named after personalities who lived not so long ago. Examples include royalty, American presidents and industrial magnates, French generals from the First World War, nineteenth-century composers, music-hall stars and politicians; Paul Bocuse recently named a soup after the then prime minister Valèrie Giscard d'Estaing.

NAMING DISHES AFTER PLACES AND EVENTS

There are hundreds of garnishes that bear place names, not only of France but of all parts of the world. Some of these are so named because the ingredients of the garnish are indigent to the place of the title such as Argenteuil in France which is famous for its asparagus and Vichy where carrots are grown, thus customers can have an association of ideas when they see dishes bearing such names on the menu. A similar system applies to Italian cooking where most pasta and pizza garnishes are named after the region or town, not necessarily where they originated, but where the main ingredient of the garnish is grown.

Poetic licence is permissible even with place names as, for example, anything served *à la Florentine* has spinach in it, yet Florence has never been renowned for the cultivation of spinach. The probable answer is that when first catching a glimpse of the Tuscan city from the surrounding hills, the traveller is entranced by the verdant greenery of the immediate surroundings in complete contrast to the arid bleakness of his journey through the centre of the country.

It is said that prosperous restaurants do not have to advertise themselves but many of them do this by creating a new garnish and giving it the name of the establishment so ensuring that not only does it go down to posterity but is also featured on the menu of rival establishments. **Café Anglais**, **London House**, **Trocadero**, **Carlton** and **Savoy** are examples but it also happens when the establishment is named after the propeietor whose name is evermore perpetuated by a garnish created by his chef.

There are also many dishes in the repertoire that bear the names of notable historic events, particularly battles, but after such things as plays, operas, books, discoveries and the more peaceful aspects of politics such as alliances or *ententes cordiales*. Not all names of dishes are necessarily authentic and many of them are fanciful names of people, events and places that existed only in the creator's imagination or came from a book he had read. Some are mythological, others could be authentic but their origins were not recorded and have been forgotton during the ages. Many people deride the use of these garnish names saying that they are outmoded or inapplicable to this country, but the fact is that they are still very widely used above a certain level of establishment and even if the names themselves convey nothing to most customers, the underlying garnishes will continue to be used because apart from a few outlandish ones that should never have been accepted, they are sound sensible mixtures that enhance the dish of which they form part.

Many historical events recorded in dish-names are those of long-forgotten wars such as Albuféra, Turbigo and Marengo where the French were the victors, but even Napoleon's disastrous retreat from Moscow is remembered in this way. The full story of how his chef, Laguipierre, concocted a new dish from a few scrounged ingredients is told in *Larousse Gastronomique* and commemorated by the name *Côtelettes à la Pojarski*.

Political events and the names of new plays, operas and ballets have all been recorded, mainly at the actual time when they took place, whether or not the outcome of the event was successful. There is even a list of garnish names used solely for cold dishes of fish, meat and chicken, aptly named after the colder parts of Europe such as Archangel, Moscovite, Neva, Riga, Suédoise and Norvégienne. The well known *Suprême de Volaille Jeanette* is named not after a girl but the ship used by a French Antarctic explorer.

There is a sense of occasion in this fascinating aspect of menu compilation which is one that is worthy of far more research than has been possible in this brief resumé.

In addition to all these classical garnish names each country possesses a list of culinary words or terms that are peculiar to it and that do not translate easily into other languages. Examples of those in use in Britain include:

> baron of beef or mutton, calipash, chine of lamb, collops, dormers, faggots, haslet, haunch of venison, kedgeree, King Harry's Shoestrings, maids of honour, megrim, pikelet, samphire, spatchcock, sundae, sirloin.

The French language is rich in technical terms for food of which these are a few examples:

> **cuissot de porc, demoiselles de Cherbourg, gigue de chevreuil, hûre de sanglier, pauillac lamb, civet de lièvre, salmis de venaison, poularde en vessie, crudités.**

By using the calendar of anniversaries it is possible to link names with dates, and vice versa and give added interest to menus by celebrating the occasion with the named dish and describing the history or meaning associated with it.

January	1	New Year's Day Lorenzo de'Medici born in 1448
	2	*Académie Française* formed by Richelieu in 1635
	3	Feast of St Geneviève, Patron Saint of Paris
	4	Australia inaugurated in 1901 Rachel the actress died 1858
	5	Twelfth Night Wassail Eve Catherine de'Medici died 1589
	6	Feast of the Epiphany Joan of Arc born c. 1412
	7	Russian Christmas Day Glasgow University founded in 1450

	9	Discovery of America in 1492
	13	Coronation of Elizabeth I 1559
	14	St Hilary's Day Death of Mme de Sévigné in 1696
	15	Molière, dramatist, born 1622
	16	Duc d'Aumale, fifth son of Louis Philippe, born 1822
	17	St Anthony's Day Benjamin Franklin born 1706
	18	William of Prussia proclaimed first German Emperor in 1871
	19	First night of *Manon* by Massenet 1884
	21	St Agnes' Day
	22	St Vincent's Day Death of Queen Victoria 1901 Lord Byron born 1788
	24	Boy Scouts organised 1908
	25	St Paul's Day Robert Burns born 1759 at Alloway
	26	Australia Day
	27	Feast of St John Birth of Mozart 1756
	28	Death of George Saintsbury, authority on food and wine, 1933
	30	Execution of Charles I
	31	Anna Pavlova born in 1885
February	1	Feast of St Bridget Chinese New Year's Day
	2	Candlemas Day in Scotland
	3	Coronation of Charles 1 in 1675
	5	St Agatha's Day
	6	Accession of Elizabeth II, 1952 National Day of New Zealand Birth of Queen Anne 1665 Mme de Sévigné born 1626
	8	Mary Queen of Scots executed 1587

	9	St Apollonia's Day
		Agnes Sorel, mistress of Charles VII, d. 1450
	10	Marriage of Queen Victoria 1840
	12	Escoffier died 1935
	13	Talleyrand born 1754
	14	St Valentine's Day
	15	Birth of Louis XV 1710
	19	Adelina Patti born 1843
	22	George Washington born 1732
	25	Caruso born 1873
	27	Foundation of the Labour Party 1900
	28	Rachel born 1821
	29	Rossini born 1792
		Leap Year's Day
March	1	St David's Day
	3	National Day of Morocco
		First Night of *Carmen*, 1875
	4	Columbus landed in America 1493
	6	National day of Ghana
	9	Birth of Amerigo Vespucci who gave his name to America, 1451
		Mirabeau, statesman, born 1749
	12	Feast of St Gregory
	14	First night of *The Mikado*, 1885
	15	Ides of March
	17	St Patrick's Day
	19	Feast of St Joseph
	21	Feast of St Benedict
	23	National day of Pakistan
	24	Death of Elizabeth I, 1603
	25	National day of Greece
		Murat, King of Naples, born 1767
	26	Sarah Bernhardt died 1923
	28	George I born at Hanover, 1660

April	1	April Fool's Day
		Brillat-Savarin born 1755
	2	Casanova born 1725
		Birth of Charlemagne 742
	4	National day of Hungary
		Death of André Massèna 1817
	7	St Francis Xavier born 1506
	14	Death of Mme de Sévigné, 1696
	15	Death of Mme de Maintenon 1719
	21	Birth of Elizabeth II in 1926
	23	St George's Day
		Shakespeare's birthday
	25	Australia and New Zealand Day
	26	Feast of St Mark
		Marie Thérèsa, Queen of France, born 1782
	29	Duke of Wellington born 1769
		National Day of Japan
	30	Feast of St Catherine
		National Day of Holland
		George Washington became first President of USA, 1789
May	1	May Day
		Labour Day
	2	Meyerbeer died 1864
	3	Richard D'Oyly Carte born 1844
	5	Death of Napoleon 1821
		Eugenie, Empress of France, born 1826
	6	Birth of Massèna 1758
	8	St Michael's Day
		V E Day 1945
	9	National Day of Czechoslovakia
		Channel Islands liberated 1945
	10	Death of Louis XV, 1774
	13	Festival of All Saints
	15	Metternich born 1773
	16	Battle of Albufréra 1811
	17	National Day of Norway

	19	Melba born 1861
	20	Balzac born 1799
	21	Queen Victoria born 1819 Oak Apple Day Everest conquered 1953
	30	Feast of St Joan of Arc Memorial Day in USA
	31	Ascension Day National Day in South Africa
June	2	National Day of Italy
	3	Birth of Sydney Smith 1771 Battle of Magenta 1859
	5	National Day of Denmark
	6	National Day of Sweden
	8	Carême born 1783
	10	Birth of Prince Philip 1921
	11	St Barnabas Day
	13	Birth of Mme d'Arblay 1752
	14	Battle of Marengo 1800
	15	Signing of Magna Carta 1215
	16	Queen's Official Birthday
	18	Battle of Waterloo 1815
	20	Accession of Queen Victoria 1837
	23	National Day of Luxembourg
	24	Feast of St John Midsummer Day Battle of Solferino 1859 Battle of Bannockburn 1314
	29	St Peter's and St Paul's Day
July	1	Dominion Day in Canada
	4	Independence Day in USA
	8	Birth of Rockefeller 1839
	9	National Day of Argentine
	12	Birth of Julius Caesar 100 BC Orangeman's Day in Northern Ireland

384

14	Bastille Day in France
15	St Swithin's Day
16	Prince of Soubise born 1715
17	J. J. Astor, of the Waldorf-Astoria, born 1763
18	National Day of Spain
21	National Day of Belgium
22	National Day of Poland

August

1	Swiss Independence Day
4	Birth of Queen Elizabeth the Queen Mother, 1900
5	Oyster season begins
12	Grouse shooting begins
14	Prince de Joinville born 1818
15	Napoleon born 1769
16	Choisy, French cleric born 1644 Feast of St Roch, Patron Saint of cooks
19	Du Barry born 1743
23	National Day of Romania
26	Battle of Crécy 1376
29	Colbert born 1619
31	National Day of Malaysia

September

1	Partridge shooting begins
2	Princesse de Lamballe murdered 1792
4	Chateaubriand born 1769
5	Birth of Richelieu 1585
6	Pilgrim Fathers sailed from Plymouth 1620
7	Birth of Elizabeth I in 1533
8	Battle of Malakoff
9	Death of William the Conqueror 1087
24	Feast of the Ingathering
26	Dominion Day, New Zealand
29	Michaelmas Day Lord Nelson born 1758 Chambord born 1830

October	1	National Day of China
	9	Birth of Comte d'Artois, later Charles X 1757
	10	Verdi born in 1813
	12	Columbus landed in America 1492
	14	Battle of Hastings 1066
	18	St Luke's Day Cambacères born 1753
	21	Trafalgar Day Death of Nelson 1805
	23	Sarah Bernhardt born 1844 Birth of George Saintsbury 1845
	25	St Crispin's Day
	26	National Day of Austria National Day of Iran
	28	Escoffier born 1846
	29	National Day of Turkey
	31	Halloween
November	1	National Day of Algeria All Soul's Day
	5	Guy Fawkes Day Mornay born 1549
	7	National Day of Russia
	10	Birth of Mahomet 570
	11	Martinmas
	15	Beaujolais nouveau release day
	20	Marriage of Princess Elizabeth and Prince Philip 1947
	22	St Cecilia's Day
	26	St Peter's Day Thanksgiving Day in USA
	27	Madame de Maintenon born 1636
	30	St Andrew's Day Andréa Doria born 1528
December	1	Birth of Queen Alexandra 1844
	3	St Francis Xavier
	4	Madame Récamier born 1777

6	National Day of Finland
7	Birth of Mary Stuart 1542
10	Grouse shooting ends
13	Henri IV of France born 1553
16	Boïeldieu, composer born 1775
17	*La Belle Hélène* first produced in 1864
21	Forefathers' Day in USA Midwinter
25	Christmas Day
26	Feast of St Stephen Boxing Day
27	Feast of St John
31	New Year's Eve St Sylvester's Eve Hogmanay

MOVEABLE FEAST DAYS

These are important dates which differ from year to year but are worthy of being celebrated by the inclusion of special dishes on the menu.

Shrove Tuesday is Pancake day; it is the day prior to the beginning of Lent and can occur on any Tuesday from 2 February to 8 March;

Ash Wednesday is the beginning of the forty-day fast for Lent.

Mothering Sunday is the mid-Sunday of Lent.

Maundy Thursday is the day before Good Friday.

Good Friday: hot cross buns and simnel cake are served.

Easter Day is the first Sunday after the full moon which happens upon or next after 21 March; if the full moon happens on a Sunday, Easter Day is the Sunday after.

Ascension Day or **Holy Thursday** occurs forty days after Easter Sunday.

Father's Day is the third Sunday in June.

Advent Sunday is the nearest Sunday to **St Andrew's Day** (30 November).

B Culinary Sayings, Proverbs and Poems

There is a wealth of sayings or *bons mots* concerned with gastronomy and many proverbs connected with food and cooking, some of them in everyday use. There is a time-honoured practice of using culinary sayings on menus and wine lists, particularly those for banquets, where their use can add considerable interest. The following are some of the better known references for general use but it is possible to classify them under more specific headings such as *bons viveurs*, cooks, courses, eating habits, epicureanism, feasts, foods, gastrology, liquor, meals, etc. where they will be most appropriate.

Good bread and good butter, good cheese and good salad make as satisfactory a lunch as the most fastidious could desire. (Burke)

A rich soup; a small turbot; a saddle of venison; an apricot tart: this is a dinner fit for a king. (Brillat-Savarin)

Cookery has become an art, a noble science; cooks are gentlemen. (Burton)

The merit of a meal does not consist in the quantity, but in the quality of the dishes. (Dumas)

> A feast prepared with riotous expense,
> Much cost, more care, and most magnificence. (Dryden)

God sends meat and the devil sends cooks. (Deloney)

A cook is known by his knife. (Fuller)

Every cook commends his own sauce. (Gerbur)

> 'Tis not the food but the content
> That makes the tables' merriment. (Herrick)

When a man is invited to dinner, he is disappointed if he does not get something good. (Johnson)

A man seldom thinks with more earnestness of anything than he does of his dinner. (Johnson)

388

A man is more pleased when he has a good dinner on his table than when his wife talks Greek. (Johnson)

> Tis a sage question if the art of cooks
> Is lodged by nature or attained from books. (King)

pour faire un civet, prenez un lièvre. (La Varenne)

> We may live without poetry, music and art,
> We may live without conscience and live without heart,
> We may live without friends, we may live without books,
> But civilized man cannot live without cooks. (Meredith)

The true Amphitryon is the Amphitryon with whom we dine. (Molière)

Strange to see how a good dinner and feasting reconciles everybody. (Pepys)

A dinner lubricates business. (Scott)

> Serenely full the epicure would say,
> 'Fate cannot harm me, I have dined today'. (Smith)

An excellent and well arranged dinner is a most pleasant occurrence, and a great triumph of civilised life. (Smith)

If you like your dinner man never be ashamed to say so. (Thackeray)

Dinner was made for eatin, not for talkin. (Thackeray)

Thirty-two religions and but one dish at dinner. (Talleyrand)

Drink wine and have the gout; drink no wine and have the gout too. (Cogan)

Eat at pleasure, drink by measure. (G. B. Shaw)

I'm only a beer teetotaller, not a champagne teetotaller. (G. B. Shaw)

L'appetit vient en mangeant. (Rabelais)

Il faut manger pour vivre et non pas vivre pour manger. (Molière)

RECEIPT TO ROAST MUTTON

> Gently stir and blow the fire,
> Lay the mutton down to roast,
> Dress it quickly, I desire,
> In the dripping put a toast,
> That I hunger may remove –
> Mutton is the meat I love.
>
> On the dresser see it lie;
> Oh! the charming white and red!

389

Finer meat ne'er met the eye,
On the sweetest grass it fed!
Let the jack go swiftly round,
Let me have it nicely browned.

On the table spread the cloth,
Let the knives be sharp and clean,
Pickles get and salad both,
Let them each be fresh and green.
With small beer, good ale and wine,
O ye gods! how I shall dine! (Jonathan Swift)

Many writers have expressed their gastronomic desires in the form of poetry. In addition to this by Dean Swift there are many others by such poets as Thackeray, Walter Scott, Ben Jonson and Shakespeare. Stanzas or verses from these can be used in appropriate places on menus and wine lists.

A man hath no better thing under the sun, than to eat, and to drink, and to be merry. (Ecc 8:15)

Go thy way, eat thy bread with joy, and drink thy wine with a merry heart: for God now accepteth thy works. (Ecc 9:7)

Let us eat and drink; for tomorrow we shall die. (Isiah XXII:13)

And wine that maketh glad the heart of man, and oil to make his face to shine and bread which strengtheneth man's heart. (Psalm 104)

Appetite comes with eating. . . but the thirst goes away with drinking. (Aesop)

A crust eaten in peace is better than a banquet partaken in anxiety. (Aesop)

If you can't stand the heat, get out of the kitchen. (Truman)

—'s idea of heaven is eating *pâté de foie gras* to the sound of trumpets. (Smith)

If God forbade drinking would he have made wine so good? (Richelieu)

Give us the luxuries of life, and we will dispense with its necessities. (Motley)

PROVERBS

The proof of the pudding is in the eating.

You cannot have your cake and eat it.

Hunger is the best sauce.

Hungry dogs will eat dirty pudding.

Too many cooks spoil the broth

A bad cook licks his own fingers.

390

Kissing don't last; cookery do.

Pour manger bien il faut savoir attendre.

Mieux vaut bon repas que bel habit.

C Education for Gastronomy

The number of great hoteliers who achieved fame in their day and are still remembered, is far fewer than that of great chefs of the past. The names of the men who brought fame to the hotels they directed or managed is limited to a mere handful and even such great men as **Sir Charles Reeves-Smith** (1855–1941) of the **Savoy, Frederick Gordon** (1835–1904) the Napoleon of the hotel world who founded both the **Gordon Hotels Company** and with **Sir Blundell Maple**, the **Frederick Hotels Group, Sir William Towle** of the Midland Railway Hotels and his two sons, **Sir Arthur Towle** who succeeded his father at the Railway Hotels and **Sir Francis Towle** who became managing director of Gordon Hotels, all are sadly forgotten or at least, overlooked by their modern counterparts. Other distinguished hoteliers were **Richard D'Oyly Carte** who created the **Savoy, Conrad Hilton** who formed the first chain of hotels, **A. H. Jones** of **Grosvenor House Hotel** in Park Lane who brought industrial relations in the hotel industry into the twentieth century, and perhaps the best known, the great **César Ritz** whose name is synonymous with luxurious living and who was in charge of the design and planning of the hotels built by the company that carried his name.

To become the good hoteliers which these people were, required keen business acumen and an ability to get on well with people so as to make customers feel important and wanted; they also had to get the best results from staff employed. The modern manager still needs to know all aspects of every job that has to be done by members of his staff, and in addition he must take a deep interest in, and have a liking for, food and wine. In today's climate of business activities, the food and beverage manager has to devote a lot of his attention to the control system of his department, possibly to the detriment of his interest in the quality of food and the calibre of service. The practicalities of the day-to-day operation may have to be left to departmental heads who will obviously operate in the way they see fit.

The routes to management of a catering enterprise are well charted, being either by direct entry as a trainee or as a student through college. Each has its advantages, the first being essentially practical and having to deal with real situations, the latter being very theoretical but leading to the award of a recog-

392

nised diploma which in turn can give admission to the professional body – the **Hotel, Catering and Institutional Management Association.**

Many people enter the catering industry with the idea of opening and running their own business and they start by going to work in a number of well-known restaurants in order to gain the necessary experience of becoming a *chef-patron* or owner-manager. Catering colleges recognises the need to fit students for this side of the business as well as that of hospitals and hotel chains. The subject of gastronomy is an ideal study for those students who see their future as being concerned with the provision of fine food and wines, whether as an entrepreneur or as a manager.

Some colleges recognise the need for more importance to be placed on the practical food and beverage subjects by appointing chefs from great hotels and distinguished *chef-patrons* to posts of visiting lecturer or advisor. Some colleges organise gastronomic societies or operate gourmet events while others, for example, the Bournemouth and Poole College, hold an annual lecture given by a well-known master chef to which local and national hoteliers and chefs are invited and the lecturer is ordinated a *Chevalier du Sautoir d'Argent* and given membership of the college culinary society. He gives a number of demonstrations of his specialities, then supervises students as they organise *un dîner dégustation gastronomique*; during this meal the visiting chef is presented with the prestigious award of a silver sauté pan.

Colleges have always had advisory committees comprised of local and national caterers to give guidance on the successful operation of the catering department, but the appointment of a quondam lecturer or the instigation of an annual visit is a fairly recent development that is to be applauded. The few days spent by an appointed professional can create closer liaison between industry and the academic world and help to make the teaching even more realistic. The problem is likely to be that there are not enough distinguished people to satisfy the needs of all the colleges.

As well as more than 250 colleges run by local authorities there are a large number of private ones that offer courses in various aspects of catering including cookery, cake decoration, the respective arts of butler and toastmaster and party catering.

Many of these colleges such as the **Cordon Bleu School** in **London** and the **Tante Marie School** at **Woking,** are for people who want to learn how to do the highest class of domestic cookery. Sometimes hotels put on short cookery courses during the off-season and the possession of a diploma from such places confers a certain cachet on the graduate. Evening Institutes offer a wide range of classes in many aspects of gastronomy including so-called 'continental cookery' and wine appreciation and these help to raise the standard of home life for the expenditure of a small class fee.

The standard of teaching at professional catering colleges in Europe is maintained at a very high level and it has long been recognised that pastry cooks in particular benefit from courses in sugar work, chocolate confectionery and specialist cake-making, as offered in Switzerland and Austria. These are held in private colleges that run on commercial lines with an intensive curriculum that produces fine craftsmen as sought after by leading establishments. The **Richemont Club** for ex-members of the **School of Confectionery** at **Lucerne** is one of the most prestigious offshoots of such élite establishments and is akin to the **Stam** or ex-students association of the **Lausanne Hotel School**.

In France a post-graduate course for chefs has been organised by the *Académie Culinaire* with the idea of putting extra polish on those who have already achieved high rank but who wish to prove their excellence still further. Such a course would be more advanced than our own **City and Guilds of London Institute No 706** Part III, which is offered in three parts – kitchen and larder, pastry, and advanced pastry. The standard is that of *chef de partie* rather than head chef but the course is very demanding.

Other advanced courses concerned with gastronomy as offered by **City and Guilds** are **Nos 113, Cocoa, Chocolate and Sugar Confectionery**; **120, Bakery** at three levels; **707, Food and Beverage Service** at two levels, **711 Patisserie (Special)**; **717, Alcoholic Beverages** and **771, Organisational Studies** for supervisory positions in catering establishments.

If departments of higher catering education are to continue to fulfil their function and justify their existence they must concentrate on the very subjects that make them different from other management courses and which are the reason students choose to follow them. These are the practical aspects of food production and food and beverage service which together with associated subjects in the spheres of human resources, finance, and science and technology help in the formation of people who will make a valuable contribution to the advancement of gastronomy and of the catering industry.

D The Menu as an Art Form

Menus are collectors' items, particularly those produced for specially notable occasions on which the names of distinguished guests are listed and those used in royal or noble houses for special meals such as those in honour of weddings or Jubilees and for visiting dignitaries.

Rare menus become museum items especially those signed by any notable people present. Some are of interest to local libraries and museums while those that are of national interest are acceptable to centres such as the *Musée Escoffier* at Villeneuve-Loubet or the *Bodleian Library* at Oxford. Most establishments keep a file of the menus they serve; this may be in an official book in which the chef or his kitchen clerk writes them for transmission to the printer or to the receptionist for typing and duplicating, or it may be a collection of the menus as printed.

The everyday menu deserves the same care in composition and production as the ones done for very special occasions; chefs and head waiters usually take pride in the menus they produce and serve because they know they are a way of representing the establishment.

At one time head waiters encouraged customers to take a copy of the menu as a souvenir but this is now done only in those places where the menu lasts for the duration of the meal or the day. Where menus are kept in use over a period of time the number is likely to be checked daily to see that none are missing and should a customer insist on keeping one as a memento of the meal he is likely to find its cost included in the bill.

Menus show the history and development of gastronomy and as with recipe books, it is possible to see from them when foods were first introduced or became fashionable. They show when particular dish names came into use and whether they lasted or were mere flashes in the pan, they also show how prices have changed. The covers of menus can show the evolution of the decorative arts as they mirror the colours and layouts adopted by designers at various times. Unfortunately the same topical scene is used to illustrate a particular time of year such as Christmas or New Year and it can be found on the menu covers of establishments all over the country, and those of such events as Ladies Nights tend to be equally stereotyped. These are not such valuable collectors' items as those done by a good artist for a particular event or particular establishment and not therefore in wide use.

A menu can not only evoke a major event but also record the interests of the proprietor and possibly of his clientele; some act as a record of the social and historical aspects of their time while others reflect aspects of the world as it then was, illustrating current fashions, means of transport, pictures of family life, sport, political changes and many other topics.

A collection of menus of the regular meetings or dinners of a society over a number of years is of particular interest, especially those of a gastronomic society. Those signed personally by the head chef are of value and the more famous he was and the more well-known the restaurant, the greater their significance. Those of places that are no longer in existence but were famous in their day, often hold more interest than places that are still thriving.

The **Ephemera Society** is concerned with preserving handwritten and printed documents and many of its members, both here and in the United States, specialise in the collection of menus and wine lists. When such rare items as, say, a Toulouse-Lautrec menu card lithograph go to auction they will fetch prices that run into several thousand of pounds.

E The Physiology of Taste

Throughout this work there are many references to **Jean-Anthelme Brillat-Savarin**'s book, *La Physiologie du Gout,* and many of its well-known aphorisms have been quoted in support of the author's theories. The sub-title of Savarin's book – *'Meditations on Transcendental Gastronomy'* – gives an idea of what the book is about but it is felt that a brief description of its aim and content will help in showing the enormous influence this great work has had over the past 150 years. The book has never been out of print since it first appeared in 1825 and it is held in high regard by all serious gastronomes and writers as being their 'bible'; it has been translated into all the major languages so is available internationally.

Brillat-Savarin was a lawyer who enjoyed good food and wine so much that he saw a need to investigate it in depth and to try to define gastronomy as a physiological study. The result was this book, written in the form of an unconnected series of thoughts, distilled from his own observations on the delights of the table. This makes it possible to use the book as a work of reference and much of its value is as a source of quotable sayings. It is hardly a book to read from cover to cover, although in most translations it is far from heavy reading. In fact, the style suits the subject perfectly. It is a book of philosophy as well as physiology.

There are two parts to the book. Part 1 contains all the well-known aphorisms or brief maxims, many of which have been cited throughout this book. They are fairly well-known and are popularly used as quotations on menus. Although they appear to be light-hearted, they are profound and can serve as a set of rules for the conduct of gastronomic occasions. There are thirty meditations on a wide variety of subjects including the senses, appetite, various items of food and drink, sleep, dreams, diet, obesity, cooking, restauranteurs and gourmandism. The thirty meditations are divided into a total of 148 separate topics that delve into all conceivable aspects of the title.

In Part II, Brillat-Savarin continues his discussions in the same vein but with a more direct approach. These are mainly instructions on the preparation of various foods and drinks, including fish, meat and vegetable dishes. There are talks on etiquette, about life in a monastery, some useful hints and some anecdotes. Songs about food convey a feeling of joy in the subject and the entire book is a work that entices the reader to develop his innate love of food into a deeper study that will enhance his knowledge and feeling for gastronomy.

Select Bibliography

THE DEVELOPMENT OF EATING HABITS

CARTER, G., *Man and the Land*, Holt, Rinehart and Winstone, 1975
DARBY *et al*, *Food, the Gift of Osiris*, Academic Press, 1977
FENTON, A. and McOWEN, T., *Food in Perspective,* Donald, 1981
HERODOTUS, Translated into French by Barquet and Russell, Gallimard, 1964
PYKE, M., *Food and Society*, John Murray, 1968
LOWENBERG *et al*, *Food and People*, Wiley, 1979
RENNER, D. H., *The Origin of Food Habits*, Faber & Faber, 1944
SILVERSTONE, T. (ed.) *Appetite and Food Intake*, Dahlem Konferenzen, 1976
TANNEHILL, R., *Food in History*, Paladin, 1975

MAN'S SENSES

AMERINE *et al*, *Principle of Sensory Evaluation of Food*, Academic Press, 1965
HILGARD *et al*, *Introduction to Psychology* (7th edn) Harcourt Brace &
    Jovanovich, 1979
OHLOFF, G. and THOMAS, H. *Gustation and Olfaction*, Academic Press, 1971
SINGER, C. and UNDERWOOD, E. A., *A Short History of Medicine*, OUP, 1962
THOMPSON, R., *Foundation of Physiological Psychology*, Harper, 1967

NUTRIMENTAL ASPECTS

BLAXTER and FOWDEN (eds) *Food, Nutrition and Climate*, Applied Science
    Publishers, 1982

BRILLAT-SAVARIN, J.-A., *The Physiology of Taste*, Penguin, 1970
CULPEPERS' *Complete Herbal*, 1826 Facsimile, Harvey, 1981
DAVIDSON *et al.*, *Human Nutrition and Dietetics*, Churchill Livingstone, 1979
ECKSTEIN, E., *Food, People and Nutrition*, AVI Publishing Co, 1980
HAMILTON, E. M. N. and WHITNEY, E. N., *Nutritious Concepts and Controversies*, West, 1982
RIETZ, C., *Master Food Guide*, AVI Publishing Co., 1978
WENZEL, G. L., *Menu Maker*, Cahner's Books International, 1979
YUDKIN, J., *Diet of Man's Needs and Wants*, Applied Science Publishers, 1978

PROGRESSION OF GASTRONOMY

BROTHWELL, P., *Food in Antiquity*, Thames & Hudson, 1969
BURNETT, J., *Plenty and Want*, Scolar Press, 1978
CLAIR, C., *Kitchen and Table*, Abelard Schumann, 1964
CHANG, K. C., *Food in Chinese Culture*, Yale, 1977
CURTIS-BENNETT, N., *Food of the People*, Faber & Faber, 1939
HARRISON, M., *The Kitchen in History*, Osprey, 1972
MONTAGNÉ, P., *Larousse Gastronomique*, Hamlyn, 1977
McKENDRY, M., *Seven Centuries of Cooking*, Weidenfield & Nicholson, 1973
MOSS, V. P. C., *Meals through the Ages*, Harrap, 1958
SIMON, A. L., *A Concise Encyclopaedia of Gastronomy*, Collins, 1952

MENU PLANNING, COMPOSITION AND WINE LIST

BEETON, I., *Book of Household Management*, Ward, Lock, 1861
BRILLAT-SAVARIN, J.-A., *The Physiology of Taste*, Penguin, 1970
CRACKNELL, H., KAUFMANN, R. and NOBIS, G., *Practical Professional Catering*, Macmillan, 1983
DUTREY, M., *Calendrier Gastronomique*, Muller, 1959
ESCOFFIER, A., *The Complete Guide to the Art of Modern Cookery*, Heinemann, 1979
FULLER, J., *Professional Kitchen Management*, Hutchinson, 1983
SEABERG, A., *Menu Design*, Cahners Books International, 1974
TSCHISKY, O., *Oscar of the Waldorfs' Cookbook*, Dover, 1973
WEST *et al.*, *Food Service in Institutions*, Wiley, 1975

HISTORY OF THE ART OF THE TABLE

HENISH, B. A., *Fast and Feast*, University of Pennsylvania, 1976
MONTAGNÉ, P., *Larousse Gastronomique*, Hamlyn, 1977
PULLAR, P., *Consuming Passions*, Hamish Hamilton, 1971
SASS, L., *To The King's Taste*, John Murray, 1976
WILSON, C. A., *Food and Drink in Britain*, Constable, 1973

THE ROLE OF ALCOHOLIC BEVERAGES

ALLEN, H. W., *A History of Wines*, Faber & Faber, 1961
DEBUIGNE, G., *Larousse Dictionary of Wines of the World*, Hamlyn, 1970
HYAMAS, E., *Dionysus: A Social History of Wines*, Thames & Hudson, 1965
JOHNSON, H., *The World Atlas of Wine*, Mitchell Beazley, 1981
LAVER, J., *Gods, Men and Wine*, International Wine and Food Society, 1966
LICHINE, A., *Encyclopaedia of Wines and Spirits*, Cassell, 1974
SIMON, A. L., *Guide to Good Food and Wines*, Collins, 1956

GASTRONOMIC PRACTICES OF NATIONS

BROWN, D., *American Cooking*, Time-Life Books, 1978
BROWN, D., *The Cooking of Scandinavia*, Time-Life Books, 1974
CREWE, Q., *International Pocket Food Book*, Mitchell Beazley, 1980
DALLAS, E. S., *Kettner's Book of the Table*, Centaur, 1968
ECKSTEIN, E., *Food, People and Nutrition*, AVI Publishing Co, 1980
ECKSTEIN, E., *Menu Planning*, AVI Publishing Co, 1978
GRIGSON, J., *The World Atlas of Food*, Mitchell Beazley, 1974
HAHN, E., *The Cooking of China*, Time-Life Books, 1973
LEONARD, E., *Latin American Cooking*, Time-Life Books, 1976
OGRIZEK, *Le Monde à Table*, Ode, 1952
RAU, S. R. *The Cooking of India*, Time-Life Books, 1974
SIMONS, F. J., *Eat not this Flesh*, Greenwood, 1981
STEINBERG, R., *The Cooking of Japan*, Time-Life Books, 1974
UVEZIAN, S., *The Best Food of Russia*, Harcourt Brace & Jovanovich, 1976

For France, Germany and Italy see individual Bibliography

GASTRONOMIC OCCASIONS

BRETT, G., *Dinner is Served*, Rupert Hart Davies, 1967
BRILLAT-SAVARIN, *The Physiology of Taste*, Penguin, 1970
ELIAS, N., *The Civilising Process 'The History of Manners'*, Basil Blackwell, 1978
LAUNAY, A., *Eat, Drink and Be Sorry*, M. J. Hobbs, 1970
LAUNAY, A., *Caviar and After*, Macdonald, 1964
MONTAGNE, P., *Larousse Gastronomique*, Hamlyn, 1977
PAGE, E. B. and KINGSFORD, P. W., *The Master Chefs*, Arnold, 1971
RAY, C., *The Compleat Imbiber*, Collins annually 1956–1972
RAY, C., *The Gourmet's Companion*, Eyre & Spottiswoode, 1963
RITZ, M. CÉSAR RITZ, *Host to the World*, Harrap, 1938

GASTRONOMY AND GASTRONOMES

ARESTY, E. B., *The Exquisite Table*, Bobbs Merrill, 1980
MORRIS, H., *Portrait of a Chef*, Oxford, 1980
PAGE, E. B. and KINGSFORD, P. W., *The Master Chefs*, Arnold, 1971
THALAMAS, P. and HERBODEAU, E., *George Auguste Escoffier*, Practical Press 1955
WILLAN, A., *Great Cooks and their Recipes*, Elm Tree, 1977

The reader is further advised to read some of the notable works of the gastronomes listed.

PLACES OF ENTERTAINMENT

ASKWITH, LORD, *British Taverns: Their History and Laws*, Routledge, 1928
BOWDEN, G. H., *British Gastronomy*, Chatto & Windus, 1975
BERTRAM, P., *Fast Food Operations*, Barrie and Rockliff, 1975
BROUDER, M. H., *The Life and Sport of the Inn*, Gentry Books, 1973
CONTARINI, P., *The Savoy was my Oyster*, Robert Hale, 1976
CURTIS-BENNETT, N., *Food of the People*, Faber & Faber 1939
FOTHERGILL, J., *My Three Inns*, Chatto & Windus, 1951
KICHENSIDE, G., *The Restaurant Car*, David & Charles, 1979
LATHAM, J., *The Pleasure of Your Company*, A. and C. Black, 1972

LUNDBERG, D., *The Hotel and Restaurant Business*, Cahners Books International, 1979

MEDLIK, S., *Profile of the Hotel and Catering Industry*, Heineman, 1978

PRIESTLAND, G., *Frying Tonight*, Gentry Books, 1972

PLATT, B. S. *et al*, *Food in Hospital*, OUP, 1963

ROBINSON, E., *The Early English Coffee House*, Dolphin, 1972

TAYLOR, D. and BUSH, D., *The Golden Age of British Hotels*, Northwood, 1974

WYCKOFF, D. and SASSER, W., *The Chain Restaurant Industry*, Heath, 1978

BIBLIOGRAPHIE FRANCAISE

AUDIGER, *La maison reglée et l'art de diriger la maison d'un grand Seigneur*, 1692

AUDOT, L-E., *La Cuisinière de la Campagne et de la Ville*, 1868

BARRAU, JACQUES, *Les Hommes et leurs Aliments*, 1984

BEAUVILLIERS, A., *L'Art du Cuisinier*, 1814

BEAUVILLIERS, A., *Le Nouveau Cuisinier Royal*, 1835

BEAUVILLIERS, A. et CARÊME, A., *La Cuisine Ordinaire*, 1848

BOCUSE, PAUL, *La Cuisine du Marché*, 1983

BONNEFONS, N., *Les Délices de la Campagne*, 1894

BRILLAT-SAVARIN, J.-A., *Le Physiologie du Goût ou Méditation de Gastronomie Transcendante*, 1834

CADET DE GASSICOURT, C. L., *Cours Gastronomique*, 1809

CARÊME, A., *L'Art de la Cuisine Française au XIXème Siècle*, 1784

CARÊME, A., *Le Maître d'Hôtel Français*, 1822

CARÊME, A., *Le Pâtissier Pittoresque*, 1822

CARÊME, A., *Le Pâtissier National Parisien*, 1815

CARÊME, A., *Le Principal de la Cuisine de Paris*, 1844

DUMAS, A., *Grand Dictionnaire de Cuisine*, 1885

ESCOFFIER, G. A., *Le Guide Culinaire*, 1903

FAYOT, A. C. F., *Les Classiques de la Table*, 1791

GOUFFE, J., *Le Livre de Cuisine*, 1807

GRIMOD DE LA REYNIÈRE, A. B. L., *Journal des Gourmands et des Belles, ou l'Épicurien Français*, 1806-7 in 8 vols

GRIMOD DE LA REYNIÈRE, A. B. L., *Almanach des Gourmands ou Calendrier Nutritif*, 1803

GUÉGAN, B., *Le Cuisinier Français*, 1938

LA CHAPELLE V., *Le Cuisinier Moderne, qui Apprend à Donner tous Sortes de Repas*, 1733

LA VARENNE F. P. S., *Le Parfait Confiturier*, 1667

LA VARENNE, F. P. S., *Le Vrai Cuisinier Français*, 1651

MENON, *La Nouvelle Cuisine, avec de Nouveaux Dessins de Table*, 1751

MENON, *La Plus Nouvelle Cuisinière Bourgeoise*, 1822
MONSELET, C., *Almanach Gourmand*, 1865
OLIVER, RAYMOND, *La Cuisine*, 1948
TAILLEVENT, *Livre Fort Excellent de Cuisine*, 1542
URBAIN-DUBOIS, F., *Cuisine Artistique, Études de l'École Moderne*, 1872
URBAIN-DUBOIS, F., *Cuisine de Tous le Pays*, 1868
VERRY, A.-M., *Le Cuisinier des Cuisiniers*, 1825

BIBLIOGRAFIA ITALIANA

This list includes most of the major works on cookery and gastronomy written in Italian from earliest times to the present day. Several of the older works have been reprinted and are available in modern covers from good booksellers in many parts of Italy. They are given here in chronological rather than alphabetical order.

ROSSELLI. G., *Opera Nove Chiamato Epularis*, 1516
SCAPPI, B. (personal cook to Pope Pius V) *L'Arte del Cusinare*, 1570
CASTELVETRO, G., *Breve Racconto di Tutte le Radici*, 1614
CERVIO, V., *Il Trinciante*, 1622
STEFANI, B., *L'Arte di Ben Cucinaro*, 1662
LIBERATI, F. R., *Il Perfetto Maestro di Casa*, 1668
CORRADO, V., *Il Cuoco Galante*, 1778
BALDINI, F., *De Sorbetti*, 1784
CORRADO, V., *Il Credenziere di Buon Gusto*, 1789
CAVALCANTI, I, *Cucina Teorio-Practica*, 1834
LURASCHI, G. F., *Nuovo Cuco Milanese Economico*, 1835
RIVA, G., *Trattato di Cucina Semplice*, 1878
PALLIOLO, P. F., *Le Feste del Conferimento del Patriziato Romano*, 1885
PRATO, C. E., *Manuale di Cucina*, 1901
AGNETTI, V., *La Nuova Cucina delle Specialita Regionale*, 1909
ROMPINI, O., *La Cucina dell Amore*, 1910
MAFFIOLI, *Il Romanzo della Grande Cucina*, 1965
CARNACINA, L. et al, *Cucina e Vino Nostrum*, 1972
DA MOSTO, R., *Il Veneto in Cucina*, 1974
GIOCO, G., *La Cucina Scaligera*, 1975
ZUCCHI, L., *Cucina Veneta*, 1977
CODACCI, L., *Civilta della Tavola Contandina*, 1981
HERRE, F., *Storia del Buongusto in Cucina*, 1981
PADOVAN, R., *La Cucina Ampezzana*, 1982
COLTRO, D., *La Cucina Tradizionale Veneta*, 1983

DEUTSCHE BIBLIOGRAPHIE

AABEL, MARIE, *Regensburger Fastenkochbuchlein*, 1897

AABEL, MARIE, *Fischküche*, 1892

BALLAUF, THERESIA, *Die Wiener-Köchin wie sie sein soll*, 1810

BEEG, MARIE, *Das Kranzlein in der Küche*, 1897

BERGNER, ANNA, *Pfalzer Kochbuch*, 1858

BOCK, HIERONYMUS, *Kreutterbuch*, 1529

DAISENBERGER, MARIA KOTHEUMA, *Vollständiges Bayrisches Kochbuch*, 1843

DIEHL, A., *Kochbuch für Fettleibige*, 1889

EIS, GERHARD, *Studien zur altdeutschen Fachprosa*, 1951

FEYL, ANITA, *Das Kochbuch Meister Eberhards*, 1963

FRIES LAURENTIUS, *Von Allerley Speysen*, 1559

GUTZ, WILHELM, *Speise und Trank Vergangener Zeiten in Deutschen Landen*, 1882

GRUNAUER, *Grunauers Vollständig und auf neue Art*, 1733

HARSDORFFER, GEORG PHILIPP, *Vollständiges Trincir Buch*, 1607

KOPPEN, ERNST, *Erstes Deutsches Kochbuch der Bürgelichen Küche*, 1905

LAUFFENBERG, HEINRICH, *Ain Nutzliches Buchlein von der Speis der Menschen* *1500*

MALORTIE, ERNST, *Das Menu, Eine Culinarische Studie*, 1878

NAUMANN, ROBERT, *Alte Deutsche Kochbücher*, 1848

RITTER, FRIDERIKE, *Wollständiges Deutsches Kochbuch fur alle Stände*, 1856

RUMPOLT, MARX, *Ein New Kochbuch*, 1581

SCHHURR, BALTHASAR, *Kunst-Hauss und Wunderbuch*, 1657

WECKER, ANNA, *Ein Kostlich New Kochbuch*, 1597

WISWE, HANS, *Kulturgeschichte der Kochkunst*, 1970

Index

407

408

411

412